P9-CQR-054

That's Hollywood

That's Hollywood

A BEHIND-THE-SCENES LOOK AT 60 OF THE GREATEST FILMS EVER MADE

Peter van Gelder

HarperPerennial

An Imprint of HarperCollins*Publishers*

For both Joes.

▦ Author's Note

I hope that what follows will inspire you to savour these great films again.

If you know any further stories – preferably true – to tickle the fancy of film-goers please drop me a line. Can You Spots – about any film at all – are particularly welcome, and I will see that anyone who contributes figures in the credits.

My thanks go to the artists and technicians of the film industry, and those who have written about them. Also, more immediately, to the British Film Institute staff and facilities, to Dave Kent and his colleagues at the John Kobal Collection, to Michael Alcock, to Sylvia van Gelder for her invaluable subbing and to Mary-Jane van Gelder for her help and patience.

Peter van Gelder
March 1990

Note: The ages for the actors, producers and directors are those at the time of filming; modesty has caused the occasional gap.

THAT'S HOLLYWOOD. Copyright © 1990 by Peter van Gelder. All rights reserved. Printed in the United States of America. No part of this book may be used or reproduced in any manner whatsoever without written permission except in the case of brief quotations embodied in critical articles and reviews. For information address HarperCollins Publishers, 10 East 53rd Street, New York, NY 10022.

First edition

FRONTISPIECE: Creating *Frankenstein*

LIBRARY OF CONGRESS CATALOG CARD NUMBER 89-46491

ISBN 0-06-055198-4

ISBN 0-06-096512-6 (pbk.)

90 91 92 93 94 MPC 10 9 8 7 6 5 4 3 2 1

90 91 92 93 94 MPC 10 9 8 7 6 5 4 3 2 1 (pbk.)

That's Hollywood

A BEHIND-THE-SCENES LOOK AT 60 OF THE GREATEST FILMS EVER MADE

Peter van Gelder

HarperPerennial

An Imprint of HarperCollins*Publishers*

For both Joes.

▦ Author's Note

I hope that what follows will inspire you to savour these great films again.

If you know any further stories – preferably true – to tickle the fancy of film-goers please drop me a line. Can You Spots – about any film at all – are particularly welcome, and I will see that anyone who contributes figures in the credits.

My thanks go to the artists and technicians of the film industry, and those who have written about them. Also, more immediately, to the British Film Institute staff and facilities, to Dave Kent and his colleagues at the John Kobal Collection, to Michael Alcock, to Sylvia van Gelder for her invaluable subbing and to Mary-Jane van Gelder for her help and patience.

Peter van Gelder
March 1990

Note: The ages for the actors, producers and directors are those at the time of filming; modesty has caused the occasional gap.

THAT'S HOLLYWOOD. Copyright © 1990 by Peter van Gelder. All rights reserved. Printed in the United States of America. No part of this book may be used or reproduced in any manner whatsoever without written permission except in the case of brief quotations embodied in critical articles and reviews. For information address HarperCollins Publishers, 10 East 53rd Street, New York, NY 10022.

First edition

FRONTISPIECE: Creating *Frankenstein*

LIBRARY OF CONGRESS CATALOG CARD NUMBER 89-46491

ISBN 0-06-055198-4

ISBN 0-06-096512-6 (pbk.)

90 91 92 93 94 MPC 10 9 8 7 6 5 4 3 2 1

90 91 92 93 94 MPC 10 9 8 7 6 5 4 3 2 1 (pbk.)

Contents

Airplane!

1980 Parody of air disaster movies with a traumatized ex-fighter pilot
saving both the day and his romance with a stewardess

▦ The talent

Robert Hays 32, as Ted Striker; film
newcomer from TV. Run-of-the-mill but
regular work since this
Julie Hegarty 25, as Elaine; model in first
film. Picked by Woody Allen for *A
Midsummer Night's Sex Comedy* (1982)
Leslie Nielsen 55, as Dr Rumack; son of a
Canadian mountie familiar from estimated
1,000 guest spots on American TV
Peter Graves 55, as Captain Oveur; Jim
Phelps in TV's *Mission Impossible* plus a
few films like *Stalag 17* (1953). He's the
brother of James Arness (but you knew that)
Lloyd Bridges 67, as McCroskey; many big-
and small-screen roles, particularly fifties
TV smash *Sea Hunt*. Father of Beau and Jeff
(but you knew that, too)

Robert Stack 61, as Kramer; Eliot Ness in
TV's *Untouchables*, of course, but made
history in *First Love* (1939) as 'the first boy
to kiss Deanna Durbin' (did you know
that?)
Howard W. Koch 64, Producer; long-
standing Paramount production executive
who made *The Manchurian Candidate*
(1962) and Warren Beatty's *Heaven Can
Wait* (1978)
Jerry Zucker 30, Writer/Director; **Dave
Zucker** 32, Writer/Director and **Jim
Abrahams** 36, Writer/Director; have
continued their three-handed approach with
some success, notably *Ruthless People*
(1986) and *The Naked Gun* (1989)

▦ The business

Jerry, Dave and Jim are two brothers and a friend who decided in the early seventies
to shun safe boring careers in Milwaukie, get their act together and take it on the
road. They evolved a homemade comedy revue called Kentucky Fried Theatre which
became a minor sensation in Los Angeles.

Having ventured thus far they further ventured $35,000 videoing their perform-
ance and touting it round the studios. This resulted in twenty-two of their skits being
filmed by John Landis as *Kentucky Fried Movie* (1977). Across America, no doubt,
many other young men fantasize about Hollywood, while across Tinseltown crusty
moguls dream of films like this which on an outlay of $700,000 gross $20,000,000.

The boys could have written their own ticket if they'd stuck to just writing after
that but they wanted more, determined never to repeat the experience of having
someone else calling the shots on their work. Landis was apparently very sweet to
them but all four got fed up with – in turn – Jerry, Dave and Jim coming up to the
director before each shot to explain just how they individually saw the joke.

The film they really wanted to make all along was a spoof on the seventies fad for
disaster movies. It had been their pet project before *Kentucky Fried Movie* and the
result of five years' work on thirty versions of a script that finally crammed in every
gag they could conceive.

Attending all their business meetings as a trio they were unable to persuade anyone to risk giving them a free hand and in any case the Directors Guild were very stuffy about three people sharing the main credit. Finally Paramount President Michael Eisner took the plunge, with the insurance of veteran executive Howard W. Koch's avuncular eye on things.

Koch minded the $3,500,000 budget and the boys returned about $80,000,000 in world receipts with a movie delivered under budget on a brisk seven-week schedule. Zucker, Zucker and Abrahams promised no sequels and moved on to sending up spies and policemen. Koch, however, was too old and too rich to for any such nonsense and re-assembled the main players for a 1982 sequel. This time there was one writer/director, Ken Finkleman, whose film was funny enough to prove that a good formula remains a good formula.

▥ Behind the screen

Three directors? It sounds like schizophrenia in stereo but in fact the trio speak with once voice: Jerry's. He is the only one who actually communicates with the crew, although he only pronounces when the three have concurred and are happy.

It also means safety in numbers. This was their first venture into film apart from what they had managed to absorb from John Landis as he directed them in *Kentucky Fried Movie*. The crew on *Airplane!* seemed to have been impressed and helpful to the newcomers; Zucker, Zucker and Abrahams at least knew what they wanted if not always how to obtain the effect. This may be why, despite the expert services of Director of Photography Joseph Biroc, *Airplane!* always has a low-budget, made-for-TV look*.

If you are wondering quite where the plot comes from just watch *Airport* 1975 and *Zero Hour!* (1957)**, both tales from the pen of Arthur Hailey. The latter, his first big screen success, is the real motherlode of inspiration. It starred Dana Andrews and Linda Darnell and has a modest claim to history in that it prompted a change in air safety rules to ensure that on any real flight not all the crew would choose fish. The boys came across it by accident when they were recording TV commercials to mock in their stage act.

The index of tolerance to ridicule in American cinema seems to be calibrated so that you can take the piss as long as you pay. *Zero Hour!* was a Paramount film but the studio had to fork out for the remake rights. And the negotiations with Universal, who were responsible for the *Airport* (1970) cycle, were very elaborate. *Airplane!* is just as close a similarity as they would allow in titles. They balked at the idea of the nun playing to the pre-pubescent stretcher case à la Helen Reddy in *Airport* 1975, which is why the stewardess does it instead.

And where do all the jokes come from? Mr Abrahams and Messrs Zucker praise the inspirational value of coffee. They apparently sit round and by the third cup the ideas are really steaming. Jim types.

---

*Also perhaps because they videoed each take to check that the final packing of jokes worked. Biroc, at 77, had been one of Hollywood's most respected and sought-after cinematographers since the 1940's and an Oscar winner for disaster pack-leader, *The Towering Inferno* (1974).

**And, to state the obvious, individual scenes take off *Saturday Night Fever* (1978), *From Here to Eternity* (1953) and, in the title sequence, *Jaws* (1975).

Kareem Abdul-Jabbar, Rossie Harris and Peter Graves: too close for Cleveland

▥ The experience

'Deliciously, inventively funny.' *Screen International* 26 July 1980

'*Airplane!* is a splendidly tacky, totally tasteless, completely insignificant flight, a gooney bird of a movie that looks as if it could never get off the ground and then surprises and delights with its free-spirited aerobatics.' Richard Schickel, *Time*, 14 July 1980

'It is all to the credit of these stock actors, who had padded out every middle quality television series and film for years that they are happy to ridicule the types they have been happy to be cast as for so long.' Nicholas Wapshott, *The Scotsman*, 9 August 1980

'The real irony of *Airplane!* (and a mark of its failure) is that the films it sets out to satirize are actually funnier and richly more entertaining.' David Castell, *Sunday Telegraph*, 10 August 1980 – typical of many critics who were superior about the film but admitted laughing a lot

'The fantasizing is fun. After that it's work.' David Zucker

▥ Can you spot . . .

* Jerry, Dave and Jim. They couldn't resist a Hitchcock-like cameo but got it over with early – on either side of their credit at the beginning. Jim is the religious zealot before and the brothers Zucker are ground controllers just afterwards.

* Some other, more famous, cameos. Ethel Merman as the man who thinks he's Ethel Merman, and José Feliciano.

* Bits which were too offensive. My video version seems to have left out the sick little girl having her drip feed accidentally yanked out by the stewardess and in a recent British TV showing Captain Oveur's hilarious oveurtures to the small boy were dispensed with. It so happened that at the time Britain was gripped by the Cleveland child-sex scandal.

Annie Hall

1977 Neurotic comedian reflects on a bittersweet romance, and on his life in general.

▦ The talent

Woody Allen 41, as Alvy Singer; for it is he . . .

Diane Keaton 30, as Annie Hall; once in a lifetime part, tailored in love. She's not been as lucky since

Tony Roberts 36, as Rob; Allen's favourite male side-kick. As with Keaton, films for others tend to be more ordinary

Paul Simon 34, as Tony Lacey; decided to stick to making records

Charles H. Joffe 46, Producer; with Rollins, Woody Allen's former agent who pushed him from just writing into stand-up comedy

Jack Rollins 61, Producer; other clients with Joffe have included Robin Williams, Billy Crystal and Harry Belafonte. Also a TV executve

Woody Allen Director; he turned rather serious after this

▦ The business

Woody Allen had a cosy relationship with United Artists that allowed him to make any sort of film he fancied if he kept the cost under $3,000,000. A dedicated core of fans would ensure modest profits every time.

Woody said then that he had relinquished hope of making millions in exchange for artistic freedom. But he wasn't exactly starving. Allen Konigsberg started out selling gags to newspaper columnists in his teens and soon graduated to TV and $1,700 a week. By the mid-sixties he could command $250,000 a year writing movie scripts.

By the end of the sixties he was directing them as well. Woody Allen films tended to be shambolic sexual fantasy-comedies but *Annie Hall* was a revelation, and a vindication of the fans who knew all along that he could deliver polished, quality goods.

It had satire, romance and very good timing. The strong female roles were just right for the mid-seventies and contributed as much to the film's impact as its timeless charm.

In particular the public fell for Diane-Annie and for her quirky wardrobe, based on Keaton's own taste, which was widely copied. Her earnings started to look up as well, although she only got $50,000 for her next, serious, lead in *Looking for Mr Goodbar* (1977).

Annie Hall broke a Woody Allen tradition by making an *im*modest profit – about $36,000,000 worldwide – but might have earned rather less with his original choice of title: Anhedonia. For anyone without the benefit of Allen's then twenty-year

---

*They spotted the rollercoaster location on a recce. Originally Singer Snr was to be a taxi driver, one of Konigsberg Snr's occupations.

experience of psychoanalysis this is a term meaning the inability to relish pleasure. United Artists head Arthur Krin didn't relish the idea to the point of threatening to jump out of the window if it wasn't changed. Woody relented during the run-up to release in the spring of 1977 but not before his co-writer Marshall Brickman obligingly trotted out a series of alternatives including 'A Rollercoaster* Named Desire'. 'Me and My Goy' and 'It Had to be Jew'.

Oscar night was a triumph with awards for Best Picture, Actress, Script and Director. But Woody was nowhere to be seen – in Hollywood at least. It was a Monday so he was playing clarinet as usual down at Michael's Pub in New York. Later he read himself to sleep with *Conversations with Carl Jung* (what else?) and only learned of the accolades from the next morning's papers. Anhedonia strikes again.

▓ Behind the screen

'There is *one* clear autobiographical fact in the picture. I have thought about sex since my first intimation of consciousness,' so said Woody Allen.

'Pull the other one,' replied his fans who swooped eagerly on a variety of obvious allusions to the truth: Keaton is Di*ane*'s (Annie's) mother's family name. Her real surname is Hall. Allen plays *Alvy* and their mutual old friend Tony *Robe*rts plays Rob. Moreover it was widely known that Allen and Keaton had been an item in real life.

Real aficionados also recognized much of the script as a rough parallel of Woody's life story including a familiar anthology of pet hang-ups spiced with a review of his best old jokes. And the millions of new Allen fans watched Diane Keaton's ingenuous performance entirely believing her to be the real Annie. In fact the actress had to use all her skills 'not to get in the way of herself', as she described it.

Not surprisingly the pair sought to play down the idea of it being a window on their private life although Allen allowed that he was playing himself in hypothetical situations. Perhaps another reason for his unwillingness to elaborate further on the precise blend of jokes and reality was the memory of being sued for $1,000,000 by his first missus when he started including ex-wife jokes in his comedy routines.

The facts are that Allen, Keaton and Roberts started socializing in 1969 when all three were on stage in Woody's *Play it Again Sam*. At the time he regarded Diane as a big Broadway star although her chief claim to fame seems to have been that she was the only one in *Hair* always to opt out of the voluntary nude bit at the end (though she did confess to peeking at the other actors' parts). Still Woody was the most famous of the trio and the other two took to calling him Max in public to lessen the chances of recognition (that scene with the Cosa Nostra branch of his fan club is another old paranoia come to life).

Diane made him laugh. He was also impressed by her artfully jumbled wardrobe though his remembered example of combat boots and oven gloves sounds pure Woody Allen. They had an affair and lived together for about a year in the early seventies.

Miss Keaton hails from California (not the Mid West) but she really does have a Grammy Hall. Allen met Grammy and the rest of the meschpruche at a Christmas (not Easter) dinner but Diane has been keen to point out that her family are *nothing* like the Halls in the film – aside from Grammy's suspicions about Jews. She also made

Diane Keaton and Woody Allen: spot the anhedonic

it clear that although she used to wash with black soap and drive a VW (skilfully, not homicidally) she gave up drugs at the time of *Hair.*

There was no Tony Lacey figure to come between them, they say, no falling out. The pair just drifted apart after deciding to resume living separately. They have remained good friends.

Perhaps the reason the film seems to dwell so much on autobiography is that what you see – concentrating as it does on the Alvy-Annie romance – was originally just one element of fifty hours of film that Woody Allen shot from April 1976. That the result didn't drift into the sort of whacky shambles typical of his earlier work is due in great part to the film editor, Ralph Rosenblum, and Allen's co-writer Marshall Brickman (certainly according to the gentlemen themselves).

Brickman described the process of writing with Woody as a protracted stylized conversation, strolling up and down Lexington Avenue. The two days worth of footage it generated contained many elements only hinted at in the cut that you see; Annie ordering pastrami on white bread with mayonnaise is one vestige of a running gag. There was science fiction, mystery and lots more besides that might have made up several further pictures. But viewing an early rough-cut Brickman recognized that the sections with Annie worked best.

Rosenblum set about editing with the necessary ruthlessness to reduce a thirty-to-one ratio. Notice how the economy of the individual scenes points up much of the film's wit.

Extra shooting was needed to fill in the jigsaw – one example being the scene with the cocaine, which explained the transition to California. In fact the point has usually been lost on cinema audiences who are busy cracking up as Alvy sneezes away $2,000 worth of drugs. The sneeze just happened and they kept the take; look in particular at Diane's reaction.

Notice, though, that still not everything fits together; for instance there's no explanation of Annie's final return from California. And right up to release there was still a question of how to finish. So in the end Ralph Rosenblum just clipped together all the most significant bits that he could remember to the backing of 'Old Times'. Allen recorded the closing monologue as he stopped off at the studio on the way to a preview. It's all a bit sloppily tacked-on – particularly the pause in the voice-over – but the film wouldn't be the same without it.

▦ The experience

'I find *Annie Hall* myself a kind of trivial, middle-class comedy.' Woody Allen, 1977

'What it comes down to finally is ninety minutes of coitus interruptus; fun but fruitless'. M. J. Sobran Jnr, *National Review*

'Whether *Annie Hall* is autobiographical or not, it has enabled Allen to progress from the realm of simple self-representation to that of the artfully shaped self-portrait.' Janet Maslin, *Newsweek*, 1977

'That Woody Allen, he's something. I can't make head or tail out of half of what he says.' (The Real) Grammy Hall

▦ Can you spot . . .

* A few soon-to-be famous faces. Christopher Walken as Annie's semi-psychotic brother, one of many supporting roles hacked to a cameo. Next year came an Oscar for *The Deer Hunter* (1978). Jeff (*The Fly* (1986)) Goldblum has a walk-on (or rather walk-past) as the Californian party guest who can't remember his mantra. And, for the sharp-eyed, Sigourney Weaver is Alvy's date at the end of the film.
* The famous taking part as themselves. Dick Cavett (pre-recorded) and Marshall McLuan (what are you doin'?) are obvious. But just look who's the winner of the Truman Capote look-alike competition.
* The spectators being held back by the New York policemen, including a horse that gets a trot-on part, when Alvy canvasses the views of passersby in the street.
* The lighting changes. Allen purposely shot New York in dull conditions and let the sun burn out all the Californian scenes. But perhaps he's not as anhedonic as he claims because all the flashbacks have a golden glow – or maybe they're meant to look faded.

Apocalypse Now

1979 A terrifying mission to kill a US Vietnam commander who has gone mad.

▦ The talent

Marlon Brando 52, as Colonel Kurtz; fifties and sixties screen giant with an Oscar as Coppola's *Godfather* (1972). Rarely seen since this

Martin Sheen 36, as Captain Willard; nervy character actor also memorable in *Badlands* (1973) and as a TV JFK. Two sons successful in films, Charlie Sheen and Emilio Estevez (the original family surname)

Robert Duvall 45, as Lt Colonel Kilgore; with Brando and Coppola in *The Godfather* – one of modern cinema's most sought-after character actors

Francis Coppola 38, Producer/Director; fresh from the acclaimed *Godfathers* and *The Conversation* (1974). His next few projects were less successful

▦ The business

Scriptwriter John Milius finished *Apocalypse Now* in six weeks but that's about the fastest stretch of an epic that took twelve years to get off the ground, four of those actually in production.

It began as a film that George Lucas, then Coppola's assistant, was going to make. With Milius he had been kicking around some of the wild tales of insanity and mayhem emerging from Vietnam, of the sort chronicled by journalists like Michael Herr* who wrote the bleary voice-over commentary for *Apocalypse Now*. Coppola's contribution was suggesting that they adapt to a Nam context Joseph Conrad's 1902 novel, *Heart of Darkness* (actually about a white hunter who goes off his head in the Belgian Congo).

When Lucas became immersed in a modest project called *Star Wars* (1977) Coppola took on a job that looked like occupying sixteen weeks of shooting and costing $12,000,000. *Apocalypse Now* actually took more than a year in the jungle through typhoons, illness and fatigue. It cost $30,000,000, the balance raised by the director hocking all his personal assets.

It recouped its costs in North America alone, raising $37,300,000. There were Oscars for Cinematography and Sound but although the critics were respectful they generally expressed disappointment at the muddled pretentiousness of the film's last quarter. Coppola himself admitted that he got too absorbed with his individual, impressive set-piece scenes, trusting them to converge in some way to a natural conclusion.

*His reports were later collected in the book *Despatches*.

These considerations apart it was an immense gamble which paid off. However Coppola's luck did not hold out with his next film, *One From The Heart* (1982) which cost $26,000,000 – $14,000,000 of his own – and returned very little. His Zeotrope studio had to go but presumably Coppola took this turn of events as philisophically as he had viewed the possibility of *Apocalypse Now* failing. He observed then that whatever happened he could get a job the next day directing any old picture for $1,000,000.

Behind the screen

The process of shooting in the Philippines was likened by Francis Coppola to the American involvement in South East Asia, except the G.I.'s had better weather. They had too much money, too much equipment and seem to have gone as loopy as Kurtz and his disciples.

It was the kind of shoot where the Italians accompanying the director of photography, Vittorio Storaro*, were provided with pasta flown in specially from their homeland. Eleanor Coppola, the director's wife, who accompanied him for much of the eighteen months on location, warned him that he was becoming like Kurtz. He was spending too much, and everyone on the set was bowing automatically to his every whim. This strained a marriage which survived several upsets and the suspicion of infidelity during filming. Mrs Coppola's method of delivering her critique was galling enough; she made her accusations on a telex with copies all round.

The craziness started in earnest in early 1976 with some of the first scenes to be shot, the attack on the village by helicopters under the command of Robert Duvall as Lt Col Kilgore. The seventy huts comprising the target had been specially constructed at a coconut plantation near Baler in the Philippines. Coppola was directing the attack – involving a force of 450 actors, extras and technicians – from one of the helicopters. It all got out of control with a successful air strike on the film's paint and prop shop. At another point Coppola had to hit the deck to avoid becoming a casualty. Can you spot Robert Duvall's acting of bravery? He hates heights and the whole sequence, especially dropping the grenade, needed much courage.

The helicopters themselves had been one of the attractions of filming in the Philippines. The U.S. military were unhappy at the sound of the film and offered no cooperation. President Marcos, on the other hand, was happy to let Coppola use the bulk of his entire force of twenty-four Vietnam War-type gunships. This generosity was all the more remarkable as he was simultaneously deploying them to put down insurgents. With a swift change of livery the helicopters were harrying the rebels by night and carrying the film-makers by day.

Filming was already in a moderate state of crisis as it was just after Harvey Keitel, originally cast as Willard, had left the production. The bone of contention seems to have been a planned lay-off while Marlon Brando spent the summer vacation with his kids. Only four days of reshooting were needed to add Martin Sheen's presence to the raid.

How does the weather look? In no time Hurricane Olga blew in, dumped forty inches of rain in six days, and blew out again leaving 140 people dead. Most of the

*Bertolucci's favourite cinematographer, hired to give the film what Coppola termed a graceful look. He was kept on for *One From the Heart.*

Apocalypse Now sets were destroyed and the crew were sent home for the two months they took to rebuild.

Martin Sheen's eerie mirror boxing scene was shot soon after filming resumed, on the actor's thirty-sixth birthday. Coppola had prepared him by keeping him drunk and confined in a room for two days. Sheen had been taking marshal arts lessons from an instructor who advised him to practise in front of a mirror. Coppola set two cameras running and let him go. He shouted 'cut' appropriately when Sheen hurt himself in accidentally breaking the mirror but they kept on filming.

It was all something of a strain. Martin Sheen temporarily separated from his wife and began a bout of heavy drinking. Three quarters through filming he suffered a heart attack. Coppola was afraid for the life of his star and also for the future of the film, but Sheen was back at work after seven weeks.

What more could possibly go wrong? Marlon Brando, Coppola's star from *The Godfather*, arrived on location after what must have been a very agreeable family summer. He was seriously overweight for the part and they had to use a leaner double for most of the long shots. In the month he was out there Brando mostly just talked, extemporizing his part as Coppola let the camera run.

Coppola had two conclusions; the one you see depends on the print you are watching. In the original 70 mm version Willard leads Clean away from Kurtz's camp. The 35 mm version ends with a series of infra-red shots of explosions, taken by many to mean an air strike on the rogue battalion although Coppola says not.

Many people thought that the real horror, apart from Brando's protracted spiel as Kurtz, was what happened to the ox near the end. The poor beast was decapitated as part of a real ceremony by the Philippine native tribesmen portraying the Montagnards, and the crew just happened to be up and rolling.

▦ The experience

'Groping to convey its size and movement, I can only say it suggests *The Bridge on the River Kwai*, *MASH* and *Catch 22* run together but transcended by the moral dimension that Coppola constructs out of the method and madness of the Vietnam War.' Alexander Walker, *Evening Standard*, 21 May 1979

'It struck me like a diamond bullet in my head that I wasn't making the film, the jungle was.' Francis Coppola

'While much of the footage is breathtaking, *Apocalypse Now* is emotionally obtuse and intellectually empty. It is not so much an epic account of a gruelling war as an incongruous, extravagant monument to artistic self-defeat.' Frank Rice, *Time*, 27 August 1979.

'The most compelling war film ever made.' Alan Brien, *Sunday Times*, 16 December 1979

▦ Can you spot . . .

* The director. He's with a TV news team playing a director.
* An ageing hippie. Dennis Hopper as the photojournalist, ending a period of comparative aimlessness following his *Easy Rider* (1969) success, with interesting films like *Blue Velvet* (1986) to come.
* Small arms. Not of the military variety; Martin Sheen's left is 3″ shorter than the other.

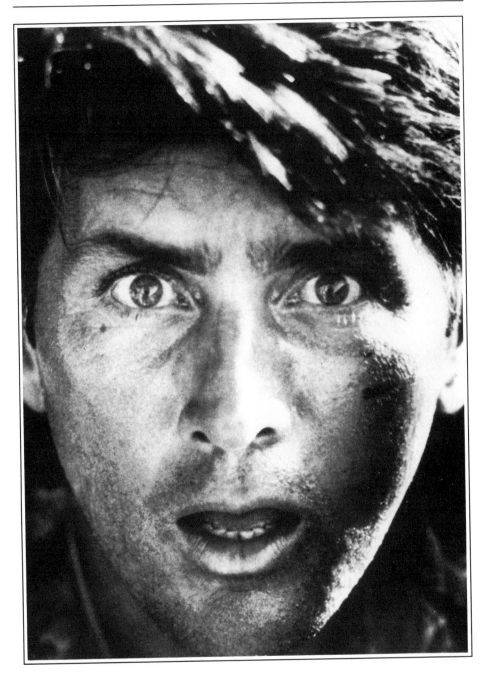

Martin Sheen: the horror

* Duvall as Coppola. When Kilgore throws away his megaphone in disgust that's a gesture deliberately lifted from Coppola's behaviour.
* What a tough life it is being a severed head. In Kurtz's camp the heads' bodies were sweltering in underground boxes from eight until six – with a break for lunch.

Batman

1989 A mysterious vigilante in bat costume fights an obsessive criminal who is terrorizing Gotham City.

▦ The talent

Jack Nicholson 52, as the Joker; the flavour of the seventies still packing them in, with an Oscar for *Terms of Endearment* (1983) and a nomination for *Prizzi's Honour* (1985)

Michael Keaton 37, as Batman; comedy star on an upward swing with *Beetlejuice* (1988) after several disappointing projects on film and TV

Kim Basinger 35, as Vicki Vale; one of the sex symbols of the eighties. You can see more of her in *9½ Weeks* (1986)

Jon Peters 42, Producer; Barbra Streisand's ex and a former hairdresser. Began in films co-producing her version of *A Star is Born* (1976). Partner with Guber since 1980

Peter Guber 47, Producer; former Columbia production chief. Responsible with Peters for a string of modern successes including *The Witches of Eastwick* (1987) and *Rain Man* (1989)

Tim Burton 30, Director; former Disney animator who had made only two previous features, *Pee Wee's Big Adventure* (1985) and *Beetlejuice*

▦ The business

When Peters and Guber first bought an option on Batman in 1979, the year of the character's fortieth anniversary, it didn't look too rich a prospect. *Superman: The Movie* (1978) had recently celebrated the Caped Crusader's stablemate at DC Comics, and the market for busybodies in tights seemed amply catered for.* Furthermore there was already a firmly-entrenched Batman image from TV, as dated as *Laugh In* and *The Mod Squad.*

This changed with a re-forging of the Batman legend in the mid-1980's by cartoonist Frank Miller Jnr with a series of adult comics, or graphic novels as they were termed. The first, *The Dark Knight Returns*, was a cult classic – moody, horrifying and very graphic indeed.

This was the stuff of a bankable screen super-hero for the late eighties, and something of a return to the original character conceived by eighteen-year-old Bob Kane in 1939. Kane was all in favour of the radical Caped Crusader and, still going strong, served as the film's technical advisor.**

Kane was in no doubt about casting the Joker. He sent the studio a still from *The Shining* (1979) of Jack Nicholson grinning maniacally, having first coloured the hair green and the face white. In any case Peters and Guber had already recruited Nicholson while he worked with them on *The Witches of Eastwick.*

Superman made more than $82,800,000 in North America alone but *Flash Gordon* (1980) struggled to cover costs.

**You can spot his signature on the cartoon of the bat handed to reporter Alexander Knox, played by Robert Wuhl.

The title role was another thing. Tim Burton had been chosen to direct because his two previous films had shown a flair for the grotesque which suited Miller's Batman vision. The producers had noted in Keaton a quality of ingratiating insanity but when Burton himself suggested his star in *Beetlejuice*, he was told by one Warner's big-wig, 'You can think of four hundred other guys before you think of Keaton.'

Fifty thousand DC fundamentalists agreed. A deluge of correspondence argued that he was too short, scrawny, bald and chinless to do justice even to the swinging sixties Batman. Bob Kane, at least, was persuaded when he saw how Keaton looked in the Batsuit – but in fact such was the iron maiden construction of the costume that it would have made Kim Basinger* look macho.

*She was a last-minute replacement for *No Way Out* (1988) star Sean Young who had been injured in a riding accident.

Michael Keaton: every inch a Batman

Gossip had the *Batman* budget at $50,000,000. Warner Brothers said it was a mere $30,000,000 – after, it seems, an extra injection of cash okayed during filming. The set alone cost upwards of $3,000,000. It was the biggest since *Cleopatra* (1963), covering most of the studio's eighteen sound stages. A man got rich just supplying the requisite sixty miles of scaffolding.

Keaton was apparently paid in seven figures, Jack Nicholson in *eight* – $11,000,000 – and that was just the start. He reportedly also took a two per cent stake in the merchandizing. The bat insignia was one of the most recognizable symbols in the world marketplace and everything possible was transformed into a setting for the motif. The stylized black-on-yellow design was the pre-pubescent fashion accessory of 1989 with sales estimated at $375,000,000. When it was used sans text or further illustration on advertising hoardings people would steal the posters.

Expectations were so high that cinema owners in the U.S. reported fans buying tickets solely to watch the ninety-second promo, then leaving before the main feature.

The film in its entirety did even better. Opening against strong competition from *Indiana Jones and the Last Crusade*, *Star Trek V* and *Ghostbusters II*, *Batman* shot into the record books as the first film ever to gross $100,000,000 in ten days.

▦ Behind the screen

The most complicated sequence to film was the Batwing crashing into the steps of Gotham Cathedral. It was one of many instances where the mega-set was supplemented by identical miniatures. The model-makers had four cameras rolling at once, they had the little streets doused with oil to mimic the hosed-down look of the set and they had a full-scale attack of nerves.

The set itself was only full-scale to a point. Anything that you can see that is higher than forty feet is either on the model, or a matted-in painting. The look was New York with no planning permission. Designer Anton Furst (who won an Oscar for *Batman* and also worked on *The Company of Wolves* (1984)) described it as if Hell had broken through the ground and kept on growing.

The Home Counties provided other locations. Wayne Manor scenes were shot at two stately homes, Knebworth House and Hatfield. The acid bath antics occurred at a disused power station.

The most difficult piece of equipment to deal with was the Batcar. Dubbed the Batpig, its handling was entirely uncooperative and once it almost flattened one of the stunt girls. Not only that, Batman kept on getting his ears caught when the roof closed. The bodywork recalled the fifties Stringray and the vintage Utah Flats speed testers of the thirties but the heart of the machines (one for stunts and one for show) was two 1968 Impalas recovered from a London scrap dealer. They had their chassis lengthened, engines dropped and various fighter aircraft bits added including part of a Rolls Royce Olympus Spey engine as the snout. This all took £160,000 and three months' construction. Even the twenty-four-inch, radio-controlled models for miniature work cost £10,000, and one was stolen.

Batman's bodywork was almost as involved. The costume was an effective disguise; for one thing you would never think it was Keaton's chin. The transformation relied on the Bat mask's vice-like design which gripped and jutted the star's under-achieving mandible. Some of the twenty-four cowls were more comfortable than others but none offered peripheral vision and all rendered the wearer partially deaf.

The body suits were armours of latex bolted together underneath the bat insignia. Keaton got extremely hot and bothered in all that rubber. He would throw things about and kick furniture in frustration. This in itself was a challenge. The cape weighted twenty-five pounds, felt like a ton and it hurt to belabour foe and furniture alike. Fortunately he had two stand-ins to help with the rough stuff and all that swooping. Kim Basinger loved the Batsuit, even though it tended to rub off on her in black globs. She said she found it sexy.

There was much speculation in the press as to what else she found sexy. Rumours, denied by the participants, linked her with both producer Jon Peters and Jack Nicholson. They were reported canoodling at the premiere. There were also reports of a subsequent romance with the film's composer, Prince. Kim merely said that she made new friends.

▦ The experience

'What's left in *Batman* is the skeleton of a nifty film. The heart got lost on Tim Burton's storyboard.' *Time*, 19 June 1989

'The movie splutters, stalls and turns inert because it's the prisoner of its set – and Jack Nicholson's relentless desire to devour it.' J. Hoberman, *Village Voice*, 4 July 1989

'Anyone who has the happy knack of sleeping through earthquakes should be able to disregard the hype encrusting *Batman* and see the film for what it is: as a moderately entertaining fantasy, with good design, some strong performances and a desperate need of a script doctor.' Adam Mars-Jones, *The Independent*, 10 August 1989

'Metaphysically the Joker was dipped in chemicals and lost his mind – not unlike the rest of society.' Jack Nicholson

▦ Can you spot . . .

* How the Joker knows Batman's identity. 'I was just a kid when I shot your parents,' he says during their confrontation in the belfry.
* Tough cards. The gunge that eats Napier's face leaves his deck of cards unblemished.
* The Flugelheim Museum is spelt two ways. There's an extra 'e' in the sign next to the tables inside.
* Someone who's happy with the costumes. Jack Nicholson helped choose the specially woven cloth for the Joker outfits; he's particularly partial to plaid. After the production he bought the lot.
* A shady character. The Joker, of course. His face was built up with prosthetic make-up – synthetic pads moulded to Jack Nicholson's muscle structure to behave like a second skin. But the make-up was so white that it would bleach out on camera so some shadowing effects are also painted on.
* Prince. He's jiving away in the 'Who can you trust?' procession organized by the Joker. The pop star was paid $1,000,000 advance for his contribution to the sound track. It made number one.

Beverly Hills Cop

1984 Unconventional Detroit detective in Beverly Hills to investigate the murder of a friend.

The talent

Eddie Murphy 23, as Axel Foley; hasn't quite maintained the momentum of *48 Hours* (1982), *Trading Places* (1983) and this
Judge Reinhold 27, as Det. Billy Rosewood; many mid-eighties comedies including *Ruthless People* (1986)
John Ashton as Sgt Taggart; Willie Joe Garr in *Dallas*. With Murphy, Reinhold and Cox in *Beverly Hills Cop II* (1987)
Lisa Eilbacher as Jenny Summers; in *An Officer and a Gentleman* (1982) and TV's *Winds of War*
Ronny Cox 46, as Lt Bogomil; familiar seventies-onwards character. In *Deliverance* (1972) and *Robocop* (1987)

Steven Berkoff 47, as Victor Maitland; an alternative force in British theatre. Got to torment Stallone in *Rambo* (1985), filmed soon after
Don Simpson 40, Producer; former ad man who with Bruckheimer produced *Flashdance* (1983) and *Top Gun* (1986)
Jerry Bruckheimer 39, Producer; oversaw Murphy's *48 Hours*. Said to preside over meetings with a loaded machine gun. In partnership with Simpson one of Hollywood's hottest executive items
Martin Brest 32, Director; despite his youth, a lot of TV and film experience

The business

It began with a trivial urban trauma suffered by Paramount President Michael Eisner. In 1975 he was stopped driving a beat-up station wagon by a very superior policeman in Beverly Hills who reduced him to feeling a hopeless out-of-towner. Eisner, one of modern Hollywood's most astute moguls, immediately recognized the germ of a film but no one could come up with a satisfactory script until the version you see on screen by Daniel Petrie Jnr.

Mickey Rourke was one of the actors approached to play Axel Foley but preparations went ahead with Sylvester Stallone as star. Sly quite liked the story but thought there were too many jokes, so he turned in a rewrite of his own which emphasized bloodshed rather than belly-laughs. Eisner – who later became head of Disney – didn't fancy the idea of Rambo Hits L.A. and as a consequence two weeks before shooting was to begin they were without a leading man.

Then somebody mentioned Eddie Murphy, who was emerging as the biggest black star since Sidney Poitier and the hottest property of any ethnic background for some time. He had started early as a night-club comedian, graduating to TV's *Saturday Night Live* when he was 19. Such was his popularity that in the course of a few years his appearance fee had climbed from $750 to reach $30,000.

He showed enough promise in the rough-cut of his first film, *48 Hours*, for Paramount to offer him a lucrative two-picture deal. When the film made $30,000,000 and his next, *Trading Places*, topped $40,000,000 they upped the ante to a five-picture deal guaranteeing him $15,000,000 plus $250,000 to set up his own production company.

At first Murphy wasn't keen on the idea of taking up arms again on screen as he had in *48 Hours* but the producers persisted. He finally accepted the role of Axel Foley, so the story goes, on the flip of a coin. Lucky for everyone concerned; *Beverly Hills Cop* was a smash, propelling the star straight into the top ten at number two (after Clint Eastwood). The film took $108,000,000 in North America alone.

Paramount's reaction? Throw more money at Mr Murphy. It is estimated that with his share of the profits Eddie netted over $14,000,000 from *Beverly Hills Cop* – roughly what the film cost to make.

▦ Behind the screen

We are talking serious ad-libbing. Although the original Petrie screenplay is intact in general plot structure and most of the action, director Martin Brest encouraged Eddie Murphy to spice it up with as much business and wise-cracking as possible.

The script was scarcely touched in the interregnum between Sylvester and Eddie so the most obvious Murphyisms are any references to the leading character being black; the exchange with the hotel receptionist and his harangue at the bonded warehouse are pure Eddie.* Critics further noted a certain improbability in the degree of Axel's uncomplicated affection across the racial divide, and his shared background with yuppie Jenny Summers. In fact Murphy was raised in salubrious surroundings on Long Island without encountering much racial prejudice, and in general keeps his act free of black anger.

The picture's individual off-the-cuff exchanges begin with the young master being momentarily beaten at his own game. We have just seen one of the most clinical motor destruction sequences since Laurel and Hardy, with tons of cigarettes spilling off the back of a lorry as it careers round Detroit. Watch Murphy miss a beat when somebody asks him if he's got a cigarette. 'Did you write that yourself?' is all he can manage as retort.

Mostly though he is leading the scene firmly by the nose and all the director can do is let the camera roll and pick up the continuity later. John Ashton quite obviously cracks up during Murphy's 'super-cops' testimonial to Ronny Cox's Lt Bogomil. Director Martin Brest gets away with it by, in the next set-up, making it seem as if Ashton's character was attempting to conceal his embarrassment.

It's one of several instances where Brest and his TV director's eye saves the day, smoothing wild material with the careful editing of shots picked up afterwards. Watch things slip gloriously out of control when Murphy encounters the only member of the company who managed to upstage him: Bronson Pinchot as Serge, the greeter at Maitland's gallery.**

Keeping the individual scenes together in these instances and then wedging them into the narrative were problems far outweighed by the benefit of Murphy's

---

*This latter example is a ringer for the notable scene in *48 Hours* where he single-handedly shakes down a bar full of rednecks.
**Pinchot later resurfaced in the TV comedy *Perfect Strangers* with Mark Linn-Baker, another young actor who made an impact in someone else's film. He co-starred with Peter O'Toole in *My Favourite Year* (1982).

dangerous screen sparkle. He even occasionally helped to stitch the original story together more securely. For example, there was the problem of how to engineer Foley's entry to the exclusive Harrow Club. As they came to shoot the scene no satisfactory version had emerged after six drafts. Murphy asked for a few seconds to think and then created the entire scam about Ramone needing to see Mr Maitland about herpes simplex ten in a mere fifteen minutes of shooting. Not everyone appreciated Murphy's way of working. To Steven Berkoff it seemed a personal challenge when the young comedian altered his lines from take to take.

A colleague on *Saturday Night Live*, Joe Piscopo, said that Murphy portrayed himself on screen, but there are a number of marked differences. For one thing Axel was a warm-hearted loner. Eddie by that time had acquired a coterie of body-guards and assistants who would attend him at his luxury trailer. Tastes in entertainment also varied between the star and his character. Teetotal Murphy would be unlikely to stop off for a beer and, unlike Axel, was rarely without the attentions of an attractive young woman. At the time of filming Murphy was engaged but they broke up about the time *Beverly Hills Cop* was released.

The most obvious difference was in deportment. Foley is a slob and Murphy can barely disguise the fact that he is in reality a fastidiously sharp dresser making the best of the unnatural costume of jeans and sweatshirt. It's said that once as he stepped from his limo outside NBC Eddie squished a dog turd. He lowered his gaze to the mess, slipped his foot delicately from the newly-bought shoe and hopped into the building.

▥ The experience

'The film's only function is to provide Murphy with the opportunity to work a dozen or so variations on his familiar and oddly endearing routine.' Richard Corliss, *Time*, 7 July 1985

'He has no zingers – he just rattles off pitifully undistinguished profanity – but we're cued to react to every four-letter word as riotous. The whole picture is edited and scored as if it were a lollapalooza of laughs. And, with Murphy bursting his sides guffawing in self-congratulation, and the camera jammed into his tonsils, damned if the audience don't whoop and carry on as if yes, this is a wow of a comedy.' Pauline Kael, *New Yorker*, 24 December 1984

'There's a lot of formula dreck in *Beverly Hills Cop* but it's still enormously entertaining.' David Edelstein, *Village Voice*, 11 December 1984

▥ Can you spot . . .

* A real cop, Gilbert R. Hill who played Foley's Detroit boss, Inspector Todd, was the policeman who showed the film-makers some of the methods of the city's constabulary. He had a quarter of a century on the force and 5,000 cases under his belt. Murphy copied Hill's practice of keeping his gun down the back of his trousers.
* A significant teeshirt. One of the cases they were taken on, in their Detroit recce, was a killing outside Mumford High School, the slogan on Murphy's top kit.

Bonnie and Clyde

1967 Outlaw couple rampage across the American South West. But the law is closing in.

▦ The talent

Warren Beatty 30, as Clyde Barrow; libidinous brother of Shirley Maclaine whose initially promising film career was going nowhere particular

Faye Dunaway 26, as Bonnie Parker; relative newcomer with sporadic subsequent success, including an Oscar for *Network* (1976)

Michael J. Pollard 28, as C. W. Moss; was about to give up acting until this hit gave him the chance to play a few quirky leading roles

Gene Hackman 36, as Buck Barrow; former marine and TV floor manager who was to become a seventies superstar

Estelle Parsons 39, as Blanche Barrow; the one who got the Oscar – and many more memorable character parts

Denver Pyle 47, as Frank Hamer; without whom no Western since the late forties was complete

Warren Beatty Producer; moved into writing and directing with an Oscar for *Reds* (1981)

Arthur Penn 44, Director; gifted film-maker from TV and theatre whose few movies include *The Miracle Worker* (1962) and *Little Big Man* (1970)

▦ The business

The story of the film starts with the two scriptwriters, David Newman and Robert Benton, who in the early sixties were working on *Esquire* magazine. They became fascinated by the American outlaw myth and in particular a breed of mobile gang unique to the early thirties, flourishing with the coming of fast Ford cars but before there was a federal police force which could chase them across state lines. Bonnie and Clyde was written in 1964 with Flatt and Scruggs' 'Foggy Mountain Breakdown', the banjo music which decorates the film, jangling away on the gramophone.

No studio wanted anything to do with such a sordid little story even though Newman and Benton managed to interest their two director heroes, Francois Truffaut and Jean Luc Goddard, in the project. The script languished on the shelf with their Flatt and Scruggs records for a couple of years until Truffaut met Warren Beatty at a party and told him about it. Beatty immediately became interested.*

In the end he is estimated to have earned himself a $6,000,000 fortune after risking $90,000 of his own money and cajoling Warner Brothers into putting up the rest of the $2,500,000 it cost to make. In North America alone *Bonnie and Clyde* has taken almost $23,000,000.

*Newman and Benton lived happily ever after, writing further successful screenplays. Benton won an Oscar directing his own script of *Kramer vs. Kramer* (1979).

Faye Dunaway: lawless and bra-less

But at first business was only moderate and critical reaction in the U.S. varied from hostile to positively vitriolic. The film offended with its pushed-boundary violence and comic/heroic portrayal of a couple who were really devoid of redeeming features. In Britain, on the other hand, the public queued for hours to see *Bonnie and Clyde* and the critics hailed it as a masterpiece.

All this persuaded America that the picture might be worth a second look and Beatty threatened to sue Warners if they didn't relaunch it. He used unconventional negotiating tactics to bully the staid studio executives, such as lying down in the middle of the office floor and refusing to move until they agreed.

Then, the unthinkable happened; the critics changed their minds. *Time* and *Newsweek* both actually published retractions of their previous reviews. Suddenly the film was taking off. By the time of the Oscars it was doing a roaring trade and had acquired nine nominations which included all the principal actors. In the event only the director of photography, Burnett Guffey, and Estelle Parsons actually won.

'*Bonnie and Clyde* is a great film, as long as you don't think about it,' wrote Jerry Richard in the *Antioch Review* summing up long-term critical opinion and everyone's uneasy aftertaste from Hollywood fantasy amalgamated with tacky historical fact. But it was a perfect film for the time, mirroring the fashionable rebellion against authority of the late 1960's with two attractive Robin Hood characters who let the poor keep their money while they robbed the banks who foreclosed on the farmers.

An indicator of the mass support for a movie is its effect on people beyond the theatre. There was bound to be some violence – as late as 1985 a man in Devon went on a shotgun spree which was linked to a TV showing of the film.

But happily the biggest influence was on fashion. Posters of the stars were on every adolescent wall. Faye Dunaway's thirties look was a break with the hard, angular lines of sixties fashion and widely copied, generating millions for the rag trade.

The costume designer, Theodora van Runkle, got this first main costume credit on the strength of her response when tested on how she would make Bonnie look sexy. Her simple answer was that Dunaway shouldn't wear a bra. Unfortunately, the multi-million dollar fashion parade seems to have passed Ms van Runkle by – she complains that all she ever saw of it was the $1,250 she was paid for the job.

But at least the people of Pau in the French Pyrennees and a Mr Ted Toddy were happy. Pau is the centre for the French beret industry, which the screen Bonnie revitalized, boosting production from 1,500 a week to 20,000. And Toddy was the owner of the 1934 grey Ford V-8 that the real Bonnie and Clyde were finally ambushed in by lawmen near Arcadia, North Louisiana. Toddy bought the car for $14,500 (it cost $786 new). It is estimated that admissions to view the Ford that wasn't quite fast enough have totalled more than $1,000,000.

▦ Behind the screen

The backgrounds and events are broadly authentic but the principal characters are pure Hollywood romance, drawing much more on Warren Beatty and Faye Dunaway than Clyde Barrow and Bonnie Parker.

The writers thoroughly researched the Barrow gang's territory. They spoke to friends and bystanders, some of whom were finally recruited for the film: bank clerks, witnesses and the like who made such believable bit players. The surname of Gene Wilder's cameo, Eugene Grizzard, comes from two elderly sisters, Mabel and

Evan, whom the writers interviewed. They are to blame for that feeble joke about the cow with laced milk.

Not only did the locals retain, and profit from, their naturalness and a fund of gory memories, they even made money on the cars they'd held onto by the dozen since the thirties, furnishing the period jalopies which bounce across the land.

What you see is generally where it happened. It seems that the little towns like Pilot Point, Midlothian and Red Oak had hardly changed in thirty-five years. The three banks which were robbed in the film were actually hit by the real Bonnie and Clyde and re-opened for the film-makers. Doesn't the first one in particular look like it has been closed for years rather than just gone broke as the teller claims?

As for the incidents portrayed . . . Well, the real Bonnie Parker and Clyde Barrow met in 1931, set about robbing banks and killed eighteen people before being peppered themselves in May, 1934. Clyde's brother, Buck, with wife Blanche, joined in, and was killed in an ambush by 100 lawmen at Dexter, Iowa. Blanche was captured and, by all accounts, was just as trying as Estelle Parsons portrays her.

Other aspects, like the earlier escape using mattresses for shields and Miss Parker's awful doggerel were also true. C. W. Moss was a composite of at least four separate gangsters who formed part of the line-up from time to time.

That's about as far as it goes. Bonnie and Clyde were plain, not a patch on gorgeous Faye and Warren (though both the girls had striking blonde hair). But the cute Hollywood Barrow gang were the planned result of Arthur Penn's technique. The characters in a film should be based on the personalities of the actors rather than the subjects, he said. 'The film is an abstraction rather than genuine reportage.'

However the families of two of the principal characters didn't appreciate his theories. Bonnie's younger sister, Billie Jean Parker Moon, tried to sue Beatty and Warner Brothers for more than $1,000,000 claiming that the film blackened Bonnie's memory. And the family of their nemesis, Texas Ranger Frank Hamer, issued a $1,750,000 suit charging the producer with portraying the veteran lawman (who had died in 1955) as inept and a vindictive killer.

Another contentious point was the pair's sexual relationship. The writers found evidence that pointed to something pretty dodgy on the nookie front but nothing specific. It might have been sado-machochism or homosexuality or even a running *ménage à trois* with other members of the gang. It seems that Warren Beatty felt most comfortable about using impotence as a sort of umbrella kink. In any case, other possibilities would have made the character too unattractive.

Similar considerations led to Bonnie's character quickly shifting in the film from crude to sensitive when confronted with Clyde's little problem. It was Faye Dunaway's idea that the couple couple successfully at last, bumping up the audience's sympathy meter another few points.

Beatty made a pact with Arthur Penn that if there were any disagreements during filming that he would defer to the director but generally they seem to have thought along the same lines. One prior conflict, though, was over the casting of the female lead. Beatty envisaged Bonnie being brought to life by his girlfriend, the French actress Leslie Caron. Gigi and Clyde?!

Arthur Penn had spotted the little-known Dunaway in a TV play. Estelle Parsons says that she never saw anyone so desperate to be a film star. Faye lost twenty pounds for the part by weighing herself down with sandbags. A double benefit was the strained look which this slimming method produced, going well with the tension of the role.*

Penn's film was made with great care and thought, as you can imagine when you watch it. By the end of 'shooting' he had accumulated 125,000 takes. Film students and reformed critics were impressed by the variety of techniques used to such great effect and the way they were intercut.

The historical facts: Ivan Melkvin, the father of gang-member and C. W. Moss component, Henry Melkvin, helped the newly-formed FBI trace Bonnie and Clyde to Arcadia, Louisiana. As in the film, he tricked them into stopping their car by pretending to fix a tyre on his truck. Bonnie Parker was eating a bacon and tomato sandwich. Clyde was driving in shirtsleeves with no shoes on. He was hit twenty-seven times. Bonnie – although she was on the side of the car away from the nest of gunmen – took twice as many bullets.

The filmed death scene took five days to complete and each take had up to four cameras running at different speeds. Beatty and Dunaway were made up with 100 or so charges containing blood paint which were fired by wire. An added touch was part of Beatty's head seeming to blow off, consciously echoing the Zapruder film of President Kennedy being assassinated. Dunaway's foot was tied to the gear shift so that she wouldn't fall out of the car.

Bonnie's death was designed to be horrific, Clyde's to be balletic. Penn got that special quality in Bonnie's last glance at Clyde by telling Faye to look toward where Beatty was standing, then quickly switching places with him. So Bonnie looks sweet and kind – and then somewhat surprised.

▨ The experience

'I wanted the film to have a certain rhythm, a nervous montage.' Arthur Penn, 1967

'A piece of shit.' The comment of one Warner executive after a preview

'It is a cheap piece of bald-faced slapstick that treats the hideous depredations of that sleazy, moronic pair as if they were . . . full of fun and frolic.' Bosley Crowther, *New York Times*, 14 August 1967

But the British view was much different: 'Make no mistake, *Bonnie and Clyde* is a film from which we will date reputations and innovations in American cinema,' Alexander Walker, *Evening Standard*, 7 September 1967

And soon the American critics began to agree. This is how *Time* retracted a previous panning review: 'Not only the sleeper of the decade but also, to a growing consensus of audiences and critics, the best movie of the year.'

'As the flowers are made sweeter by the sunshine and the dew,
So this world is made much brighter by the likes of folks like you.'

Couplet by Bonnie Parker on her gravestone.

▨ Can you spot . . .

* Some of the snapshots in the opening titles were actually of or by Bonnie and Clyde.

* A musical relative from TV. Lester Flatt and Earl Scruggs are probably best known for their theme music to TV's *Beverly Hillbillies*.

---

*She is also reported to have repaid $25,000 of her $50,000 fee in return for having her name over the title.

Brief Encounter

1945 Lovers at a train station who put duty before desire.

▦ The talent

Celia Johnson 36, as Laura Jesson; stuck mainly to the stage and blissful middle-class homelife

Trevor Howard 28, as Dr Alec Harvey; hardly a toyboy. Became one of Britain's most dependable film stars, usually as a toughie

Cyril Raymond 47, as Fred Jesson; typical role for specialist in leading ladies' solid husbands. Just demobbed as RAF Wing Commander

Stanley Holloway 54, as Albert Godby; Doolittle in *My Fair Lady* (1964) of course

but the war was a peak in more than fifty years of great character parts

Joyce Carey 46, as Myrtle Bagot; turning from stage to film work. More usually in upper-class roles

Noel Coward 46, Producer; multi-talented theatrical with high wartime film output. Future cinema work was almost all as actor only

David Lean 37, Director; last film with his mentor, Coward. A decade later he moved into spectaculars

▦ The business

This serves as warning to be wary of selling off the rights if you are fortunate enough to own a saleable literary property.

Brief Encounter started out as *Still Life*, one of twelve playlets in a series called *Tonight at Eight-Thirty** that Coward wrote for himself and Gertrude Lawrence in the mid-thirties. Then it had seemed a good idea to sell the screen rights to MGM. In the early forties Noel Coward and David Lean set up a company called Cineguild to produce films of the Master's works and it seemed like a good idea to do *Still Life*. The problem was they had to buy the rights back from the latest owner, British producer Sydney Box, for a whopping £60,000.

The film cost £270,000 to make. Finance – including the cheque to Mr Box – came from distributors Rank. As this wasn't Hollywood there was no frittering away the budget on the actors' fees: Celia Johnson got £1,000 and Howard £500 with not a penny for the frequent television repeats which were to come.

Brief Encounter was instantly recognized as something special by the critics – ensuring future opportunities for Celia Johnson, who didn't really take advantage of them, and for Trevor Howard and David Lean, who did. But initially the cinema box office receipts (unlike the Sydney Box office receipts) were poor.

---

*We Were Dancing (1942) and *Meet Me tonight* (1952) belonged to the same collection and were sold separately.

Celia Johnson: that hat

At an ominous preview in the docks of Rochester outside London a woman in the front started a ripple of laughter that became audience hysteria. Cineguild co-founder Anthony Havelock-Allen reckoned it was triggered by embarrassment at the emotional strain of the piece but David Lean felt like burning the negative.

Response abroad was variable. In the United States, as in Britain, it was a critics' film with Oscar nominations for the script, for Celia Johnson and for David Lean.

In occupied Germany the reaction was positively hostile. A British military spokesman archly explained that the native population were unable to comprehend the moral scruples on which the plot hinged.

But the French loved it and success there boosted British audiences; the film was re-issued in 1948. And why the French enthusiasm? There were two schools of thought. One held that they saw *Brief Encounter* as an exposé of British hypocrisy. But critic Dylis Powell said the French found it charming that a woman could be loved wearing a hat like that.

▦ Behind the screen

Milford Junction was really Carnforth Station, at the foot of the Lake District, chosen partly because of its distance from the German airfields. Unfortunately this had already been spotted by numerous southerners escaping the V2s so the cast and crew had to be spread through five different hotels around the area.

The three months of filming started in early 1945 and had to be conducted when the local trains weren't running. So if the lovers look somewhat strained it could have something to do with a shooting schedule that ran from ten in the evening to eight the next morning. They only stopped filming for the Luftwaffe and for the express trains roaring past, at this stage unenhanced by Rachmaninoff's Piano Concerto No 2.

David Lean envisaged using one of the fast trains to jazz up the shot at the beginning of the film when station master Stanley Holloway checks his watch and notes that the express is on time (itself a charming reminder of a bygone era). What a shot it would be, down next to the track as engine sped by! But Holloway wouldn't do it. He could bear the nights and the nagging cold you can see in the actors' breath but he was afraid of loud noises and an express train screaming into his ear was too much.

The cold probably helped the atmosphere, as the actors huddled together between takes round the real waiting room fire. The unit were used to working successfully together. This was Lean's fourth film with Noel Coward, and Celia Johnson had been in two of them, *In Which We Serve* (1942) and *This Happy Breed* (1944). It was Trevor Howard's first major role after being spotted by Lean in *The Way To the Stars* (1945) epitomizing the solid English gentleman.

When interviewed many years later both Howard and Johnson seemed cool about their brief encounter. Celia Johnson's memories of it were vague though she said it took a long time to shoot. Howard balked at any questions about an initial success that he felt had threatened to overshadow a long, distinguished career. The pair were reunited in 1980 on television for *Staying On*. At that time Howard remembered his co-star as the best actress he'd ever worked with.

Unlike their tortured screen characters both stars had good, lasting marriages. Celia Johnson lived in middle-class bliss in Oxfordshire with her husband Peter Fleming, brother of James Bond creator Ian.

Bemedaled paratroop officer Trevor Howard had a breezy way with women which might not bode well for married life. His attitude is illustrated by one of the few disagreements between star and director. Howard couldn't understand his character's remarks about the wood for the fire being damp in the friend's flat, as they move towards consummating their affair. 'I want her, and there she is. What am I doing messing about?' blustered Howard. Lean began to expostulate on the psychological motivation of uneasy small talk, but the ex-soldier was quite unconvinced. 'You're a funny chap,' he said.

Notwithstanding this seeming lack of sensitivity Trevor Howard's then recent marriage to actress Helen Cherry lasted until his death in 1988, despite rumours of much after-hours heavy drinking and extra-marital heavy petting. Mrs Howard remained Mrs Howard, she said, because rooms tended to be more interesting when Trevor was in them.

▦ The experience

'A shining example of how good a film can be when all idea of making it smart, snappy or glamorous has been discarded from the start.' *The Guardian* 19 March 1946

'Nowadays I am rarely moved to tears in the cinema and during *Brief Encounter* I found my handkerchief a sodden ball without having noticed I was crying because I was too absorbed in what I was seeing.' E. Arnot Robertson, *Daily Mail*, 23 November 1945

'One of the most emotionally honest and deeply satisfying films that has ever been made in this country.' C. A. Lejeune, *The Observer*, 25 November 1945

'Two characters in search of a bed.' Anon

▦ Can you spot . . .

* When the story takes place? It is set six years in the past. You wouldn't find a railway cafe full of all that tuck during the War or for a decade after. Dolly Messiter's laboured choice between milk and plain chocolate was a deliberate tease at contemporary audiences, who tittered enviously at the dummy sweets, the mock icing on the cakes and all that lovely plaster fruit.

* Some ropey dialects. You can see the Carnforth Station signs for local trains across the Pennines to Leeds and Bradford but the accents of the locals are pure celluloid cockney.

Butch Cassidy and the Sundance Kid

1969 Two lovable Western outlaws rob one too many trains.

▦ The talent

Paul Newman 44, as Butch Cassidy;
sixties superstar at peak form and
popularity
Robert Redford 33, as the Sundance Kid;
straight into the bigtime. Also successful
producer but he got his Oscar for directing
Ordinary People (1980)
Katherine Ross 27, as Etta Place; made
Tell Them Willie Boy is Here (1970) next

with Redford but this was the end of a
great start in films
John Foreman, Producer; has produced
several Newman and John Huston films
since
George Roy Hill 46, Director; from the
stage and TV. Made first film, *The World of
Henry Orient* (1964), at 40. His few movies
are mostly notable

▦ The business

At the time it was compared to *Bonnie and Clyde* (1967) (the title and the cute-
criminal concept) but really the closest similarity is in the way the two were written.
Both came from a fascination with outlaw legend against the backdrop of a vanishing
era. In this case scriptwriter William Goldman* spent six years researching Butch
Cassidy, a twinkle-eyed, turn-of-the-century bandit who, with his shadowy cohort,
the Sundance Kid, led the Hole in the Wall gang. Goldman's reward was a record
£400,000 for his screenplay and an Oscar.**

The writer always had Paul Newman in mind for the film, though in the role of
Sundance. That's not too hard to imagine so you might like to turn your mind to the
partners who were approached or considered: Steve McQueen, Warren Beatty,
Marlon Brando and, originally, Jack Lemmon. George Roy Hill stuck out for Robert
Redford.

They seem to have shared a fractious streak. Hill had been fired from his two
previous movies, *Hawaii* (1966) and *Thoroughly Modern Millie* (1967), after disagreements over editing. Redford had spent a year unemployed after quitting the Western
Blue (1968) a week before filming started. He was broke – but not for long. The
prickly actor who had turned down roles in several big sixties hits (*Who's Afraid of*

---

*He'd done *Harper* (1966) for Newman and went on to script Redford's *All the President's Men* (1976) and
other biggish films.
**There were Academy Awards as well for the photography, music and for 'Raindrops Keep Fallin' On My
Head'.

Virginia Woolf? (1966), *The Graduate* (1967) and *Rosemary's Baby* (1968)) was suddenly noticed, becoming an instant and lasting superstar.

Paul Newman was there already. But even though his fees were more than $1,000,000 a picture he was finding it tricky to hold on to his cash so was easing himself into the business side of film-making. *Butch Cassidy* was one of his first productions through a company he had formed with John Foreman, who had been his agent.

It was a good way to start off. The touching, amused comradeship of an appealing pair of villains was a great hit at the time, making this the highest-grossing Western ever. For the $6,270,000 it cost to make *Butch Cassidy and the Sundance Kid* has attracted world rentals of about $60,000,000. There was a spin-off TV series, *Alias Smith and Jones*, and Goldman knocked up a prequel, *Butch and Sundance: The Early Years* (1979). Neither involved Redford or Newman, who instead reunited for more lovable larceny in *The Sting* (1973) – which earned twice as much as *Butch Cassidy*.

▦ Behind the screen

If they look as if they really were enjoying each others company it is because they really were. Paul Newman and Robert Redford formed an immediate, lasting friendship. They joked and bantered along with George Roy Hill; and they drank – or at least Paul Newman did. Several visitors to the set remember his steady progress through six-packs. No one, however, remembers him tipsy. You might even spot the can opener he kept around his neck under the costume.*

Newman could be forgiven for being in a mood to take things easy. He had spent much of the previous year involved in politics, supporting the unsuccessful presidential aspirations of Democrat Eugene McCarthy. He was also basking in the critical acclaim for his first shot at directing: *Rachel Rachel* (1968) starring Joanne Woodward, to whom he had been married for the previous eleven years.

Their's has continued to be one of the most durable marriages in the business but at the time there were rumours of a rift to the extent that the couple spent $2,000 on a half-page ad in the *Los Angeles Times* attesting to the fact that they were still together. The stable homelife was something he shared with both Hill and with Redford, who had one of Hollywood's other legendary happy marriages. Robert Redford had wed Lola van Wagenam, a Utah Mormon, when he was twenty-one and she seventeen. Their daughter Amy was born in the year following *Butch Cassidy*, but unhappily the couple split after twenty-six years in 1984. You can see wedding rings on both Butch and Sundance. Redford kept his on because he couldn't get it off and Newman's is on his right hand not his left because of a recent motorcycling injury.

Newman wasn't too sure about playing Butch, which he regarded as a comedy part, because he didn't think he was a convincing funnyman (to understand his feelings at the time see *The Private War of Harry Frigg* (1967)). He was finally brought round by the concept of Butch as an ordinary nice-guy in comic situations. Redford on the other hand identified with Sundance from the start. He said in interviews that he admired the outlaws of the time for their sense of fun and, according to Hill, he shared his character's hard-nosed independence and passion for privacy.

*Costumes by Edith Head, one of Hollywood's most frequent names in the credits over five decades, mainly at Paramount and Universal.

Hill made a feature of the story's supposed authenticity; there's the claim in the titles and the allusion of the opening high-contrast colour shots processed to sepia. But much is fictional, including the centre-piece chase by the superposse commissioned by the Union Pacific Railway's Mr Harriman. The posse existed, Mr Harriman existed, even Woodcock existed cowering in the train's strong-room. But Butch learned about their plans and took off to Bolivia before they picked up his scent.

It seems that the real Butch and Sundance were together for about twenty years in all, robbing trains and banks in Utah and Wyoming. Butch never killed anyone during these escapades and appears very amiable, even Paul-Newman-like, in photographs. Almost all that is known of Sundance or Etta Place is their images in the studio portraits taken at the time of the escape with Butch to Bolivia. Etta may have been a prostitute, which perhaps fits better with the story. It *is* known that the real reason for her return to the States was appendicitis rather than premonition.

One unlikely but authentic touch is the bicycle in the 'Raindrops' sequence. Apparently this was one of the boys' favourite modes of inter-brothel transport. The scene was also included to fill out Katherine Ross's character to some extent. She gives the appearance of bravely enjoying herself amidst all those chummy men but perhaps her true position can be derived from Paul Newman's encapsulation of the *Butch Cassidy and the Sundance Kid* story. 'It's a love affair between two men,' he said, 'The girl is incidental.'

All three musical sequences were written into the script but the New York section of stills (modelled on the existing shots of the real Butch and Sundance) was planned as live action. *Hello Dolly* was in production at the time and Hill was going to borrow their turn-of-the-century New York sets but this was vetoed by Fox's chief Richard Zanuck who didn't want to cloud the glory of *Dolly*'s (later) release.*

Necessity has often been the mother of imaginative sequences. George Roy Hill obtained some vintage views of New York from local museums and got the photographer doing the publicity snaps for the film, Lawrence Schiller, to shoot the principals in matching light for later superimposition. And as it was only stills, Zanuck relented and let them onto the *Hello Dolly* stages for the final snaps in the sequence.**

Although the bicycle sequence in particular was one of the more memorable bits of the film it shared with the dialogue one of the principal contemporary criticisms of a picture that set itself up as having a documentary basis. It all felt too modern for 1906. Would the real Butch and Sundance have used phrases like 'Who are those guys?' Hill and writer Goldman countered that their *characters* were contemporary. Besides, they didn't believe people ever talked as in a John Wayne Western either.

Edwardian outlaws certainly wouldn't have been larking about to 'Raindrops Keep Fallin' on My Head'. This and the other two music sequences were written by Burt Bacharach after shooting had finished, so all the sequences were filmed without the director knowing what he would be cutting to. The final effect has an enchanting

---

*It might have done the reverse. *Hello Dolly* and *Tora! Tora! Tora!* contributed to huge losses for Fox that year which even profits from *Butch Cassidy* and *M*A*S*H* couldn't cover. Fox finances have often bounced and shuddered like this – *The French Connection* (1971), the *Star Wars* (1977–83) cycle and lots more money-spinners were to come.

**This is the director's version of the story. Schiller claims to have 'directed' the sequence himself with an $89,000 budget.

Robert Redford, Katherine Ross and Paul Newman: the girl is incidental

improvisatory look with Paul and Katherine clowning on the bike but you will notice that a stand-in is used when Mr Newman is attempting anything the least bit strenuous here and throughout the picture.

Robert Redford did do some leaping around and off trains himself but one stunt in particular needed the professional touch. The second, over-dynamited railway carriage seems to blow up right in front of the lens because that's how they shot it. They battened down four cameras in a bunker and shot at three times normal speed to slow the blast down. The figures in the foreground make it all look like a tragic mistake but the superstructure of the box car was only balsa wood and the stuntmen knew *exactly* where to stand.

Director Hill could hardly stand anywhere. He had put his back out and went round on a stretcher for much of the shoot. It was while musing during longueurs enforced by his recumbent state that he came up with the freeze-frame ending which gave the picture a heroic, non-violent finish.

Things look pretty hopeless but don't fret. According to his sister, Mrs Lula Parker Betenson, the real Butch Cassidy (né Robert Leroy Parker in 1867) returned to settle in Washington State where he died peacefully in the late thirties.

▦ The experience

And never was heard a discouraging word . . .

'It's a lovely week, and indeed a lovely year, that contains a picture like *Butch Cassidy and the Sundance Kid*.' Penelope Mortimer, *The Observer*, 8 February 1970

'I doubt that you have ever been held in your cinema seat at gunpoint by such amiable rogues as the couple featured in this highly entertaining Western.' Ian Christie, *Daily Express*, 3 January 1970

'The film does wonderful things with mood and atmosphere. The touches are fleeting, but they are there.' Hollis Alpert, *Saturday Review*, 27 September 1969

'It was a perfect example of film-making as a community experience. Nobody had to defend their position and everybody was geared to invent and create.' Paul Newman

'The most consistent fun of any film I've ever done.' Robert Redford

▦ Can you spot . . .

* The absence of music. Although 'Raindrops' and the rest of Burt Bacharach's score was a great hit there's only twelve minutes of it in the whole film. Hill avoids music for the sake of it.

* A tricky shot. It's where Butch comes riding past the windows of the cabin where Etta and Sundance are sleeping. Simple and effective enough – but how do you get the exposure right so that you can see inside and out? The cabin was a purpose-built set on location near Grafton, Utah, and specially lit so that the interior and exterior intensity balanced.

* A famous floozie. Paul Newman's bird in the brothel is Cloris Leachman, later widely known for her TV work in the *Mary Tyler Moore Show* and *Phyllis*.

* Robert Redford's best side. He has three prominent moles on the right of his face and prefers to be filmed from the left.

* The vintage of the silent outlaw movie in the opening titles. Though it has the appearance of genuine age these were sequences shot by Hill for a section in the film that was never used, when Butch and Sundance see an exaggerated report of their deaths at a Bolivian cinema.

Carry On Cleo

1964 A doltish slave from Britain is mistaken for a great fighter and becomes Caesar's bodyguard.

📧 The talent

Kenneth Williams 38, as Julius Caesar; highly popular British comedy star, active in all media. Carried On in all but four

Sidney James 51, as Mark Antony; with Williams in Tony Hancock's radio and early TV shows. Many more character parts and leading comedy roles

Charles Hawtrey 50, as Seneca; son of theatrical knight of same name. Often in Will Hay movies

Kenneth Connor 46, as Hengist Pod; a serious actor as well but best known for comedy including most recently TV's *Hi-de-Hi* and *'Allo 'Allo*

Jim Dale 29, as Horsa; pop musician who wrote lyrics to *Georgy Girl* (1966), more recently on Broadway

Joan Sims 34, as Calpurnia; in all but five *Carry Ons* and many more comedy films since the early 1950s

Amanda Barrie 24, as Cleo; former dancer and *Double Your Money* hostess. *Coronation Street*'s Alma Sedgwick in the eighties

Peter Rogers 48, Producer; husband of equally successful producer Betty Box who made the *Doctor* series

Gerald Thomas 44, Director; former editor who worked on *Hamlet* (1948) and *The Third Man* (1949)

📧 The business

No one ever lost money by underestimating the British public's taste – a sound showbiz adage to which the wealthy men behind the *Carry On* movies are fit testimony.

In 1958 producer Peter Rogers and his director friend Gerald Thomas raised the money to film a property no one else was interested in. It was an army farce called *The Bull Boys* which they played about with a bit and retitled *Carry On Sergeant*. Rogers and Thomas spent £74,000. Their film was number three at the British box office that year.

There was nothing for it but to carry on. So, at a rate of two or three a year, they started to churn out a series of pictures using a variation on the same old title, a corps of the same old actors and many of the same old music hall jokes.

The second, *Carry on Nurse* (1959), was even more successful than *Sergeant*. Unlike its predecessor it was even a hit in the United States, running for more than two years at one Los Angeles cinema.

By the time they made *Carry On Cleo* for a still minuscule £160,000 the series was well into its stride and a British institution. It contains some of the best performances by the *Carry On* team, although stalwarts Hattie Jaques and Barbara Windsor are absent. Rogers and Thomas were taking about £15,000 up front and each kept a third of the profits, which at £500,000 per film meant they were soon millionaires.*

*Nor was this series their only source of income. Separately and ensemble both Rogers and Thomas have been behind umpteen other low-budget British films.

Not so the *Carry On* stars. A key factor in the films' profitability was ruthless budget management. Top earners of the company were Kenneth Williams and Sid James and they only got £5,000. Charles Hawtrey, who complained that he hadn't received a pay rise since 1960, was probably on about £3,000. The rest were paid even less. Apparently Rogers *did* offer the central core of regulars a share of the profits in the early days but they couldn't decide how to divide the money and nothing ever came of it.

Carry On Cleo was another money-spinner. The series continued until the mid-seventies and the arrival of the muckier *Confessions Of . . .* films. The competition restricted *Carry On* audiences to teenagers (the staple had been youngsters with their naughty old daddies) and production was suspended. Rogers and Thomas moved deftly into television compilations and carried on coining it.

▦ Behind the screen

Rogers and Thomas would come up with a theme, then hand the project over to a writer, often Talbot Rothwell.* For their tenth *Carry On* they tapped into the freely flowing hype for *Cleopatra* (1963), which had been doing the rounds. Not only that, the original classy sets remained at Pinewood ready for economical re-use.

Fox, the makers of *Cleopatra*, were happy to go along with the gag but drew the line at the *Carry on Cleo* poster. This had Kenneth Williams, Sid James and a reclining Amanda Barrie in the same pose as Rex, Dick and Liz had been adopting to promote their modest effort. Despite a doughty defence from Quintin Hogg, later Lord Chancellor, the *Carry On* boys were legally bound to change their publicity.

Objections also came from Marks and Spencers who didn't mind them taking the mickey** but wished they hadn't used their trademark colours of green and gold. For them an apology was enough.

As usual the schedule was a tight eight weeks for *Carry On Cleo* although unusually they were starting in July; normally they tended to avoid filming during summer season or panto time – the cast had to earn a living somehow.

The company knew what they were in for, a production line of shots called up by a director obsessed with speed and efficiency. Comedy was a serious business and the script was the bible. There was very slight tolerance of joking on set; anything too uproarious would slow down the process. The regulars all abided by the rules of arriving word-perfect and avoiding ab-libs. Anyone who didn't was never seen carrying on again.

So keen was Gerald Thomas about getting it in on time that he would use the first take wherever possible, scoffing at any suggestions of a novel effect or angle. Why bother with anything which didn't make it more funny? These lickety-split production values litter the films with minor loose ends which are fun to spot – like the substantial country house in the background as the Roman legions approach the ancient Britons' settlement at the beginning of *Cleo*.

This didn't necessarily mean that filming was a solemn affair. You can see a lot of barely suppressed, first-take smiles from the extras, and Francis de Wolf playing Agrippa, the galley captain, looks as if he is really creasing up when Kenneth

---

*He had provided jokes for the Crazy Gang and would later script Frankie Howerd's *Up Pompeii* on TV.
**Warren Mitchell, playing Spencius, was just starting the TV series that was to make him famous as Alf Garnet, *Till Death Us Do Part*.

Sidney James and Kenneth Williams: we're in the money . . . comparatively

Connor's visor falls unceremoniously. Kenneth Williams claimed that he goosed Connor and Jim Dale with his short sword during the shot of them protecting him at the end and they couldn't get back at him until after the take.

At the time the series was grinding to a halt in the mid-seventies there were a number of newspaper exposés which painted a darker portrait of the lives and times of the *Carry On*-ers.

Oddest seems to have been the delightful Charles Hawtrey. Gay sixties playwright Joe Orton, a friend of Kenneth Williams, seemed to have his number. Orton called him a very sad man indeed, unable to have sex properly with a man or a woman and at his best when exhibiting his hilarious personality. Hawtrey was apparently often sozzled on set, once even passing out entirely. He left the *Carry On*s in 1972 after an argument over billing and died in 1988 a tragic recluse.

Of the other regulars Joan Sims also seems a far sadder and more isolated figure than the laughter that she brings would suggest. Sid James was an inveterate gambler who at one point was said to be carrying on with Barbara Windsor. He would get his £5,000 filming fee in two portions: £3,500 for his bank account, the rest as a secret gambling fund. There seems to have existed a degree of resentment toward the wealthy, thrifty producer who would visit them all on the set once a day, like a lord, in his yearly-changed Bentley. Peter Rogers is credited, nevertheless, with helping Sid out of his gambling debts.

▦ The experience

'The *Carry On* series is the exact film equivalent of a seaside postcard.' Isabel Quigly, *Spectator*, 11 December 1964

'Blimus! Burton and Liz were never like this!' *Daily Mail*, 8 December 1964

'In the canon of *Carry On*, *Cleo* is one of the best, providing, for me, Kenneth Williams' most outstanding, and definitive, performance in a *Carry On* as Caesar and one of Kenneth Connor's most entertaining portrayals as Hengist Pod. In addition, writer Talbot Rothwell never excelled this script for the audacity, cleverness and profusion of puns, the swagger and cheekiness of the double entendres, or the absurd logic of the plot.' Kenneth Eastaugh, *The Carry-On Book*, 1978 (a must for devotees)

'Cheap, dull and British.' *New York Times*, on a TV showing in 1971

'They are the model for my own films,' Andy Warhol

▦ Can you spot . . .

* The most noteworthy joke at the time. The critics all remembered Sidney James biting off the head of the asp.

* A concession to the censors. Rogers and Thomas were adept at edging into the big-money A certificate bracket to target their core audience, children accompanied by their fathers. So they always seeded in a few over-the-top jokes for cutting back painlessly if the authorities insisted. Joan Sims's mouthing of 'Piss off' during a dissolve seems to have been a borderline case.

Casablanca

1942 Of all the gin joints in all the towns in the world, she walks into his . . .

▦ The talent

Humphrey Bogart 43, as Rick; tough-guy turns romantic lead turns screen legend
Ingrid Bergman 24, as Elsa; 'luminous' newcomer from Sweden. Success, scandal, Hollywood exile and rehabilitation followed
Claude Rains 42, as Captain Louis Renault; fine stage professional who led the ranks of supporting players for three decades after *The Invisible Man* (1933) debut
Conrad Veidt 49, as Major Strasser; gay when drunk, straight when sober, according to friends. Died the following year
Paul Henreid 34, as Victor Laslo; European heart-throb. Had just created the classic double cigarette lighting bit with Bette Davis in *Now Voyager* (1942)
Dooley Wilson 48, as Sam; nightclub singer and bandleader who started in pictures the previous year
Hal Wallis 42, Producer; one of Hollywood's most solidly commercial producers from the thirties through to the seventies
Michael Curtiz 53, Director; former actor. A Warners stalwart who could direct any sort of film

▦ The business

Warner Brothers had only recently woken up to the fact that they had a major star in Humphrey Bogart. Following the success of *The Maltese Falcon* (1941) he was now at the start of a new seven-year contract that brought him into the first division of Hollywood earners at $3,500 a week, guaranteed for forty weeks of the year.

He was worth every cent. The following year he entered the top ten where he stayed for the rest of the decade – and Bogie became one of those few Hollywood stars to be even more fervently embraced by the public after his death.

Casablanca was, at $878,000, a big budget picture* and Hal Wallis, Warner's head of production, was willing to supplement the top Warners supporting players and back-room boys with high-rent talent from other studios. Ingrid Bergman was on a long contract with David Selznick who got a weekly fee of $3,125 for lending her services. Dooley Wilson came from Paramount at a knock-down $500 a week but really good villains cost dear and the authentically teutonic menace of Conrad Veidt** was worth a massive $5,000 a week to MGM. Wallis himself received $52,000 for his efforts while the best paid of the company was director Michael Curtiz, who received $73,400.

The $20,000 paid for the screen rights to an unproduced play called *Everybody Comes to Rick's* was itself a record but the whole venture proved a good investment. The gross for the first year alone was $3,700,000. Today *Casablanca* figures near the

*It finally came in at $950,000.
**He was only acting. Though born near Berlin Veidt was a vehement anti-Nazi who became a British citizen in 1939 and donated much of his salary to war relief.

Humphrey Bogart and Ingrid Bergman: how will it all end?

top of many lists of all-time favourite films and is the most frequently shown movie on American television.

Popularity at the time was greatly helped by the current of patriotism in an America about to enter the War. One of the first major blows against the Third Reich was the Allied landing at Casablanca in November 1942. Warners had originally planned a leisurely 1943 release but rushed the picture out in selected theatres just 18 days after the troops moved in. Churchill, Roosevelt and Stalin further contributed to the *Casablanca* effort when they held a summit in the town coinciding with the film's January 1943 general release.

Academy Awards for Best Screenplay, Picture and Direction still came as surprise, at least to Michael Curtiz. After the experience of getting his own family out of his native Hungary he must have identified with the hopeful refugees in *Casablanca*'s first scenes. And he must have identified with all the Central European accents too; when it came to fracturing the English language Curtiz could out-Goldwyn Goldwyn. On the stage at the Academy Awards ceremony he had no words prepared for the night he won the only Oscar in an illustrious film career. 'So many times I have a speech ready but no dice. Always a bridesmaid, never a mother,' he explained.

▦ Behind the screen

One of the magical things about *Casablanca* is that the actors have no more idea of how the story is going to end than you do on first viewing. By the time of the scene where Rick lets the young refugee couple win the price of their freedom at roulette the script pages for the day were arriving in the morning and no one knew what tomorrow would bring.

Nevertheless a high percentage of what you see in the way of basic story-line and dialogue is from the original play by Murray Burnett and Joan Alison. With some notable improvements: 'Here's looking at you, kid,' was originally the rather limp 'Here's good luck to you', and even if you use your best approximation of the Bogart lisp on 'Of all the cafes in all the towns in the world, she walks into my cafe,' *Casablanca* wouldn't have been the same without the final version. Both pieces of rephrasing are attributed to Bogart himself.

Who really deserves the Oscar for best script? Well, the credits went to Julius and Phillip Epstein and Howard Koch, who set about knocking the original into a screen-play. Koch stayed on set most of the time to contribute anything extra that was needed but as shooting went ahead (in sequence) others were brought in for specific tasks. One example is Casey Robinson who wrote the Paris flash-back sequence, partly accounting for its rose-coloured soppiness, nicely at odds with the contemporary scenes. The onscreen credits – as so often in Hollywood films – were dictated by the Screenwriters' Guild who stipulated a limit of two writers or teams.

Bogart spent a lot of the time with the writers discussing the fine points of plot and dialogue, cosseted in his dressing room over a drink. It must have been a pleasanter atmosphere than he was getting at home. His wife, Mayo Methot (see also *The Maltese Falcon*) was becoming increasingly unstable and even threatened to kill him. On hearing this the star's loyal agents discreetly took out a $100,000 life insurance policy on him. It got to the point where Bogart would spend the odd night in his dressing room and he was once caught in the early hours riding a bicycle around the Warners lot trying to sober up.

One of Mayo's problems was that she was particularly jealous of Ingrid Bergman, which on the beautiful face of it doesn't seem so daft – although Ingrid herself was then happily married to fellow Swede, Dr Peter Lindstrom. Consequently Bogart kept his distance from Bergman, whose reaction to her co-star mirrors Elsa's comment about Rick, that she couldn't say what he was like, though she saw him quite often.

Otherwise things were fairly chummy. Conrad Veidt and Paul Henreid, far from being hunter and quarry, were actually the best of friends. Veidt had intervened on Henreid's behalf to prevent the Austrian refugee from being interned in Britain near the beginning of the war.

Bogart enjoyed having his old drinking companion Peter Lorre along, although his time on the film was comparatively brief. And when Lorre left Claude Rains kept him amused. The scene where Rains as Renault comes rushing into Rick's office was shot in the morning at a stage in the day when Rains found it difficult to get sufficiently keyed up. Curtiz kept calling for more pace and piled on the retakes so for variety Rains came bursting through the door on a bicycle. Perhaps it was the one Bogie had been riding on round the lot.

If Elsa appears confused imagine what Ingrid Bergman was going through in the last chaotic stages of filming. She was particularly aggrieved at having to weigh her character's motivation in the moments during which she absorbed the day's script.

Bogart seemed to mind less, perhaps because of his involvement in the writing. One day all he had to do was come to the cafe balcony and nod, not knowing until much later that he had been cueing the Franco-German battle of the anthems. It's a scene that can still bring a lump to the throat so imagine its impact on wartime audiences. Murray Burnett said that he wept after writing it for the original play.

The tension mounted toward the end of filming, as it does onscreen, with no one sure the whole souffle wasn't going to collapse into a badly-resolved mess. Still to be addressed were questions of who should get the girl, how to avoid one of the goodies dying and the moral dilemma raised if Elsa dumped her heroic hubby.

Perhaps the Epsteins, who hadn't been involved with the filming, were fresher to the task. While Bogart and Curtiz quarrelled over the director's idea that Rick should kiss Elsa one last time at the end (Bogie won) and that he should shoot Strasser in the back (two-nil to Bogie) the answer came to the Brothers Epstein in a joint flash of inspiration while driving home from the studio. Recalling an otherwise minor line of dialogue they had given Renault early on in the film they looked at each other and chorused, 'Round up the usual suspects.'

After all the bickering, confusion and improvisation it was Wallis who got the final word – he's credited with coming up with Bogart's last line, 'This could be the start of a beautiful friendship.'

It's a friendship that has lasted with audiences ever since.

▦ The experience

'The atmosphere of uneasy distrustfulness makes a sharp background for swift action, the characterization is clear cut and credible and the strong cast drop into their places without even an audible click.' *Manchester Guardian*, 23 March 1943

'The love story that takes us from time to time into the past is horribly wooden and clichés everywhere lower the tension.' William Whitebait, *New Statesman*, 16 January 1943

'The happiest of happy accidents.' Andrew Sarris

'It is as folklore rather than as a cinematic masterwork that *Casablanca* is likely to survive.' John Baxter, writing in *Films*, 1984

▦ Can you spot . . .

* Some unconvincing miming. Dooley Wilson was a drummer not a pianist. The music is being played off camera by Warners staff musician Elliot Carpenter. Incidentally, 'As Time Goes By' was an old hit that was specified in the original play but Warners' resident composer, Max Steiner, tried to veto it in favour of one of his own compositions. Luckily Ingrid Bergman had already been shorn for her next part in *For Whom the Bell Tolls* (1943) – or at least that's the excuse they used for not reshooting it. Notice how Steiner makes the best of things weaving what became a romantic classic into the themes he himself supplied. And notice a golden oldie from Steiner's own catalogue; the title music is a reworking of his theme for the *Lost Patrol* (1934).
* Two teams from other films. Peter Lorre and Sydney Greenstreet played with Bogie in *The Maltese Falcon*. And Claude Rains and Paul Henreid were fresh from *Now Voyager*. They would have felt comfortable in the railway station – that was from *Now Voyager* as well.
* A typo in the credits. S. Z. Sakall has his middle initial changed to K. Most people knew his as Cuddles.
* A famous montage-maker. The opening sequence is by Don Siegel of *Invasion of the Body Snatchers* (1956) and *Dirty Harry* (1971) fame.
* Bogie's ring. A legacy from his doctor-turned-drug-addict father (it came with $10,000 in debts).
* Some touches to test the suspension of disbelief. The back projection dissolves between scenes in Paris. The letters of transit are signed by de Gaulle who as Free French leader was hardly likely to be moonlighting for Vichy. And Leslie Halliwell points out that if our hero was in Paris until the Germans arrived in 1940 he's done well to establish everybody coming to Rick's by 1942. And what about the weather at the end; fog and rain . . . in North Africa?
* Bogie's magic cigarette. Do yourself a favour and don't try to keep track of how it shrinks, extends and occasionally disappears altogether between shots – you'll end up doing nothing else and miss one of cinema's great romances.

Chariots of Fire

1981 Two British rivals overcome adversity and stick to their principles triumphing in the 1924 Paris Olympics

▦ The talent

Ben Cross 33, as Harold Abrahams; ex-RADA, Royal Shakespeare Company player. After *Chariots* turned down $100,000 to play Prince Charles for American TV. More films and TV followed, including *The Far Pavilions*

Ian Charleson 31, as Eric Liddell; another RSC player. Parts in *Gandhi* (1982) and Hudson's *Greystoke* (1984) followed. Died of AIDS in 1990

Nigel Havers 29, as Lord Andrew Lindsey; son of then British Attorney General and big TV star of the eighties

Ian Holm 49, as Sam Mussabini; familiar supporting actor, starred in TV's *Game, Set and Match*

Cheryl Campbell 30, as Jennie Liddell; also in TV's *Pennies from Heaven*, and in *Greystoke*

Alice Krige 27, as Sybil Gordon; South African actress mainly on TV

David Puttnam 39, Producer; key British film executive of the seventies and eighties. *Bugsy Malone* (1976) and *Midnight Express* (1978) before; much else since, including a year as president of Columbia Pictures

Hugh Hudson 35, Director; veteran of more than a thousand commercials, also shot location footage for *Midnight Express* – made *Greystoke* next

▦ The business

David Puttnam found himself at a loose end in a rented house in L.A. with nothing better to do than read a book about the Olympics. He was drawn to the entries for 1924 which recorded Harold Abrahams, as the last Briton to win the 100-metre dash, and Eric Liddell, who had triumphed in the 400.

Puttnam immediately recognized commercial potential and commissioned a script from Colin Welland.* Despite the producer's track record of solid profit no one else in Britain shared his enthusiasm except Goldcrest, a new production company gearing up for the advent of TV's Channel Four. They contributed £25,000 to fund the development of the idea. Puttnam finally secured his backing from Dody Fayed, the owner of Harrods, and from Twentieth Century Fox.

Puttnam held them to using both Colin Welland's script unaltered and his protégé, Hugh Hudson, to direct. The financiers in turn held Puttnam to a tight schedule and a budget that allowed $2,500,000 for lensing (as filming is called in the trade press) and $3,500,000 for prints and publicity.

---

*The writer of *Yanks* (1979) but then better known to British audiences as a copper on TV's *Z Cars*.

Promotion was a problem, or so it seemed. The Americans feared that a film about sport would fail to attract a female audience. Puttnam was made to bring a rough cut of the picture to the States for the Fox bigwigs to ponder. It turned out as something of an embarrassment to the restrained Brits. Hardened American money men were moved to tears and, more incredibly, to open their wallets with generous offers of finance for future projects.

Their rapture was matched by that of the British critics when the film was released, and the public were caught in the wave. This was the aftermath of the 1980 Moscow Olympics where the British government's disapproval had put a cloud over the achievements of home-grown athletes who had completed. A chocolate box representation of British sporting grit and triumph was just what the nation needed. It was the year's top money-maker.

The United States was a tougher market to crack. Critics expressed a detached admiration for the technically expert performance on heart-strings by Messrs Hudson and Puttnam. The Fox promotion team fervently took on the challenge of making the film succeed, even going so far as to dub a profanity into Ian Holm's otherwise unsullied dialogue so as not to put off adult attendance with a pure-U rating.

The American public lapped it up. *Chariots of Fire* became history's biggest non-U.S. money-maker, grossing £30,000,000 in North America.* Oscar night was memorable for the British film industry. The film won Best Picture, Best Art Direction, Best Score – and Colin Welland walked off with the Oscar for Best Screenplay, issuing a famous hostage to fortune: 'The British are coming'.**

However as with much else in *Chariots of Fire* this was not as straightforward a triumph for Britain as it appeared. Aside from the artists' fees and the prestige value of being associated with a hit, Goldcrest were the only British interests to share materially in the immense revenue derived from *Chariots of Fire*. They retained a percentage which has earned more than $800,000. According to financial analysts of the time, the remaining chariots of cash – including £1,000,000 paid by the BBC for TV rights – stayed firmly with the backers in the United States.

▦ Behind the screen

Hugh Hudson was an advertising man, and in casting *Chariots of Fire* he was concerned with the look of the film. The younger actors were chosen for their features rather than their celebrity. Ben Cross, for example, is of Irish Catholic extraction but was called after a browse through the actors catalogue, *Spotlight*, for Jewish types. Ian Charleson knew he had the part of Eric Liddell as soon as Hudson clapped eyes on him. The director seemed startled and commented that he looked just like him . . . and that was that.

Their faces may have jumped the hurdle but could their bodies? To get all these thirty-something actors to look convincing in running kit as world-class athletes they were put through up to two months of rigorous training. Ben Cross learned to do five hundred push-ups at a go. By the time the cameras started rolling all of them were very fit.

---

*A record snapped up in 1986 by *Crocodile Dundee.*
**And indeed they came back in even greater style next year with Richard Attenborough's *Gandhi* which won eight Oscars including Best Picture.

As with their characters, Cross and Charleson hardly met each other during filming as the story followed their separate paths to glory. Each considered himself the central character in the picture and the onscreen handshake before their first major competition had some of the tension of the relationship between Liddell and Abrahams.

Picking young unknowns for the leads saved money, as did the choice of locations. Much of what is presented as Paris is in fact Merseyside. Liverpool Library and Town Hall served both inside and out for the elegant British Embassy in Paris. They were all running for Britain at Bebington Sports Centre across the Mersey, which was particularly attractive because there was no modern lighting to take down. With some stands added on and tinkering with the track it took on what looked like the size and form of the Paris Stade de Colombes in 1924.

For much of the shooting at Bebington they relied on a hundred or so extras padded out with a few dummies. They were at the stadium a month but they allowed themselves just one day to film both races and the opening Olympic ceremony. For this they needed a big crowd so they advertised a Bank Holiday event which attracted 7000 people with a raffle, the chance to see how film folk work and an itsy-bit part in a feature film.

The repeated slow-motion photography of the sporting climaxes became a tech-n' jue cliché, and irritated the critics. However nobody seemed to offer an alternative way of spinning out events which are over in ten seconds yet must serve as the pinnacle of two hours dramatic build-up. Also there was only one day's footage to play with.

The music helped. It was composed by Vangelis Papathanassiou* early on in the project and was used as a rhythmic template for the production. The technicians listened to it walkman-like while filming the Broadstairs beach run sequence of the opening titles so that, in theory, they would be influenced to move the camera with instinctive musical sympathy. The main theme has now become as firmly identified with the opening titles of TV sporting events as 'Also Sprach Zarathustra' with televised space travel. Surprisingly, though, aside from broadcast music libraries the soundtrack album was not a big seller.

Filming in Paris had been ruled out by cost. The Trinity Quad, and all other Cambridge University location work, had been ruled out by the college authorities, after reading the script. Notice the crowded Cambridge street scene with the adjacent academic precincts empty. The reason given for the non-cooperation was that it would have disturbed the tourists and, besides, none of the crew had been students. Fortunately Hugh Hudson *had* been to Eton and they were allowed to stage the race there.

The apparent Cambridge snobbishness or embarrassment about the script may simply have been an expression of regard for the truth. The scamper round the quad before the bells finished tolling made a memorable scene but, like much else in a film that purported to be biographical, the real events were rather different.

Harold Abrahams never ran around the courtyard at Trinity or anywhere else; he didn't like distances over 200 meters and furthermore the right-angle corners were lethal. It was actually a feat accomplished by Abraham's friend, Lord Burghley, Fifth

---

*Former partner with Demis Roussos in Aphrodite's Child.

Marquis of Exeter – the model for the fictional Lord Lindsey.* Nor was Abrahams possessed of a special mission against anti-semitism. He is more likely to have been motivated by the achievements of his two older brothers who were both noted athletes. One, Sir Adolphe Abrahams, was also the Olympic team doctor.

The incident where American runner Jackson Scholz passes Liddell a note blessing his endeavours seems another figment of Colin Welland's imagination. When *Chariots* came out the old champion, by then 84 and retired from a second career writing sports fiction, found himself deluged with requests for spiritual guidance. Despite being credited as a consultant Scholz is said to have refused to see the film.

Researchers found fifty errors of fact in the narrative. Some, like Abrahams not meeting his future wife until after the Olympics, are harmless shifts for dramatic effect. More fundamental was the fact that the real Eric Liddell knew months in advance that the 100-metre heats were scheduled for a Sunday and had ample time to prepare instead for the 400 metres. And while it is true that Liddell and Abrahams won their races, thus claiming their mention in record books left lying around rented accommodation in Los Angeles, they were amongst the small fry of the Paris Olympics. The athletics were dominated not by the two Britons but by Paavro Nurmi, a flying Finn who won five golds in the long distance events. Also making a splash was a five-times swimming gold medallist who would make it into pictures long before Liddell and Abrahams – everybody's favourite Tarzan, Johnny Weissmuller.

▓ The experience

'As opiate and bewitching a piece of movie-making as Britain has lately produced.' Nigel Andrews, *Financial Times*, 3 April 1981

'It shows that they still do make them like they used to, only better.' Alexander Walker, *New Standard*, 2 April 1981

'This film is full to bursting with the impersonal, go-to-the-mountains poetry that sells products.' Pauline Kael, *New Yorker*, 26 October 1981

'*Chariots of Fire* is a hymn to the human spirit as if scored by Barry Manilow.' Richard Corliss, *Film Comment*, September/October 1981

'By the time I had finished *Chariots of Fire* I hated running.' Ben Cross, 1981

▓ Can you spot . . .

* Where the title comes from – William Blake's words for Britain's most imperious hymn, Jerusalem; sing along:
  Bring me my bow of burning gold,
  Bring me my arrows of desire
  Bring me my spear, oh, clouds unfold,
  Bring me my chariot of fire . . .
* Some famous faces. John Gielgud and director Lindsay Anderson as the Master of Trinity and Master of Caius respectively. And comedienne Ruby Wax is Bunty.
* A persistent autograph hound. The little girl seeking Liddell's signature at the meeting in East Wemyss has followed him across the Firth of Forth for a much later gathering in Edinburgh. And she's still wearing the same outfit.

---

*Burghley took all of forty-six seconds to complete it as well; not as fast as Nigel Havers and Ben 'Push-ups' Cross who nip round in thirty-four-and-a-bit.

Citizen Kane

1941 The life of an American newspaper magnate as told by the people who knew him.

The talent

Orson Welles 25, as Charles Foster Kane; revelling in cinema's flashiest debut
Joseph Cotten 35, as Jedediah Leland; the most successful of the *Kane* novices
Dorothy Comingore 22, as Susan Alexander; never fulfilled this promise of stardom
Everett Sloane 30, as Bernstein; a rich career of character parts followed

Ruth Warrick 24, as Emily Norton; became a minor star of the forties
Agnes Moorehead 33, as Kane's mother; a PhD whose career after *Kane* brought five Oscar nominations – and the role of Samantha's mother in TV's *Bewitched*
Orson Welles Producer/Director; never again got the studio backing he deserved

The business

Orson Welles, with no real experience in films, had been brought over from New York to help renew a movie company's fortunes. RKO was one of Hollywood's major studios but prone to financial problems and, at the time, going through some management changes. The new studio boss, George Schaefer, felt the company needed new blood and was prepared to pay for it. Equally, Welles needed money to help keep afloat the Mercury Theatre company which he had founded with John Houseman.* Welles' contract with RKO gave him $100,000 for one picture each year which he would produce, direct, write and perform in. Plus he was to have complete artistic control and would have been able to do any project he wanted costing less than $500,000 – about $100,000 over the odds for the time. Not bad for a twenty-five year old.

Pre-shoot costings showed *Citizen Kane* coming in at just over $1,000,000 and the studio intervened with their only real exertion of control over the picture – they kept the budget pegged at $723,000 although its costs finally edged up past $800,000.

The film and its boy wonder author were the talk of Hollywood during production and the result has delighted the critics from the time of release to the present. But an outraged William Randolf Hearst, the newspaper tycoon whose life the film partially mirrored, used all his power to ensure that it could play in only a few cinemas, and so it wasn't a great audience puller.

Citizen Kane was up for nine Oscars but there were boos when the nominations were read out at the ceremony. Many in scandal-sensitive Hollywood were unwilling to antagonize the muck-raking Hearst empire by showing support. Others were fed up with the film's trumpeting publicity and Welles' brashness. Despite this Welles and Herman J. Mankiewicz shared the Oscar for best screenplay.

*Distinguished producer who became a star actor at the age of seventy-one as a law professor in *The Paper Chase* (1973).

It was withdrawn from general release after a year and registered on RKO's books of the time as a $150,000 loss. They must have wished they had taken up Hearst's pre-release offer to pay for them to burn the prints and negatives.

It was TV that revived the film's fortunes. *Citizen Kane* mostly languished in the vaults for its first fifteen years but RKO gave up its film interests in the early fifties and the catalogue was the first to be sold to television. With innumerable airings the film found a wider audience than ever before and regained the prominence the critics had given it all along.

It has consistently featured in shortlists of the favourite films of all time, been extensively analysed and documented – and in the long term turned out to be a good earner for RKO's beneficiaries.

 Behind the screen

Orson Welles had arrived in Hollywood with the best initial contract in the history of films and a whizz-kid reputation. He had shown a variety of early talents and enough gab to talk himself into a stage, radio and now film career – all as the head of his own production company. His principal claim to fame was a 1938 radio version of H. G. Wells' *War of the Worlds*. It was made to sound like real reports of a Martian invasion and caused widespread panic.

Orson Welles: welcome to heaven

When he arrived in Tinsel Town Mr Welles was highly pleased with himself and didn't care who knew it. 'The biggest train set a boy ever had,' he commented while being shown round the RKO lot.

'There but for the grace of God, goes God,' commented Herman Mankiewicz, the wit who was his co-author on 'Kane'.*

The young genius found trouble fulfilling his contract. His first project – an adaptation of *Heart of Darkness* – had been shelved because of cost, and a thriller by Welles called *The Smiler with the Knife* was knifed because the intended star, Carole Lombard, wouldn't do it. She said that if it was a success Welles would get the credit and if not she'd get the blame.

Mankiewicz had worked with Welles before in radio. In contrast to his youthful collaborators he was in his mid-forties with a largely pedestrian screenwriting career behind him (despite involvement as uncredited scriptwriter for some of the greatest Marx brothers films). He also had a drink problem and it was John Houseman's main task to keep him off the bottle long enough to do his bit.

Just what his bit was has been the subject of some controversy. Welles tried to claim sole credit for writing the film and was only persuaded to make it a joint credit after the intervention of The Screenwriters' Guild.

Where Welles' ideas start and Mankiewicz's leave off is hard to determine. There seems to be evidence for both of them discussing similar original ideas, Mankiewicz providing one or two draft scripts and Welles the rest. Welles also maintained that John Houseman contributed significantly to the Mankiewicz efforts. The central dramatic device – the search for the meaning of Kane's dying word 'Rosebud' – was always acknowledged by Welles to be Mankiewicz's

It is clear that the film is a pastiche of the life of newspaper magnate William Randolph Hearst despite a lone bit of script early on which self-consciously seeks to deny it. 'How different was he (Kane) from Ford – or Hearst, for that matter?' asks someone looking at the newsreel of his life. Answer: not very different at all.

William Randolf Hearst built up one of America's most powerful newspaper chains based on the proceeds of a silver mine. He is said to have influenced the election of two presidents and to have forced the United States into the Spanish American War to improve circulation. All this is the same for Charles Foster Kane except that in the film it was a gold mine.

Perhaps the cheekiest parallel is Kane living in a vast one-man Disneyland called Xanadu, in Florida. Hearst had something very similar, San Simeon, in California (200,000 acres, 50 miles of ocean front, largest private art collection, zoo, etc). In fact the interiors in the film of Kane's Xanadu are based on magazine photos of San Simeon, where Welles and Mankiewicz had both been guests. However the exteriors, actually only paintings on glass, are judged to have been influenced more by the castle in *Snow White and the Seven Dwarfs* (1937).

Where real life and celluloid diverge rather concerns the love interest. In the film Kane divorces his wife and marries an ordinary girl whom he tries to turn into a star against her will. He even has to build an opera house for her to sing in. Hearst's real relationship with the actress Marion Davies was far more touching and bizarre.

---

*Or so he's almost always quoted. But other sources, including Welles himself, attribute the coinage to another wit, Winston Churchill, describing Sir Stafford Cripps' conduct as Chancellor of the Exchequer several years later. It's a good line, anyway.

In 1917 Hearst was in his fifties when he spotted and fell for nineteen-year-old Marion, a model who had made one film. He determined to make her a star, and set up a special production company for her, Cosmopolitan Pictures. He instructed his papers to sing her praises every day – an order not rescinded until his death in 1951, well after her film career ground to a halt (the talkies revealed a definite stutter).

She had still done pretty well in the silents and probably would have made it without Hearst's attentions. In the event almost all her pictures lost money because of the expensive detail that he insisted on. He parted with about $7,000,000 all told on Cosmopolitan productions.

Unlike Mrs Kane, Hearst's first wife wouldn't give him a divorce and so the lovers never tied the knot. Marion's only marriage came after Hearst's death, and although their relationship was well known in Hollywood it was never mentioned, even in Hearst's rival scandal sheets.

Welles himself was between wives at the time of *Citizen Kane*. He had just divorced Virginia Nicholson, an actress from Chicago, and would marry Rita Hayworth two years later.

Perhaps if Hearst had been at the height of his powers he would have succeeded in suppressing *Citizen Kane* but he was nearly eighty and had been suffering financial reversals.* Nevertheless the film was shot in secret. Welles was mindful of the influence that Hearst retained and of his likely reaction – to say nothing of the hype value of mystery. The set was closed during filming and no one working on the film spoke publicly about the detailed subject matter until after it was completed.

It would still have been recognized as a great film achievement without all the mischief. The production combines so many then-new techniques used so effectively that it has often been cited as their first airing. An example is overlapping dialogue, which, in fact, had been used the previous year in *His Girl Friday*. The magic synthesis of *Citizen Kane* came through Welles' natural flair and imagination driven with a power to inspire those around him, including many experienced technicians.

Welles puts his main screen credit at the end of the film alongside cinematographer Gregg Toland, the colleague who did most to make it a stylish triumph. They were able to make full use of two new developments which were pioneered in the movie; faster film and much more powerful lighting which made it possible to get the deep focus shots that characterize *Citizen Kane*. Toland also used the first self-blimped (self-muffling) camera which meant that Welles had the freedom of greater camera movement. One of the main departures noticed at the time was Welles' prominent use of ceilings, needed as background for the low shots he favoured. That in turn added to the dramatic lighting because he couldn't shine lamps more conventionally through the top of the set.

Welles even used budgetary restrictions to his advantage. The scenes at Xanadu between Kane and Susan were supposed to be played in a drawing room but they saved money by making do with the great hall set instead. The huge spaces and oversized hearth are a far more eloquent setting for the deterioration of their relationship.

Budgets are always a problem. The first scenes to be shot were filmed in secret because the overall costings hadn't quite been finalized. They were listed in the

---

*In the mid-thirties Marion repaid some of his largesse with a $1,000,000 personal loan to get him out of some immediate difficulties.

returns as tests. None of these needed special sets. The very first set-up was the reporters watching the newsreel. They used the RKO projection room. The second was inside Susan's nightclub, normally a set seen in Westerns.

The third scene looks like a deep focus shot, when Kane bursts in on Susan's attempted suicide. This isn't really a set at all – just a couple of flats (boards serving as walls). It isn't really deep focus either although you can see the pill bottle inches from the camera, then Susan, and then Kane bursting into the room in the background. It's actually a double exposure, the first focussing specifically on the pill bottle. Tricks and special effects of this sort pop up all through the film. It has been estimated that up to 80% of the shots in *Citizen Kane* employ some degree of trickery.

It even comes between the shots, with the flashback sequences. The scene appears to fade progressively from background to foreground. This is done by lowering the lights on the set in sequence.

At the end, as a conciliatory gesture, George Schaefer sent a print of the film to William Randolf Hearst at San Simeon. It was returned unopened, proving once and for all that he wasn't Kane, who would have watched and enjoyed it.

▦ The experience

'*Citizen Kane* is as drastic an innovation in film production as the arrival of the talkies. It is the beginning of a new era in camera work, in set building and in performances.' Elma Ferguson, 1941, summing up the general elation amongst critics which sometimes went over the top . . .

'. . . a job of intensely graphic vivisection of a hypothesis.' *Motion Picture Herald*, 1941

'Everybody denies that I am a genius – but nobody ever called me one.' Orson Welles summing up his career

'Genius is definitely the word for Mr Welles.' *Citizen Kane* souvenir programme, 1941

'In a way it is a sad film . . . for with it Welles went straight to the top and he has never gone higher or even (except, as it were, retrospectively and respectfully) kept his position there.' Isabel Quigly, *The Spectator*, 1965

'I started at the top and worked down.' Orson Welles

▦ Can you spot . . .

* Despite 800 extras Welles was short of people when he secretly began shooting with the projection room scene. Joseph Cotten is used as an extra sitting in the corner.
* Another extra who made good. Alan Ladd is in several bits but most easily spotted in the final sequences when they are dismantling the Xanadu collection. He's holding a pipe. Ladd was soon to marry his agent and make it big in *This Gun for Hire* (1942).
* How they aged the principal actors fifty years. The make-up artist, Maurice Seiderman, made plaster casts of the actors' faces and used these to build rubber bumps and folds which were stuck back onto the real thing and covered with make-up. Otherwise lighting and use of shadow disguise what is unconvincing.
* If that was really the end of Rosebud. No, it found a good home. Two examples were burned for the film but Stephen Spielberg recently acquired the remaining one at auction; a snip at $60,000.

Crocodile Dundee

1986 Ingenuous outback toughie takes New York by storm.

▓ The talent

Paul Hogan 46, as Michael 'Crocodile' Dundee; Australia's most famous comedian **Linda Kozlowski** 28, as Sue Charlton; Broadway stage actress who has since worked on TV **John Meillon** 52, as Wally Reilly; another Aussie legend, familiar from *On the Beach*

(1959) and many other films. Here in a part included especially for him to play **John Cornell** Producer; Hogan's manager and partner. He directed *Crocodile Dundee II* (1987) **Peter Faimar** Director; first feature for Hogan's TV director

▓ The business

Paul Hogan had made his fortune from TV comedy and TV commercials but he did a series of 'Visit Australia' ads aimed at United States consumption for no fee. Patriotic altruism? Rather a calculated marketing manoeuvre in a determined, if homespun, assault on the international film industry by Hogan and his manager, John Cornell. *Crocodile Dundee* was soon to be released and they wanted to ensure that the American public were presented with a familiar face.

He had already used the technique to good effect to crack Britain with a celebrated series of commercials for Australian Lager. However Hogan had no need to convince his fellow antipodeans. Over the previous decade he had risen from a stand-up comedy debut masquerading as a tap-dancing, blindfolded knife-thrower on a local TV talent show to a national institution.

Hogan recognized that the films coming out of Australia, apart from the *Mad Max* (1979) series, tended to win considerable critical regard but be relegated to playing art houses. There was an opening for an affordable, mass-popularity picture creating a new national folk hero to replace the existing naff line-up of no-hopers like Ned Kelly.

Australians were so keen to be in on the action that a public offer of shares towards the film's A$8,900,000 budget was oversubscribed by A$3,500,000. Hogan had already given a few sporting friends a piece of the action but he owned 65% of the film with Cornell. They provided real money from their TV fortunes and also paid their own fees back into the production. Hoges retained himself and Ken Sadie on A$218,000 for the script and he got a further A$450,000 for his appearance*; Cornell likewise was paid A$150,000 but invested far more.

*The fees for the rest of the cast collectively, including Linda Kozlowski, came to about A$120,000.

It all made for an optimistic shoot; during production Cornell confidently predicted they would recoup outgoings in Australia alone. In fact the film razed all existing box-office records in Oz, earning A$100,000,000 in two months. Domestically, it was easily bigger than *E.T.* (1982) which is still world financial champion.

Cornell and Hogan arrived in the United States with no distribution deal and without the customary entourage of business advisers but they impressed the Yanks with their powers of deal-making. Paramount won the rights and spent the original budget over again on publicity. They also submitted the film to detailed market research which led them to excise seven minutes from the first half including more impenetrable Australianisms such as 'Stone the bloody crows.' There was also much weighing up of alternative titles. It was decided that the simple addition of quotation marks around the word 'Crocodile' would ensure that American moviegoers would not mistake it for a natural history feature.

The U.S. reviewers on the whole damned it with faint praise but Paramount publicity and word-of-mouth worked fast. *'Crocodile' Dundee* was the most popular film ever released in autumn. It was the same story in Britain and the rest of the world with a gross of US$375,000,000 worldwide, the most successful non-American film ever.

The lucky Australians whose venture money was not part of the over-subscription made five or six times what they put in. But Cornell and Hogan made sure that they owned 100% of the sequel which came out the following year.

▦ Behind the screen

They were going to use a real, sedated crocodile for Dundee to save Sue from but the insurers wouldn't hear of it. So the croc you see is a A$50,000 model which looks all the more realistic because they were able to mould its latex skin from the hide of a real five-meter-long killer. Tons of mud were dredged from the hollow to accommodate the hydraulic plungers which launched the monster up rails at Linda Kozlowski.

Not that there weren't enough real crocodiles ready to try out for the part. Two heavily armed guards were hired to fend off the creatures at the Kakadoo National Park in Australia's Northern Territory and Hogan was given instructions in case of attack.*

Tourism in this stark wonderland doubled after the film's release. There were even pilgrimages to the unprepossessing town of McKinley in the Queensland interior, the location for Walkabout Creek. Bemused locals took the hint and changed the name of the local Federal Hotel to the film's Walkabout Creek Hotel. The proprietors were soon able to sell out for twice what they had paid not so long before.

Linda Kozlowski was a film newcomer who had been recommended by Dustin Hoffman and hired over the objections of the Australian actors' union who wanted them to use local talent. This native New Yorker acquitted herself well with the crew, keeping cheerfully professional on outback locations which only offered the most basic standads of comfort. They were particularly impressed by her refusal of stand-in grub; those unpalatable bush yams that she munches are the genuine article. She says as a consequence the unit elected her an honorary bloke.

---

*Assuming you can still command the use of your legs the trick is to run in a zig-zag. Then the beast's deep-set eyes won't be able to follow you, mate.

Paul Hogan: A$50,000 croc and A$559,000 Croc

That's not exactly the way Hogan voted. The nights in the Australian bush were generally the most boring times of the production, but not it seems for Paul and Linda. It was later said to be an open secret that they had a fling while making *Crocodile Dundee*. They became more obvious about it during a press call for *Crocodile Dundee II* when they smooched passionately for the cameras. Shortly afterwards Hogan left wife Nolene (whom he had married in their teens) and their five children for Linda.

Hogan plays a character which he has refined to an extension of his own attractive personality. You can see that, despite his age, he is also as fit as a croc hunter, but the pursuit of Dundee's physique almost led to tragedy. Shortly after filming Hogan suffered a mini-stroke after lifting one too many 250-pound weights. Australia was on tenterhooks but Hoges made a swift and full recovery. He claimed the haemorrhage affected a part of his brain he never uses.

The seven week's *Crocodile Dundee* filming in Australia was followed by six weeks in the United States. When it came to the final scene in the subway they used several hundred extras who doubled as an impromptu preview audience. It proved welcome confirmation that the Americans would get the jokes.

The film's U.S. locations gained attention from the film's fans though, as with McKinley, expectations were sometimes unduly raised. There were many complaints at the Plaza Hotel from guests who could not find their bidet, one of many cultural puzzles encountered by Dundee on his travels. Time and again the reception desk had to explain that although the set used in the film was fitted with this civilized accoutrement they had yet to grace loos at the Plaza.

▥ The experience

'About the worst thing that can be said about *'Crocodile' Dundee* is that it's nice – not overly genteel, but nice. It's a movie doggedly designed to make you feel good.' Vincent Canby, *New York Times*, 16 November 1986

'Dundee wearing his Australian version of the stetson acts like some representation of the old cowboy and thus reminds the American cinema of its more manly, heroic and (at least in his case) good-humoured past.' Peter Ackroyd, *The Spectator*, 3 January 1987

'One reason the Americans bought it must be because Hogan is nice about them in a way they would never presume to be nice about themselves.' Victoria Mather, *Daily Telegraph*, 12 December 1986

'It's not full of boob jokes or lavatory wall humour and the guy looks at the world through rose-coloured glasses and gives everyone the benefit of the doubt.' Paul Hogan, analyzing the film's appeal

▥ Can you spot . . .

* The imported crocodile teeth. Much deliberation went into the colour and shape of Mick's hat but they had to get the teeth from South-east Asia.
* Lousy directions from the Plaza doorman. To follow Mick to the subway Sue has to go west to Columbus Circle – and be photographed attractively against the backdrop of Central Park – whereas a closer station is just east or round the corner.
* The embarrassment of their first screen kiss. Perhaps. There was a lot of ribbing from the crew as Paul and Linda went into their third or fourth take. 'Calm down, Hoges,' they cat-called. Isn't there a slight tremor as his hand reaches for her chin?
* The production designer. Graham (Grace) Walker plays Angelo in the Australian scenes.
* Some threatening weather. They lost a day's shooting as the ghost of Hurricane Gloria brushed New York.

The
Dam Busters

1955 Dr Barnes Wallis' invention of a bouncing bomb and the men who used it to soak wartime Germany.

▦ The talent

Michael Redgrave 47, as Dr Barnes Wallis; distinguished Cambridge-educated theatrical, knighted four years later. Wife Rachel Kempson, children Vanessa, Corin and Lynn, some grandchildren: all actors
Richard Todd 35, as Wing Cdr Guy Gibson; ex-Sandhurst and a war hero himself in the Para's, also in Michael Anderson's *Yangtse Incident* (1957)

Robert Clark 49, Producer; long-time Associated British executive
Michael Anderson 34, Director; his first major assignment after distinguished apprenticeship. Later made *Around the World in Eighty Days* (1956), *The Quiller Memorandum* (1966) and *Logan's Run* (1976)

▦ The business

'Not another war picture,' was the general reaction to the prospect of *The Dam Busters*. It was a decade since the German surrender, ten years of how-marvellously-we-did-during-the-war movies, and the British public were cooling to the genre.

The Dam Busters reversed the tide. Its scrupulous, proud (and much-self-publicized) authenticity, presented with few frills, brought a lump to the collective throat in Britain and the Commonwealth.* It was the biggest British money-maker of 1955.

The American public was less enthusiastic and there were rumours (which the makers Associated British went so far as to deny in newspaper ads) that the distributors, Warners, hadn't pulled their weight sufficiently in promoting the film.

As if that wasn't enough, Warners employed an editing short-cut in the U.S. version that raised questions in the House of Commons. In two years of preparation for filming the makers aspired to absolute accuracy about the raids, even going so far as to send a copy of the completed script to every surviving member of the Squadron for vetting. But in trimming the action down for the American market the Warners editors spliced in an extra shot of a plane crashing. The only example they could find was a USAF Flying Fortress. This was immediately seized upon by pedantic, mid-fifties Can You Spot-ters and the two offending seconds were promptly excised.

The original footage had genuine aircraft to spare. The RAF, confident of a good showing in the film, readily supplied bombers and pilots to Associated British – at a price. In 1954 their charge for a cinematic bomber wing was £130 per hour per plane. The 150 hours of flying time accounted for roughly 10% of the budget.

*The script by R. C. Sheriff was particularly praised.

Michael Anderson's direction won him his break in Hollywood. After seeing the film, wide-screen cinema mogul Mike Todd abandoned his original plan of dividing his epic *Around the World in Eighty Days* between directors in each of the countries Phileas Fogg was to travel through. Instead he left it to the young Englishman. And the Air Chiefs seem to have been equally impressed. Anderson was awarded the C. P. Robertson Trophy for the year's best interpretation to the public of the RAF.

▦ Behind the screen

This is very much a Barnes Wallis picture. As a consultant for the film-makers he was on set for much of the time and allowed Anderson to use (repeatedly) his own grainy shots of the bouncing bomb being tested.

Redgrave and Wallis hit it off at once. The first time they met the great engineer burst out laughing, perhaps because of how little the actor resembled him in physical stature. You can see that Redgrave towers over his fellow actors. Dr Wallis was shorter and more slight.

It was more of a meeting of minds, recognized when Redgrave told Wallis that he wasn't going to attempt to mimic him in his portrayal. They agreed that the task was one of creation rather than imitation. Redgrave said that it was one of his favourite parts, particularly because it was completely removed from his own character.

Unlike Redgrave the remainder of the cast were chosen partly because of their resemblance to the people they were to represent. Filming was done as much as possible in the locations where everything happened, particularly the airfield scenes which were shot at the original base at Scampton in Lincolnshire. However they didn't go so far as to repeat the flights over the Ruhr, settling instead for a simulated attack on Lake Windemere.

If the flying scenes with Lancasters of the correct model were convincing, the model-work and special effects certainly were not to the critics of the time. The flak attracted particular flak from know-it-alls who surmised it had been scratched directly onto the film stock. The model targets were considered similarly obvious by some.

Those with first-hand experience disagreed. Veterans of the raid were strong in their praise of the combat realism – apparently flak actually looks like scratches on celluloid. The American Motion Picture Academy agreed to the extent that art director Robert Jones got an Oscar nomination for the dinkie dams.

The real thing had been breached twelve years to the day before *The Dam Busters'* premiere. The raid on the Moehne and Eder dams on the Ruhr, of 16 May 1943, was one of the most effective single Allied actions on the Western Front. Seventy-seven flyers survived of the 133 who had set out from Scampton that clear evening. Guy Gibson was awarded the VC for his part in the operation.

The Germans set 2,000 slave labourers to work and had the dam rebuilt within five months but the power station just downstream that the first bomb bounced on to was not recommissioned until 1953. They were still mopping up the area while *The Dam Busters* was in production.

In the course of two years' preparation for the part of Britain's most decorated fighter of the war – Wing Commander Guy Gibson, VC, DSO and Bar, DFC and Bar – Richard Todd contacted many friends, colleagues and even the hero's father. But unlike Barnes Wallis, who was knighted in 1968 and died in his nineties in 1979,

Gibson did not survive the war. The brass kept him away from action for a time but he was shot down over Holland after a mission to the Rhineland eighteen months following the Dam Buster raid.

▦ The experience

'Excuse me while I rave about the finest flying picture I've seen.' Reg Whitley, *Daily Mirror*, 20 May 1955

'*The Dam Busters* is a picture without a blemish. It is thrilling. It is moving. It is true. I think you should be proud to see it.' R. Nash, *Star*, 20 May 1955

'Mr Anderson has handled the final scenes in particular with sympathy, and understatement is never allowed to become the cliché it often is in British films of this kind.' Dilys Powell, *Sunday Times*, 22 May 1955

'From the very beginning, the production ruling for *The Dam Busters* was "authenticity and accuracy" – stick to the facts.' Associated British blurb, 1955

'There is not a single scene in the film which taken on its own is the truth – but take them all together and the whole thing *does* add up to the truth.' Dr Barnes Wallis

▦ Can you spot . . .

* Lots of latterly famous faces. Robert Shaw plays Flight Sergeant Pulford, George Baker is Flight Lieutenant Maltby, Tony Hancock's Aussie radio co-star Bill Kerr is Flight Lieutenant Martin and I'm sure that's Patrick McGoohan guarding the door to the Squadron's briefing room and redirecting Nigger.
* Some miraculous navigating. How could they get the height right using the convergent-beam principle that first occasion they're trying it out – while the aircraft is banking at the same time.
* Any sign of the enemy. All you see are the animated flak patterns; no mention is made of the countless civilians swept away by the ensuing floods, apart from one fairly sanitary shot of workers scurrying out of danger. Director Michael Anderson said that like his subsequent *Yangtse Incident*, which showed little of the Chinese, the narrative perspective concentrated on the British men involved.
* A troublesome dog. No, not the individual hound playing Nigger but the name itself and the actual inclusion of the character. Sure enough, Guy Gibson's dog got run over on the day of the action. There were nevertheless raised eyebrows at featuring the mut's demise more prominently than most of the human casualties. And the name was understandably dubbed to Trigger for some American states.

Dirty Harry

1971 Tough San Francisco cop hunts a crazed killer.

▦ The talent

Clint Eastwood 41, as Inspector Harry Callahan; from TV's *Rawhide* via the Leone spaghetti Western classics. Continued to dominate the box office as a latter-day John Wayne

Andy Robinson 29, as Scorpio; many TV guest spots and Siegel's next film, *Charley Varrick* (1973). Returned to TV

Don Siegel 59, Producer/Director; American but Cambridge- and RADA-educated former editor whose other films include the classic *Invasion of the Body Snatchers* (1956) and *The Shootist* (1976)

▦ The business

Dirty Harry might have been Frank Sinatra's film but he was recovering from an operation on his hand and wouldn't have been fit for the action. So the screenplay – entitled *Dead Right* – by husband and wife team Harry and Rita Fink went the rounds until Paul Newman, who didn't fancy the shabby, Columbo-like character originally conceived (hence Dirty Harry), suggested they approach Clint Eastwood.

Eastwood had formed his own production company, Malpaso, in the late sixties to harness a career that was more profitable for others than himself and type-laden with Westerns. He needed both a new image and a surefire hit, especially after the moderate business for *The Beguiled* (1971) directed by Siegel and his as yet untested debut as a director with *Play Misty for Me* (1971).*

Sharing Newman's view of the first-draft Harry Callahan, Eastwood brought in writer Dean Riesner – who worked with Siegel on *Coogan's Bluff* (1968) and *Charley Varrick* (1973) – to rework the Finks' character into a suitably Clinty hero. This included changing the ending from the original coup de grace by a marksman at the airport to Eastwood's vengeful personal intervention. How does he suddenly materialize on that railway trestle?

Eastwood also hired his friend Don Siegel to direct their fourth venture together.** With the help of Siegel and Sergio Leone, and yet almost unnoticed by the critics, Eastwood had risen to the point where he had just been featured on the cover of *Life* magazine under the banner headline, 'The world's favourite movie star – no kidding.'

The righteous tone of the film, opening as it does with the tribute to fallen San Francisco police officers, caused a stir at a time of fashionable student radicalism in the United States. Some looked on *Dirty Harry* as a paean to police piggery but a

---

*Yes, a three-picture year. As it turned out *Misty* did well. Eastwood was praised as a director and has continued in that role from time to time.

**Their others were *Coogan's Bluff* (1968). *Three Mules for Sister Sarah* (1970) and *The Beguiled* plus *Escape from Alcatraz* (1979) to come. They had reversed roles in *Play Misty For Me* with Siegel playing a bartender.

penetrating review in radical chic *Rolling Stone* articulated another current reading of the film as a sensitive portrayal of a man trapped by the system and circumstance. The Philippines police certainly had no doubt where their sympathies lay. One of their branches asked for a sixteen-millimetre print of the film for use in their training programme.

Whatever the arguments, *Dirty Harry* struck a chord with audiences, proving the biggest money-maker so far for both director and star, and the fifth highest grossing film of 1972 ($16,000,000 in the first two years). It began a series of so far five portrayals by Clint Eastwood of Harry Callahan,* the backbone of one of the most successful screen careers of the seventies and eighties.

The real Scorpio was also a high achiever. The film was based on a psychopath calling himself Zodiac who terrorized San Francisco in the late sixties. He killed five people at random and wrote letters to the police with threats echoed in the film, targeting minority groups. He also threatened to hijack a busload of kids. But the S.F.P.D. had no Harry Callahan and Zodiac, mercifully inactive since 1969, has never been caught.

When another nutter dubbed 'The Zebra Killer' started operating in 1974 graffiti appeared around San Francisco asking, 'Dirty Harry, where are you now that we need you?'

▦ Behind the screen

This was the new, urban Clint Eastwood but even if the image was changing there was a certain comfortable familiarity about the shoot. He was with a director he liked and trusted, filming on his old stamping ground; he had grown up in Oakland across the Bay. *Dirty Harry* was a location picture aside from the shoot-out at the beginning when Inspector Callahan pauses from his hotdog to demolish a gang of armed robbers.

Because of the nature of the stunt, with the hydrant making the car's day, the scene was entirely staged on a set at Warner Brothers. It is a striking demonstration of the film-makers' ability to match back lot with real life. The only give-away is the passers-bys' aptitude for ignoring the camera.**

Literally shooting on the street had its problems, chiefly in the reaction of local residents to Scorpio's afterhours machinegun fire. The film-makers found themselves restricted to a schedule which normally meant wrapping by midnight.

Once when they *were* able to work all night there was another problem. The director had flu so it fell to the star, with his experience of making one film, to stand in for Siegel. The scene was where Harry saves the would-be suicide from the roof. As it turned out, the greatest impediment was the crowd of sensation seekers, particularly one woman who was annoyingly persistent in her pursuit of the Eastwood autograph. She left him alone after he whipped out his blank-loaded magnum and fired over her head.

Eastwood completed the whole scene in one night, not the best part of a week predicted by the studio. When you see him walking away exhausted at the end it's

*Magnum Force (1973). The Enforcer (1976). Sudden Impact (1983) and Dead Pool (1989) – none directed by Siegel.
**But see also Can You Spot . . .

five thirty in the morning. He directed another brief segment as well, the encounter with the gay lad in the park.

For the suicide scene and elsewhere, Clint Eastwood insisted on doing his own stunts, the most notable and risky being the leap onto the roof of the hijacked bus. But take a careful look at Andy Robinson, playing the psychopathic Scorpio as he is belting the children inside. The tender-hearted actor didn't have the stomach to go through with it until Don Siegel started demonstrating what he wanted using the young actors with such convincing viciousness that Robinson got on with the scene just to get Siegel to lay off.

Did liberal director and conservative star fight about the politically charged subject matter? No, they just wanted to make a pacy, commercial film. There was nevertheless speculation at the time about possible arguments between the old friends on set.

One of the few actual disagreements came with the last scene when Harry throws away his badge.* Eastwood didn't want to perform what he interpreted as a gesture of abdication but Siegel persuaded him that he was merely demonstrating his disgust.

Perhaps it was Eastwood's business instinct rebelling against chucking the prospect of profitable sequels. In any case, as Eastwood put it, the badge must have been attached to a piece of elastic because Harry Callahan was soon back in the S.F.P.D. keeping the streets dangerous for perps.

▓ The experience

'Don Siegel's latest film, *Dirty Harry*, is an elegiac, necrophiliac, fascist love poem.' Anthony Chase, *The Velvet Light Trap Revue of Cinema*, 1972

'I was telling a story about a hard-nosed cop. That doesn't mean that I condone hard-nosed cops.' Don Siegel, 1973

'Don Siegel is an expert director who moves things along with pace and tact – the sort of tactfulness that knows instinctively when to cut a shot and when to linger. If he had used a better lead than Clint Eastwood, who is really more of a blessing to a lighting cameraman than a director, he would have made a film to remember.' Christopher Hudson, *Spectator*, 8 November 1972

'I felt bored rather than sickened, and hope my feeling is registered at the box office.' Fergus Cashin, *The Sun*, 30 March 1972

'When I go to the movies it's to have a few laughs and a couple of beers afterwards. I don't worry about social injustice.' Clint Eastwood

▓ Can you spot . . .

* What's on at the movies. The cinema on the set-bound bank robbery shoot-out is showing Eastwood's latest *oeuvre*, *Play Misty For Me*.
* The critics' favourite shot. It's the end of the scene in the stadium as the helicopter carrying the camera hovers out into blackness.
* The love interest. There isn't any – unless you count the squeaky-clean encounter between Harry and his partner's wife. Director and star had had enough of women in the female-laden *Beguiled*.
* Big Al's. You can see its front hoarding briefly as Harry and partner are cruising for the killer in San Francisco's sleazy Broadway area. Although you can't tell, it was next

*cf. *High Noon* (1952).

Clint Eastwood and stuntman: stand-in director who didn't use stand-ins

door to where they filmed the nightclub scenes, an establishment called 'The Roaring Twenties'. Outside, the barker was enticing potential customers with the pitch: 'Come and see what the movie leaves out.'

* Convenience blood. Warners publicity blurb puffed the gore substitute used for Scorpio's first victim in the pool. It was especially developed on an oil base by the studio SFX boffins to scoop cleanly out of the water after each murder like seaweed.

Duck Soup

1933 Freedonia is in peril and only Rufus T. Firefly can save the day . . . maybe.

▦ The talent

Groucho Marx 42, as Rufus T. Firefly; the smart one – became one of TV's early big stars

Harpo Marx 44, as Brownie; the intellectuals' pet

Chico Marx 47, as Chicolini; the gambling playboy

Zeppo Marx 32, as Bob Rolland; bailing out of the act

Margaret Dumont 43, as Mrs Teasdale; Groucho's favourite foil, perhaps because she didn't understand the jokes

Louis Calhern 38, as Ambassador Trentino; mid-career between romance in the silents and key character parts in the fifties

Herman J. Mankiewicz 35, Producer; normally a scriptwriter whose greatest moment was *Citizen Kane* (1941)

Leo McCarey 34, Director; triple academy award winner who made comedies with most of the greats

▦ The business

The change to sound invigorated the balance sheets of most Hollywood studios sufficiently to get them through the 1929 Wall Street Crash but somehow Paramount was in trouble. The studio needed to jettison anything that wasn't sure-fire commercial material, and their sights were on the Marx Brothers.

The Marxes could earn $3,000 a week each from their Broadway comedy revues but Chico and Zeppo regularly staked that much on a single bet, and Groucho had lost his entire $240,000 fortune playing the stockmarket. They would miss the $150,000 the act was paid per film.

Unfortunately, although the fifth Marx Brothers Paramount release, *Duck Soup*,* is today considered to be their finest effort the critics and public of the day were unimpressed. The film grossed about $1,500,000 – not enough for the studio, which had seen revenue fall with each successive picture, and they dropped the Marx contract.

Despite still being hits on stage and radio the Brothers were despondent and Zeppo quit the act. But help was at hand from an unexpected source. Chico, the inveterate gambler, happened to get into a card game with MGM chief Irving Thalberg and afterwards parleyed the act straight into one of the best deals of that time. Their salary, according to Groucho, was $200,000 a film between them plus 15% of the gross.

But the comedy was never as sharp again. Thalberg's influence was to dilute the Marxist mayhem with romance and plot. Nevertheless it made economic sense: *A*

*Preceded by *The Cocoanuts* (1929), *Animal Crackers* (1930), *Monkey Business* (1931) and *Horse Feathers* (1932).

Night at the Opera (1935), the first of their MGM period, doubled the gross of *Duck Soup* and the Brothers were getting their royalties from re-releases for years, enough to finance Chico through many more card games.

⊞ Behind the screen

The world around the Marx Brothers was in upheaval. While the studio was near bankruptcy, America was reeling from the effects of the depression and Germany was electing Hitler to power – a context which has prompted theories, setting up *Duck Soup* as a politically lampooning precursor to Chaplin's *The Great Dictator* (1940). Harpo certainly remembered the atmosphere being coloured by the sound of the Fuhrer's fulminations over the radio but most of those involved agree with Marx biographer Joe Adamson: 'There are political satires and there are political satires. *Duck Soup* is neither.'* As usual the only aim was at readily identifiable targets, strictly for laughs.

The Marxes themselves needed a laugh. They were worried about the impending end of their contract as well as grieving for their father, Frenchie, who died a few weeks before filming began in the summer of 1933. Also the act was breaking apart. Zeppo, who always looked expendable, was preparing for partnership in a theatrical agency with brother Gummo (the one who had left the act before their film days).

Groucho had the additional burden of helping to set up the Screen Actors Guild in the face of sniping opposition within the industry while at home his wife, Ruth, was starting to drink heavily, straining their previously happy marriage.

But at least Harpo was on a high. He was falling in love with his future wife, Susan Fleming – a happy first marriage in his forties. And he was being flattered as well by the attention of leading American wits who admired his skills as a pantomimist.

With all this going on Harpo said he had never felt under so much pressure to perform well. One day the normally straightforward vaudevillian found himself asking Herman Mankiewicz to explain the motivation of his character. Mank helpfully replied that he was playing a middle-aged Jew who goes around picking up shit.

That against this background emerged the best Marx Brothers film is due in part to the presence of director Leo McCarey, later acknowledged by Groucho as the only really great director they ever had. And that is quite something coming from the old stage comic who in general reviled directors for their hackneyed technique, their reliance on copious retakes (rarely necessitated by the nimble-tongued Groucho) and their predilection for starting work early ('This is a hell of a time to have to be funny!').

For directors and other back-room boys the feeling was mutual. How's this for a recommendation, from writer S. J. Perelman: 'Anybody who ever worked on any picture for the Marx Brothers said he would rather be chained to a galley and lashed at ten minute intervals until the blood spurted from his frame than ever work for these sons of bitches again.'

But the domineering McCarey – a veteran of Hal Roach, and the Laurel and Hardy shorts – was a match for the four Megalomania Brothers. There was little confrontation. Instead they all spent the production in a sharp but generally good-natured exchange of practical jokes, bets and great comic ideas.

*Mussolini didn't agree with Mr Adamson's view and the film was banned in Fascist Italy. All their flicks were already *verboten* in Germany.

It was McCarey's sense of humour that the Marxes admired most. He came up with Harpo's running gag of snipping everything with his scissors, and himself snipped away at any material in the script that was extraneous to Marx Brothers lunacy. Gone were romance (Zeppo and Raquel Torres) and solo musical spots (Chico and Harpo) – but you can still see where they would have fitted. Some of the gaps were filled by scriptwriter Arthur Sheekman who came up with a lot of last-minute gags (such as 'Go and never darken my towels again!'), whispered into Groucho's ear just as the cameras rolled.

Harpo, Groucho and Chico: refugees at MGM

The rest came direct from McCarey. The force of his personality can most clearly be seen in the untypical comic touches that he managed to impose on the Marx Brothers style. One was his use of the minor script device of Chico being a peanut salesman as an excuse for the lemonade seller sketch, a scene of deliberate mutual destruction straight out of Stan and Ollie. Chico and Harpo's adversary, Edgar 'Slow Burn' Kennedy, was himself straight out of Laurel and Hardy – he co-starred in many of their Hal Roach films and even directed a couple. They all took their time over the scenes: four days of loving improvisation.

But it took only a quick-fire two hours to record one of cinema's most famous bits of comedy business – the mirror scene. It was another of McCarey's ideas based on an old vaudeville routine. They were able to knock it off in one Saturday morning thanks to Harpo taking perfect, instantaneous cues from Groucho.

If the big unanswered question for you now is the exact meaning of *Duck Soup*, Groucho (who claimed that he could explain the titles of all their shows bar one*) explained, 'Take two turkeys, one goose, four cabbages but no duck and mix them together. After one taste you'll duck soup for the rest of your life.' Hello, I must be going.

▦ The experience

'The same tricks can't be worked over and over again. The comedy quartet has a rather set routine.' Edwin Schallert, *Los Angeles Times*, 1 January 1934

'If you were asked to name the best comedies ever made, and you named *The Gold Rush* and *The General* and a half dozen others, *Duck Soup* is the only one that doesn't have a dull spot.' Woody Allen

'In our early pictures we were hilariously funny fellows, knocking over the social mores and customs of our times, but with each succeeding picture the receipts slipped just a bit. The reason we switched from being anarchistic in our humour to being semi-lovable was simply a matter of money.' Groucho Marx

'The most surprising thing about this film is that I succeeded in not going crazy.' Leo McCarey

▦ Can you spot . . .

* Marxist continuity. Leo McCarey went for the funniest takes and never mind the matching. It is most outrageous in the opening reception for Firefly when Groucho's coat changes from grey with braids to tails and back again in the twinkling of a cut.

*Apparently their first Broadway hit, *I'll Say She Is*, puzzled him.

Easy Rider

1969 Two hippies encounter good times and hostility on a journey across America.

▦ The talent

Peter Fonda 30, as Captain America; least distinguished of the Fonda clan
Dennis Hopper 33, as Billy; Hollywood rebel pal of James Dean. Re-emerging as character star of the eighties
Jack Nicholson 32, as George Hanson; hold on to your hats – here comes a superstar
Peter Fonda Producer; has directed a couple since
Dennis Hopper Director; his next effort *The Last Movie* (1971) has been acclaimed as one of the worst films of all time

▦ The business

The whole enterprise seems rather unlikely. Peter Fonda conceived the germ of the plot as an antidote to the tedium of a promotional trip to Toronto. He based it on a few factual incidents which survive in the film as the reference to hippies' hair being trimmed with rusty razor blades and in the violent end.

What a far-out idea! Fonda called his friend and sometime co-star Dennis Hopper at three in the morning to enthuse about it and then preserved his thoughts on a tape recorder. These mutterings were sufficient to induce Bert Schneider of the fledgling Raybert Productions to part with the $375,000 spent on *Easy Rider*.

It wasn't really such a wild gamble. Both Fonda and Hopper had a sufficiently well-established notoriety from their roles in *The Trip* (1967) and other unorthodox entertainments to make any flick of theirs featuring hippie bikers certain to turn some sort of profit. But just to make sure the budget wasn't all dreamt away, Raybert sent along one of their scriptwriters, also a minor actor, who was preparing to direct his first film. His name was Jack Nicholson and he was kind enough to step in when no one else was available to play the drunken lawyer.*

It might have turned out so differently but *Easy Rider* was one of the unexpected hits of the sixties. If you compare the Raybert outlay with the estimated $40,000,000 worldwide gross, *Easy Rider* comes out as one of the most profitable films of all time. Fonda and Hopper each got a third of these profits, and not content with this Hopper later sued for a further 3% for his contribution to the screenplay.** Nicholson also got a very small percentage for securing some financial deal along the way, but his main prize was the good fortune to fall into a part which so brilliantly showcased his appeal. He became one of the biggest stars in the seventies and eighties.

*They were all great pals. Bert Schneider's partner in Raybert was director Bob Rafelson. Together they had been the driving force behind TV's *The Monkees* and had made the group's movie, *Head* (1968), with script by Jack Nicholson. The trio made several notable films including *Five Easy Pieces* (1971) and *The King of Marvin Gardens* (1973). Nicholson had scripted *The Trip* for Roger Corman.

**Terry Southern is a third credited writer whose contribution seems to have been the prestige of his name (he wrote *Dr Strangelove (1963) and Barbarella* (1967)), the title and a little shaping to the Fonda concept and Hopper script.

Fonda and Hopper, on the other hand, were unable to repeat the formula and largely squandered the further opportunities to produce and direct offered them on the back of this Triumph. Or was it a Harley-Davidson?

⊞ Behind the screen

They started off with a sixteen-millimetre camera, lots of marijuana and a script that was really little more than a pipe-dream. But they knew that somehow the New Orleans Mardi Gras would fit into the narrative and made that their first location, shooting the rest of the film in sequence. Can you spot how Hopper's hair, in particular, looks six weeks more kempt as soon as they move out into the street for the Mardi Gras scenes?

This and the LSD sequence are typical of a production where even when things went wrong the final product remained undiminished and sometimes greatly enhanced. The New Orleans street scenes look specially processed for far-out effect but are actually just plain old fogged through a technical fault. And part of the psychedelic soundtrack in the LSD sequence comes from Hopper's microphone being left on by mistake. With three cameras rolling at once and a flashy fish-eye lens this at least was familiar ground for novice *auteur* Hopper. His only previous directing experience was the psychedelic sequences for *The Trip*.

Time and again the directorial bacon was saved by the services of two inspired technicians: film editor, Don Cambern, and cameraman Laslo Kovaks. It was Cambern who coped with Hopper's debut touches as director, principally the six-frame flashes between some scenes. Hopper felt these to be more challenging to the audience than regular cuts and fades. Cambern also managed to snip around the worst omissions in the available material.

An least he had some beautiful shots to work with. Kovaks provided the panoramic study of south-west America, shot from the back of a Chevy convertible. Can you spot it reflected in the yards of elongated motorcycle chrome? This footage attracted a far wider audience for *Easy Rider* than the hippie biker fraternity and Kovaks went on to film *Paper Moon* (1973), *Close Encounters of the Third Kind* (1977), and *Ghostbusters* (1984).

In some respects the adventures of Fonda, Hopper and their twenty-three man filming entourage mirrored the drug-sodden passage of Captain America and his mate Billy, particularly in the reaction of the locals. This mingled an instant loathing of the, by modern standards, rather muted alternative look and an undisguised admiration for anyone making movies. Most seemed to have given them the benefit of the doubt, assuming them to be in costume rather than expressing a genuinely pursued lifestyle.

These small-town attitudes were used to particularly good onscreen advantage in the cafe sequence, filmed in Morganza, Louisiana. Some citizens had already been recruited by the film's advance men but the characters you see passing comment on our heroes were some even more ornery individuals spotted by Hopper.

As with much of the rest of the film, the structure of the scene was planned in advance but the precise dialogue was left to improvisation. So as to inspire the good 'ole boys to the proper pitch of eloquent bigotry Peter Fonda explained that he and Hopper were playing a pair who rape and murder children. 'Say anything you want,' he advised. The local lads needed little further encouragement. The female talent, on the other hand, were more self-conscious and a little puzzled as to what was expected of them. At last the penny dropped: 'You mean you-all want us to flirt with you? Oh we know how to do that!' Who needs expensive professional supporting players?

Jack Nicholson was another matter. It was his skill that made the fireside soliloquies about the State of the Union and UFOs (an obsession of Hopper's at the time) fit seamlessly with the improvised, naturalistic dialogue of the rest of the film. These sections closely followed a script by Dennis Hopper. It's right there, hidden underneath Nicholson's coat.

What a convincing job they all made of being stoned: a case of method acting. Whenever you see any of the characters smoking a joint it's the real thing, and whenever you see Fonda or Hopper, *period*, chances are they have just been inhaling inspiration. By all accounts they spent the whole shoot, and several following years, in a hemp-induced haze. One story had it that Nicholson consumed 155 joints during the fireside scenes but he denied it. He does admit, however, to smoking a fresh joint for every take and set-up (purely for the sake of continuity, of course). This presented him with the unusual dramatic challenge, occasioned by the need to seem progressively more zonked during the scene, of having to act stoned while relatively straight in the early takes and relatively sober when completely out of it later on. The director doesn't seem to have helped much. When Nicholson bursts out laughing at the end of the UFO speech it is because of Hopper mugging off camera.

An incident alluded to in the film put Nicholson off trying anything much more mind-blowing than pot. He had a bad LSD experience when he went tripping with Hopper and Fonda at D. H. Lawrence's tomb in the New Mexico desert during a break in shooting. His character, George Hanson, toasts Lawrence with his first drink of the

Peter Fonda and Dennis Hopper: everybody must get stoned

day. Hanson's squawking-duck gesture that punctuated the impact of alcohol on innards became something of a fad in Los Angeles at the time.

For Nicholson the character of George Hanson was just an act but Hopper and Fonda had something in common with the outlook of their characters, and some notable differences. Their home lives were more conventional. Hopper was in the midst of a divorce and though that would come to Fonda as well at the time he was happily married with two children. He felt himself to be more relaxed and gregarious than his character, Captain America, and Hopper to be more articulate than Billy. And despite the critical and public acclaim for Nicholson's performance, Fonda judged Hopper's to be the more skilled if less cute.

Aside from Jack Nicholson and the scenery, *Easy Rider*'s attraction lay in sex, drugs and rock-'n-roll. This last feature was carefully woven into the film by Fonda and Hopper with the generous cooperation of many of the era's top rock acts. The only dissenter seems to have been Bob Dylan who refused to allow them to use his 1965 recording of 'It's Alright Ma I'm Only Bleeding' over the end of the film. Bob, by that time in his mushy John Wesley Harding/Nashville Skyline phase, was possibly uncomfortable with the sound and sentiments of his old hit. Fonda claims he might have relented if they had changed the ending to the one Dylan himself devised: Captain America ramming the pick-up truck with his bike, immolating its murderous occupants! Peace, man.

▦ The experience

'It made my career. A few days work for a personal friend and I became a star.' Jack Nicholson

'Even if you can't go along with the slightly fatuous self-importance of the hippies, or Fonda's tendency to bless all he approves of like a teenage pope the film remains one of the most perceptive in years to have come from the direct experience of its makers.' Alexander Walker, *Evening Standard*, 4 September 1969

'The amazing, confusing thing about *Easy Rider* is that it really is eloquent in almost every passage that isn't marked "Hush – Eloquence at Work".' Joseph Morgenstern, *Newsweek*, 21 July 1969

▦ Can you spot . . .

* The weakest scene? According to Fonda it's the farewell from the hippie commune.
* An unobtrusive camera. Hopper asked Kovaks to use a long lens during the fireside scenes so that the technology wouldn't impose itself on all the meaningful philosophizing.
* What the title means. Peter Fonda: 'Easy Rider is a Southern term for a whore's old man. Not a pimp but the dude who lives with the chick. Because he's got an easy ride. Well, that's what's happening to America, man. Liberty's become a whore and we're all taking the easy ride.'
* Two likely lasses at the house of Blue Lights. Karen Black and Toni Basil both became stars of the seventies, on film and record respectively.
* Another famous face. Phil Spector, the master sixties record producer, played the big wheel at the beginning buying the cocaine. He was apparently genuinely frightened of the planes coming in to land just overhead but gives a very convincing impression of calm after sampling the 'goods'.

E.T.: the profits were out of this world, too

E.T.:
The Extraterrestrial

1982 A stranded visitor from space befriends a young boy but is homesick and seems to be dying.

🖽 The talent

Henry Thomas 8, as Elliott; Texas farm boy in one previous film

Drew Barrymore 6, as Gertie; 6 'going on 29'. Scion of great Barrymore acting clan with much film and TV experience, and many troubles since *E.T.*

Robert McNaughton 16, as Michael; a respected stage veteran

Dee Wallace as Mary Taylor; former ballerina with bit part in *10* (1979)

Peter Coyote 40, as Keys; just missed the job of Indiana Jones. Also in *Jagged Edge* (1985)

Kathleen Kennedy 28, Producer; Spielberg's personal assistant from *1941* (1979) who went on to become his partner

Steven Spielberg 36, Producer/Director; has continued to produce, mainly other people's work, including *Poltergeist* (1982) and *Back to the Future* (1985). Hasn't lost his directorial talent for money-spinning despite branching out from pure kids' stuff

🖽 The business

In the first weekend that it was released *E.T.* grossed rather more than the $10,500,000 it cost to make – the first rumble in an avalanche of revenue that has made this film the biggest money-maker ever.

That summer of 1982 it was taking about $20,000,000 a week and within a few months had broken all records. When last seen the figures for North America alone were heading towards $300,000,000. Spielberg, hardly short of spare change when he embarked on the project, was soon reported to be getting a cut of $1,000,000 a day.

E.T. was the third Spielberg film – with *Jaws* (1975) and *Raiders of the Lost Ark* (1981) – to enter the all-time top ten of money-makers. They were soon joined by the Raiders sequel, *Indiana Jones and the Temple of Doom* (1984). Another Spielberg film, *Close Encounters of the Third Kind* (1977), hovers just outside the top ten having grossed only a paltry $80,000,000 or so.

MCA, the parent company of Universal Pictures, were naturally anxious to retain the services of their young golden goose and rewarded him with a special retreat on the Universal lot. Styled to look like a New Mexico Indian dwelling, it is filled with the electronic games and gadgetry that Spielberg employs to keep his childish muse fully stoked. It cost $3,600,000. Steven queried the expense but was told that it represented the rentals for *E.T.* from Bolivia and that he shouldn't worry about it. He uses it as the headquarters for his company, Amblin' Productions, and has adopted as the logo the image of Elliott and E.T. flying across the moon on their bicycles.

The film touched the critics' hearts as much as those of the general audiences and they praised it as an instant classic of children's movies. Hard-baked cinema hacks at the 35th Cannes Film Festival who were treated to a preview cried like babies and gave the film a tremendous ovation . . . and this was a screening at 8.30 in the morning!

Not quite everyone was so appreciative, though. In Sweden, anyone under eleven was banned from the film because it showed children being hostile to their parents.

The greatest single expense on the film was the little creature from space: $1,500,000 worth of pullies, levers, electronics and latex. But Spielberg, pointing out that E.T. had to carry the bulk of the two-hour film, said that he came cheaper than the admittedly established Marlon Brando who wheeled $3,500,000 out of the producers of *Superman* (1978) for a cameo lasting a few minutes.

The producers took full advantage by creating a whole parallel fortune with dolls, books and other products to cash in on the E.T. legend. And with all that money and attention flying about, others were bound to benefit as well, not least the lucky manufacturers of a number of products featured in the film. The people who market a chocolate and peanut butter confection called 'Reese's Pieces' saw sales rocket by 85% after their product was featured.

Behind the screen

This was one from the heart for Steven Spielberg, the most personal of all the movies he had made since he started filming model train crashes with an 8mm camera as a boy.

A close student of his technique might notice a more fluid style than in his previous pictures. It was here that he abandoned the use of story-boards, apart from the special effects scenes which are so expensive and so detailed, each source of light and the minutiae of movement having to be specified, that they need to be planned out exactly.

Previously he would have used anything up to 2,500 drawings in a production, which would have covered each shot, but on *E.T.* he would arrive on set with only a general idea of what he wanted to do. For the most part the film has been shot chronologically, enabling the children to develop the parts and improvise to a certain extent. Part of this new approach was on the advice of François Truffaut, whom Spielberg featured in *Close Encounters of the Third Kind*. The French director maintained that it was particularly necessary to keep flexible when making films with children.

Spielberg often uses experiences and impressions from his own childhood, one example here being the trick of faking a temperature by holding the thermometer to a lightbulb. Elliott uses it when he wants to stay home with E.T. and years ago Steven used it when he wanted time to edit his films on a schoolday.

At the time of filming *E.T.* Spielberg was going through the emotional low of separation from Amy Irving, the actress who was to later become his wife. They ended a four-year relationship shortly before work on the project started and didn't get back together again until the year after it was released when they were both in India – she playing in *The Far Pavilions* and he researching locations for *Indiana Jones and the Temple of Doom*. They soon came up with a new production, son Max, but have since split.

During the fifty-eight days of filming *E.T.* Spielberg built up a close relationship with his young stars. He seems to have a natural gift for working with children and that is of course the way he started out – directing his friends and their wrecked train sets. One of the elements of the rapport he built up with the human star of E.T., Henry Thomas, was a shared enthusiasm for the electronic game, Pacman. Spielberg would never talk down to the youngsters or underestimate how perceptive they were. But he said that all they wanted to know was what they were to do and why; anything deeper was just a bore.

For the most part the young actors – of 200 or so auditioned – were picked for their spontaneity. Drew Barrymore proved the greatest teller of tall tales at the auditions, making up a variety of stories including her adventures in a punk rock band. A mature six, she had her own definite ideas about being in pictures. 'I wanna be a star because it makes you feel good,' she said. She later turned to supplementing the thrill of celebrity with drink and drugs and, following a period of detoxification, attempted suicide at the age of thirteen.

Just after making *E.T.* Drew had neatly summed up a common attitude to the star of the picture; 'When I first met E.T. I was scared because he was icky. But after a while I thought he was real and I fell in love with him.'

That's the magic of E.T. So subtle and complete was the special effects package that produced the film's star player that everyone on the set thought he was real as well. The dozen or so operators who had to practise hard to coordinate the hundreds of separate movements he was capable of, added to this by playing tricks on their fellow studio workers. So, the story goes, it ceased to be a surprise to see E.T. relaxing off camera smoking a cigar and once he even pinched the behind of the writer, Melissa Mathison. It got to the point where people would start to speak to him as if he were alive. One special effects man who had the task of spraying E.T. to keep him looking properly icky asked the contraption to move its head to one side. Like any obliging star the little alien gracefully complied.

The universal experience of initial revulsion at the sight of the creature, and subsequent affection, was a key element of the planning. Spielberg said he wanted the character to earn love.

His original concept called for a creature from a hot planet with a strong gravitational field. Hence E.T. was to be short, fat and sweaty. Spielberg was specific that the alien should have a rear like Donald Duck's. He came up with the face by taking the photograph of a newborn baby and pasting Albert Einstein's eyes and forehead over it.

Another specification was the extendable neck, so that no one could think that it was just a midget in a suit. In fact, any time you see E.T. walk that *is* someone in a suit. A walking E.T. would have meant an extra $1,000,000 and, more importantly, too much time.

So how do you go about fashioning these scraps of a concept into a photogenic and believable creature? Take several million dollars and the special effects skills of Carlo Rambaldi, whose other triumphs include the expressive face of King Kong in his 1975 incarnation.

The film actually uses three E.T. bodies with four interchangeable heads offering different effects. If you look carefully you can see that the E.T.s change from shot to shot.

The most crude package was the body which would contain a tiny human for the walking sequences. The head has only six points of movement which, along with the arms, are radio controlled.

The most complex was the head used for close-ups. It has eighty-five bits that move: eyes, eyelids, throbbing veins, lips and all the rest of the blend of muscles which animate our expressions. The eyes themselves were so complicated and time-consuming to construct that they were done by separate specialists. E.T.'s eyes dilate and contract as the light changes, thanks to someone crouching some way away operating a cable. And that's the way the rest of E.T.'s expressive face works as well. He is a mass of hand-operated, radio-controlled or otherwise electronic cables being coordinated between up to a dozen operators twenty feet or so off camera. His bodies are aluminium skeletons covered with latex and painted by a make-up expert.

One of the torsos also had hand-operated bellows to help create E.T.'s glowing heart. It's actually a plastic called Hot-Melt illuminated by a 1000 watt bulb and kept cool by a hairdrier. Someone forgot to turn on the hairdrier during the intensive care scene and the leading alien caught fire.

So complex and expressive is the close-up head that E.T. has a lot more acting left in him. His vocabulary was limited in the film but he was capable of saying anything. The voice was provided mostly by a former school teacher called Pat Welsh who was overheard ordering something in a supermarket. Her croaky tones, matured on forty cigarettes a day, were the perfect basis for a little electronic jiggery-pokery and extra vocal input from actress Deborah Winger.

Talking aside, the most difficult thing to coordinate was E.T. eating. His lips and tongue were controlled by different people and so tongue biting was a hazard. In fact it took a lot of time to perfect any of his movements and although the humans tended to get it right in a few takes E.T. needed anything up to fifteen.

The little alien even had a special tube so that he could drink beer in the drunk scene . . . but that's one of the occasions that he got some help from a human.

If you see him moving someone's inside. The one teetering around the kitchen is twelve-year-old Matthew de Merritt, who looks very much like Henry Thomas except that he was born with no legs. He is inside the most basic E.T. body, walking on his hands. Mostly, though, Matthew had a far easier way of getting around the set; he is an expert skateboarder.

E.T.'s human element was actually something that Stephen Spielberg had been trying to keep quiet but one of the other E.T. actors called attention to herself by saying she was the one who had brought E.T. to life. In fact the actress Tamara de Teaux (who is an inch under three feet and was 22 when *E.T.* was made) appears in only one scene: when E.T. returns to the spacecraft near the end of the film. All the other scenes with movement were played by 2' 10" Pat Bilon who suffered greatly from heat in the tight confines of E.T. during the shoot. He died of pneumonia soon after.

But that's not all – E.T. has human hands. Although they look impossibly thin and extra-terrestrial they are in fact the very earthly property of mime artist Caprice Rothe who answered an ad calling for someone with 'long, graceful fingers'. Any hand movement is hers apart from when E.T. covers his face in the corn field and as he reaches out when dying. She is in a glove that comes all the way from her armpit to an extended special effects finger. This has a tiny imbedded red bulb which lights when E.T.'s healing powers are required. Caprice could have used some of that healing herself; she was normally bent double so as to keep out of sight of the camera. Being scrunched up against a practical refrigerator in the drunk scene was bad enough but worse was when E.T. and Elliott are saying goodbye. She had to keep her arms stretched out awkwardly for ages so as not to disturb the atmosphere when Spielberg was explaining this key emotional moment to Henry Thomas.

It is thanks to Caprice Rothe that E.T. has a slight tremor. It originated from the first shot she was involved in when a certain nervousness was heightened by the effects of a recent cup of coffee, a beverage to which Ms Rothe's system is unaccustomed. She got the shakes and it showed on the take but Spielberg liked it and asked her to keep it up.

It's not really surprising that E.T. was a model (as was his spaceship, a ball of special effects two feet across) but the trickery didn't stop there. It is perhaps disappointing to learn that Elliott and his friends didn't really go flying around on their BMX bikes. These intricate models were made and filmed by Industrial Light and Magic, the special effects firm run by Spielberg's fantasy partner George Lucas. The figures are less than two feet tall but are constructed so as to appear to shift their weight as real bicyclists do and with a wealth of detail, including specially made clothing, which it is impossible to pick out when watching the film.

But after all this multi-million dollar attention to detail there was something about the special effects that still niggled Stephen Spielberg: E.T.'s eyes looked too glassy. He wanted them to have moist red rims but the special effects experts persuaded him that anything which would have made the eyes wet would also have perished the latex skin and damaged the $400,000 worth of gizmo guts within. Which is perhaps why E.T. ends up having the only dry eye in the house.

▦ The experience

'I think I'm Peter Pan – I really do.' Stephen Spielberg

'Working from a sensitive, slangy script by Melissa Mathison, Spielberg shows himself to be a personal artist with all the uncanny intuitive force of a space-age Jean Renoir. Watching this vibrantly comic, boundlessly touching fantasy you feel that Spielberg has, for the first time, put his breathtaking technical skills at the service of his deepest feelings.' Michael Sragow, *Rolling Stone*, 1 July 1982

'Magical yet wrenching, *E.T. The Extraterrestrial* is the most moving science fiction movie ever made on earth.' Pauline Kael, *New Yorker*, 14 June 1982

▦ Can you spot . . .

* Almost all the film is shot from child-(or E.T.) height.
* A rather menacing plant amongst the collection of specimens gathered in E.T.'s spaceship. It's a triffid.

The
Exorcist

1973 A young girl is possessed by the Devil.

▦ The talent

Linda Blair 14, as Regan; a troubled adolescence followed, with roles in *Airport 1975* (1975) and *Exorcist II* (1977) plus lots of minor films

Ellen Burstyn 40, as Chris MacNeil; one of several notable films of the seventies including *The Last Picture Show* (1971) and Oscar-winning *Alice Doesn't Live Here Any More* (1975)

Max von Sydow 43, as Father Merrin; distinguished Swedish favourite of Ingmar Bergman. Not too scared to return for *Exorcist II*

Jason Miller 33, as Father Karras;

Broadway playwright who has continued to act

Lee J. Cobb 62, as Lieutenant Kinderman; the original Broadway Willie Loman and the first boss of Shilo Ranch in TV's *The Virginian*. Leading character actor in one of his final roles

William Peter Blatty 44, Producer; wrote *A Shot in The Dark* (1964) and *Darling Lili* (1969)

William Friedkin 34, Director; fresh from an Oscar for *The French Connection* (1971). Known more widely since for messy divorce proceedings than his films

▦ The business

William Peter Blatty was a successful writer, mainly of light comedy scripts, but he decided now to explore something darker. He wrote *The Exorcist* first as a novel, with the screen rights sold to Warner Brothers for $641,000 before it was even published. This proved shrewd speculation on the part of the studio; *The Exorcist* stayed at the top of the charts for 20 weeks, finally selling six million copies.

Blatty's contract also stipulated his participation in the filming as producer and a reported 40% of the profits. With the director on $175,000 up front, plus bonuses and 10%, one wonders what was left in it for poor old Warners.

The budget was to be $4,000,000 and the shooting to be done in 95 days. But a number of serious problems cropped up – deaths, injuries and accidents – which doubled the shooting time and the costs. Finally over $10,000,000 was spent.

The Warners' hype machine exploited these tragedies to help turn *The Exorcist* into something of a public issue. Might seeing the film unleash sinister forces? The papers followed up deaths which coincided with a trip to the pictures. Would there be mass fainting, alarm or nausea? Instances were widely circulated in the press.

Reports to psychiatrists and churchmen of demonic possession increased noticeably. The Catholic Church had been consulted by the film-makers, and Warners produced a detailed press fact-pack about supposed examples of devilment, the history of exorcism and even the ceremony's form of words – just in case.

The critical response to the film was united. It was judged obscene, exploitive and morally ambiguous. Strangely, though, the United States licensing authorities granted *The Exorcist* an R rating, permitting a possessed teenager to see it if accompanied by an adult.

The public was immensely titillated by a spectacle which, in the thrill-weary seventies, packed the power to shock in the same way as the likes of *Frankenstein* (1931) had another generation. Blatty won an Oscar for his script and *The Exorcist* became one of the top films of the year, one of the biggest money-makers ever, taking $89,000,000 in North America alone. As well as its sequel, the far more modestly-received *The Exorcist II: The Heretic*, there followed a revolting resurgence of big-money film horror.

▦ Behind the screen

Blatty based his novel on the last official exorcism in the U.S. sanctioned by the Catholic Church. He had read about the case as it unfolded in the late 1940's while a university student at Georgetown in Washington D.C. where the film is set.

The real case concerned a fourteen-year-old boy from Mount Ranier, Maryland, who attracted poltergeist phenomena of the shaking pictures/jumping fruit variety. Mysterious red writing appeared on his body. 'Go to St Louis,' it said. Curiously the boy had a favourite aunt in that town. He was duly taken to St Louis where he gave vent to some very strange noises and was treated to a course of exorcism lasting two months. The lad soon settled down, happily and permanently dispossessed.

Blatty's model for Ellen Burstyn's character was closer to home, his next-door neighbour, Shirley Maclaine. She was said to be less than happy about the screen characterization, a displeasure compounded by Blatty's willingness to expound freely on the topic.

Almost as soon as they started filming, things began to go wrong. There were deaths: Linda Blair's grandfather and Max von Sydow's brother both died in the first week, delaying production as Max returned to Sweden for the funeral.

There were losses: the ten-foot-high model of the demon Pazuzu went missing on its way to location filming in Iraq and ended up in Hong Kong. Bits of the film itself went missing as well.

There were accidents: Jason Miller's young son was hit and seriously injured by a motorcycle. Ellen Burstyn hurt her back in the flying sequence and was off work for two weeks. A carpenter lost his thumb building the Georgetown house set which in turn mysteriously caught fire one night. As it was central to the production there was a further stoppage of six weeks while it was rebuilt.

To cap it all, a week after he had finished his filmed death scene in the *The Exorcist* Irish actor Jack MacGowran died. It was all a devilsend to the publicists; the production was jinxed and Satan was really at work.

It was the special effects and make-up people who were *really* really at work. One of the most impressive manifestations was achieved using a duplicate of Regan's room, surrounded by $100,000 worth of refrigeration equipment. This brought the temperature on the set down to $-10°$, the only method of achieving the visible breath of cold. It was numbingly raw for the actors although Linda Blair had the comfort of a suit under her bedclothes and an electric blanket. The crew worked in ski gear.

Max von Sydow: *What* did you say, little girl?

Another key article of equipment was a complete, accurate model of Linda Blair which was used both for cinema's most famous liturgical wank, and for the head revolution that immediately followed it. This is the appropriate point in the film to faint or retch. At least you're now past the worst bit.

Most of the attention focused on Linda Blair's make-up but Max von Sydow's is the artier job. It was all the work of greasepaint master Dick Smith, who had convincingly aged Dustin Hoffman a century for *Little Big Man* (1970) and Marlon Brando twenty years for *The Godfather* (1972). Father Merrin's age spots and wrinkles were much admired by the cosmetic cognoscenti, as was the subtle battering which the experience inflicted on Chris MacNeil's face.

One thing that made Linda's make-up job difficult for Smith was that she was, as he put it, 'Healthy, healthy, healthy'. Her chubby, wholesome features were difficult to putrefy, especially as it is a make-up maxim that plastic surgery is not an option, however tempting.

They used everything but. Her mouth was stuffed with braces to sinisterize her expression and irritating contact lenses provided her demonic glare. On exorcism mornings she would have to endure hours of make-up, passing the time watching reruns of *The Flying Nun*, which may have enhanced her portrayal of satanic fervour.

Only a few shorts actually feature the dummy. Mostly it's Miss Blair, with inflatable bags around her neck or festooned with make-up wounds revealed when a suitable false covering is whipped away. The raised letters reading 'Help me' were actually on foam rubber which puffs out when in contact with solvent.

Linda seems to have sailed through this without complaint, except apparently turning a bit precious when it came to gunking up her hair, of which she was very proud. Another niggle was the vomit. It's constituents, oatmeal and pea soup, are two of her least favourite foods travelling either way.

Filming the full-face puking took some thought. For your regular peeing and semi-profile spewing it was sufficient to use a concealed tube connected to a reservoir. Linda had no control over these events; her sf-excretions were fired by the director using a remote control. In the head-on shot you are looking at (or trying to avoid looking at) a mask with sick-delivery tubes concealed beneath the surface.

However it was the stream of foul language emerging from Linda Blair, rather than the thickened broth, that was the real shocker for some people. Max von Sydow was one of them. Although he was privy to all the technical secrets, Friedkin had purposely not prepared him for this onslaught, confident that the great actor's concentration would carry him through in character. In fact von Sydow was so stunned by the detailed, if somewhat disorganized, instructions for self-abuse from his fourteen year old co-star that he stopped dead.

One of the most cutting reviews of the film came from the distinguished *New Yorker* critic Pauline Kael. In her column she wondered what sort of parents would allow their child to take part in such goings-on.* Linda's mother said she simply thought it looked like a fun part. Miss Blair was a bright young sportswoman who had been in commercials since the age of six. She was chosen from amongst 500 hopefuls because of her resemblance to Ellen Burstyn.

The little girl grew up fast. A year following the general release of the film, at the age of fifteen, she was reported as living with a future soap opera star. By the time Linda was twenty she was on probation for drug offences. However, at the time of *The Exorcist* she seemed quite unfazed by her role or the ensuing fame, preferring talk of horses. 'The funny things weren't hard to do because I didn't believe the story,' she explained.

▦ The experience

'Vile and brutalizing.' Jay Cocks, *Time*, 14 January 1974

'*The Exorcist* is nothing more than a religious porn film, the gaudiest piece of big-budget schlock this side of Cecil B. DeMille (minus that gentleman's wit and ability to tell a story).' Jon Landau, *Rolling Stone*, 14 February 1974

'A well-made film, admittedly, but why it had to be made at all is another matter.' Cecil Wilson, *Daily Mail*, 14 March 1974

'I want to see what everyone is throwing up about.' A contemporary moviegoer

▦ Can you spot . . .

* The simplest special effect. To get the whole room to shake, the set had been mounted on something the size and shape of a bowling ball. The props men would simply take the supports off and man-handle the set around.
* Two real priests. Revd William O'Malley who played Father Dyer and Revd T. Bermingham who played the University president were two of the advisers on the film, and defended it afterwards.
* What the film Chris MacNeil was working on was about. In the book it is supposed to be a musical version of *Mr Smith Goes to Washington* (1939), perhaps an even more horrifying prospect than *The Exorcist* itself.

---

*In fact the final voice you hear delivering the lines as Regan the Devil is fifties star Mercedes McCambridge, who raised hell when Warners at first did not acknowledge her in the credits.

Fantasia

1940 Eight pieces of classical music illustrated by animation

▦ The talent

Walt Disney, 38, and his staff.

▦ The business

At the time of production the Disney studios were monied and in good spirits after the success of *Snow White* (1937) and *Pinocchio* (1939). *Fantasia* cost $2,280,000 to make of which $400,000 went on the music and the new recording techniques.

But it wasn't typical Disney. Both the critics and the public were unsure, and the film wasn't an immediate success. Nevertheless it won several special Academy Awards for the new sound techniques and a number of other commendations.

As with all the Disney features it was regularly re-released, but cut down from the original 126 minutes to 81 with the intermission and much of the commentary removed. Still, it didn't recoup its cost for another fifteen years.

A turning point in *Fantasia*'s fortunes came with its 1969 release when it was rediscovered by the psychedelic generation. As a mind-blowing experience it has steadily brought in $2,000,000 a year to the Disney studios since then.

All told it has attracted more than $28,000,000 in North American rentals (and so about double that in worldwide business).

▦ Behind the screen

Fantasia really starts with The Sorcerer's Apprentice. Deems Taylor, the film's narrator (and at the time the host of American radio opera programmes), spread the story that it was to be a comeback vehicle for Mickey Mouse, as a two-reeler on its own.

Not at all, say the folks at Disney. It's true that Mickey's immense popularity during the early thirties had been partially eclipsed by that of Goofy and Donald Duck but the world's greatest mouse certainly didn't need to make a comeback. No, the Disney version is that Mickey was second choice for the part. *The Sorcerer's Apprentice* was to have originally starred Dopey, the most popular character from *Snow White*. However for some reason Walt wasn't keen on resurrecting any of the Snow White stars and suggested Mickey as an ideal alternative.

Whatever its origins, it might have stayed a two-reeler if Disney had not met Leopold Stokowski who was a distinguished figure in classical music and the conductor of the prestigious Philadelphia Symphony Orchestra.* Stokowski suggested to Disney a full animated concert and under his influence The Concert Feature, as it was called, grew and grew.

*Incidently, he was also having an affair with screen goddess Greta Garbo, then thirty-two and at the height of her fame. They parted before actual filming began.

As with all the Disney cartoon features Walt was the oracle. Every gag, movement, character and background is there because he either approved it or thought it up in the first place. He would hold long creative meetings with a stenographer present to record his extempore visualizations.

This was carried to its logical conclusion with the first main section, the Toccata and Fugue in D minor. Disney had discovered that Bach was an improviser as well, allowing his mood to carry his recitals. With Stokowski he listened to the work and they compared their impressions. One woodwind passage seemed to Disney like a hot kettle with spaghetti floating in it but that image doesn't figure in the film.

This section caused bitterness because Oskar Fischinger, the artist who had developed the abstract designs, didn't like his ideas being changed (Disney thought them too avant-garde). Fischinger is said to have originally suggested the animated concert to Stokowski who in turn passed the idea on to Disney. He had, in any case, made an animated abstract version of Paul Dukas' *The Sorcerer's Apprentice* several years earlier. Fischinger was hired to direct the Toccata and Fugue but he walked out before filming started. He stayed in Hollywood though, dividing the rest of his career between painting, experiments in abstract animation and making commercials.

All the musical works but one were chosen first and the ideas for animation added later, but Disney particularly wanted something to illustrate the dawn of time and Stokowski suggested Stravinsky's *Rite of Spring*. Stravinsky was the only living composer whose work was used, and his reaction depends on whose version you believe. The Disney histories quote him as saying that he 'supposed that was what he had meant' when he saw the animated section his work inspired. But he is also quoted as agreeing with many critics who objected to the often trite visual images being imposed on jumbled snatches of great music. 'I will say nothing about the visual compliment as I do not wish to criticize an unresisting imbecility,' is a quote from outside the Disney canon.

There were also complaints from purists about the music being restructured for the purposes of the film. The latest re-release has a newly recorded soundtrack which is closer to how the composers wanted their work heard. The conductor for the new version, Irwin Kostal, had to match exactly Stokowski's original improvised changes of tempo using a special cueing system. Now it matches the pictures better than ever – they found that *Fantasia* had been playing for forty years with the soundtrack two frames out of synch.

As with all those big features in the golden age of Disney, there was a remarkable atmosphere of dedication and purpose during the making of *Fantasia*. Disney was already planning a follow-up but it never materialized, partly perhaps because of *Fantasia*'s initial lack of financial success. This corporate elation was one of the reasons that people like Stokowski from outside the film industry were so eager to work for Disney. 'It's like living in Santa's workshop,' said Deems Taylor.

Part of this feeling came from Disney always pushing forward techniques. He used the multiplane camera fully for the first time in *Fantasia*. This was a towering structure developed by Disney's longtime collaborator Ub Uwerks (the man who actually drew Mickey Mouse) which allowed animation to be carried out on several glass screen layers. It gave an increased impression of perspective, allowing the camera to zoom through scenes. It had been used before in some sequences of *Snow White and the Seven Dwarfs*.

Walt Disney (sitting, right) and staff: Santa's workshop

The original sound system for *Fantasia* was completely new, dubbed Fantasound by Disney. He recorded the music in Philadelphia's Academy of Music, a hall renowned for its acoustics. They used thirty specially placed microphones with the aim of replaying the soundtrack on thirty identically arranged speakers in the cinema.

This was by all accounts very effective but as it necessitated rigging each cinema especially for Fantasound it was only demonstrated fully at a few venues. So subsequent generations have only heard a re-mixed version of the original and, with a new soundtrack as well, all that's left of Stokowski, apart from his tempo, is that silhouette making like a conductor.

As with *Snow White*, live models were used to refine the animation of natural movement in various characters. The pirouetting hippos and their partners in the Dance of the Hours were a few good-natured members of the Ballet Russe.

Little ceramic models were made to give the animators the three-dimensional feel of non-realistic characters in this and other Disney cartoons. But they kept on disappearing, a favourite souvenir for visiting dignitaries.

Disney himself was the model for the Sorcerer (who is called Yensid – get it?). The real give-away is the raised eyebrow of disapproval when he takes his magic hat back from Mickey. This was recognized by all at the studio as a cheeky re-creation of one of Disney's best-known expressions. The joker was Bill Tylta, who was also given the important task of animating the Devil in the 'Night on Bald Mountain' sequence.

For this he asked one of the directors, Wilfred Jackson, to film Bela Lugosi as the model for the part. But Tylta wasn't happy with the result and after the great screen Dracula had left he got the skinny, young Jackson to go through the motions instead.

The last scene of the film which follows is one of the most effective – the procession of monks to the music of *Ave Maria*. The sequence seemed jinxed, needing to be reshot many times. It all finally came together two days before the premiere and was rushed off to the cinema to be tacked on the end of the show print.

▧ The experience

'*Fantasia* will amaze-ya.' Contemporary publicity blurb

'*Fantasia* was made at a time when we had the feeling that we had to open doors. This medium was something we felt we had a responsibility for, and we just felt that we could go beyond the comic strip, that we could do some very exciting, entertaining and beautiful things with music and pictures and colour.' Walt Disney

'In *Fantasia* he lifts the art of drawing movement right out of the "comic" and essays for the first time serious studies of a higher plane.' Sir David Low

'The atmosphere of *Fantasia* is a little chill, a little rarefied, a little self-conscious; the immense skill is undeniable, but it is the music rather than the animation which evokes emotion and sympathy.' Leslie Halliwell, 1982

▧ Can you spot . . .

* Where they had to exercise a little censorship – or is it centaurship? The centaurettes as first drawn for the Pastoral section were thought a bit too obviously female for one half of a courting couple. Strategically placed bra-flowers were added later. Still, if it's a cheap thrill you're after you've got the glimpse of the centaurettes bathing, and the Nutcracker Nymphs are worth a second glance. Plus, if you're a quick-eyed necrophiliac 'A Night On the Bare Mountain', as the piece is normally called, is aptly named.

Fatal Attraction

1987 A one-night stand leads to jealousy, revenge and horror.

▦ The talent

Michael Douglas 42, as Dan Gallagher; TV star (*Streets of San Francisco*), star producer (*One Flew Over the Cuckoo's Nest* (1975), eighties film superstar, *Wall Street* (1988) was next

Glenn Close 39, as Alex Forrest; after late-ish start in movies, changing image from prim to raunchy. *Dangerous Liaisons* (1989) was next

Anne Archer 39, as Beth Gallagher; experienced film and TV actress

Stanley Jaffe 47, Producer; president of Paramount at 30. Returned to production with *The Bad News Bears* (1976) and *Kramer vs. Kramer* (1979)

Sherry Lansing 42, Producer; former actress, later Hollywood's first female studio chief as president of Fox. With Jaffe she has since made *The Accused* (1988) and *Black Rain* (1989) with Michael Douglas

Adrian Lyne 46, Director; graduate of the British TV commercial school who made *Flashdance* (1982) and *9½ Weeks* (1986)

▦ The business

In 1979 British writer James Dearden (son of Ealing director Basil) made a 42-minute short called *Diversion* for £30,000 which hardly diverted anyone except production partners Lansing and Jaffe.

They bought all sixty prints of *Diversion* for £5,000 and got Dearden to expand the screenplay to a full-length movie. Michael Douglas became involved at an early stage after meeting Stanley Jaffe on a plane. Comparing notes they found that they both were working on a concept which had a husband coming to grief because of an illicit affair.

It took more than four years to find the finance, partly due to studio fears that the audience would find the husband too unsympathetic. *Fatal Attraction* cost $13,000,000 to make, including an extra $1,300,000 for a new ending. Dearden's original version had Alex committing suicide to the strains of *Madame Butterfly* but getting back at Dan in death because his fingerprints were on the knife she used to end it all.* Preview audiences treated to this scenario were left wanting revenge. Some screamed 'Kill the bitch,' so as to eliminate any doubt as to their feelings. Dutifully the necessary cast and crew re-assembled at the Westchester, New York, location house to enact the more familiar transitive finale. The original harikari version was released and played successfully in Japan.

*Hence the pair's morbid dwelling on *Madame Butterfly* over Sunday lunch and the significant shot of Dan getting his dabs all over the knife handle at her flat after their penultimate fight.

Glenn Close: lunatic truck driver

The film was perfectly timed for the market. 1987 was the Year of the Bimbo when presidential candidates and TV evangelical performers tumbled like nine-pins following revelations of previous, naughty tumbles with young women. It was also the height of the AIDS scare which, though not directly alluded to in *Fatal Attraction*, contributed to an atmosphere where sex was seen once again to be potentially life-threatening.

The gross in North America had topped $150,000,000 by the end of the year and it broke box office records in Britain, taking £1,000,000 in the first week. In analyst-ridden New York it was reported that 70% of patients with marital problems were claiming to be obsessed with *Fatal Attraction*.

▦ Behind the screen

Glenn Close wasn't originally considered for the role of Alex but she fought for an audition and, according to Adrian Lyne, got the part within twenty-five seconds. They were doing the restaurant seduction scene and before the director's eyes Close transformed the straight-laced image he had always associated with her to lunacy-unearthed.

He nevertheless insisted that she lose ten pounds. With all that bared flesh, one can understand. One dissatisfied reviewer commented that Miss Close still retained too much the look of a truck driver for his taste.

The sex scenes seem to have been a focal point for the production. Adrian Lyne described the days leading up to filming them as being fraught with pent-up energy. Here and elsewhere during the production all concerned seem to have found the director's approach, honed at the erotic workbench of *Flashdance* and *9½ Weeks*, extremely helpful and sensitive. He seems to have just let the cameras roll, abandoning the 'Quiet on the set' traditional separation between a take and what was naturally going on.

In considering where to stage these frolics (floors and taxis were other possibilities) Lyne paid close attention to the comic as well as erotic potential. The tap going on during the kitchen sink scene and the man walking past the lift were planned, central elements of the encounters.

Douglas seemed anxious to treat it all as simply part of the job ('I just showed a little tush, that's all.') but he has admitted to enjoying sex scenes for their intuitive freedom. He reckons that, like action sequences, you are free to just let it all hang out, so to speak, without worrying about camera angles and casting a shadow on your co-star. He expressed disappointment that they didn't go ahead with a full sex scene he was originally to do with Anne Archer as well.

Glenn Close was rather dreading it. She arranged with a props man to be furnished with margueritas at forty-five-minute intervals during filming but says that in the end she didn't need them. It went fine. She described the scenes as exhilarating; she had never felt so abandoned in a role.

So what about the Mutual Attraction? It was a question gossip columnists were asking, with a firm 'no' in response from Michael Douglas. He had been married for more than ten years to a girl he proposed to and wed within six weeks of meeting. Although they had a trial separation in the early eighties (a domestic situation resolved by the decision to move up the coast from Los Angeles to the less 'Hollywood' Santa Barbara) Douglas firmly denied that he had ever even had a one-night stand. Anne Archer was similarly firm about her domestic situation.

Glenn Close had a less settled private life. Soon after *Fatal Attraction*, though newly married for a second time, she was pregnant by someone else's husband. She left her own hapless spouse to be nearer to the father of a girl who was born in early 1988.

The two co-stars seem to have felt some affinity for their characters. Michael Douglas said that Dan was the closest role to himself he had played, and Glenn Close based Alex in part on memories of being a lonely career woman.

She also consulted three separate shrinks for an inner profile of her character, who is meant to be suffering from a form of the obsessive condition known as De

Cherambault's Syndrome. After completing the part Close had herself to seek psychoanalytic help as the pressures at home were exacerbated by her public identification with someone dubbed the most hated woman in America.

Adrian Lyne's sympathies were all for Alex. She was to him a pathetic, tragic figure. One indication of this is the way he emphasized Dan's weak-willed stupidity by making Beth look as sexy and inviting as possible. Lyne said that Dan got what was coming to him but both he and Glenn Close felt that Alex deserved better. They agreed with critics who said that the end forced on the film-makers by the previews was out of character. Ms Forrest would have bailed out the Japanese way.

The experience

'Fatal Attraction is just about the worst dating movie imaginable – a movie almost guaranteed to start sour, unresolvable arguments – but long lines of people curl around the block waiting to see it.' Pauline Kael, *New Yorker*, 14 October 1987

'The film is compelling because, ultimately, there's no such thing as safe sex.' J. Hoberman, *Village Voice*, 29 September 1987

'The reason for the film's extraordinary popularity is not obvious for, although it is slickly made and the actors are well cast, it contains little genuine suspense and the plot is full of irritating little holes.' Alexander Chancellor, *The Independent*, 12 November 1987 (who was also shocked at the reaction of a mainly black audience in Washington who laughed throughout the film)

'I wanted to take every situation to the worst-possible-case scenario and see what happened.' James Dearden

Can you spot . . .

* Herman Munster. Arthur, the avuncular head of Dan's law firm is played by Fred Gwynne of TV's *The Munsters* and *Car 54, Where Are You?*
* How old the Gallagher's daughter is. Mum says five at one point and Dad says six at another.
* The staying power engendered through kitchen sink sex. According to the wall clock, they start at 4.45 and are bonking away till 6.35. No wonder the coffee boils over.
* Mr Chancellor's 'irritating little holes'. Why does the daughter go off with a strange woman and how could her teachers permit it? And how does Alex suddenly appear in the Gallagher house at the end once Dan has made a point of going around locking everything up?
* Some familiar shots. Michael Anderson, who made *The Naked Edge* (1961) with Gary Cooper (in his last role) and Deborah Kerr, was incensed at the knife/bath finale saying it was 'difficult to determine the line between homage and theft'. Lyne indicated that it was neither but did admit borrowing the image where Beth clears the bathroom mirror to see Alex in the reflection from the Czech film, *Closely Observed Trains* (1966). Critics also reckoned that Lyne was trying to do a Hitchcock but the director says he prefers Chabrol.

42nd Street

1933 The classic tale of how a Broadway musical was brought to the stage in the early 1930's.

▦ The talent

Warner Baxter 42, as Julian Marsh; survived the advent of sound with an Oscar for *The Cisco Kid* (1929) remaining in the big time during the thirties

Bebe Daniels 31, as Dorothy Brock; this has-been role fitted her Hollywood fortunes at the time but with husband Ben Lyon she became a big radio star in Britain

George Brent 28, as Pat Denning; Irish-born leading man of the thirties and forties

Ruby Keeler 23, as Peggy Sawyer; chorus girl whose film career began and ended with husband Al Jolson in the mid-thirties

Dick Powell 28, as Billy Lawler; starting on a film career as second-string Bing, turned movie tough-guy then rich TV executive

Ginger Rogers 22, as Anytime Annie; asked back to star in *Gold Diggers of 1933* and paired the same year for the first time on film with Fred Astaire

Una Merkel 28, as Lorraine Fleming; former Lillian Gish stand-in; frequent supporting comic actress best-known for *Destry Rides Again* (1939)

Guy Kibbee 50, as Abner Dillon; moved into a few leading roles after this but mainly familiar as a character in films before 1950

Hal B. Wallis 33, Producer; one of Hollywood's most successful and prolific studio executives

Lloyd Bacon 32, Director; top Warners hack – three films a year until 1956

Busby Berkeley 37, Dance Director; setting a style that has continued to define pure 'Hollywood'

▦ The business

Warners had pioneered talkies with *The Jazz Singer* (1927), making a killing and establishing the studio as a real force in Hollywood. But the flood of stagy, ex-Broadway musicals which followed soon became a glut. By 1933 Warners were losing money and hardly a single 'all-singing, all-dancing' film had been made in two years.

Time for the pendulum to swing back, thought Darryl F. Zanuck, Warners Production Chief. Head Brother Jack disagreed so Zanuck had to back his hunch in secret. All the musical numbers you see were apparently filmed at night after Jack Warner had gone home. The boss's first inkling was when he viewed the finished product. Perhaps it was Zanuck's attempt at compromise that the bulk of the film is a docu-drama with most of the song and dance concentrated at the end.

However it was this musical finale that had the greatest impact (although the saucy back-stage soap opera was appreciated as well). For one· thing it was shot so differently to film musicals of the past, which had treated the camera as if stuck in a theatre seat. The mobile point of view was the inspiration of a dance director who had grown up in the theatre, Busby Berkeley. The veteran of more than twenty Broadway musicals, he had been imported to Hollywood by Zanuck and set about this, his first major film project, with zeal.

George E. Stone, Warner Baxter, Ginger Rogers and some of the 200 female extras: marching orders

As the movie went into production in late 1932 word got to Zanuck about the elaborate sets and innovative camera rigs his protégé was requesting, so he decided to visit the set and investigate for himself. He demanded to know why, for instance, Buzz needed three concentric circular platforms for the 'I'm Young and Healthy' number. Berkeley, who planned every detail of a scene in advance, took the executive through his concept shot by cut. Zanuck was convinced. He turned to his aides and told them that in future they were to give Berkeley anything he requested. He also put him on a $1,750 a week, seven-year contract. Berkeley later estimated that his routines cost a hefty $10,000 a minute – about $120,000 of the $379,000 spent on *42nd Street*.

The remainder was down to Lloyd Bacon, who had little to do with Berkeley during the production, and is now chiefly remembered for his association with this film. Nevertheless at the time Bacon was a Warners mainstay, the studio's highest paid director on $4,225 a week.

Of the players, Warner Baxter was the only major attraction. He got a fee of $31,000. As for the rest, you are witnessing a number of youngsters coming back stars. This was Ruby Keeler's first picture but she had a splendid introduction to the industry in her husband, superstar Al Jolson. Ginger Rogers, too, chose her partners well. A boyfriend, Mervyn LeRoy, had been rostered to direct *42nd Street* but fell ill – not before he had recommended that Ginger, then a small-time player in sweetie roles, branch out by going for the tart part of Anytime Annie.

Released on 4 March 1933, the day of Franklin D. Roosevelt's inauguration, *42nd Street* traded successfully on a theme of success through cooperative effort. This, plus the frank references to the Depression, suited the election-winning philosophy and optimism of the incoming President's New Deal. *42nd Street* was one of the top box office attractions of the year and Warners' most profitable movie of the decade, finally grossing upwards of $5,000,000.

Jack Warner had an immediate change of heart about musicals and two more Busby Berkeley extravaganzas followed in the same year – *Gold Diggers of 1933* which played up the Depression angle even more strongly and *Footlight Parade* – both with Keeler, Powell and Kibbee. As a consequence the Warners accounts went into the black again by 1935.

Meanwhile the man with the hunch, Darryl Zanuck, had gone off to form Twentieth Century Fox leaving his replacement, Hal B. Wallis, to cop the producer credit. Busby Berkeley's contribution went largely unnoticed by the public but he was launched on a thirty-year career of directing and choreography.

By the 1960's he had acquired a cult status as his work was rediscovered by a generation more appreciative of the back-room stars. He was reunited with Ruby Keeler at the end of the decade for a successful Broadway adaptation of *No, No, Nanette*.*

It continued a financial record that Berkeley described with a degree of modesty for which he was well known. 'No one ever lost a dime on any of my pictures because all of them were so great,' he crowed.

---

*42nd Street, which was based on a novel rather than an actual show, reversed the conventional adaptive process as the basis for a successful stage production in the eighties, which also used songs from other Warners' musicals of the time, notably 'We're In the Money' from the equally watchable *Gold Diggers of 1933*.

▓ Behind the screen

If you think the film as it stands is racey, you should get hold of the original book by Bradford Ropes. There is considerably more overt bed-hopping and drunkenness* plus smidgins of blackmail and anti-semitism. But perhaps the most interesting plot difference is that in the original Marsh, the impresario played by Warner Baxter, and Lawler, the juvenile played by Dick Powell, were gay lovers. Note the scene where the unattached Marsh pleads with dance director Andy Lee, played by George E. Stone, to come home with him.**

The Hays office production code had been in force since the birth of the talkies but really only got geared up a few years after *42nd Street* was made. That accounts in part for so many surprisingly frank sexual references and some delightfully skimpy cossies. Of course the original storyline would have caused a ruckus as late as the 1960's. The novel's themes, atmosphere and backstage cheesecake remain but few specific plot details, one exception being the crack about Anytime Annie only saying no once and then she didn't hear the question. The classic line from Julian Marsh to Peggy as she is about to go on stage 'You're going out there a youngster but you're going to have to come back a star,' didn't appear until the last draft of the script.

After that it was all down to Busby Berkeley. Though born in a trunk he had cut his choreographic teeth during service in the Great War when he was a Second Lieutenant under General Pershing – a drill master, training battalions of men, 5,000 or so at a time, in complex square bashing. Lt Berkeley's speciality was marches in perfect time without the cue of a musical accompaniment. Say, let's do the war right here!

If you look carefully at his movie routines you will see that there is really very little dancing. Berkeley himself admitted to hardly knowing the first thing about dance; the spectacle of mass movement is his bag.

He also recognized, on arrival in Hollywood, the crucial difference between the multi-faceted but static viewpoint of a theatre crowd and the single, but movable eye of the camera. He exploited the freedom it gave him, to the delight of his new audience who were particularly impressed by the surreal experience of the first truly cinematic dance numbers – routines and images which could not possibly be contained on a stage. One of Berkeley's favourite examples was Ruby Keeler's dance on the taxi.

Berkeley retained a military precision in the displacement of his shapely troops. He claimed it meant hardly ever needing more than one take, and indeed part of the sport in viewing the films is the occasional cog not quite in mesh with the rest of the Grand Plan. He achieved the camera movement with some inventive rigging and the odd structural alteration to the Warners sound stages. Berkeley designed a suspended track which took the camera dolly where none had previously ventured, carrying just one grip and the operator. The high shots, which were to become his trademark, were mostly achieved by erecting scaffold sixty feet into the rafters and using a wide-angle lens, but in some cases even that wasn't enough and he had holes drilled in the sound stage roof to poke the camera through.

*Remember when watching the film that Prohibition wasn't repealed until the following year.
**In the novel, touchingly, Marsh and Lawler lived happily everafter.

The number which caused Berkeley the most problems was 'Shuffle Off to Buffalo'. The railway carriage which could split down the middle had already been constructed, but what to do with it? What you see is off-the-cuff Berkeley creation: the result of three days' deliberation on the set, sudden inspiration – and in the can within a couple of hours.

▦ The experience

'This song and dance show, which has brought back song and dance shows "has everything" – a fine cast, tuneful song numbers (which I am afraid have been done to death by the dance bands by now), spectacular ensembles, and a story that has always been sure-fire.' Lionel Collier, *Picturegoer*, 2 September 1933

'A New Deal in entertainment.' Cinema advertisement

'Ruby Keeler's debut as a picture personality and make no mistake about it, a new star is born.' *Photoplay*, 1933

'When Keeler sings one imagines there's something wrong with the soundtrack; when she dances she's a klutz; when she acts, she runs the gamut of two expressions: a blissful smile and a worried frown. As for Powell, he simply grins his way cheerfully throughout the musical. And if his singing is better than Keeler's his dancing is worse.' Rocco Fumento in *42nd Street*, 1980

'The backstage musical par excellence.' Edward Sorel, *Esquire*, October 1970

'What I mostly remember is stress and strain and exhaustion.' Busby Berkeley

▦ Can you spot . . .

* What the musical-within-the-musical, *Pretty Lady*, is all about. The dance numbers don't seem to have any logical connection.
* The men who wrote the words and music. Tubby Al Dubin, the lyricist, and Harry Warren, the composer, make an appearance – as the lyricist and composer. Lloyd Bacon's visible somewhere too.
* A star of the silents. The old actor who helps Peggy when she almost faints again on the bench, backstage at rehearsals, is Henry B. Walthall, who starred in Griffith's *The Birth of a Nation* (1915). He was to have had a scene where he died on stage but they cut all but this brief walk-on.
* The days when Canada Dry ginger ale was a sophisticated dinner beverage. It is advertised on the back of Dorothy Brock's copy of the *New Yorker*.
* A ropey tracking shot. It looks like a bumpy ride to the top of the Empire State Building at the climax to the '42nd Street' number.
* Who Julian Marsh was based on. It could have been Julian Mitchell, a prolific Broadway producer of the day, or impresario Florenz Ziegfeld who died that year complaining of being sick and broke.
* The over-dubbing. No, because there isn't any. This was so early in the history of sound that the techniques weren't perfected. The orchestra are always just off camera or actually seen playing in the pit.

Frankenstein

1931 A young scientist creates a monster man from bits of corpses. His experiment goes tragically wrong.

▦ The talent

Boris Karloff 43, as the Monster; né Pratt; beginning a monstrously lucrative, forty-year reign of terror

Colin Clive 33, as Dr Henry Frankenstein; also in *The Bride of Frankenstein* (1935). Died of alcoholism aged 37

Mae Clarke 24, as Elizabeth; née Klotz; the same year Jimmy Cagney pushed half a grapefruit into her face in *Public Enemy*, her most memorable screen moment

John Boles 35, as Victor; WW1 spy and Broadway singing star with a long steady movie career

Edward Van Sloane 49, as Dr Waldman; stock 'professor' character actor

Dwight Frye 32, as Fritz; a horror film regular. Like Van Sloane, also in *Dracula* (1931)

Carl Laemmle Jnr 23, Producer; career fizzled out in the next five years

James Whale 35, Director; British Broadway director new to Hollywood. Quit mid-film ten years later for comfortable retirement painting

▦ The business

The Universal production of *Dracula* earlier in 1931 had been one of the most popular movies of the year and the new studio boss, Carl Laemmle Jnr, was eager to repeat the success.*

He got his wish. The audiences loved *Frankenstein* the movie. More than that, then and since, they greatly sympathized with Boris Karloff the monster. He was so horrific, so touching and so fascinating that the anxious studio officials monitoring the all-important previews observed sections of the audience wandering out in shock, walking round the block and then coming back in for more.

The story had always been a money-spinner. It was the most successful novel in English for thirty years after nineteen-year-old Mary Shelley wrote it in 1817 as a sort of bet with her husband Percy Bysshe Shelley and Lord Byron. It has never been out of print and for many years Mary was generally regarded as a successful novelist who married a minor poet. During her lifetime it spawned nine plays and brought in far more income than Percy's poems.

The film, in turn, is estimated to have earned more money compared to its production costs than practically any other. It finally came in at $291,000 (at least $100,000 more than the average film of its day) and has earned a reported $13,000,000.

---

*He had just taken over the running of the studio from his father who had founded it in 1912. Evidently nepotism was rife at Universal if Ogden Nash is to be believed: 'Uncle Carl Laemmle had a very large faemmle'.

Business was just as good when it was re-leased in 1938 on a double bill with *Dracula*. In one instance a crowd of 4,000 people broke into a cinema, so anxious were they to see it. The theatre manager promptly hired the hall opposite and started showing it there too.

Frankenstein launched Boris Karloff on a long and prosperous career of villains quite at odds with his real gentle, courtly personality. And, of course, it has continued to add to the fortunes of Universal Pictures and studios all over the world with sequels, remakes, take-offs and a pandemonium of allied horror creations.

▦ Behind the screen

'I think it will thrill you. It may shock you. It might even . . . horrify you!' So you're warned by Edward Van Sloane (Dr Waldman) in an introductory announcement. This was tacked on at the insistence of Carl Laemmle Jnr and probably the result of very mixed motives.

The film is still pretty creepy now so imagine the impact that the sight of brains and stitches – and the concept of a man revelling in playing God – must have had on the tender audience of 1931. Imagine also how many extra seats were likely to be sold if the makers played up warnings about all the horrors.

If *Frankenstein* has retained some of that impact over the years then the key must be Karloff's sensitive performance under layers of chillingly effective cheesecloth and greasepaint. But he was only the third choice for the part.

Lon Chaney, the man of a thousand faces in innumerable silent horror films, was to have played both Dracula and Frankenstein's monster but he died of throat cancer. So the next choice for the two roles was Bela Lugosi, who had been playing Dracula on stage for three years.

But Lugosi was no Lon Chaney. He couldn't stand the lengthy monster make-up job and didn't want a non-speaking part. It is said that he saw himself as a new Valentino who just happened to have made his debut with fangs. After seeing tests in make-up the Universal bosses agreed that he wasn't the best choice for the part and the search was on for a new monster.*

The film already had a director, a genius according to the typically low-key film publicity of the time. What that probably meant was Universal reckoned he could handle dialogue. Talkies had just taken over and Broadway directors like James Whale were much sought after by Hollywood. He was offered his choice of project and snatched *Frankenstein* from under the nose of the French director Robert Florey who had done all the ground work.

Although Whale's film is an undoubted classic some critics are ungenerous about his level of contribution to its success. He *is* credited in *Frankenstein*, however, with being the first director to make use of off-camera dialogue – the audience seeing the reaction of others instead of the speaker – and introducing cinema's first 360° pan.

But Whale's real gift to posterity was the discovery of Boris Karloff, then the veteran of minor roles in sixty films. The director spotted him eating in the Universal canteen. Whale later said that what drew him was something he could see in Karloff's face. The physique was lacking but could be altered easily – the key was his 'queer, penetrating personality'.

*Lugosi, who had a troubled, tragic career did play the monster in *Frankenstein Meets the Wolfman* (1943) but without much conviction. When he died he was buried in his Dracula cape.

Boris Karloff: the full treatment

How any personality managed to penetrate the great hunks of greasepaint stucco is a tribute both to Karloff and to the real creator of the Frankenstein monster, make-up man Jack Pierce. He spent three months ploughing through a selection of gruesome historical and medical texts, deciding for instance that of the six possible ways of removing the brain from the skull a trained surgeon would probably have used the easiest method (slicing around the top like a pot lid).

The result was a triumph for the cameras but an ordeal for Boris Karloff. There are various estimates of how much it all weighed, starting at about fifty pounds. The boots with their four-inch soles alone weighed eighteen pounds each. The monster's skin was built up from layers of cheesecloth which gave the impression that it had pores, an effect which greatly impressed Karloff. After some experimentation they found that a blue-grey colour produced the appropriate lurid shade on film.

Boris's contribution to the make-up was the eyelids. He wanted the monster's eyes to lack intelligence; they should be half-closed. To get the effect they weighed his eyelids down with repeated coats of mortician's wax. It added nicely to the actor's ordeal, but that wasn't enough for Pierce. He inflicted wire clamps on Karloff's lips, fitted to pull the corners of his mouth out and down, and coated his fingernails with black boot polish. The costume was shortened to make him look even taller and his two pairs of trousers had legs stiffened with steel braces.

Who would be a movie star? Poor Boris sweated buckets underneath all that superstructure during the hot months of August and September 1931 when the film was shot. The heat and perspiration tended to make his head melt and so there were constant running repairs on set from Pierce. Karloff kept his sense of humour though. He said that the clammy interior of the costume gave him the right atmosphere for his performance.

Although the pre-release posters of the film showed how the monster would look, Publicity made great play of keeping the details secret, even from the rest of the Universal lot. Boris was led under a sheet between the make-up rooms and the set.

It took four hours to slap it all on and another two hours to tear it all off plus infrared treatment and massage for Karloff's tired bones. Starting point for make-up removal was the scar on the monster's forehead, just the place for getting a good grip. Even harder to get rid of, though, were the marks from those bolts on the monster's neck (electrodes for starting him up). Karloff had scars there for ages.

▦ The experience

'Because of his restraint, his intelligent simplicity of gesture, carriage, voice and make-up, Karloff has truly created a Frankenstein monster. Had he yielded to the temptation to melodramatize as the opportunity offered, the dramatic effect would have been far less formidable.' Leo Meehan, *Motion Picture Herald*

'My dear old monster, I owe everything to him. He's my best friend.' Boris Karloff

[It is] 'difficult to understand why Universal thought it had a gem of a director in James Whale. His direction is primitive at best. The film is really shot as a stage play.' Richard J. Anobile, 1974

▦ Can you spot . . .

* Some familiar scenery. The village had been built for previous Laemmle hit, *All Quiet On The Western Front* (1930). Frankenstein's lab thrilled again in numerous episodes of the *Flash Gordon* serials.

* Frankenstein can make a man but he can't count. When Elizabeth, Victor and Dr Waldman visit his lab he calls it a good scene with one man crazy (himself) and three very sane spectators. He then points to *four* spectators (including Fritz).

* Something the monster is missing. Jack Pierce made Karloff remove false teeth he had on the right side of his face to leave his cheeks looking more sunken.

* The vintage of the print you're watching. The original version has young Dr Frankenstein's crazed exclamation at the moment of creation: 'Oh! In the name of God! Now I know what it feels like to be God!' But by the second release with *Dracula* in 1938 the moral climate in Hollywood was more oppressive and this whiff of blasphemy was cut. Some of the original prints were tinted green, 'the colour of fear!'

* A cut that made the film even more horrific. As originally filmed the monster meets a little girl, Maria, and joins her game of floating flowers on the water. When they run out of flowers the monster puts Maria in the water to see if she will float too, an experiment which proves unsuccessful. But Carl Laemmle Jnr thought that too explicit and so all the first generation of Frankenstein watchers saw was a cut as the smiling monster reaches out for the girl. The next we see of her is lifeless in her father's arms, implying a fate even worse than accidental drowning. The dunking shot was restored for later releases. (The studio also insisted on a happy ending. Incredibly Frankenstein survives being thrown off the top of a windmill by his creation. It looks pretty bad for the monster, though, stuck in the flames . . . but don't worry – remember all the sequels to come.)

The French Connection

1971 Two tough New York narcotics cops track a Gallic drug smuggling gang.

▦ The Talent

Gene Hackman 40, as Popeye Doyle; about to become a brief, unlikely superstar after long obscure apprenticeship. Few memorable roles since
Roy Scheider 36, as Buddy Russo; felt his early career blighted by George C. Scott resemblance. Leading roles to come included *Jaws* (1975) and *All That Jazz* (1979)

Fernando Rey 56, as Alain Charnier; familiar Spanish star of European movies, especially those of Luis Bunuel
Phillip D'Antoni 41, Producer; also made *Bullitt* (1968) and later directed some minor films
William Friedkin 31, Director; was a TV director in his teens. Next came *The Exorcist* (1973)

▦ The Business

The heroin in question was worth about $30,000,000 – enough to carry the junkies of New York for several months. *The French Connection* made more than $50,000,000 (on a $2,200,000 budget) and was enough – with the help of Gene Hackman's next high-earner, *The Poseidon Adventure* (1972) – to carry Twentieth Century Fox to better times in the seventies.*

The plot was based on writer Robin Moore's account of an investigation dating back to 1962. Initial interest in the film was boosted by a timely repetition of history when a further 230 lbs of heroin was intercepted stashed in a car on a boat from France about a month before the premiere.

Friedkin's innovative documentary technique using unfamiliar character actors made a great impact, attracting awards as well as long cinema queues. Oscars came for Best Film, Director, Screenplay and to Gene Hackman as actor, one of three major acting awards he got that year for the part.

The public and the industry had started noticing Hackman after his supporting roles in *Bonnie and Clyde* (1967) and *I Never Sang For My Father* (1969). Suddenly at the age of forty *The French Connection* turned his success curve vertical. He was soon in the $1,000,000-a-picture league and undertook a punishing three-film-a-year schedule through the seventies including *French Connection II* (1975), with Fernando Rey the only other original participant.

---

*Hello Dolly (1969) and *Tora! Tora! Tora!* (1970) had dragged the company into a $100,000,000 deficit at the end of the sixties.

One familiar side-effect of success was the strain on his fourteen-year-old marriage. There was a brief separation shortly after *The French Connection* and a messy divorce in 1985.

By the time of his portrayal of Lex Luthor in *Superman* (1978) the thrill of second-rate starring roles had palled. Hackman retired exhausted, spent a lot of money and was back again at a frantic pace in the eighties.

Things soon began to connect, as well, for Roy Scheider and William Friedkin. But the big loser was the man who had inspired the film, Eddie Egan, the tough New York narc who was the real Popeye Doyle. Egan made precisely $240 from the whole project, and lost his job as a result.

▦ Behind the screen

Eddie Egan introduced himself to William Friedkin thus: 'I drink beer, I lay broads and I bust heads.' *The French Connection* is Eddie Egan's story. The language, attitudes and idiosyncratic working practices are his. All the incidents, apart from the car chase, are supposed to be based on Egan's own experiences.

The real case began in late 1961 when Eddie Egan (Jimmy 'Popeye' Doyle in the film) and his partner Sonny Grosso (Buddy Russo) were at the Copacabana Club celebrating a successful minor bust. They spotted a group of drug dealers paying court to one Patsy Fuca (Sal Boca). Although they had been on duty for twenty-seven hours the duo followed Fuca to his fleabitten snack bar in Brooklyn. Four months of further surveillance culminated in the arrest of a number of drugs figures and a record-breaking seizure of smack.

The poor sap who owned the car was in real life Jacques Angelvin (Henri Devereaux in the film), who presented one of France's most popular TV shows of the fifties, *Paris Club*. He got six years, but the Alain Charnier kingpin figure played in the film by Fernando Rey got away with it because de Gaulle wouldn't allow him to be extradited from France.

You can compare for yourself the real crimebusters with their screen counterparts. Friedkin retained Eddie and Sonny on secondment from the N.Y.P.D as technical advisers and gave them both parts. Egan was undoubtedly the bigger show-off of the two. That's him acting for all he's worth as Doyle's boss, Simonson. Sonny Grosso is buried away as the little-seen Fed, Klein. Klein's FBI partner, the ultimately unfortunate Mulderig, is played by Bill Hickman, who was also the film's stunt coordinator and stand-in for Hackman. So in those three-way arguments it's the original Popeye arguing with the film Popeye arguing with the stand-in Popeye (and Hickman with Hackman). The other authentic copper on screen is police mechanic Irv Abrahams. He got to play himself as the dickhead who didn't think to check under the rocker panels.

Gene Hackman formed his characterization of Popeye Doyle on a frightening crash course in police work Egan-style – several weeks on the beat with Eddie and Sonny. Egan was initially cool toward Hackman (he was miffed that Rod Taylor hadn't got the part) but this evaporated as he got stuck into his unconventional sleuthing. He took Hackman and Friedkin on a raid similar to the one Popeye makes on the drugs bar. Egan threw the director a gun and barked at him to cover the door. Both film folk were shaken but able to apply the experience to the film, including the Egan phonebooth method of suspect restraint.

Gene Hackman, Roy Scheider and Alan Weeks: victim of gentleness

These frightening sorties also produced most of the dialogue. The Oscar-winning screenplay by *Shaft* author Ernest Tidyman seems little more than a framework for improvisation on the profane theme of Messrs Egan and Grosso's phraseology. Audiences who saw the film on first release – before Hackman and Scheider were at all familiar – felt as if they were watching a fly-on-the-wall documentary.

The real Gene Hackman wouldn't hurt a fly-on-the-wall. Completely at odds with this brutal role he is a gentle man, raised in a small town in Illinois where his father was the local newspaper editor. He claimed to be almost unable to go through with the establishing small-time bust where he intimidates the pusher with accusations of picking his feet in Poughkeepsie. He was meant to hit his suspect for real and although Alan Weeks, playing the pusher, smiled and reassured him between takes

Hackman hadn't the stomach to make it convincing. He pummelled the long-suffering Weeks through more than twenty takes before getting it right.

Both Hackman and Friedkin started off the *French Connection* experience with liberal views about police brutality but came away ambivalent, having seen first-hand some of the tough reality of the job that had to be done. Friedkin went so far as to advocate legalization as the only course in dealing with the drugs problem. Ironically in the eighties he was in a very public custody battle with his second wife, British actress Lesley-Anne Down, during which he accused her of drug-taking.

William Friedkin didn't just rely on the police to provide material for *The French Connection*. The eighty-six genuinely sordid New York locations were found by Mr Fat Thomas, reportedly a wheelman for local drug gangs who had been arrested countless times but always let off for lack of evidence. Another realistic touch was three months of winter filming, the season when the real events had taken place, with the additional benefit of aiding Hackman and Scheider's convincing portrayal of two cold, tired men.

The nitty-gritty acting and location work was skilfully packaged in muddy photography and sound. Cinematographer Owen Roizman won an Oscar for a Hollywood movie that he largely shot himself, using a hand-held Ariflex camera without any blimp to mask its whirr. Who would have heard in any case? With all the ambient noise of New York it was a challenge for the audience to understand the soundtrack. Friedkin hardly recorded anything after the event but there's one really obvious instance of bad looping in the exchange between Russo and Angie in the Boca greasy spoon. Can you lip-read what they're really saying?

Roizman's repertoire of tricks to disguise any trace of technique was avidly followed in the cinema technical magazines of the time. He lit the interiors to look as if he was using available light, concealing sophisticated rigs all over the place – often replacing the bulbs in ordinary sockets with photo-floods or fixing tiny incandescent lamps (known in the trade as dinkie-inkies) in the table lights. On the street he would under-expose and correct the print in processing to get the coldest, greyest-possible tones.

There was never an attempt to disguise the camera from the blasé New Yorkers who gave the film-makers nary a second glance. Perhaps it was the low-tech accessories. Instead of dollying the camera with specialist rolling stock on little train tracks for his moving shots, Friedkin just looked for a reasonably unbroken stretch of pavement and shuttled the Ariflex along on a wheelchair. There was also a sort of outrigger camera platform fixed to the side of a car. You can see it for yourself reflected in the windows as Popeye stakes out Frog One outside the Westbury Hotel.

The most challenging street filming was the car-train chase, approached by Friedkin in a conscious attempt to outdo the famous spin around San Franciso in his producer's previous smash(-bang-wallop), *Bullitt* (1968). This was a hurtle down twenty-six blocks of Brooklyn's Sitwell Line, shot during snatches of matching weather over five weeks.

The sequence is based on five individual stunts, shot out of order because the first one they tried went wrong. When the white car noses out and hits Popeye's commandeered Pontiac that's a stunt driver getting his mark wrong. But never mind the error, what a great action shot! Bill Friedkin must have half expected something of the kind to happen because he had a spare Pontiac, and up to five cameras dispersed to cover the action from all angles. As one, the operators revived the gag where Cecil B. DeMille asks the cameraman to confirm he's got the shot of some unrepeatable set-piece disaster that everyone else has missed. 'Ready when you are, B.F.,' they all chimed.

Roizman's favourite shot (which is used twice) was the tilt up from Hackman's face to the train on the track above. Most of the driving you see was done by Gene Hackman himself, a pussycat to his friends but a tiger behind the wheel. He shot along at between 70 and 90 miles an hour making it scarcely necessary to slow the camera motor down so that the final shots would look faster.

That was with the intersections blocked by a contingent of assistant directors and old buddies of Egan and Grosso. It took the skill and daring of stunt coordinator Bill Hickman to shoot the backbone of the sequence, Popeye's point of view of the road. This time they didn't bother to restrict public access to the route. So every time you're staring out the front window with Popeye between the stunts it's twenty-six blocks of real traffic with Hickman improvising his lane changes as dictated by necessity.

The train crash at the end of the chase is a very simple piece of trickery. It was performed to circumvent the wishes of the transport authority who got very sniffy at the idea of portraying an accident which they maintained was impossible. Friedkin simply shot the train moving away from the camera and reversed it, with sound effects. Crunch.

The transport people can't have been pleased. The New York Police Department certainly weren't happy at a film which appeared to tarnish the badge, and which had been made with the assistance of two serving policemen.

After sixteen years on the force and 8,000 arrests, Egan was called into his superior's office to be confronted with charges over cutting too many corners in his paperwork. He was fired, just hours before he was due to retire on a full pension.

▓ The experience

'The only thing this movie believes in is giving the audience jolts, and you can feel the raw, primitive responses in the theatre.' Pauline Kael, *New Yorker*, 30 October 1971

'The film has all the depth of a mud puddle but director William Friedkin sets such a frantic pace that there is hardly a chance to notice, let alone care.' *Time*, 1 November 1971

'The only social significance as far as I can see is that we have allowed tough cops like the one I play to grow up.' Gene Hackman, 1972

▓ Can you spot . . .

* A lot of loose ends, pointed out by Pauline Kael and others. What was the purpose of the episode at the beginning when the Marseilles detective is shot? What did the crooks go to the New York motor auction for? How could Charnier and Nicoli (Frogs One and Two) fail to see Popeye noshing pizza just opposite their window when they were lunching at Copain, the posh restaurant? Why on earth did Boca leave the Lincoln out in a back street to get stripped rather than snug in its garage? And how did he drive it there in the first place with its rocker boxes filled with heroin instead of valve oil?

* Prince Charles' favourite pop act, The Three Degrees, of course, providing the musical accompaniment to the celebrations of the cops and their prey at the Copacabana.

Genevieve

1953 Two young couples on the London to Brighton Vintage Car rally.

▦ The Talent

Kenneth More 38, as Ambrose; big British star of the fifties. Better known around the world from TV's *Forsyte Saga*
Dinah Sheridan 32, as Wendy; apart from *The Railway Children* (1971) her last starring comedy role before eighties TV career revival in *Don't Wait Up*
John Gregson 33, as Alan; many great British films of the fifties but little cinematic luck subsequently apart from TV's *Gideon's Way* in the sixties
Kay Kendall 26, as Rosalind; unique and memorable talent. This is where she made her mark
Henry Cornelius 39, Producer/Director; German refugee much influenced by René Clair

▦ The Business

Doesn't it remind you of an Ealing Comedy? Hardly surprising considering the director and the writer.

Scriptwriter William Rose went over to Ealing straight after *Genevieve.** Director Henry Cornelius was a distinguished graduate of that gentle school; he'd produced *Hue and Cry* (1946) and directed *Passport to Pimlico* (1948). But now he was out on his own with a private production company, Sirius, that had already made a forgettable comedy, *The Galloping Major* (1951). Profit from that and money from the National Film Finance Corporation funded *Genevieve*.

Or rather it nearly did. The budget that Cornelius the producer had assembled was beggared by Cornelius the director and his insistence on numerous retakes. The money ran out near the end of filming, but fortunately they were insured for this and the show went on. The only real problem was an invasion of insurance company men looking for lights to turn off and other ways to save some of the premiums.

At least salaries don't seem to have been a drain on the budget. Kenneth More was the best-known at the time and probably the best paid. He got about £3,000 as a flat fee. Dinah Sheridan got a flat fee as well. The film was made in association with the Rank Organization and John Gregson and Kay Kendall were both Rank contract players, with Kay starting out on about £100 a week. If only they'd been offered repeat fees!

Not that anyone thought it was anything special while they were shivering through the filming. And the reaction of a kindly film mogul after an early, high-powered screening was to attempt reassurance. He told Cornelius and Rose he was sure they would make a good film sooner or later.

---

*He scripted *The Maggie* (1953) and *The Ladykillers* (1955) before going back to his native America where he wrote a string of hits through the sixties, winning an Oscar for *Guess Who's Coming to Dinner* (1967).

But this light, sexy comedy soon recovered its cost in Britain alone and went on to become a worldwide favourite, one of the most financially successful British films ever. Larry Adler's catchy solo harmonica theme music became a substantial hit.

Sadly Henry Cornelius had little time to capitalize on his success. This was his last notable film and he died of a coronary five years later in his mid-forties. The four stars had mixed fortunes. It made Kay Kendall a minor star and Kenneth More's film career took off like never before. But John Gregson just drifted through his Rank contract before being dumped at the end of the decade. Dinah Sheridan quit the movies for love and marriage, and *Genevieve* was little help when that went sour a decade later.

And, by the way, the Veteran Car Club loved it. They seem to have made all concerned honorary members.

▦ Behind the screen

You're looking at four very cold actors. The action is meant to be over a weekend of changeable weather in September. It was actually filmed during fifty-seven bitter days between October and February. Dinah Sheridan claims that if you look carefully you can see the actors sneaking on more and more clothing as the film progresses.

Henry Cornelius anticipated the technical problems and relied heavily on what he termed his own special brand of sunshine: a battery of twenty four arc lamps hooked up to a portable generator. That's why the foregrounds always look so pleasant while beyond the sky is filled with the menace of a British winter.

The director either didn't anticipate or didn't much care about the actors' comfort. He did gather them for a tot of brandy each morning but that was just expedient in bringing colour to their cheeks. His insistence on retakes was a bane and caused what seems to have been the one big ruction of a chill but otherwise jolly few months.

The shot should have been simple: Kenneth More driving the 1904 Spyker, with Kay Kendall as passenger, up to the camera. But Cornelius was never satisfied. The day was drizzly and the portable sunshine was at full dazzle, but because it was supposed to be fine weather the actors couldn't do their trick of bundling up. Finally Kay Kendall cracked and began belabouring the director with an umbrella.

Cornelius' perfectionism carried on far beyond what is visible on the film. Preparation work on the characters with William Rose was so detailed that it even ran to jokey life histories. Kenneth More's Ambrose, for instance, was the son of a kidney pill manufacturer. Kay's Rosalind had a grandfather who had crossed the Alps at the age of three. In fact, Kendall and More's real stories were far more interesting. Both were making a key bid for stardom – and both would succeed.

Kay Kendall's film career had almost ended before she was twenty with the failure of her first picture, *London Town* (1946). Seven years later she had fought back through work in rep to a new contract with Rank. Her first film for them was *Genevieve*, and she clicked. Kendall was a favourite with the reviewers, who dwelt particularly on her trumpet playing. She took lessons so as to handle the instrument convincingly but the soundtrack you hear came from jazzman Kenny Baker.

Her screen partner Kenneth More was also at a turning point. His greatest success so far had been on the stage, with a string of film roles that were mostly minor and fairly serious. In *Genevieve* he showed his flair for breezy comedy and went on to a varied career as one of the big British stars of the next twenty years.

Michael Medwin, Kenneth More and Kay Kendall: it's that beastly little man with the portable sun

It says something for his stamina that he seemed so bouncy during filming. At the time he was also playing in the West End, and each evening was a frantic dash to the theatre. As if that wasn't enough to sap his energies, he had also just married. But it was his new bride, Billie, who advised him to take the role of Ambrose. She said that he needed a screen role with real personality to make his mark. Although he didn't let it show the double booking put a great strain on More. He described his hectic schedule to Chaplin who made him promise never to do such a thing again: 'It takes years off your life,' warned the master comedian. It was a vow More never broke.

John Gregson, too, was happily married and – unlike More – remained so, fathering six children. The personal lives of their leading ladies were rather less settled.

Perfect screen wife Dinah Sheridan was going through a protracted and very messy divorce. Three years previously her petition to part with actor Jimmy Hanley on the grounds of his adultery and heavy drinking had been thrown out by the judge. His view was that she was just weary of the ties of marriage and wanted to concentrate on her acting career. Finally, during the filming of *Genevieve* the divorce came through, but this time it was Hanley claiming she had deserted him. Later in the year Dinah announced she was quitting films to marry Rank executive John Davis but ten years later there was another acrimonious divorce and she had to work hard to rebuild a career. She finally found personal happiness with Canadian actor Jack Merivale whom she nursed for years through kidney disease and married in 1986.

Kay Kendall's story is tragically brief. She was to meet her future husband, Rex Harrison, the following year. He married her in 1957 knowing that she was fatally ill with leukaemia but saw to it that Kay herself never knew. She died six years after *Genevieve*, at the age of thirty-two. During the production, though, she was having an affair with Jim Sainsbury who was just starting with his family's giant foodstore chain. He never married and apparently never told his family about the relationship but when he died in 1984 – by then one of the firm's directors – he left almost all of his £18,000,000 fortune to a leukaemia research fund founded in her name.

Over the few cold months they were filming *Genevieve* the four stars seemed to have hit it off. Kenneth More remembered it as a 'high spirited time altogether' and, particularly, glamorous Kay Kendall – all tight jeans and shoes with ostrich trimmings. It hardly seems the gear for weeks of frozen motoring in vintage crocks.

Dinah Sheridan was as prepared as anyone, the hardy veteran of trans-continental safaris by car. But John Gregson couldn't drive at all. They sent him for lessons but his efforts scared Dinah half to death. Tuition in a modern car is scant preparation for the idiosyncrasies of a model half a century old. Doesn't he look particularly shaky that first time he sets off down the Strand from opposite the High Court?

In fact Gregson and More didn't need to do too much driving. As well as his portable sun Henry Cornelius had equipped himself with a pair of long loaders. They were big enough to accommodate personnel, cameras, lights and mock-ups of the cars, and haul them about for much of the close-up dialogue work. You can spot how much higher the two jallopies appear compared to other traffic. The snarls that the huge vehicles caused as they lumbered around the pre-motorway countryside were discreetly kept off camera.

And the real star of the show? You'll be pleased to hear that Genevieve, a 12 horsepower Darracq made in Paris in 1904, is enjoying a happy retirement. Pay her a visit at the Giltrap Museum in Queensland.

▦ The experience

'Car comedy fires on all cylinders.' *Daily Mail*, 29 May 1953 – reflecting the very favourable press reaction in the UK and abroad

'A top-ranking comedy which will get laughs wherever it is shown, this latest British entry should prove to be a top money maker.' *Variety*, 8 July 1953

'No one dreamed it would be a hit.' Kay Kendall

▦ Can you spot . . .

* Some shocking continuity. You can often spot limbs and expressions jumping about across shot changes in any film, if you want to be picky, but this one is worse than most. Perhaps all the retakes meant that the actors lost track of exactly how they'd played the previous action. The most glaring example is at the beginning of the trumpet sequence. Cringe when the original trumpet player – suddenly not sitting any more – shrugs at himself.

* A shadowy film crew. In the newsreel sequence as the McKims drive up to genuine BBC man Leslie Mathews, the crew appear as shadows at the bottom of the frame.

* The disappearing Westminster Bridge. When they came to film the sequences where the Spyker gets stuck in the tramlines at Westminster Bridge they found that workmen had just taken them up. That's why in a twinkling of a shot change the background becomes nearby Lewisham, where tramlines were still *in situ.*

* It's certainly not the road to Brighton. Cornelius found that the Buckinghamshire surrounds of Pinewood Studios looked more like Surrey than Surrey so most of the exteriors are here, around the Moor Park Golf course. This caused a good deal of confusion as bewildered motorists and the odd disgruntled policeman puzzled at road signs showing thirteen miles to Brighton.

The
Godfather

1972 Transition and crisis in one of the powerful Mafia families of post-war New York.

▦ The talent

Marlon Brando 46, as Don Vito Corleone; always the biggest star of the cast, still an object of fascination. His career and bank balance made much headway following this timely success

Al Pacino 31, as Michael Corleone; very choosey about films. Few successes since the mid-seventies

James Caan 32, as Sonny Corleone; became a star of the seventies but couldn't hold on

Robert Duvall 40, as Tom Hagen; star supporting actor, shone again in Coppola's *Apocalypse Now* (1979), and beyond

Albert Ruddy 38, Producer; former producer of TV's *Hogan's Heroes. The Cannonball Run* (1981) is probably the most notable of his projects since

Francis Ford Coppola 31, Director; a prodigy partly raised in the Roger Corman sleaze end of film-making who has continued to display an immense, if erratic, talent

▦ The business

It began as an exercise in getting out of debt. Mario Puzo found himself in his mid-forties with two well-received but only moderately-selling novels behind him and $20,000 worth of unpaid bills. So he decided to sell out and write a sensational block-buster about the Mafia. The plan worked, with *The Godfather* a worldwide best seller: 500,000 hardcover copies and ten million paperbacks.

At an early stage, before the royalties actually started flooding in, he placated some of his creditors by selling an option on the film rights cheap to Paramount: $12,500 up front with a total of $50,000 if they went ahead with the project. Eventually he got $80,000 because there was a clause linking the fee to book sales.

He wasn't the only one who began the project with money troubles. Francis Ford Coppola had run into problems setting up his own production company and owed $300,000. Despite an Oscar for his script of *Patton* (1969) Coppola's record as a director was indifferent* and, of course, he was quite young. Coppola was awarded and retained the *Godfather* project partly because of the faith shown by Paramount production chief Robert Evans. His ethnic origin also helped. Evans wanted an Italian-American in charge who would have an inbred feel for the way the central characters should embrace one another and stow their pasta.

Coppola pressed home his advantage by talking Paramount into significantly upgrading what had been envisaged as $2,500,000 worth of gunplay filmed in con-

---

*His biggest assignment, *Finian's Rainbow* (1968), had shown promise but insufficient receipts.

temporary St Louis. *The Godfather* was to be a full-blown $6,000,000 epic in period costume with a recommissioned, more thoughtful Puzo script. He also insisted on Marlon Brando, a Nebraska-born WASP, for the role of Don Vito Corleone,* this at a time when the star was generally regarded as a troublesome hasbeen.

The studio finally agreed while imposing stringent conditions. Brando was to be offered only expenses in advance, and to give various guarantees of cooperation. He was also to submit to the indignity of a screen test.

The first two could be lived with but Coppola couldn't stomach inviting the illustrious star to try out. Instead he took a video camera to Marlon's house under the pretence of doing a make-up check. Brando shadowed his eyes with shoe polish and stuffed his cheeks with Kleenex,** then just sat down in front of the camera eating fruit and drinking demitasses of coffee. The effect was so startling that it instantly persuaded the powers that were Paramount. Besides, the other principal contender, Lawrence Olivier, was indisposed.

All was ready to go except for rumblings from a group called the Italian-American Civil Rights League. Their disquietude merited particular attention by virtue of the leadership of one Mr Joe Columbo, a nonfictional New York Godfather. Producer Albert Ruddy earned his keep, when summoned before a gathering of 1,500 members. He agreed to delete all references in the script to Mafia or Cosa Nostra, a painless concession as the names were only invoked a couple of times in the working screenplay. There was also a contribution to the League's hospital building fund. And finally Ruddy earnestly undertook to cast some of the membership as extras.

The most prominent of the intake was Gianni Russo, who played loathsome Carlo Rizzi. Russo had a regular gig as a Las Vegas night club MC. He was also a chum of Columbo's son Anthony, a jolly good friend to have. Russo had to lose 78 lbs for the film, a feat he reportedly achieved on a diet of one meal a day plus all the white wine he could contain. He is remembered toting a gallon jug around on set.

With the Italian-American Civil Rights League placated so, magically, was everyone else. League members acted as unofficial liaison for the location work ensuring that anyone not offering suitable cooperation was presented with a counter-offer they couldn't refuse.***

The Godfather was an instant success with the public, re-establishing Brando's dominance and catapulting Al Pacino, James Caan and Francis Coppola into the spotlight. The movie established itself as the industry's record money-maker, displacing *The Sound of Music* (1964). It had grossed $330,000,000 worldwide by mid 1974, the year NBC paid a further $10,000,000 for one TV screening. When Coppola amalgamated *The Godfather* and its 1974 sequel into a TV mini-series the network forked out a further $15,000,000.

Brando, having foregone a fee, was on a healthy percentage though a contractual clause put a ceiling on his earnings at $1,500,000. More money-spinning assignments

*In fact the cast was estimated to be 95% ethically authentic, notable exceptions being Brando and James Caan, whose family was German Jewish. However Caan had grown up in an Italian neighbourhood in New York and reckoned himself an honorary member of the clan.

**Much effort was made during production to keep the details of Brando's make-up the worst-kept secret in hypedom.

***This particular euphemism for coercion achieved wide currency from its use in the film. A critic overheard it being discussed by a group of London hoods emerging from a screening. 'What a nice way of putting it,' one of them remarked.

were on the way and Brando became a specialist in exacting colossal fees for virtual cameos. Coppola, in addition to $100,000 up front and $1,500 a week in expenses, was on 6%. Ruddy the Mouth got 7.5% and Puzo a further 2.5%. The more junior members of the cast like Caan, Keaton, Pacino and Duvall were each paid $35,000.

There were good pickings at the Oscars as well. Both *Godfathers* won Academy Awards for Best Picture and Best Screenplay. Brando won Best Actor for *The Godfather** and Robert de Niro Best Supporting Actor in *The Godfather Part II*. There were also Oscars for *The Godfather Part II* for Best Director, Best Art Direction and Best Musical Score.

Fine, but what would the mob think? No worries . . . Mario Puzo had discovered a new circle of supporters when the book was published. Sturdy, heavily bejewelled fellows in shades would hail him in the street and, more practically, he found gambling debts in Las Vegas mysteriously marked 'paid'. However, when it came to the film the generally-felt, flattered amusement was not universally shared as witnessed by the odd bomb threat and Mr Ruddy's (unoccupied) car being sprayed with bullets. Perhaps he should have reacted more positively to complaints from prominent underworld figures that they were not invited to the premiere.

The leader of the Italian-American Civil Rights League, Joe Columbo, never made the premiere either. Presumably following the ill-judged refusal of some offer he was shot in the head a few blocks from where they were filming, shortly before *The Godfather* was completed.

▥ Behind the screen

Filming began a week earlier than planned in March 1971 because the forecast said snow and Coppola wanted to shoot Christmas Eve outside Best and Company on Fifth Avenue. The snow didn't show and so instead they used special effects ice machines. This was the first of 120 locations where New Yorkers were treated to a slightly puzzling free show. The confusion in this case arose from Best's being re-opened a year after closedown with Christmas windows at Easter displaying 1945 prices.

Look at all the detail. Coppola had won his battle for a period piece and was determined to carry it through meticulously. Everything down to the lipsticks, pencils and wall posters has been carefully scrutinized for stray anachronism. Coppola even adjusted his direction to the forties and fifties mood, shooting without modern zooming and rapid cuts.

This was not understood by the crew who had little confidence in him. His cinematographer, Gordon Willis, dared to respond to instructions about how to shoot a scene by saying, 'Oh, that's dumb.' There was a mini-rebellion which threatened to oust Coppola from the picture and studio chief Robert Evans feared his young protégé would suffer a breakdown. But Coppola had the backing of head office and the loyalty of Marlon Brando; it was the renegades who got the boot. Willis toned down his act and stayed (along with production designer Dean Tavoularis) for *Godfather II*.

The most difficult scene of all to film was the attempted assassination of the Don outside the Olive factory. They set themselves up in Mott Street, a Little Italy thoroughfare which retained a look untouched by the decades. For three days Brando

*He caused a furore by sending a native American calling herself Saskia Littlefeather along to the ceremony to refuse his statuette. He was at Wounded Knee at the time on another Indian protest.

chose his fruit and took his bullets before an enthusiastic audience who crowded every available vantage point from fire escapes and windows. It was this lively involvement which apparently wasted time; the onlookers were unable to conquer the impulse to applaud the actors before a take was completed.

Brando didn't much mind. It is said that this was his favourite production in twenty years. He confounded the pre-filming anxieties with his cooperative attitude and immersion in the part, slouching into the quiet menace of Don Corleone as the make-up and mouth-brace went on, just as he had for his surreptitious screen test.

Brando lifted the performance of his gifted young co-stars who wondered at finding themselves playing alongside a key influence on their craft. Al Pacino was particularly awe-struck filming the first scene with his hero, when he is protecting his shot father in hospital.

What could Brando learn from his co-stars? They introduced him to the sophisticated humour of mooning. This was altogether a very cheeky production, most frequently the cheeks being James Caan's. They were exposed from car windows on occasion and also in the middle of the wedding scene, one of several pranks during this sequence.

Take a keen look at Luca Brassi, played by Lenny Montana, paying his respects to the Don. As Brando was doing his close-up Montana stuck out his tongue to which was affixed a piece of surgical tape bearing the message, 'Fuck you, Marlon.' The Don was gone. It perhaps accounts for Montana's own startled hesitation that when it came to his delivery to camera he was confronted with Brando's tongue which by that time had acquired its own piece of tape reading, 'Fuck you, too.'

Montana was an ex-wrestler who had been recruited from the ranks of hangers-on in the location crowds. Another non-actor prominent in this scene, which featured many of the League extras enjoying the rare sunshine, was singer Al Martino as Johnny Fontaine. This character in Puzo's novel had been construed by some to represent Frank Sinatra, whose view of the book was vitriolic. The original candidate for the role, Vic Damone, pulled out citing the familiar line that the film was likely to be detrimental to the image of Italian Americans. Martino's attempts at acting look hopeless but the performance was saved by Marlon Brando. The original script called for the Don to admonish the singer by tugging his hair affectionately, a piece of business abandoned because Martino's toupee couldn't take the strain. Instead the Don was to gently cuff his face. The unexpected force of Brando's slap elicited an expression of shock which was the highlight of Martino's performance.

Brando was full of tricks and techniques, one being the use of flesh-coloured earplugs which muffled extraneous noises, forcing him to concentrate more completely on his fellow players. He also came up with the idea of cut-out orange peel teeth to amuse the boy playing his grandson. The little lad hadn't been responding very well, and the teeth scared him witless, but somehow they got it in the can. This was one of several cases where Brando's help provided classic shots but threw up added problems. A memorable image* is Don Corleone stroking the cat. It was a resident of the East Harlem Studios where they were filming, seized upon by Brando just before the cameras rolled. As you can see the puss was enraptured by Brando's caresses, to the point that its purrs dominated the soundtrack forcing a redub.

---

*Already explored as sinister counterpoint to Bond villains.

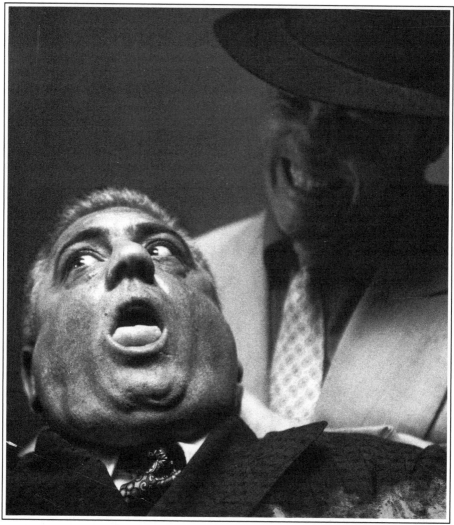

Lenny Montana and unidentified Tattaglia assassin: could you just repeat that message for the Don?

The most bothersome Brandoism was his refusal to learn lines. This was not sheer laziness but rather method acting, practised by Brando since *On the Waterfront* (1954) and based on his observation that in real life people don't know their lines, the words come as a surprise. In this case they come from cue cards. Can you spot where they are? A few examples to get you going: on the camera, inside drawers, under the grapefruit – and what's that on the desk blotter.

Despite all this everyone was very impressed, and the relationship between the re-established star and his young director was so good that Brando was moved to forego $50,000 due to him because filming, particularly of the wedding scene, was delayed by rain. One of the contractual clauses working in the actor's favour provided for the money to be paid if he was kept over six weeks. Brando agreed to the extra filming for free so as not to prejudice Coppola's efforts.

The film representation of the ageing gang lord was not entirely satisfactory to the other set of professions involved, the real-life mobsters minding the production. Two of them articulated their displeasure during the assassination scene in Mott Street. It was mainly a question of wardrobe. A don of Corleone's stature and vintage would have sported snappier outfits featuring diamond-studded belt buckles and the like. His hat would never have been pinched; Italian Block style was de rigeur. And if Brando looked like an old shlepper, the wouldbe assassins were worse. 'They hold their pieces like flowers,' was the disparaging professional assessment.

▦ The experience

'Marlon Brando's historic performance in this ferocious picture of the American Mafia "families" at war amounts on screen to surprisingly little, but in dramatic power it dominates everything.' Cecil Wilson, *Daily Mail*, 22 August 1972

'Best performance comes from newcomer Al Pacino. I rate him as one of the biggest screen finds since . . . well, since the young Marlon Brando.' Fergus Cashin, *The Sun*, 22 August 1972

'In its blending of new depth with an old genre, it becomes a rarity, a mass entertainment that is also great movie art.' Jay Cocks, *Time*, 3 April 1972

'Couldn't bear it.' Sir John Gielgud, 1972

▦ Can you spot . . .

* The family. No, not the Mafia family – the Coppola family. The director's sister, Talia Shire, played the Don's beat-up daughter Connie. His father provided the background music and was the piano player in the mattress sequences.
* Some injuries. Al Pacino was forced onto crutches after tearing a ligament. He misjudged his jump on to the getaway car following his hit at the restaurant (where the owner and his wife played themselves). James Caan was stunned by all the explosive rigging that gave him the effect of being shot at the motorway toll. You can see that it hurts, and despite the use of a stand-in during the beating-up scene, Gianni Russo reportedly suffered two cracked ribs and a chipped elbow.
* Why Brando's voice is lighter near the end of the film. It is supposed to signify the Don being shot in the throat but Coppola forgot to establish this in the film, apart from the brief appearance of a throat bandage.
* The trouble with Diana Keaton. Five years before her triumph as *Annie Hall* they were thinking of taking her off *The Godfather* at an early stage. Her movements were considered gawky and she was too tall for Al Pacino. Notice how when Michael and Kay meet after he comes back from Sicily he walks up on the crown of the road and she's down next to the gutter. Pacino has recently been quoted as indicating that the two were then lovers. She was apparently instrumental in curing him of a drink and drug habit that was fogging him at the time of *The Godfather*.

Some also-rans for the part of Don Corleone as supporting actors. Both John Marley (who played the producer Jack Woltz) and Richard Conte (Barzini) were considered.

Goldfinger

1964 British superspy James Bond must stop master criminal Goldfinger from turning the United States gold reserves radioactive.

▥ The talent

Sean Connery 33, as James Bond; managed to outpace the type-casting trap to the point where he could re-visit Bond in *Never Say Never Again* (1983)

Gert Frobe 51, as Auric Goldfinger; great German heavy hamming it in *Those Magnificent Men in Their Flying Machines* (1965) next

Honor Blackman 38, as Pussy Galore; at her peak after TV's *Avengers* – reunited with Connery for *Shalako* (1968)

Albert (Cubby) Broccoli 55, Producer; has made the rest of the James Bond series his extremely profitable life's work

Harry Saltzman 49, Producer; split with Broccoli in the seventies. Also made the sixties Harry Palmer films with Michael Caine

Guy Hamilton 42, Director; made *Funeral in Berlin* (1966) next for Saltzman and three more seventies Bonds

▥ The business

Ian Fleming started writing the James Bond books during a yearly two-month vacation in Jamaica from his regular work as a Fleet Street newspaper executive.

Much of his inspiration came from wartime service as assistant to the Director of Naval Intelligence, when Fleming himself held the rank of Commander. The decorative details about vodka martinis, ballistics and fast cars were provided by wine waiters and other essential journalistic contacts. The name James Bond was that of the author of *Birds of the West Indies* which graced the Fleming coffee table.

The Bond books sold well and seemed ripe for film exploitation but the impediment was that no star would commit himself for a run of pictures. Finally two North American independent producers working in Britain, Harry Saltzman and Albert 'Cubby' Broccoli, decided to chance buying an option from Fleming for $50,000 and managed to persuade the respected boss of United Artists, Arthur Krim, to back the project with or without a leading actor. Fleming's cut was $100,000 per picture plus a percentage.

That still left the choice of a leading man. Sean Connery was a relatively unknown actor; a former navy gunner (invalided out with ulcers) and aspirant-Mr-Universe. He arrived at his audition wearing a lumber jacket and growled at Mr Broccoli 'You either take me as I am or not at all.' Cubby took him.*

Connery signed up for six pictures with a clause that let him do one non-Bond film a year – which is initially where he made his big money. He got just £6,000 for his first mission, *Dr No* (1962). Its success, and that of *From Russia With Love* (1963),

---

*Why, you might ask. Both Saltzman and Broccoli had noticed his promise in Disney's *Darby O'Gill and the Little People* (1959) and *On the Fiddle* (1961). Besides, Cubby liked his Edinburgh brogue and Mrs Broccoli thought him good-looking.

Sean Connery and Honor Blackman: what a lot he's got

established Connery as a bankable commodity. He was paid $400,000 for Alfred Hitchcock's *Marnie* (1964) just before starting work on *Goldfinger*. His Bond earnings were not keeping up.

Then a curious thing happened. It was during the scene in the Fontainebleu Hotel where Oddjob sneaks up and karate chops Bond on the back of the neck. According to a story later told by *Goldfinger* publicist Tom Carlisle, Connery slumped down at the end of the take, complained of a headache and had to leave the set. How does it look to you on screen? The incident surprised and worried those present as the professional wrestler playing Oddjob, Harold Sakata, was a precision chopper, not given to causing damage when none was called for. In any event, so the story continues, by the time Connery had recovered sufficiently to return to the set he had a new contract which brought him £50,000 up front and 5% of the profits.

The profits were immense. *Goldfinger's* budget was $2,900,000 but it took money faster at the box office than any previous film, finally grossing about $45,000,000 worldwide. Contributory factors were the unleashing of United Artists' first Bond publicity bonanza, the absence of any significant competition at the time of release in late 1964 and the revelation that the Fleming collection had been on the late President Kennedy's reading list.

The *Goldfinger* image was strongly marketed, epitomized by the alluring figure of Shirley Eaton as the gild-fated Jill Masterson. Merchandizing covered everything from eau (eau seven) de cologne to toy Aston Martins.

The next Bond, *Thunderball* (1965), was even more profitable and Sean Connery leapfrogged straight into the number one spot in the standard U.S. 'Quigley' chart of the top cinema draws. Broccoli and Saltzman had found a formula which continues to make big money today – a total of $2,000,000,000 and rising.

Alas Ian Fleming missed his creation's greatest screen successes. He died of a heart attack a few weeks before *Goldfinger* was released.

▥ Behind the screen

The moment James Bond removes a stuffed seagull from his head and unzips his wet suit to reveal pristine evening dress we are clearly departing from both the original literary character and his previous two screen incarnations. *Goldfinger* was the birth of the jokey Bond that dominated the series until the late eighties when Timothy Dalton returned more to the root of the character.

The crew thought it was all too silly and blamed their new director, Guy Hamilton. *Dr No* and *From Russia With Love* had been made by Terence Young who stalked off when Saltzman and Broccoli turned down his demand for a cut of the profits.* Young shared something of the action-man qualities of 007 and his early Bonds were more in keeping with the preoccupied gentleman-killer of the Ian Fleming novels. But the idea of a Bond you could laugh with seems to have been the producers' (and scriptwriter Richard Maibaum's) strategy for coping with the rash of imitators and potential send-ups.

Most of the location work on *Goldfinger* went ahead in early 1964 without the stars being present. Apart from a week's material shot in Switzerland anything you see with Sean Connery was done at Pinewood Studios outside London, where they had constructed a $100,000 mock-up of Fort Knox.

Hamilton even got permission to film at the real thing in Kentucky as well, plus the use of any number of extras in uniform. Those are all real soldiers falling down under the influence of the supposed nerve gas. The army liaison man for the film-makers at Fort Knox was retired Colonel Charlie Rushon, credited as technical advisor at the end of the film and welcomed as *General* Rushon on a banner you can see at the end of a pan as Pussy's glamorous flight of aviatrixes bomb by (a glamour that would not

---

*He stalked back for the next one, *Thunderball* (1965).

have stood closer examination; they were lads from the local flying school perfunc-
torily disguised in black jumpsuits and blonde wigs).

Outside was close enough to America's gold reserves for the Treasury Department
to extend its welcome to the film-makers and Col Rushon, but production designer
Ken Adam* was just as happy. Bullion storage presents a unique set of engineering
problems best solved by tucking it away in little rooms connected by small corridors,
hardly a sufficiently spectacular backdrop for Bond and Oddjob to slug it out.

Hamilton's matching of the real Gold Depository with his Home Counties version
(complete with wire fencing and mile-long drive) was more successful than the stuff
at the beginning at the Fontainebleu. They filmed at the famous Florida hotel on the
same trip as Kentucky, using *in situ* only Cec Linder as Felix Lighter and Austin
Williams as the cheated-and-repaid Mr Simmonds. It matches well initially as Lighter
strolls round the pool in Florida to find Bond in the Pinewood cabana area – but the
later back-projection shots must have made them wish that Connery hadn't been tied
up with *Marnie* while they were in the States.

Hamilton also filmed some of the car chase around Auric Enterprises without
Connery. You can treat this as a Pinewood tour. They were actually tearing around
the studio buildings and, so as to minimize the risk both to brickwork and Aston
Martin, shot some in slow motion to accelerate the action.

The Aston Martin DB5 was the flashest thing on four wheels at the time, all the
more so for the £5,000 worth of refinements added for the one-off version in the
film.* In the book gadgetry was limited to the odd secret compartment and a homing
device. *Goldfinger* started another regular feature of the Bond films: Q in the person
of actor Desmond Llewellyn with his arsenal of progressively more outlandish strains
on the public purse.

Much of the gadgetry on the DB5 really worked. The smokescreen and oil-slick
dispenser were relatively simple modifications. A similar device which sowed three-
point nails in the path of would-be pursuers was fitted but unused in the film for fear
of imitative vandalism. The man delivering the car to the studios allegedly got into
trouble when a policeman rumbled the revolving numberplates. The ejector seat,
cannibalized from a fighter plane, also worked but had to be fitted specially for the
action shot, as did the Boadicea-style hubcap scythes. On the other hand, although
the machine guns barked fiercely they were no more lethal than puffs of acetylene
gas being ignited by the car's distributor and the spring-up shield was proof against
little, certainly not bullets.

The appearance of this sleek armoured personnel carrier in the film did no harm to
Aston Martin sales (even Prince Charles bought one) and demand was boosted for
Ford's new sports model, the Mustang, as driven by Tillie Masterson. Thereafter
firms competed heavily to have their products placed.

The first scenes to be shot after Connery's arrival on March 19 were in the cafe,
with so many people crowded into the set that the sweat you see is real. But that's
about all. Inconsistencies start with the dinner suit and continue with the fight
upstairs from the cafe. The conditions are supposed to be tropical, so why does the
girl have an electric heater in her bathroom conveniently placed for Bond to broil the

---

*He's done most of them, plus *Around the World in Eighty Days* (1956) and many more spectacular films.
**This brought its price to a hefty £11,000. It was worth £140,000 at auction in the eighties.

opposition? This, the threat of death by gloss emulsion paint, and any number of other catalysts for precipitation of disbelief abound.

For Connery it was all familiar stuff, a doddle after the challenge of working with Hitchcock on *Marnie*, and he was eager to be rid of his obligations to play a part he had lost interest in.

Fortunately there were other things to divert him, including his older-than-usual Bond girl, Honor Blackman. In the book Pussy was a lesbian, vestiges of which remain in some of the dialogue and inadvertently in the stuntman's butch hands, pitching Bond over when he's eavesdropping from the model of Fort Knox.

The chemistry between them on screen seems to have continued between takes. Connery had married actress Diane Cilento two years previously when she was pregnant with their son Jason, who grew up to be an eighties screen heart-throb. The couple separated a few months after *Goldfinger* came out.

Honor Blackman's comments have the ring of experience when she describes Connery as confident, attractive and virile, 'I think he's got a pair of the best eyes that have ever been seen on screen, apart from anything else he might have that's good and there's plenty of that!'

▦ The experience

'My only grumble about Bond films is that they don't tax you as an actor. All one really needs is the constitution of a rugby player to get through all those nineteen weeks of swimming, slugging and necking.' Sean Connery, 14 February 1965

'The whole film is quite fantastic, with the plot striking a precarious balance between the impossible and the ridiculous, but the outrageous mixture is irresistible.' Iain Crawford, *Daily Express*, 20 September 1964

'It's all incredible and terribly sinister but you can't help watching.' Hollis Alpert, *Saturday Review*, 12 December 1964

'Ian Fleming would have enjoyed it.' *Time*, 17 September 1964

The Queen Mother thought it the best film she had ever seen.

▦ Can you spot . . .

* Some rather un-Bond tattoos. 'Scotland forever' and 'Mum and Dad' emblazoned on Connery's right arm are masked with make-up. But I'm sure you can see something on his forearm under the manly mat of hair.
* The toupé. One of the least vain stars, Connery stopped worrying much about the family tendency to baldness in his twenties.
* Who's not really speaking. Gert Frobe is dubbed and so is Shirley Eaton, who sounded less posh in her usual comedy roles. She was dubbed by Nikki van der Zyl, who also did Ursula Andress and practically all the other female voices in *Dr No*. She once asked Bond director Terence Young for a part in her own right, a request he dismissed with the observation, 'You wouldn't stop the traffic.'
* A familiar name. The producers thought so and stopped NBC using the chief gangster's surname as the title for one of their new shows going to air shortly before *Goldfinger*'s release. So the network changed it from *Solo* to *The Man from U.N.C.L.E.* NBC successfully argued that the programme's dashing protagonist was quite different from the film's hood-with-a-pressing-engagement, so he was allowed to keep the name of Napoleon Solo.

Gone With the Wind

1939 The story of a tempestuous love-hate relationship against the backdrop of the South's struggle in the American Civil War.

▦ The talent

Clark Gable 38, as Rhett Butler; the King at the height of his popularity

Vivien Leigh 26, as Scarlett O'Hara; a dazzling Hollywood debut

Olivia De Havilland 22, as Melanie Hamilton; already a veteran of fifteen films

Leslie Howard 49, as Ashley Wilkes; died four years later when the aircraft carrying him from a British Government mission to Portugal was shot down

Thomas Mitchell 47, as Gerald O'Hara; former reporter and playwright. Many character roles including drunken doctor in *Stagecoach* (1939) for which he won the Oscar

Hattie McDaniel 44, as Mammy; screen veteran, previously first black woman on U.S. radio. With Best Supporting Actress here, the first black to win an Oscar. The next was Sidney Poitier 25 years later

Butterfly McQueen 28, as Prissy; soon got fed up with repeat roles and left films. Obtained political science degree aged 64

David O. Selznick 37, Producer; one of Hollywood's most stylish and successful moguls – behind many great films

Victor Fleming 56, Director; lucky to get the Oscar for this – lucky to direct more great films

George Cukor 40, Director; with a slew of successes, one of Hollywood's premier craftsmen

Sam Wood 56, Director; made *Goodbye Mr Chips* (1939) – on his own

▦ The business

Gone With the Wind cost the then princely sum of $3,700,000 to make. The producer, David O. Selznick, knew whom he had to have as the male lead but Clark Gable was an MGM player and a deal needed to be struck. They agreed to share the distribution rights which, it turned out, were worth at least $25,000,000 to MGM.

Afterwards Gable said he was aggrieved that he never received a single bonus from MGM for securing one of their most lucrative deals. Even so, his salary did go up in a new five-year contract from $4,500 a week to $7,000 which must have taken some of the sting away and it's also been reported that he *did* get a healthy bonus. The practically unknown Vivien Leigh only got $30,000 for the whole picture, and she had the most work of any of the other featured players.

Almost all the other financial statistics for the film involve previously unheard-of figures . . .

Margaret Mitchell, who had written the book in an attempt to get over the boredom of a sprained ankle, received $50,000 for the film rights and another $50,000 after the film was released.

Selznick had never actually read the book before shooting – he had a synopsis prepared for him by an employee – and he bought the rights against all advice. Whizz-kid MGM production chief Irving Thalberg had already given it the thumbs-down. 'No Civil War picture ever made a nickel,' he said. Similarly, Victor Fleming refused the offer of a percentage of the profits because he didn't think they'd be worth having.

The American public were clamouring for the film of one of the country's biggest best sellers. It was an immediate hit, grossing almost $1,000,000 in its first week, and has since taken at least $76,000,000 in North American rentals (worldwide the figure would be about double that).* It was only overtaken in the highest-grossing stakes a quarter of a century later by *The Sound of Music* (1964).

It had the longest ever run for a film in a British cinema, four years and twenty-nine weeks at the London Ritz. It was re-released over and over, including a fifty-years-on version in 1989, and always did good business. Almost forty years after its premiere it attracted the biggest-ever television rights deal when CBS paid $35,000,000 to screen it twenty times over the following twenty years.

▦ Behind the screen

The first scene of the film to be shot was the spectacular burning of Atlanta. It was done before Selznick had officially cast the female lead, Scarlett O'Hara. 'Atlanta' itself is many bits of redundant set that were due for destruction anyway. They were repainted and disposed of in one of cinema's most spectacular set pieces.

Tradition has it that Selznick, who personally supervised this, and practically every other aspect of the film, turned round from all the blazing backdrops to be introduced to Vivien Leigh, the little-known English actress who was finally cast for the part. However it seems that the producer had kept his eye on Vivien for some time and this meeting was staged as a fitting end to the two-year, publicity-rich talent hunt that led to her taking the role.

As many as 2,000 hopefuls were interviewed for the part and more than 160,000 feet of film were shot testing ninety of them. The cost of the test film alone would have been enough to finance a decent second feature.

But there was no doubt in anyone's mind who should play Rhett Butler although Gable wasn't too keen. He said that everyone had their own image of Rhett and he didn't see how he could please them all. It's said that his increased salary convinced him. He needed it to finance the divorce he was finishing at the time of the filming. His first two marriages had been to older women – one fourteen, the other seventeen years his senior. But he was separated by now from wealthy Texas socialite Ria Langham and wanted to marry his dream match, Carole Lombard. He got his wish during the filming (and was allowed two whole days off for a honeymoon) but Lombard was to die in a plane crash three years later. Gable never fully recovered.

Vivien Leigh was also going through a divorce and was to marry *her* dream match, Laurence Olivier, the following year. They had met during the filming of *Fire Over England* (1937). She was never fully to recover from their final breakup in 1960.

---

*It also dominated the Academy Awards in one of cinema's strongest years. In addition to Hattie McDaniel's win there were Oscars to Vivien Leigh and Victor Fleming, and for Best Picture, Editing, Art Direction, Screenplay and Cinematography.

The marital musical chairs of the two stars is ironic in that one of the other main contenders, Paulette Goddard, was barred from the part by the powerful morality movement in the States because she was living openly with Charlie Chaplin. Perhaps Clark and Carole and Vivien and Larry were more discreet.

But America still found cause to be outraged, at the casting of an Englishwoman as bookland's favourite Southern Belle. This caused some strain during the filming as did the attitude of Leslie Howard, who never seemed to have wanted the role of Ashley. He thought he was too old for the part and objected to another typical outing as a weak dreamer. Does he look distracted in the film? He was working on *Intermezzo* (1939) with Ingrid Bergman at the same time and wouldn't learn his lines for *Gone With the Wind.*

Then, of course, there was the succession of directors.

The first, George Cukor, was fired after a couple of weeks of filming and following two and a half years of pre-production work. Traditionally it has been said that he clashed with the interfering Selznick over the script and that Gable objected to him because he was known as a 'woman's director' who would shoot the movie to favour its female stars.

Recently, though, there have been allegations of a deeper and more personal grudge. Cukor was a homosexual, a close friend of a former MGM star-turned-interior decorator, Billy Haines. Hollywood gossip-monger Kenneth Anger says that Cukor knew of some homosexual activity between Haines and Gable when Clark was first trying to make it in Hollywood. Gable couldn't stand being directed by the man who knew too much . . .

Cukor's hand is still very much in the picture though. Both Vivien Leigh and her co-star Olivia de Havilland went to Cukor for coaching sessions in secret throughout the making of the film.

Another two directors took over. Victor Fleming was the main one and he won the actual director's credit on the film. History has judged him a fairly minor talent despite some notable successes including *The Wizard of Oz* (1939), which he was working on at the same time. Fleming was a gung-ho type who appealed very much to Gable but who horrified the women. He had quite a bit of help, not just from Cukor. Sam Wood also shot some of the scenes. There were some days when Wood would shoot in the mornings and Fleming in the afternoons. Watching over them all the time – and often running them ragged – was Selznick, a hands-on producer if ever there was one.

Other old directorial hands shot isolated sequences. B. Reeves Eason staged action sequences in Atlanta. One contains the most dangerous shot of the whole film for Vivien Leigh. It's one of many risky-looking set-ups during the panicked evacuation of Atlanta, when she is almost knocked over by a horse bolting backwards. She refused to use a stand-in and backstage hearts were racing.

The most dangerous shot for Gable only imperilled his macho image. It's the one where he weeps when he learns that Scarlett has had a miscarriage. Gable said crying was for sissies and didn't want to do it. But he was persuaded to shoot the scene both ways and had to admit afterwards that the crying take was the more effective.

Another scene that caused more than its share of bother was during the final moments of the film when Rhett says the immortal line 'Frankly, my dear, I don't give a damn.'

Vivien Leigh, Clark Gable and Victor Fleming: I've got my director now

Not so much immortal as immoral. 'Damn' was almost unheard of on the screen at that time and Selznick had to fly to New York specially and spend four hours convincing the industry's guardian of morals, Will H. Hays, that *the word* was essential to convey the full force of Rhett's feelings. Hays wanted him to say 'Frankly, my dear, I don't give a darn' but Selznick prevailed. They still got fined $5,000 by the American censors for technically violating the production code – but for the highest-grossing film for the next twenty-five years, who cares? America had to wait twelve more years for another onscreen damn.

And so we come to the end of one of Hollywood's longest films – three hours and forty minutes – and the first to have an intermission. Selznick thought it essential, his promotions manager disagreed. They settled it by a simple experiment: putting an intermission in one of the screenings and counting the grateful patrons who used the break to make for the toilet. Selznick was right again.

▦ The experience

'Surely the most over-rated film of all time.' Robert Ottway, *Daily Sketch*, 1968; reflecting a mainly cool reaction to a remixed, wide-screen version issued that year

'Still a banquet.' Ian Christie, *Daily Express*, 1968

'A British actress who is comparatively unknown in the United States made such an impression on the critics that she is now hailed as one of the outstanding figures of the screen.' *Daily Telegraph*, August 1939

'When I first read *Gone With the Wind* I was determined to play Scarlett. Everyone said I was mad to try for the part but I knew I'd get it.' Vivien Leigh

'I have seen the film sixteen times and it still moves me to tears each time.' Olivia de Havilland

▦ Can you spot . . .

* Rhett and Scarlett, seen in silhouette during the burning of Atlanta, are stand-ins (they hadn't picked a Scarlett yet).
* Unsymmetrical Tara. The O'Hara family home, a studio backlot frontage like the set of a Western, is rarely seen directly from the front because the main door is off-centre. Almost all the surrounding trees and shrubbery are fake as well. As are many of the prostrate Confederate soldiers in the spectacular crane shot of Atlanta – not dead, just dummies.
* A wrenched limb. One of the few scenes that George Cukor shot before being fired was Melanie's birth pains. He cued fresh sets of contractions by twisting Olivia's leg.
* Rochester. Aunt Pittypat's coachman, Uncle Peter, is played by Eddie Anderson. He had just started a long partnership with Jack Benny as the manservant with a sandpapered larynx.
* Superman. Take a good look at Stuart Tarleton, alias George Reeves, who played the superhero on TV. And there's even a superhorse. Thomas Mitchell's mount is none other than the Lone Ranger's Silver, once dubbed 'the smartest horse in movies'.
* Every principal character but one has their own particular theme music in the score supplied by Max Steiner. Leslie Howard's Ashley is the only one who misses out. Tara, of course, has the main theme.
* The electric street lamp. This useful innovation seems to have reached Civil War Atlanta well in advance of Edison's prototype lightbulb of 1879.

The Graduate

1967 He is seduced by the wife of his father's business partner but then falls for her daughter.

▦ The talent

Dustin Hoffman 30, as Benjamin Braddock; struggling character actor who has reasserted his stardom with almost every subsequent film

Anne Bancroft 35, as Mrs Robinson; fifties B movies, an Oscar for *The Miracle Worker* (1962), very selective since

Katherine Ross 25, as Elaine Robinson; Miss Most-Promising, next came *Butch Cassidy and the Sundance Kid* (1969) but she prefers horses and gardening to Hollywood

William Daniels 40, as Mr Braddock; former dancer, ubiquitous character actor, in TV's *Soap* and *St Elsewhere*

Murray Hamilton 44, as Mr Robinson; stock character actor. Lots of TV and the man who didn't want the beaches to close in *Jaws* (1975)

Lawrence Turman 41, Producer; made a few more films you'll have seen but nothing remotely as memorable as this

Mike Nichols 35, Director; seemed to falter in the seventies, back in force in the eighties

▦ The business

Mike Nichols was entering his third successful career, after taking America by storm in a late-fifties stand-up comic partnership with Elaine May and shining again in the sixties as a Broadway director. Now he was moving on to films – but what should he choose?

Producer Lawrence Turman gave him Charles Webb's new Catcher-in-the-Rye-type novel. Nichols got hooked by the scene in the hotel where Ben would rather make conversation about art with Mrs Robinson than make love.*

Webb was paid $20,000 for the screen rights. Buck Henry got $35,000 for the six months he spent transposing it to screenplay with Nichols** – and a succulent bit part: the hotel clerk.

Unknown Dustin Hoffman only got $17,000 and signed on for unemployment insurance after shooting finished in August 1967 but the part and his unchiselled appeal attracted immense cultish popularity. His next screen role, super-seedy Ritzo in *Midnight Cowboy* (1969), earned him $250,000, and hinted at the versatility and skill which would make him one of cinema's most respected actors. And most remunerated: by the mid-eighties he could command more than $5,000,000 for *Ishtar* (1987).

*Nichols actually made *Who's Afraid of Virginia Wolf* (1966) first but chose *The Graduate* before that.
**Calder Willingham, who is co-credited, bailed out early but made sure he got a credit.

Simon and Garfunkel made big money even faster. Their soulful ditties – old hits, apart from Mrs Robinson – were woven skilfully into the narrative and found an audience far wider than their largely campus following.

However the prize earner at the time was Mike Nichols. He got a record $1,000,000 of the $3,100,000 budget, but would seem to have been worth it considering the film has made one hundred times that. *The Graduate* was top American earner in 1968, charming the critics and packing in the baby-boomers – who were just starting their rebellious phase and, like Ben, not sure what to do about it.

▦ Behind the screen

Does it strike you that a short, Jewish, thirty-ish character actor is the last person you would cast as Benjamin Braddock, athletic star of the college debating society? Well, that's one reason you're reading about great films rather than making them.

Hoffman couldn't understand being chosen either and pointed out the obvious to Mike Nichols: the role called for a young, Californian 'beach nazi'. But Nichols said that Ben was short and Jewish inside and that it was appropriate for him to look like an outsider as well (which actually smacks of rationalization considering that the WASP-ish likes of Robert Redford were considered).

Hoffman's screen test was cringe-making, a love scene with Katherine Ross. Dustin arrived looking pale, distracted and – as Miss Ross recalled it – about three feet tall. Both realized that he was the last sort of person she'd have a love scene with in real life. As the cameras rolled, in a moment of confused desperation, Hoffman grabbed at his co-star's bottom. She gave him what-for but it was this outburst that got him the part. Nichols had seen a mixture of awkwardness and aggression that would transcend physical type-casting.

It seems that Nichols preserved that spark of power and hesitation you can see in Hoffman's performance by pressuring him during the filming. The actor remembers Nichols' insistence on every colour, texture and nuance conforming to his wishes. Both men were recent immigrants from the theatre and Hoffman thinks this added to the tension. Nichols' directing was still based on his stage work. He rehearsed the players for three weeks before shooting so that they knew their lines off pat. And, see, particularly at the beginning, how long the takes are – blocked out like a play.

Hoffman's paranoia went from bad to worse. He formed the impression that Nichols regretted his choice in casting him. But in fact the director knew he was on to a winner when it came to shooting the scene where Ben books the illicit hotel room. Nichols came back from the rushes saying 'We may have a decent picture'. Hoffman had got the effect by remembering the time he bought his first packet of condoms.

Even if Dustin was finding work a bind there was the solace of a stable homelife. His future wife, dancer Anne Byrne, had just moved in with him (they divorced in 1979 about the time he was recreating marital break-up in *Kramer vs. Kramer*). And Anne Bancroft was as helpful to him as Mrs Robinson was to Ben, though in screen rather than sexual technique. Hoffman wasn't the only screen novice she had on her hands. Her husband, Mel Brooks, was also breaking into movies with *The Producers* (1968)* which ended shooting just after production started on *The Graduate*.

*Small world department: Brooks was leaving the hit TV comedy, *Get Smart*, which he created and scripted with Buck Henry.

Dustin Hoffman and Anne Bancroft: she gave him a few pointers

After filming, Hoffman knew the picture would be a great success but felt he never wanted to do another and hit the psychiatrist's couch. Perhaps it steeled him against repeating the same dominated relationship with a director. Ever since he has been seen as an actor who knows his craft, and his own mind.

And what about the real Benjamin? Charles Webb's novel, written when he was in his early twenties, was autobiographical – all the way down to his refuge in the swimming pool and the 'plastics' conversation. Webb's parents, a rich L.A. doctor and wife, were outraged by the book and suspiciously scrutinized their friends for the real Mrs Robinson – but that element, claims the author, was fictional. He in turn was outraged at the only major alteration Nichols and Buck Henry made to his plot: Ben arriving at the church too late but still running off with the bride. Webb's Ben got there in time to stop the marriage vows and keep tidily to the moral high ground.

Nichols said that his favourite scene was that last long look at them in the bus, Ben in sweaty street clothes and Elaine in her wedding dress. In a few minutes she would realize she hadn't anything else to wear and their troubles would really begin.

Charles Webb and his Elaine (Eve, who prefers to be known as Fred) rejected the trappings of materialism – the vice that Nichols sees as the central theme of the film – and embarked on a nomadic existence in a mobile home. Last seen they were temping for a cleaning firm called Mr Mop. They have three kids and a dog called Mrs R.

▦ The experience

'*The Graduate* represents a breakthrough of sorts in the Hollywood scheme of things . . . it has taken aim, satirically, at the very establishment that produces most of our movies . . . it is a final irony that it has been rewarded with a shower of gold.' Hollis Alpert, *Saturday Review*, 6 July 1968

'The kids kept standing on line for a) Dustin Hoffman and b) Simon and Garfunkel. The adults stood on line to find out why the kids stood on line.' Andrew Sarris, *Village Voice*, 20 December 1973

'Looking back, I have no sense of achievement.' Dustin Hoffman

▦ Can you spot . . .

* Richard Dreyfuss as the student in Ben's Berkeley digs making a meal of his eagerness to call the cops.
* A lot of heavy symbolism: Ben under glass. You could spend the whole film spotting the metaphors for isolation that Nichols churns out in fish tanks, scuba masks, and windows. Note the way the reflection of Anne Bancroft's naked stand-in obscures the face of Elaine's portrait when she comes in the door (just before all those quick cuts which give a new meaning to the term flash-frame). Or how about the way black-and-white clothing and decor predominate for the bad guys while Ben and Elaine favour soft colours. This and much more significant stuff for the film-art buff (the shot that dwells on the clown portrait, the keys thrown in the fish tank, etc) is interpreted in *Mike Nichols* by H. Wayne Schuth.
* The change in rhythm. A lot of people preferred the film before Elaine came on the scene but the effect was planned by Nichols in his representation of the story purely from Ben's perspective (he's in every set-up). When romance arrived Nichols changed the pace and colour scheme, and brought out the long lenses.
* An offensive ethnic reference. A group called 'Americans of Italian Descent' wanted the film-makers to cut the reference to Ben's new Alfa Romeo as a 'wop car'. It would have been a simple matter of clipping some voice-over but the intention to disparage the Braddock circle rather than Italians was felt to be clear.
* Sunshine and showers. The weather was very contrary – endemic, it seems, to location work even in balmy California. They were dogged by rain but Nichols' difficulties are most obvious in the sunny backgrounds to the driving sequences when it's *supposed* to be pouring. The wop car was being tailed by a sprinkler van.
* Someone you once met at a party. The celebrants at the Braddocks' home were real Hollywood bon viveurs who were let loose with the entertainment budget.
* Where you've seen the two dotty hostesses at the 'affair' in the hotel. From TV's *Bewitched*, of course. Alice Ghostley – Mrs Singleton – was Esmerelda, the housekeeper, and Marion Lorne (the elderly Miss de Witt) was Aunt Clara.

Grease

1978 Musical of high school romance and associated traumas in the fifties.

▦ The talent

John Travolta 23, as Danny; one of a brood of six, all actors. Comparatively few subsequent films, none very exciting
Olivia Newton-John 29, as Sandy; success continued on disc through eighties but not in films
Stockard Channing 32, as Rizzo; classy debut in *The Fortune* (1975) and the critics' choice in *Grease*. Pops up on film only occasionally

Robert Stigwood 44, Producer; pop entrepreneur also behind *Hair* on stage and *Jesus Christ Superstar* (1973) on film
Allan Carr 38, Producer; agent to Peter Sellers, Tony Curtis and Ann-Margret
Randal Kleiser 30, Director; from television, including *The Boy in the Plastic Bubble* with Travolta. Moved on to *The Blue Lagoon* (1980) and *Flight of the Navigator* (1986)

▦ The business

Hollywood's biggest money-making musical began as a clever little fifties parody at a Chicago theatre specializing in experimental productions. You can still detect the flavour of the show whenever they slip into the original songs (there are lots – check the credits).

Grease was the creation of unemployed actor Jim Jacobs and bra salesman Warren Casey. It was souped-up by Broadway promoters into one of New York's longest-running musicals. The show had been on for seven years by the time the movie came out.

Theatrical agent Allan Carr bought a film option early in the run. It seemed a natural for the Fonz, but Henry Winkler of TV's *Happy Days* didn't want to use another fifties JD impersonation for his break into films. So how about John Travolta, who had become a TV star in America through his role as Vinnie Barbarino in *Welcome Back Kotter*? He had been signed to a $1,000,000, three-picture deal by rock promoter Robert Stigwood who was branching into movies at what seemed like a good time – this was the first year in thirty that cinema audiences hadn't declined. He had just brought another one of his acts, sixties singing trio The Bee Gees, together with Travolta for *Saturday Night Fever* (1978). Travolta agreed to the new project, which would also include music by Bee Gee Barry Gibb, although he had reservations similar to Winkler's about repeating the role of a working class lout which he had thoroughly explored in *Fever* and *Kotter*.*

Allan Carr met Olivia Newton-John at a party. He was impressed by her sense of humour and thought she might be right for the part of Sandy. Olivia Neutron-Bomb, as she was nicknamed, was then better known for her voice than her wit. She was an

*He had also been in the Broadway version of *Grease* as Doody.

internationally established pop singer who had cracked the American Country music market* and had a wall covered with gold and platinum discs.

Olivia was eager to venture back into films after debuting as part of a naff manufactured group called Toomorrow who appeared in a 1970 film of the same name and instantly disappeared again. She certainly wasn't in *Grease* for the money. Up front she got less than the cost of the press launch.

This opulent affair (held on three sound stages set as school gymnasia, whereas they had shot the film on location) was typical of a production where filming was almost secondary to the immense marketing effort which accompanied it. The budget was $4,000,000 for the movie but another $5,000,000 was spent on hype. In Britain the TV ads alone cost £400,000.

The songs were the promotional shock troops with John Travolta and Olivia Newton-John being propelled together into pop history as the first combo to reach number one with all of their records. 'You're the One That I Want' – by ONJ's producer, and sometime member of the Shadows, John Farrar – was a nine-week number one before the film was released and 'Summer Nights' from the original stageplay was top for seven weeks when it opened. In Britain 'Hopelessly Devoted to You' (also by Farrar) and 'Sandy' (another number written especially for the film) reached number two. 'Grease' – Barry Gibb's contribution, recorded by Frankie Valli – reached number three and even 'Greased Lightnin'', which sounds merely like a poor excuse for a dance routine, got to number eleven.

All were accompanied by clips from the film as videos, providing lashings of 'free media' and priming the public as well for a concomitant fashion blitz. With *Happy Days* bobbing high in the Neilsen ratings plus big audiences for pop's rock-'n'-roll revivalists there were fortunes to be made flogging everything in nifty-fifties fashion and accessories, including the unimaginable *Grease* shampoo.

It all worked. When the film was finally released cinemas were mobbed. The premieres, particularly in London and Chicago, turned into riots. *Grease* earned $96,000,000 in North American rentals, the most successful musical ever. Even poor little Olivia, who started the project with just a measly advance and the proceeds of eight previous mega-hit albums to sustain her, earned an estimated $10,000,000 from a percentage of the profits and the immense record sales.

Despite all this success everyone seems to have fallen out. Carr and Olivia parted with mild acrimony when she refused to do his follow-up, *Can't Stop the Music* (1980) camping it up with The Village People. Carr and Stigwood had to make *Grease II* (1984) without either Olivia or John.

The pair were reunited in 1983 for *Two of a Kind* which Leslie Halliwell dismisses as 'totally unsuccessful'. By then it seemed as if Travolta's star had peaked and Olivia had moved back into records topping the American charts for ten straight weeks in 1981 with 'Physical'.

Carr and Stigwood also parted company, apparently after Robert criticized Allan's dress sense. It was described by one report as the biggest battle of movie queens since Bette Davis and Joan Crawford on the set of *Whatever Happened to Baby Jane?* (1962).

---

*Hence the steel guitar accompaniment to 'Hopelessly Devoted to You', and the greater confidence in her performance any time she is singing.

▦ Behind the screen

The public delirium was accompanied by critical derision, much of it heaped on the young director, Randal Kleiser. It wasn't necessarily his fault as he was not in a typical director's control of the production. He had arrived at a late stage when most of the shots had been mapped out for him in advance by cinematographer Bill Butler* who wanted to make sure of some groundwork to prevent the whole enterprise from falling apart. Kleiser was also subjected to the constant guiding influence of Allan Carr who insisted, for example, on banning soft focus and muted lighting in order to evoke the technicolour look of the fifties. Deprived of using these effects, Kleiser could not adequately disguise what looks like an epidemic of arrested development, producing the most senior crop of high school seniors imaginable. It was also Carr who adapted the script to accommodate ONJ's antipodean lilt.

Kleiser's inexperience was also blamed, and possibly with more justification, for inadequately staging the background and other details. Notice, as the critics did, all the kids lounging about with little to do, and the appalling lip-synch.

Travolta, as well, was said to be under-used by the director to the point where he spends much of the film just looking on. This brief respite may have been just what he needed. John had completed *Saturday Night Fever* only ten days before beginning *Grease* and he was still making occasional appearances on *Welcome Back Kotter*. But in the midst of this apogee in his fortunes was personal tragedy. A few weeks earlier, during *Saturday Night Fever*, his lover Cynthia Hyland had died in his arms from cancer. They had met – he in his early twenties she in her late thirties – while making *The Boy in the Plastic Bubble* (directed by Kleiser).

Travolta was said to channel his sexual drive into his screen charisma but he seems to have directed it elsewhere too. He claimed, in a perhaps unfortunate interview in 1980, that he had slept with all his leading ladies. Olivia denied this both at the time of the film, when there were rumours, and following publication of the interview. She was especially sensitive to suggestions regarding her relationship with Travolta, as you see them flirting on screen, because at the time she was temporarily split from her long-term boyfriend, British entrepreneur Lee Kramer. It seems that the co-stars were good companions, going off horse-riding and the like, but that was about as far as it went.

Whether or not you can sense the inner unhappiness in Travolta's performance by all accounts he was very easy to work with, despite a certain obsessiveness which meant the odd call to the director in the middle of the night to go over which take was best. He fitted in well with the rest of the cast; the John Travolta in *Grease* was still unaffected by the success of the yet-to-be-released *Saturday Night Fever*. He was also in dancing trim. John is a man who likes to eat but he had lost twenty pounds working out for his debut.

Filming went ahead on the first day of the summer vacation at one of the three Los Angeles schools used for the locations. Can you spot how hot they all are? It was well in the nineties as the dancers trooped through their numbers again and again.

Olivia did some training but seems to have found it all a bit of a doddle. She liked being lifted most and, after choreographer Pat Birch was kind enough to say she

*Veteran of many better-looking films including *The Conversation* (1974) and *Jaws* (1975).

John Travolta and Olivia Newton-John: you're the one that I want, uhn uhn uhn

moved well, compared her performance with John to Ginger with Fred. Her fellow hoofers, the cream of an open call in New York and Los Angeles, did not all endorse the comparison.

Aside from this sort of minor, chorus line bitchiness it appears to have been a happy shoot. Stockard Channing, picked in part because she was a client of Carr's, was particularly enthusiastic. She claimed to have learned to relax more on screen and in private through working on the film. Carr and Stigwood vied to spread the more relaxation through the company, treating the enterprise as a continuous party. Travolta got in on the act by purchasing a DC3 and flying a bunch of them to Las Vegas for a weekend.

They were also eager to share the joy of the *Grease* party atmosphere by leaving the sound stage doors open so that the music would blare all over Paramount. At one point it became so deafening that Jack Nicholson, who was making *Goin' South* next door (and was himself eminently qualified to teach the finer points of neighbour disturbing), sent a note requesting them either to put him in the picture or turn down the noise.

▦ The experience

'If white bread could sing, it would sound like Olivia.' Anon

'At times I feel like the 1978 equivalent of Doris Day.' Olivia Newton-John

'In an enterprise that seems to be all mistakes the basic one may be that director Randal Kleiser doesn't know what he is talking about. He has no feel for the times when kids were trying to resolve the contradictions between an inherited style of surviving adolescence and the radically different, new possibilities.' Richard Schikel, *Time*, 19 June 1978 – one of many critics who found that *Grease*, the film, missed the point of Grease, the original

'It's a coarse, graceless production, though there is some fun to be had in watching the nervy attempts of the producers to juggle two moralities for the sake of the family audience: for the adults, that sex is all right if you're in love, and for the adolescents, that sex is all right if you're in love with it.' Ted Whitehead, *The Spectator*, 23 September 1978

▦ Can you spot . . .

* What country you're in. If *Grease* is called *Gummina* you must be in France, *Brilliantino* in Italy and *Vaselina* down Mexico way.
* John's car. At the drive-in it's marked 'John', appropriately in grease, on the back of the jalopy. His character, of course, is called Danny.
* Authentic faces of the fifties. Eve Arden (much appreciated by the critics), Frankie Avalon, Sid Ceaser, Edd Byrnes – Kookie of TV's *77 Sunset Strip* – and a face of the thirties, Joan Blondell.
* Faces of the eighties. Jeff Conaway starred in TV's *Taxi* and Didi Conn was in *Benson*.
* A family connection. The waitress on the left watching the TV is John's older sister Ellen Travolta. Watch her enthusiastic recognition of Danny when the camera picks him up.

A Hard Day's Night

1964 Twenty-four hours in the life of the Fab Four at the height of Beatlemania.

The talent

John Lennon 23; also acted in another, non-Beatles, Lester film: *How I Won the War* (1967)

Paul McCartney 21; has stuck to playing himself in his few films: *Help* (1965), *Let It Be* (1970), *Give my Regards to Broad Street* (1986)

George Harrison 21; became one of Britain's most successful film producers in the seventies and eighties

Ringo Starr 23; hailed as the best Beatle

actor in this film. He went on to make a string of mixed-quality features

Wilfred Brambell 52, as Paul's Grandfather; senior partner in the TV hit *Steptoe and Son*

Walter Shenson 44, Producer; also an American in Britain, also made *Help* with Lester and the Beatles

Richard Lester 32, Director; went on to churn out many financial successes but here he was at his freshest

The business

United Artists were keen to knock off a quick, black-and-white exploitation film of the group so they could market the resulting soundtrack album.

The producer, Walter Shenson, kept the budget tight at £180,000 and Lester had everything shot in a six-and-a-half week window between Beatle commitments. The whole production was at breakneck speed – just a little over three months from shooting the first frame until the premiere.

Before it was even finished the film was in profit from advance sales of the album and with the Beatles at the crest of their popularity was a runaway success in its own right. To date it's taken more than $5,500,000 in North American rentals (thus at least double that worldwide).

It made Shenson a millionaire and the Beatles organization got 30% of the profits but Lester, whose genius helped make the film such a lasting success, only pocketed a modest fee. Later a grateful Shenson gave him a $\frac{1}{2}$% of the profits.

Behind the screen

Richard Lester filmed most of the sequences that open the movie himself, knocking off shots with the Ariflex camera hand-held while his substantial crew looked on.

One of the main difficulties in making the film was that Beatlemania was at its height and any shots done in the open were liable to attract an uncontrollable mob of fans. It meant that they had to go with the first take for almost anything outside.

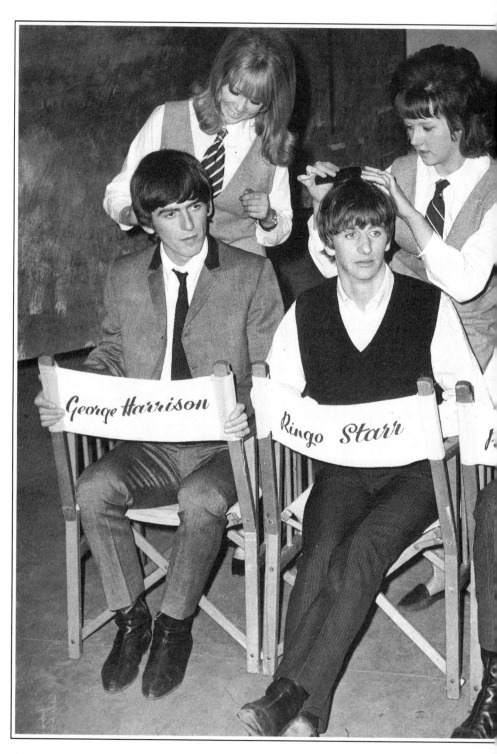

The Beatles plus extras: George meets Patti (left)

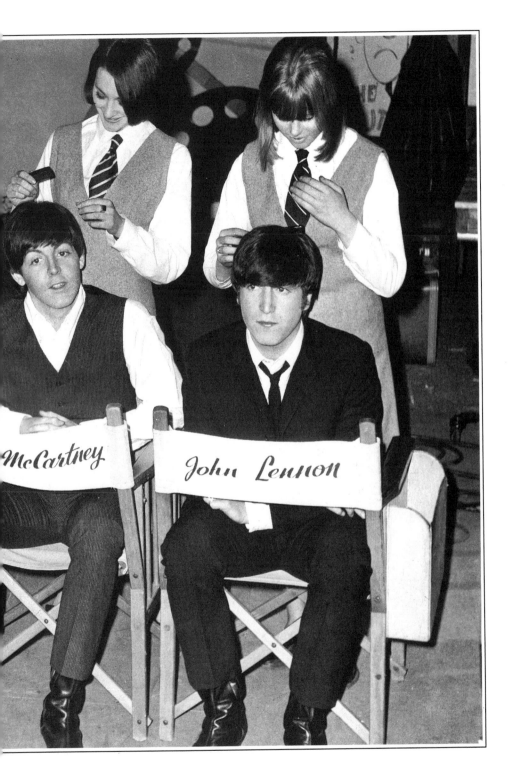

But it was sometimes helpful in casting the film. Lester used some of the fans who were hanging around as extras if they showed any spark. They were given £3 15s a day plus a free lunch but they'd have probably paid Lester for the privilege.

These recruits could be pretty scary. During those first few sequences as the young gods are running from the fan extras through London's Marylebone Station (hired on two consecutive Sundays for the purpose) the Beatles were really quite frightened. Richard Lester's only direction to the fans had been to try and get them. Try they did. George in particular was scared and furious. He shakes his fist at Lester's camera in the shot inside the train as they're pulling out of the station.

And if the paid extras were a menace, what about the ordinary fans? The final concert sequence was filmed in the Scala Cinema in London but the teenies outside sawed through the bars on the windows and streamed in. Lester grabbed his Ariflex and used the tripod to fend them off.

Lester was also doing much of the shooting on the train sequences which follow the opening shots. He didn't use a 'blimp' to house the camera and muffle the sound of its mechanism so that whole section is post-synched, though you'd hardly know it.

Romance rode that train with George. He met his future wife Patti Boyd – then a nineteen-year-old model – during those sequences. She's the blonde in the pair of schoolgirls (called Rita and Jean in the script) that John, Paul and George start eyeing up in the dining car.

George's romance with Patti meant that all four Beatles – despite the over-ready supply of would-be groupies – were fairly well attached around the time of the filming. John was already married to the long-suffering Cynthia, Ringo was to marry childhood sweetheart Maureen Cox in eleven months time and Paul was ensconced at Jane Asher's family's house. George and Patti married in January 1966 but she left him for Eric Clapton in 1974.

One of the winning elements in the film was the witty, natural script by Alun Owen; comparatively little in the film is actually adlibbed (a notable exception being the news conference scene). Owen was suggested as scriptwriter by Paul because he was from Liverpool. To get the idea for the film he joined the Beatles entourage for a weekend's commitments in Dublin. His conclusion: they were the prisoners of their own success, cocooned in hotel rooms by their Merseyside mafia. Their sense of fun and yearning for freedom emerge as the film's central themes.

The Beatles' wit and their sharp delivery of a plethora of one-liners were natural gifts that helped their music conquer the world – but for the film they had some important help from Richard Lester. An American who was a successful television director by the time he was twenty, Lester gave it all up to bum around Europe busking on the guitar and piano. That was one of the things the Beatles liked about him: he could play along with them.

The script is written so that they don't have to remember any long speeches. Lester would point the camera at a Beatle and say the one-liner to him. The Beatle would say it back. If it wasn't right Lester would say it another way and the Beatle would alter the delivery.

For most of the time it was being made the film had no real title – it was just called Beatles Number One. 'A Hard Day's Night' came from John telling the producer about how Ringo was apt to mangle the English language. 'A hard day's night' is Ringo-ese for an all-night recording session. United Artists, who had been hassling for a title so they could promote the film, were unimpressed but Shenson thought it was great and asked John to write a title song.

John called him into the dressing room the next morning and he and Paul played the song, reading the lyrics off the matchbook that John had scribbled them on. It became the group's fifth number one in a row – the second number one from the film (the other was 'Can't Buy Me Love').

The experience

'First shot taken while I was in the ladies' toilet. I have no idea who was in it. I think they were the Beatles but they were wearing the clothing they came in, and not what was supposed to be worn. It was photographed by the director. I trust this is not the way we intend to go on. God help me.' continuity girl Rita Davison's notes from the chase-to-the-train scene that opens the movie

'No matter what I do after this, it's all downhill. No matter what films I make or what service I do for the community, when I die the placard will read "Beatles director in death drama".' Richard Lester, 1971

'A whale of a movie . . .' Bosley Crowther, *New York Times*, 1964, reflecting the almost unanimous critical acclaim

'The Citizen Kane of jukebox movies.' Andrew Sarris, *Village Voice*, 1964

Can you spot . . .

* In the initial running-onto-the-train sequence the Beatles wear different clothing from one shot to another (see continuity girl quote).
* Is Ringo looking a bit peaky in the film? He went down with tonsillitis just after filming was completed. Unknown drummer Jimmy Nicol accompanied the fab three on a world tour and quickly resumed being unknown.
* Some well-known faces as extras: Bob Godfrey, the animator, and TV personality Robin Ray (playing the floor manager) are both in the television studio. Derek Nimmo plays a magician in one sequence. Comedy actor and writer Jeremy Lloyd starts imitating Ringo's dancing at the disco. Lionel Blair plays a dancer – what else?
* And Richard Lester is in a shot walking across the television stage (he's the one in the black corduroy suit).

Henry V

1944 Shakespeare's version of the young king's victory over the French at Agincourt.

The talent

Laurence Olivier 36, as Henry V; film star who had only recently been recognized as a brilliant Shakespearean

Felix Aylmer 55, as the Archbishop of Canterbury; many character parts into the sixties including Polonius in Olivier's *Hamlet* (1948)

Leslie Banks 54, as the Chorus; Oxford educated theatrical who became minor star of the thirties after his debut in *King Kong* precursor *The Most Dangerous Game* (1932)

Robert Newton 39, as Pistol; unique British character actor. Bill Sykes in *Oliver Twist* (1948) and arrh, Jim lad, the classic Long John Silver in *Treasure Island* (1950)

Harcourt Williams 64, as Charles VI;

another Olivier stage crony. Head of the travelling players in *Hamlet*

Max Adrian 42, as the Dauphin; stage and revue star. Returned to character parts in films in the sixties and early seventies

Esmond Knight 38, as Fluellen; Londoner fighting back to work after being blinded in 1941 on Naval service against the *Bismark*

Renee Asherson 24, as Princess Katherine; a few more films into the early fifties, when she married Robert Donat

Laurence Olivier Producer/Director; Oscar-winning *Hamlet*, and *Richard III* (1956), amongst other screen Shakespearean ventures

The business

Henry V must be the most successful film ever to sink a production company. The company in question was Two Cities, founded in the thirties by an Italian immigrant to Britain, Filippo del Giudice.

Four months' internment at the beginning of the War didn't dampen del Giudice's loyalty to his adopted country and he dedicated himself to the propaganda effort. He persuaded Noel Coward to make *In Which We Serve* (1942) and courted the services of Olivier after hearing him on radio entertaining the troops with the great speeches from Hank Cinque. Del Giudice had himself been pointed to this most bullish of Shakespeare plays by a man from the Ministry of Information, Dallas Bower.

Olivier demanded full control as producer. After the likes of William Wyler, Carol Reed and Terence Young declined the invitation he decided to direct it as well. But wisely cautious of setting himself up entirely as a one-man-band on this, his first venture into film production, Olivier retained the services of Bower, who normally worked for the BBC, as Associate Producer. The Ministry of Information tie-in helped secure the release from active service of the cream of technicians and younger stars. Many of the cast were Olivier's illustrious stage colleagues, mingled with some of the best-known entertainers of the day – music-hall giant George Robey as Falstaff and ballet star Robert Helpmann as the Bishop of Ely, for example.

One important player was missing. Olivier cast his wife, Vivien Leigh, to play Katherine but her *Gone With the Wind* (1939) mentor David Selznick wouldn't release her to play what he considered to be a minor role. Renee Asherson filled her shoes admirably – and exactly: she was picked partly because she was just Vivien's size and the costumes had already been made.

Once filming had started Olivier's chief collaborator was Reginald Beck, who helped plot the camera movement, edited the footage and directed the shots you see Olivier in. It is perhaps his editor's eye and planning that kept the shooting ratio to 1.25:1 – the Hollywood standard is more like 15:1.

But that's about as far as the economy went. Olivier's entire budget from del Giudice was £300,000 but £80,000 went on the first scenes to be shot, the Battle of Agincourt. Del Giudice's main financial backer took this as a cue to pull out, which might have scuppered the project had J. Arthur Rank not come to the rescue – at a price. That price was Two Cities, which became a Rank subsidiary. Del Giudice later retired from films and went into a monastery.

Olivier continued on *Henry V* as he had started, going hugely over the budget that Rank, too, had wanted to keep to £300,000. The final cost was £476,000 – of which the cast got a collective £65,000, less than was spent on costumes. In fact a quarter of that wages bill must have gone to the 650 Irish soldiers and farmers who were the extras in the battle scenes. They were on £3 10s a week with a £2 bonus if they brought their own horse.

Rank was able to recoup this in Britain alone. The critics were keen from the start and soon the public discovered that here was an approachable Shakespeare film with visual excitement, emotion, humour and a patriotic message which, though released too late to rouse the nation through D Day, fitted the end-of-wartime spirit. Receipts were helped as well by the state in the form of huge parties of school children.

Henry V was big box office beyond this Sceptred Isle; especially in America where takings exceeded $2,000,000. Olivier's credits for the script, production, direction and acting gave him the reputation of a new Orson Welles and he was awarded a special Oscar. More Academy Awards – for Best Film and Best Actor – came for Olivier's next venture into movie Shakespeare, *Hamlet*. And in 1989 Kenneth Branagh dared to attempt a little touch of Larry, starring in and directing a new filmed version of the play. Lord Olivier just missed the opportunity to compare it for himself. He died a few months before *Henry V* II was completed.

▦ Behind the screen

The battle scenes are a thrill to watch but were a pain to shoot, a fair measure of it suffered by Laurence Olivier.

In part he brought it on himself. It was June 1943 and they were filming in neutral Eire, chosen because able-bodied male extras were plentiful and low-flying planes were few. Olivier drew on his experience as an officer in the Fleet Air Arm and now, as commander of a regiment of extras, actors and technicians he resolved to lead from the front.

As they approached the battle scene stunts he announced to the company that he wouldn't ask anyone to do something he wouldn't do himself. The prudent Irish took him at his word. The literal crunch came when he was called on to demonstrate the ease with which the English soldiers could drop in ambush from trees onto the French knights. It took all his immense thespian powers to make the drop look straightforward, and disguise spraining his ankle.

Knight mares

Worse was to come. He was lining up the shot where one of the French who is sacking the English camp leans off his horse close to the lens. The nag collided with the heavy Technicolor rig which in turn split Olivier's lip, marking the actor for life. Can you spot the scar through the make-up in the close-ups during the fireside soliloquy? He tended to mask it with a moustache in later life.

They were in Ireland for thirty-nine days and it rained for at least two weeks of that. When there *was* sun it would mostly dodge between those mischievous little clouds you can see in most shots. The only compensation was acres of mud to fight in and puddles galore for arty reflection shots.

The spectacular charge of the French Knights* was filmed in a field on the estate of Lord Powerscourt in Enniskerry near Dublin. It had a road on one side where a half-mile track was laid to carry the camera. The knights were drilled for ten days to keep in line and the archers were taught how to launch their papiermaché, felt-tipped shafts with conviction. Not all of them got the message. In particular can you spot the pathetic arrow that goes nowhere as the English tactical retreat lures the French horsemen under the trees?

Audiences at the time were particularly struck (as indeed were the French knights) by the flight of arrows. It is actually a drawing being reduced optically accompanied by the multi-dubbed whoosh of a willow switch. Also very impressive to audiences accustomed to the privations of war was how colourful and grand it all was.

*Spectacular and derivative, according to film buffs. Next time you're settling down to Eisenstein's *Alexander Nevsky* (1938) compare Olivier's Agincourt with the charge of the Teutonic knights across frozen Lake Peipus.

The lush costumes were pieced together from bits gathered by designer Roger Furse, one of the key talents Dallas Bower had been able to wangle away from more conventional war service. The painted-on embroidery is the most obvious case of making do. Less apparent onscreen is the scarcity of theatrical chain mail. Instead Furse improvised with knitted twine sprayed with aluminium. Gaps and imperfections were masked as much as possible with banners and pennants but fortunately there was no rationing on good scholarship – the motifs you see were the ones at Agincourt.

Colour was a rare luxury in a wartime British film. It was said that one of Olivier's chief concerns when he got nutted by the Technicolor camera was that his face hadn't damaged the only such piece of equipment in the whole of the British Isles. The process's appetite for light demanded every lamp they could muster and thus relighting for every different shot you see. This may have influenced Olivier's theatrically-derived use of long takes, and certainly contributed to the whopping thirteen-month schedule.

They began by shooting the climax and ended by filming the models: the ships and the representation of London as it appeared to the seventeenth-century map maker J. C. Visscher, which opens the film. This was 3,500 square feet of wood and plaster tinkered together over several months in the workshops at Rank Studios in Denham.

A Standard model-maker's technique for enhancing the illusion is to speed up the camera so that when played back normally the movement of small things seems laboured and massive. But the Technicolor motor had only one speed so they had to slow up the models themselves, using especially heavy smoke from the tiny chimneys and the thickest oil for Old Father Thames. The shots of Henry's flotilla relied on the skill of the puppeteers, and the allowances that the audience would be making in view of the production's stylized design.

The problem in presenting Shakespeare on screen had always been the translation of Renaissance theatre to the more naturalistic medium of film. A key to *Henry V*'s popularity, beyond the obvious appeal to contemporary fighting patriotism, was Olivier's successful gimmick of transitions of setting.

The mainly comic preliminaries at the Globe Theatre served to tidy away fiddly plot details and accustom the twentieth-century ear to the seventeenth-century verse, while retaining interest with the documentary re-creation of an Elizabethan day out. It also got over the awkwardness of conveying the Chorus as a Renaissance voice-over announcer.

The Globe scenes caused some difficulties, mainly because of the extras. This was Denham, not Eire, and able-bodied men who were free to lounge around a film set were rare and somewhat suspect. The audience, apart from the especially demobbed leading actors, was reputedly either Britons who were deemed unfit for the forces or Commonwealth deserters.

They proved a surly lot and largely unresponsive until it came to the King's defiant rebuttal of the Dauphin's insulting gift of tennis balls.

In the first take Olivier misquoted, 'When we have matched our rackets to *his* balls . . .' and the whole audience broke up.

Olivier was furious. On the retake he corrected the 'his' to 'these' playing the standing flourish for all its worth to shock any visions of the Dauphin's wedding tackle from the mob. You can see they were also tickled by Felix Aylmer's Archbishop of Canterbury casting aspersions on the morals of German women, as he holds forth on Salic Law.

The medieval backdrops which dominate most of the scenes that follow were actually from an art magazine, a feature in the April–July 1940 issue of *Verve*. That was the only way that the film-makers could get at a fifteenth-century manuscript, *Les Très Riches Heures du Duc de Berri*, at the Conde Museum in occupied Chantilly. The idea was to present the image of the historical period as normally illustrated and Olivier must have felt some debt to the man who commissioned the masterpiece because he added the character of Duc de Berri as Ambassador, played by Ernest Thesiger, where none exists in the original play.*

Committing all this to film was cinematographer Robert Krasker, famous for his monochrome work** but then a newcomer to colour. He broke the rules of colour cinematography in several instances, consequently breaking new ground, particularly in the way he shot the 'little touch of Harry' sequences and the English marching by the stream to their encampment on eve of battle.

Krasker understood the point of using the *Très Riches Heures* designs even less than he understood colour. Each time he was presented with a new set, he would shrug and comment, 'Looks terribly phoney'.

---

*Neither does Falstaff's death with the King's voiced-over parting put-down. Olivier transplanted this fragment from the end of *Henry IV Part 2*.
**He also shot *Brief Encounter* (1945) and *The Third Man* (1949).

▦ The Experience

'The movies have produced one of their rare great works of art.' *Time*, 8 May 1946

'A great play has been made into a great film and Shakespeare has survived the transition.' *The Times*, 23 November 1944

'This is a production finely felt and finely played in which there is movement for the eye to glance at in the great speeches but not so much as to blur appreciation of their delivery.' Dylis Powell, *The Sunday Times*, 26 November 1944

'Of all my films I'm fondest of *Henry V* because in its time it was such an adventure.' Laurence Olivier, 27 January 1970

▦ Can you spot . . .

* Arthur Daley. British viewers may recognize the youthful George Cole playing the boy. He was nineteen. And in his mid-forties – just the age for *Dad's Army* – John Laurie as Captain Jamie.

* Leo Genn's worst moment. No, because of Olivier's tact and skill as a director. It was just before the shot where his character, the Constable of France, is introduced in the tableau along with the rest of the degenerate French royal circle. This was his first time on a film set for some years because of war service and he was very nervous. Olivier walked past him and taking Genn's chin in his hand straightened his jaw. Genn said this simple physical note from the director gave him the poise and confidence you can see on the screen.

* A dodgy dissolve. What went wrong just before the 'Into the Breach' speech?

* How they cut the original down by half. Olivier, Reginald Beck and Shakespearean scholar Arthur Dent chipped away hundreds of stray lines and passages spottable only by constant reference to the original text. The comic subplots that ease you between the Globe and France are very much trimmed once the action starts. Notice the way Bardolph, Nym and the Boy suddenly drop out of the proceedings. Their crimes and come-uppances were edited out as was an exchange of gloves and challenges which rounds out the debate between the cheeky commoner at the fireside and the incognito sovereign. Liberal cosmetic surgery has smoothed Henry into a hero entirely acceptable to twentieth-century sentiments with much of the Elizabethan bloodlust and the worst references to the French removed. And in the U.S. you're saved hearing such Shakespearean terms as 'damn' and 'bastard'.

* Olivier's way of filming the great speeches. He believed that the normal Hollywood formula of starting in long shot and moving to climax in close-up was wrong for Shakespeare. At the peak of any of Henry's great rallying cries he would want to belt it out, not feel the restriction of tight framing. You can spot that this is the way he did all the big scenes and that aside from a lot of camera moves to contain substantial sections in one theatrical shot he kept his camerawork plain. Olivier felt that you only needed to use fancy camerawork to enhance a weak script.

* A change of horse in mid battle. Because he was unsure of Leo Genn's equestrian prowess, as a safety measure Olivier switched horses for the fight sequence – from his usual matinee-idol thoroughbred, Blaunche Kyng, to a streetwise polo pony.

* The sex of the horses. The film was shown to a bunch of Oxford scholars to test their reaction to the textual cuts and the presentation. The only remotely adverse comment came from one learned lady who pointed out that the horses should all have been stallions.

High Noon

1952 Marshal Will Kane has to face alone a gang of criminals after the town desert him.

▦ The talent

Gary Cooper 50, as Marshal Will Kane; former cartoonist, son of a senior Montana judge, Hollywood Western idol, here ensuring more good films in his last decade
Grace Kelly 22, as Amy Kane; Philadelphia princess whose beauty won a meteoric film career and, five years after *High Noon*, Prince Rainier of Monaco
Thomas Mitchell 59, as Jonas Henderson; familiar Western character with memorable parts in several great films including *Stagecoach* (1939) and *Gone With the Wind* (1939)
Lloyd Bridges 38, as Harvey Pell; TV star and father of a brood of actors, he returned

to prominence spoofing his customary heroic roles in *Airplane!* (1980)
Katy Jurado 24, as Helen Ramirez; Mexican ex-Hollywood correspondent also in Brando's *One-Eyed Jacks* (1961). Later Mrs Ernest Borgnine
Stanley Kramer 38, Producer; many further interesting films as diverse as *It's a Mad, Mad, Mad, Mad World* (1963) and *Guess Who's Coming to Dinner* (1967)
Fred Zinnemann 45, Director; Austrian cinema craftsman who won Oscars for *From Here to Eternity* (1953) and *A Man For All Seasons* (1966)

▦ The business

Stanley Kramer was a pioneer of independent production, normally bringing his films in at a thrifty $1,000,000 or less. Gary Cooper had been one of Hollywood's biggest stars for more than twenty years and his normal price could have been a quarter of that. But he noticed that other stars around him were going in for a new fee structure which gave them fresh opportunities and sometimes even more cash than they would have normally made. They would take an almost token payment before shooting and make their real money from a percentage of the profits.

Another reason for Cooper's approachability was that he seemed to be on the slide, slipping out of the top ten for the first time in a decade. Indeed, he was well down the list of those considered for the part of Will Kane but, according to Cooper biographer Stuart Kaminsky, the lettuce magnate financing the film was a fan. He stipulated that either they use Cooper or he would withdraw the green stuff. Cooper took a modest $60,000 in advance and a percentage. The budget for the rest of the company totalled a thoroughly abashed $35,000.

High Noon was a big hit with public and critics alike, winning four Oscars, including Best Actor for Cooper.* This second Academy Award bounced Coop right back up the charts where he stayed for another five years.

The rest of the company had more mixed fortunes. Kramer says that the film grossed $18,000,000 but nevertheless the following year he was forced to throw in his lot with Columbia pictures. Writer Carl Foreman was one of the victims of the

---

*The other Academy Awards went for Editing, the Score and the song, 'Do Not Forsake Me'.

McCarthy witch hunts. His script for *High Noon* was seen as an allegory for Hollywood's relationship with the investigations.*

It was his last work for a while. Directly afterwards he was shunned by the industry in general and dropped by Kramer and Cooper who stopped doing business with him. Carl took shelter in Britain until the seventies during which time he wrote *The Bridge on the River Kwai* (1957) and *The Guns of Navarone* (1961).

Aside from Coop the only other well-known cast member was Thomas Mitchell. Great things were expected of the female lead, Katy Jurado, but during filming the attention of the director, Fred Zinnemann, shifted to a prim young stage actress who had attended his audition wearing white gloves. Grace Kelly attracted no critical praise from the film and was herself displeased with her $750-a-week performance but she went on to become one of the most memorable of Hollywood's fifties stars.

▓ Behind the screen

These were difficult times for Gary Cooper. You can see it in his face and his walk – and Fred Zinnemann used it to good effect in making this such a powerful film.

One problem was Cooper's health. He had just undergone a hernia operation and was soon to need another. It made his fight with Lloyd Bridges particularly painful, although he never caused any delay in filming. Audiences accustomed to dashing leading men were impressed at the time by his realistically battered portrayal of a worried Will Kane. In fact his expression of anxiety was partly drawn from another nagging pain, a duodenal ulcer which had to be removed three months after filming.

His private life was enough to make anyone wince. His eighteen-year-old marriage to Rocky was . . . you guessed it. They had recently separated and she had been seen in public with other men. Not that Cooper had reason to complain; he was at the time in the fourth year of a relationship with Patricia Neal. To make things even more complicated it seems that Cooper had a fling with Grace Kelly during filming though *she* at the same time was in the midst of a long affair with actor Gene Lyons.**

Meanwhile back at the set, Katy Jurado was jealous of what she saw as Fred Zinnemann's excessive attentions to Grace Kelly. This, at least, seems only to have been professional jealousy, at the close-ups the director was lavishing on the young beauty.

Even if one couldn't say the same for the relationships, filming went smoothly in a tight thirty-two days during the autumn of 1951. The extent and exact timing of the post-production surgery that followed depends on who you believe. Carl Foreman, for one, held that tales that have emerged of a radical re-edit merely slandered Zinnemann's original direction.

The other version is that all concerned were quietly confident on the way to the previews, but their *oeuvre* was greeted with yawns. Apparently the song by Dmitri Tiomkin and Ned Washington was composed and added at a late stage along with the concept of real-time base. Film editor, Elmo Williams claimed that *High Noon* was then completely overhauled with out-takes of Coop looking particularly rough included and much of Grace Kelly's rougher acting removed (imagine).

---

*John Wayne was particularly disgusted at the sheriff flicking away his badge at the end (cf. *Dirty Harry* (1971)). His *Rio Bravo* (1958), directed by Howard Hawks, is said to be a rejoinder.
**Neal soon left to marry Roald Dahl. Cooper stayed with Rocky and Lyons never made it beyond Commissioner Randall in TV's *Ironside*.

▦ The experience

'Surely the most perfect Western ever made.' Alexander Walker, *Evening Standard*, 3 April 1986

'The atmosphere of violence is clothed in a kind of drawling, easy-going foreboding.' Hollis Alpert, *Saturday Review*, 5 July 1952

'Gary Cooper was the personification of the honour-bound man. He was in himself a very noble figure, very humble at the same time, and very inarticulate. And very unsure of himself.' Fred Zinnemann

'Looks like she could be a cold dish with a man until you get her pants down and then she'd explode.' Gary Cooper on Grace Kelly (commenting on, that is)

'I loved every minute of it except when the wife was on the screen. I just wasn't in the same class with the rest.' Grace Kelly

▦ Can you spot . . .

* How a real time Western which runs eighty-four minutes covers over ninety (the narrative-proper starts with the wedding at 10.30 and finishes just after high 12.00). We lose a minute here and there with a sizeable chunk going when Kane makes his abortive escape from the town. On the other hand it seems to be 11.20 for ages.

* The critics' favourite shot. It's the crane close-up that starts with the Marshal and pans up to show the empty streets and him alone – and some telephone poles making an early appearance that far west in 1888.

* An old line. Gary Cooper's first words in *High Noon* were the same as in his debut in *Shopworn Angel* (1928).

* The scenery. No, this is a Western with no Fordian panoramic backdrop. Cinematographer Floyd Crosby studied Civil War photos and wanted to recreate their feeling of a burnt-out sky. It was shot near Sonora, due east a ways from San Francisco.

* The son of a thousand faces. Lon Chaney Jnr plays Martin Howe. And *The Good, the Bad and the Ugly* (1968) star Lee van Cleef is Jack Colby.

* A second star. When Kane dispenses with his badge of office at the end isn't there a second star half buried in the sand behind his foot?

Grace Kelly, Katy Jurado and Fred Zinnemann: look who's getting all the attention

High Society

1956 On the eve of her wedding a socialite is torn between three suitors.

▦ The talent

Grace Kelly 27, as Tracy Lord; enjoying her last Hollywood outing
Bing Crosby 51, as C. K. Dexter-Haven; the world's favourite singer in his last screen success
Frank Sinatra 40, as Mike Connor; the world's other favourite singer, then securely entrenched on a new wave of song and screen popularity after rough times in the early fifties
Celeste Holm 36, as Liz Imbrie; an Oscar for *Gentleman's Agreement* (1947) and nominated for *All About Eve* (1950). From the sixties, more often on TV
Louis Armstrong 55, as Himself; jazz great whose film appearances span thirty-three years until his memorable rendition of the *Hello Dolly* (1969) theme
Sol C. Siegel 53, Producer; soon to become Head of Production at MGM, he had already produced many interesting films including *I Was a Male War Bride* (1949) and *Gentlemen Prefer Blondes* (1952)
Charles Walters 44, Director; former dancer, and choreographer of *Meet Me in St Louis* (1944)

▦ The business

This was Siegel's first movie for MGM after a movie from Fox and he scored something of a coup getting together three of the brightest stars of the day and persuading Cole Porter to turn out his first batch of film songs for eight years.*

For Sinatra it was a chance to appear with his idol** and make $250,000 on the side. For Bing it was an opportunity to renew an old acquaintance with Grace Kelly and collect $200,000 plus about the same again as a percentage of the gross. And as for Grace herself, this was just part of her MGM contract which brought her upwards of $1,000 a week plus bonuses. Other, personal, business was more on her mind at the time. This was to be the last of Grace's eleven films. One month before filming *High Society* she became engaged to Prince Rainier of Monaco. They married a month after the production finished. She still had four years of her MGM contract to come but had made it clear she would not be fulfilling it.

How did the studio take this breach and the departure of a star who had been number two in the popularity ratings the previous year? With sensible equanimity. They were benefiting from priceless publicity which could only bode well for the two Grace Kelly pictures still to be released, *The Swan* (1956) and *High Society*. Dore Schary, the head of production, waived her contract (which continued to be paid for several weeks after she was married) and threw in all Tracy Lord's wardrobe as well.

---

*Siegel's powers of persuasion extended, in Porter's case, to an offer of $250,000.
**They had sung together on TV – on Bing's first show – and Crosby made a brief appearance again in Sinatra's *Robin and the Seven Hoods* (1964).

The critics preferred *The Philadelphia Story* (1940) with Katherine Hepburn, Cary Grant and James Stewart based on the same play by Philip Barry. But they loved the songs, particularly the Crosby-Sinatra duet and 'Now You Has Jazz'.

The public loved it all. *High Society* cost about $1,500,000 to make but returned $5,800,000 in North America alone. The duet 'True Love' between Grace Kelly and Bing Crosby was a million-seller. It was Bing's twentieth gold disc, Grace's one and only. The award hung proudly in her palace at Monte Carlo. Even the royalties were regal; her share was $50,000.

▦ Behind the screen

It was never true love between Bing and Grace but they did have an affair; not while making *High Society* but rather during Grace's more flighty stage, before her whirlwind royal romance. Their trysts were reportedly at Alan Ladd's place in 1952 – at the time when Bing's first wife, Trixie, was dying of cancer. The romance didn't last but it was apparently rekindled a couple of years later when they were co-starring in *The Country Girl* (1954).

As they began filming *High Society* it all became rather embarrassing – and in a way echoed the film's plot. Somehow Grace's mother back in Philadelphia* had been persuaded to give a very intimate account of her daughter's past, including allusions to her relationship with Crosby, in an interview with the Hearst newspapers. It had just been syndicated. To make matters worse Prince Rainier visited the set on the day she filmed the snuggling duet with old fling Bing. There was an awkward lunch afterwards where Dore Schary was rude about the size of Rainier's principality. The film was banned in Monaco. Rainier explained that it 'wasn't quite the thing'.

While Grace was all fixed up her two co-stars, Sinatra and Crosby, had more open-ended love lines. Sinatra had to endure news stories about the wild times of his estranged wife, Ava Gardner. Crosby and Kathryn Grant, the starlet he had been dating since 1953, were having a protracted dither about whether to tie the knot. The Crosbys finally married and the Sinatras finally divorced the following year.

This was accounted by all a very happy five weeks of filming with Charlie Walters swearing like a trooper and everyone enjoying themselves. Crosby had an easy rapport with Sinatra similar to the one he enjoyed with Bob Hope. Apparently Crosby's nickname on set was Nembutal – Sinatra's was Dexedrine.

There was an initial reserve towards Grace Kelly from the company because of her impending royal status, but the ice was broken by ice. Grace asked if she could wear her own engagement ring in the film. Director Walters joked that they would have to see if it was good enough. She then displayed the stone** which Celeste Holm described as the size of a skating rink. When everyone oohed and ahhed Grace said 'It is sweet, isn't it', and was teased happily for the rest of the production.

Grace Kelly was praised for a comedy flair not previously displayed. After the initial traumas she relaxed more than ever before into what she knew would be her last role. Wouldn't she miss it? No, she was said to be disillusioned with the gossip of

---

*Grace, the daughter of a wealthy industrialist was type-cast for *The Philadelphia Story*. The reason *High Society's* location was moved to Newport – home of the jazz festival – was, of course, to allow Satchmo and his musical numbers to trickle into the story.

**Most clearly appraised when she crosses her fingers behind her head after promising to behave with the reporters, and when she examines it herself on the sofa whilst sobering up.

Bing Crosby and Grace Kelly: didn't we meet at Alan Ladd's?

Hollywood and to have achieved all that was possible, although there were plans for a film with Hitchcock in the early sixties which never came off.

Later Grace confided to Gore Vidal what may have been the main reason she was pleased to quit while ahead. She looks as lovely as ever in *High Society* but that's after spending longer than ever before in make-up. Her call time had been put back from eight in the morning to seven-thirty. Grace noticed that Joan Crawford's call was at five, Loretta Young's at four. It was time to get out before the days got longer.

The experience

The critics fancied Grace but preferred *The Philadelphia Story.*

'*High Society* is simply not Top Drawer.' *Time*, 6 August 1956

'A dispirited re-hash of the earlier movie with practically all of its charm gone and with its cast seemingly aware of the fact. The principals perform, most of the time, with a kind of glum cheeriness.' Hollis Alpert, *Saturday Review*, 11 August 1956

'*High Society* is not the zippiest musical I have seen. Often it strikes a falling note and breaks awkwardly into tune. But it is certainly one of the zaniest due, incredibly, to the melting enchantment of that cool beauty Grace Kelly.' Edward Goring, *Daily Mail*, 14 December 1956

Can you spot ...

* Who is singing Grace Kelly's part in 'True Love'. She is. They wanted to replace her but she had been taking singing lessons for months and insisted. She did fine.
* A civil rights breakthrough. This was apparently the first time that black people came to the front door. Louis Armstrong and his band had just completed a highly successful tour of Europe which had included gigs behind the Iron Curtain – hence Bing's reference to it at the opening of the film.
* Frank Sinatra in a droll role. He was renowned for his antipathy to the press and in one celebrated incident had punched a press agent who asked him if a certain 'broad' was with him. The broad in question was Judy Garland. (And the answer was no.)
* Who's learning to fly. The aerial footage of Newport that opens the picture is as shaky as you get.

It Happened One Night

1934 An heiress escaping the threat from her father to annul her recent marriage is helped by a brash journalist.

▦ The talent

Clark Gable 32, as Peter Warne; hitting his peak star decade
Claudette Colbert 27, as Ellie Andrews; French-born melodrama star – DeMille's Cleopatra the same year – finding a new niche in comedy
Walter Connolly 46, as Alexander Andrews; one of many memorable character appearances near the end of a distinguished acting career

Roscoe Karns 38, as Mr Shapely; another character favourite who popped up in pictures from the silent days to the mid-sixties
Alan Hale 39, as Danker; jolly screen fixture, most memorable as Little John. Lookalike son carries on the tradition
Frank Capra 37, Producer/Director; the first of three Oscar winners in five years

▦ The business

To start with no one was very keen. The two stars were assigned to the film as punishment, the studio had it pegged as a loser ('bus movies are dead') and when it was first released the critics were largely unimpressed.

It was the public that had the good taste. They loved *It Happened One Night*, came to see it time and again, told their friends about it. The film's success saved Colbert's career and helped consolidate Gable's ascent to screen royalty. And for a minor studio and its star director, Frank Capra, it meant a foothold in the major league. Then barely ten years old Harry Cohn's Columbia was a minnow compared with big fish like Colbert's home studio Paramount or Gable's MGM. Lending the talent out to the down-market newcomer was a way of keeping the stars in line.

Clark Gable was then a contract player at MGM on a healthy $2,500 a week but he had been unhappy on his previous picture, *Dancing Lady* (1933), and the studio suspected him of trying to dodge returning for some retakes, so they decided to pack him off for a spell in filmland's Siberia. He took this rap on the knuckles pretty sorely and was drunk for several days. But as it turned out, aside from the awards and acclaim, *It Happened One Night*'s success practically doubled his income in the next year to more than $200,000.

Paramount were equally eager to be shot of Claudette Colbert for a while. It looked as if her popularity was sagging and they were fed up with her headstrong, difficult attitude. But it was Claudette Colbert, the spitfire, that made Capra want to offer her the female lead in *It Happened One Night*. That and the fact that practically everyone else who was at all suitable in Hollywood had already turned down the role. Capra had directed Colbert's first film, *For the Love of Mike* (1927). It was an unhappy experience and the resentment she harboured must have transmitted itself to her dog, who bit Capra's bum when he came to her house for a parley. Anyway she was about to go off for a holiday with friends so to get rid of him she demanded $50,000 – twice her normal fee - and an impossibly rushed four-week shooting schedule which would enable her to join her friends for Christmas. Capra told her to start the next week.

The stars' fees meant that the $325,000 budget was as tight as the shooting schedule but the film was completed in time for Colbert's Christmas holidays – partly thanks to the crew working through the night.

When Gable went on a nationwide promotional tour he got his first taste of the sort of treatment we associate nowadays with pop stars. He was mobbed by fans who stole his handkerchiefs, cufflinks and anything else they could remove from his person for souvenirs – and those were just the shy ones! At least one female fan offered her bra for him to autograph and by all accounts numerous others offered much more besides.

The fashion spin-offs from the film are well known. Every visible Gable touch was mimicked: the pipe, the trenchcoat with the tied belt and rest of his get-up. And it was a famous black day for the underwear industry when Gable revealed a bare chest during his dissertation on how a man gets ready for bed.*

But mostly there were winners. The film industry, quick to a good thing, continued the successful vein of so-called screwball comedies and the writers of *The Daring Young Man on the Flying Trapeze* found they had a hit on their hands. Even the bus companies benefited. They noted a markedly increased trade from single young ladies – all hoping, no doubt, to find themselves sitting next to that Mr Right without a vest.

Popular acclaim, however, is no guarantee of film industry respect; the test would be the 1935 Oscars. Claudette Colbert wasn't even going to attend the awards. Always apparently just off somewhere she had a train to catch for the east coast. Friends persuaded the railway company to hold the express for ninety minutes and got her to the ceremony in time to collect her Oscar along with Gable and Capra. In her acceptance speech she had the grace to say she owed it all to the director. It was another forty years before another film, *One Flew Over the Cuckoo's Nest* (1975), was able to match the record of Best Picture, Actor, Actress, Director and Screenplay.

▦ Behind the screen

It didn't bode well. Gable was still drunk and pretty abusive when he had his first meeting with Capra but even at that comparatively early stage of his career he was not an asset to be turned down by the director.

Judge for yourself whether he looks a bit rough around the edges. MGM reckoned he had been malingering but it seems that Gable really had been quite ill and had lost a lot of weight during nine weeks in hospital where his tonsils and appendix were removed. He was also having recurring trouble with his teeth.

---

*Capra claims the effect of the absence of undershirt was unforeseen and unavoidable. It seems that the removal of a vest is incompatible with screen dash and if Gable had left it on he would not have seemed a sufficient sexual threat to carry off the scene.

Clark Gable and Claudette Colbert: the worst picture we've ever been in

Then, of course, there was marital turmoil. Gable was about to leave his second wife, Ria Langham, and had just met Carole Lombard who was to be his third wife and greatest love. He left Ria the following year and started dating Carole.

Nevertheless Gable soon unwound and began enjoying the first comedy role of his career. He delayed the tight shooting schedule again and again by breaking up during scenes that only showed their full funny side when actually played. He had a few jokes of his own, as well. Displaying his typical sophisticated sense of fun he hid a hammer down his trousers for one setup and then drew Colbert close. Her startled scream and his ensuing laughing fit meant that Capra had to call an extra break.

Claudette Colbert probably needed a laugh. Her career was in the doldrums, her five-year-old marriage to actor/director Norman Foster was on the rocks – and she was having sinus trouble. But things were just about to look up. She killed the last two birds with one stone, divorcing her husband soon after the film and wedding the man who was treating her sinuses, Dr Joel Pressman. They were together until his death thirty-five years later. Her career ceased to be a problem as well. The success of *It Happened One Night* gave it the boost of a lifetime, leading to a string of fashionable comedy roles through the thirties. She was a star for at least the next twenty years.

But no one knew what a winner they were working on at the time and Colbert continued to spar with Capra about the filming. In an autobiography written more than thirty years later, Capra described her through clenched typewriter as 'a tartar, but a cute one'. For one thing she refused to cooperate in one of the most memorable scenes, where she shows a leg to hitch a ride. Capra just shrugged and called for a stand-in to do the close-up, which had exactly the desired effect. Colbert took one look and shouted 'Get her out of here. That's not *my* leg!'

She also refused to take off any clothes on screen, which meant that Capra got what he considered a far more sexy effect. Instead her character modestly undressed behind the Wall of Jericho, draping it with her undies.

All along Colbert complained about the speed of the shoot, at how slap-happy it all was, though this was in part due to her own insistence on dashing off for Christmas.

In fact *It Happened One Night* is filled with ad-libs, even if there are not as many as the public believed. So natural was the impression created on film, that the piggy-back across the stream, the hitch-hiking scene and the Man on the Flying Trapeze sing-along were all widely rumoured to be spontaneous.

In fact the sing-along just about qualifies. Capra had simply planned for there to be a bridging number from two hillbilly singers but during the set-ups he noticed that the rest of the extras were joining in. So he ordered more cameras and shot almost all of it in one with the passengers contributing solo verses and the two stars' reactions as they happened. You can see how he covered the close-ups and the master shot almost like a multi-camera TV production, and a couple of very tentative pans. The extra equipment meant even less room than normal for manoeuvre in the real bus they were forced to use in those days before the widespread use of cut-away sets. Even the actor playing the irascible driver joined in and so provided Capra with the perfect plot device of running the bus off the road.

It was *all* just about perfect, not that a drained Capra – nor anyone else – realized it. When Colbert finally joined her friends for that belated holiday her only comment was 'Am I glad to get here. I've just finished the worst picture in the world.'

▦ The experience

'A film about the making of *It Happened One Night* would have been much funnier than the picture itself.' Frank Capra

'I was brought into the motion picture business as a heavy but I knew I had to play *It Happened One Night* cool and relaxed. And that's exactly how I went about it.' Clark Gable

'What I believe is that he was playing himself, and maybe for the only time in his career. That clowning, boyish, roguish, he-man *was* Gable.' Frank Capra

The American critics were unimpressed with the film when it first came out although by the time it had reached Britain the word had spread.

'The story scarcely survives print, but it is exceedingly well told, some of the incidents being positively brilliant.' *Monthly Film Bulletin*, September 1934

'An overlong account is kept entertaining through Capra's persuasive direction and the interpolation of several quite brilliantly observed sequences of which the hitch-hiking episode is chief.' *Cinema Quarterly*, Spring 1934

▦ Can you spot . . .

* Special attention to Clark Gable's image. He still looked too babyish in his early thirties and so Capra fixed the lighting carefully to add a bit of maturity. And he appeared taller in this film than ever before. Capra let him tower naturally over his fellow actors. Always before directors had put everyone else on boxes when they were near him.
* An outdoor scene that wasn't. The night in the haystack was filmed in a circus tent during the day with the sounds of crickets dubbed in afterwards, the first time this technique was used.
* Claudette Colbert's right side. She had once been told that her left was best and always fought to get photographed from that angle.
* Bugs Bunny. Apparently animator Bob Clampett was inspired in his creation of this famous cartoon character by Gable's way with a carrot.

King Kong

1933 An adventurer brings a gigantic ape back from the East Indies which terrorizes New York.

▓ The talent

Fay Wray 25, as Ann Darrow; retired nine years later. This was by far her most famous role

Robert Armstrong 42, as Carl Denham; busy character actor. Also with Bob Hope and Jane Russell in *The Paleface* (1948)

Bruce Cabot 28, as John Driscoll; his first year in films, after meeting David O. Selznick at a party. Still working in the early seventies

Willis O'Brien 46, Animator of King Kong; an Oscar for Kong re-hash *Mighty Joe Young* (1949), one of thirty more years of special effects productions. Tutored latterday animated model wizz, Ray Harryhausen

Merian Cooper 39, Producer/Director; air hero in both World Wars who continued to work with Selznick and John Ford

Ernest Schoedsack 39, Producer/Director; continued to direct spectacles including *Mighty Joe Young*

▓ The business

Impresario adventurer Carl Denham was a screen composite of the two men responsible for *King Kong*, Merian Cooper and Ernest Schoedsack, a pair of documentary film-makers who travelled the globe looking for amazing things to photograph. They were new talent recruited to RKO by David O. Selznick who himself had been brought in to get the studio out of Depression troubles. Studio salaries had been scythed and all production halted while budgets were re-examined; in future $200,000 was to be top-whack for any picture.

Cooper and Schoedsack were allowed to make a jungle action film, *The Most Dangerous Game* (1932) with Fay Wray, Robert Armstrong and Noble Johnson. Then Cooper saw some footage that might make possible a concept he had been nurturing for some time. The shots were from an epic stop-frame animation movie called *Creation* that was being created by one of the pioneers in the field, Willis O'Brien, in his own corner of the studio.

After a word with Selznick, Cooper hijacked the unit and set them about test shots for *King Kong*, the film that had germinated from his initial mental image of a gigantic ape scaling the Empire State Building. O'Brien – or O'Bie, as he was known – quit on the spot, but reconsidered after a stop at the local speak-easy. During the fifty-five stressful weeks of production that followed he was to repeat the performance several times.

Selznick let them stretch the budget to $650,000 including the money already spent on *Creation*. In any case Merian Cooper himself took over from Selznick as head of production before *King Kong* was completed. It was one of the first films the studio released following his promotion, and Cooper was able to bask fully in its immense success. To the public its convincing blending of actors with the monstrous mayhem was a technical miracle on a par with *Star Wars* (1977).

It grossed $2,500,000, keeping the wolf from RKO's door until Fred and Ginger danced to the rescue a couple of years later. There followed an immediate forgettable sequel and, in 1977, a duff remake but the original film continued to be shown at profit for some years. With television re-runs it has become a classic. In 1983 Kong loomed over New York once more, as a giant inflatable hoisted to celebrate the film's fiftieth anniversary.

▦ Behind the screen

Stop-frame animation, the most obvious special effect in *King Kong*, had been around for some time. The technical advances that made the film such a breakthrough at the time and so enjoyable still today are less obvious, and consequently more successful.

Chief among them was the perfection of a new synthetic back-projection screen and a system which synchronized the camera and back projector (cf. *2001* (1968)). Together they widened the scope, size and credibility of the effect. Optical printing too entered a new phase with the travelling mattes pioneered on *Kong*. They made possible, for instance, the examination of the dinosaur killed at the start of the search for Ann on Skull Island.

A number of techniques that the Cooper/Schoedsack crew came up with themselves weren't widely adopted until some time later. The multi-plane arrangement of backdrops used to introduce a sense of depth to *King Kong*'s jungle scenes was further developed by Disney for *Snow White* (1937) and *Fantasia* (1941). And in sending the camera buzzing down a wooden ramp for the scenes where Kong is dislodged from the Empire State Building the film-makers pioneered the mobile camera techniques of *Star Wars*.

However it was the bringing to life of Kong himself that was the object of most curiosity at the time. As recently as the mid-seventies someone popped up asserting he was the man in the gorilla suit whereas, despite a number of such claims since the production, the studio always maintained that it was all done with models. Nevertheless if you look carefully at the long shot of Kong climbing the Empire State Building the figure does have the fluid movement of a gorillagram.

A fanciful Kong exposé appeared in a contemporary *Time* magazine article, describing him as a fifty-foot-high Trojan Gorilla, coated with thirty bearskins and housing six men operating eighty-five different motors.

In fact for head and shoulders shots (apart from Kong looking in the skyscraper window) they *did* use a mock-up with a six-foot-wide smile and foot-long teeth. Only three men were needed inside but they commanded a complex array of levers and bellows which produced a range of expression more varied, in the view of one critic, than that achieved by other leading cast members.

There was also an eight-foot articulated hand for Fay Wray to wriggle about on as she was divested of her clothes by the lascivious simian. The giant mitt was raised ten feet off the ground and the reason that Fay is clutching on so is that she's afraid she is going to fall off.

However the main Kong was eighteen inches high, the creation of model maker Marcel Delgado. He first made a reference sculpture in clay and then fashioned the figure you see around a skeleton of aluminium alloy called Dural. Rubber sections that would expand and contract like muscles were attached, then tissue paper to fill out the rest of the body.

Kong's skin was latex and his coat, rabbits' fur – a cheap, weak link in the chain of illusion. The ruffling of the ape's fur you can see in almost every sequence is from the animator's hands as he repositions the model. This imperfection was rationalized with ease by RKO publicists: the monster's fur is bristling because he is so riled.

It's a safe bet that those tell-tale handprints belonged to Willis O'Brien who personally animated most of Kong's role. The movements, expressions and reactions you see are those of O'Bie himself.*

His triumph was similar to that which Boris Karloff had achieved two years previously with his sympathetic portrayal of Frankenstein's monster from within a stiff casing of make-up. O'Bie also delivered a compelling performance but whereas Karloff could emote in real time the stop-frame animator had to act step by tiny step, twenty-four a second, while changing the details of the scene as well.

The animated sequences you see took up to an hour's work per second of film. One reason that many of the shots are so short is that it all had to be done as a continuous process, otherwise something would jolt out of place or the minute live shrubs would wither. For similar reasons all the light bulbs were replaced before starting a sequence, as any changed lamp would have different intensity.

It took a twenty-hour day to complete many of the shots. Sequences took even longer. The most challenging, Kong's battle with the flying dinosaur, needed seven weeks. The pterodactyl-type adversary with a forty-inch wingspan was a refugee from *Creation* and trickier to handle than the land-based creatures, which were secured through pegs in the thick wooden bases of the miniature sets. They would perform in a landscape of plasticine and painted toilet paper, forested with grape roots and carpeted with copper foil ferns. The workroom was kept sealed as they beavered away lest a slight draught cause the jungle to appear to jump.

Because the animation took such a disproportionate amount of time it couldn't possibly keep up with the live action. The actors were laid off for weeks at a time and several, including co-director Schoedsack, were able to shoot other films during gaps in a production schedule that was at least five times longer than normal for the era.

Most of Kong's human victims were specially made six-inch figures, articulated and weighted to writhe convincingly. In the scenes where live action and animation mix you are looking at a patchwork of images. Sometimes the actors are playing to back-projected monsters – but the film-makers also cleverly worked it in reverse. The *King Kong* production team devised their own miniature projection screens by stretching material normally used for surgeon's gloves over small wooden frames. They were then able to get their models to interact frame by frame to live action footage. It was first used for the scene where Cabot hides underneath Kong in a cave.

The landing on Skull Island was filmed at San Pedro. The water, beach and the players are real but the wall and the mountain behind are a painting on glass which is actually very close to the lens. The rather obviously cartoon gulls were added later to reinforce an impression of depth.

Filming the events at the island settlement paired huge sets with miniature models. Ever conscious of the RKO budget clampdown they used a native village set

*This according to Orville Goldner, another special effects man on *King Kong* whose memoir, *The Making of King Kong* written with George E. Turner and published by Tantivy Press, gives a real insider's view of the mechanics of the production.

King Kong and islanders: how frightened do they look?

left over from *Bird of Paradise* (1932). The giant wall was from C. B. DeMille's *King of Kings* (1927). The villagers who seem to be up on the parapet are actually on top of one of the RKO studio buildings with a lower-half model matted in. The strange lighting effects and general carrying-on convinced some local residents that the buildings were on fire.

The giant doors and altar existed in miniature and full size. The full-size doors were dragged open by tractors. Just how frightened do the natives look? All they could see in the opening was a blue screen, quite lacking the motivational incentive of a fully riled and ruffling Kong. The producers were worried that the natives didn't look convincingly traumatized.

Talk about gratuitous violence; much of the destruction wreaked by Kong on his whirlwind tour of New York was included as an afterthought because they were a reel short. By this time the backroom boys were demob happy and not beyond a little fun. Watch out for special effects surnames; the Delgado building and Goldner's Chocolates, for example.

The shoot-out on the Empire State Building was another blend of live action and model work. Pilots from the local air field were hired at $10 each to swoop and dive, but there were also models with wingspans that ranged from four to fifteen inches so they could themselves be mixed to force the perspective.

It was here, at the end, that the creators of Kong decided to treat themselves to a brief appearance. Take a look at the Flight Commander and his observer, respectively Merian Cooper and Ernest Schoedsack. They had agreed after all that work, in Cooper's words, 'We should kill that son of a bitch ourselves.'

▥ The experience

'Miss Fay Wray and Mr Robert Armstrong are in the cast but the real hero is the ape, who rolls his eyes, roars and gnashes his teeth with a violence and abandon which are delightfully in accord with the spirit of the whole film.' *The Times,* 12 April 1933 – one of many reviews to warn that it was not a film for children

'King Kong, two years in the making behind locked doors, is the mechanical marvel of this Technocratic age.' *Picture Goers Weekly,* April 1933

'They said it couldn't be filmed – but it was! See it and ask – what if such a thing could happen?' A breathless RKO publicity department's suggested newspaper catchlines

▥ Can you spot . . .

* Where you've seen the backgrounds before. The film-makers based them on Gustav Doré's nineteenth-century illustrations for the Bible and *Paradise Lost.*
* A tipsy Bruce Cabot. He got drunk during the preparation of the scene where they search for Fay Wray in the ship. If he looks rather more sobered up when you see him it is because Schoedsack slapped him around.
* A pair of pliers. I haven't yet, but they are apparently visible in one shot with dinosaurs, at the bottom of frame. To save the take they animated it out of the scene as if it were a snake burrowing in the undergrowth.
* Suicidal natives. As is the tradition with cinema's victims, from before *Kong* to the more recent Cong of *Rambo* (1985), natives who are canny enough to survive on a jungle island don't know to run away when a monster is coming for them.
* Kong is bigger in America. Skull Island is on a one-foot-to-one-inch scale and so he's eighteen feet high. The sea voyage has done him such a power of good that in New York he is the equivalent of twenty-four feet tall.
* Where you've heard Kong before. In the zoo, of course. Sound man Murray Spivack stitched together and slowed down all the peaks from lions and tigers roaring at feeding time.
* Is Fay Wray cold or is she just glad to see Bruce Cabot after her conversation on culinary matters with Charley the cook.

The Lavender Hill Mob

1951 A mild bank clerk plans an ingenious gold bullion theft.

▥ The talent

Alec Guinness 36, as Holland; moved to more serious characters. A percentage of *Star Wars* (1977) made his million
Stanley Holloway 60, as Pendlebury; music-hall and film character favourite. Alfred Doolittle was still to come
Sidney James 38, as Lackery; became one of Britain's best-loved comic actors with the *Carry On* series and Tony Hancock
Alfie Bass 41, as Shorty; familiar comic character actor, memorable in TV's *Bootsie and Snudge*
Michael Balcon 55, Producer; key British stylist, father of Ealing films
Charles Crichton 40, Director; turned to television and corporate videos after abortive American film venture. Bounced back with *A Fish Called Wanda* (1988) in his seventies

▥ The business

Ealing Studios in West London was a cosy place to work, with its stable of directors, technicians and writers under the tutelage of Sir Michael Balcon.* The deal the company had with the Rank Organization was cosy too, giving independence and guaranteed wide distribution.

The Lavender Hill Mob earned Ealing and Rank about what 'Dutch' Holland and his fellow non-desperadoes netted in their heist: £1,000,000. Alec Guinness was paid £6,000, considered then to be a fair sum for a British actor in Britain. One of the industry's brightest assets, he could earn up to £25,000 a year in films during this period.

Ealing's star writer, T.E.B. Clarke,** got an Oscar for *The Lavender Hill Mob* and Alec Guinness went to number six in the British box office charts, but this was the high watermark for Ealing. Although several more great comedies with Guinness were to come, including *The Man in the White Suit* (released two months after *The Lavender Hill Mob*) and *The Lady Killers* (1955), the gentle Ealing blend was soon out of step with the gritty fifties. Family members started drifting away, often to less rewarding stages in their careers, and the company did not see out the decade.

---

*A leading light in the British film industry for more than fifty years and the man who discovered Alfred Hitchcock.
**His flat fee for this film was £1,500 and not a penny in royalties or TV repeat fees, a frequent moan of those in pictures before the accommodation of the new medium in contracts.

Alec Guinness: fubsy

▦ Behind the screen

If the robbery seems to work ingeniously well it could be partly because of the help the Bank of England gave in devising the method. It says something of the age of innocence which produced the Ealing Comedies that an ad hoc committee including the Bank's transportation and bullion managers was convened when Tibby Clarke presented himself at the Old Lady of Threadneedle Street with an appointment form which stated: Information required on means of stealing gold bullion. The officials got so engrossed in their scheme that they quite forgot Clarke was still in the room.

He was supposed to be researching a serious number about the London waterfront but he had been struck instead by the comic possibilities in a quayside gold foundry he visited. There was an insignificant little man in charge of a glittering fortune, and an attitude of familiar nonchalance amongst the workforce. The only seeming acknowledgement of the raw material's value was a careful examination of the mens' boots for any specks as they left. This attention to footwear and the general harbour atmosphere are retained in the film. The original concept emerged as *Pool of London* (1951) completed by Clarke's fellow Ealing scribe, John Eldridge. They even used some of the same locations simultaneously. A shot in *Pool of London* was spoiled by Alec Guinness being chased by a policeman past a camera that turned out to be filming for the sister production.

Clarke got stuck when he was plotting out what to do with the gold once it had reached the foundry. Then he happened to clear out an old drawer at home and what should he find but a small, gold-coloured model of the Eiffel Tower. Eureka!

Michael Balcon employed an earthier epithet as Clarke presented him with *The Lavender Hill Mob* when what he was expecting was *Pool of London*. However he calmed down after Tibby's tactical retreat from his office and gave the go-ahead a little later like nothing had happened.

Some elements of scripting proved difficult. The scene where Holland seduces Pendlebury to a life of crime is the eleventh rewrite. All told when it came to filming, Charles Crichton eliminated everything that wasn't absolutely necessary from the narrative to reduce a 110-minute script to a lean 78 minutes.

Alec Guinness got involved with the writing process in so far as it affected his character. He got the mannerisms for 'Dutch' – the slight speech impediment, the walk, the gestures – by strolling the streets observing people. He described his character as 'fubsy', a favourite Guinness buzz-word at the time, by which he meant chubby and somewhat squat. He insisted on slight padding, and you can see how he tried to give the character a double chin by looking down as much as possible – and how he sometimes forgot.

Guinness said he enjoyed making the film but a contemporary interview with Kenneth Tynan had him making 'few artistic claims for it'. In fact his art seems to have been something of a worry at the time. He was said to be going through self-doubts about his acting, to be sick of playing his oddball characters and looking for a change in his films to something closer to his more substantial stage work. These doubts can't have been helped directly after filming by his *Hamlet* season in the West End which flopped.

Stanley Holloway was attracted by the prospect of work with Guinness, and by the week's location filming in Paris. But the centrepiece of the Paris sequence, the run down the spiral staircase, was done in the studio. Charles Crichton had an eighty-foot high staircase built of laminated wood and mounted his camera on a high crane. Parisians were still treated to the bizarre spectacle of Crichton and his crew careering down the Tower to get the shots for the back projection.

It was the only time Stanley Holloway and Alec Guinness appeared together but Guinness obviously enjoyed the experience because he asked Holloway to be in his ill-fated *Hamlet*. Holloway recalled years afterwards that rushing madly up and down the Eiffel Tower was one of his more unusual auditions for Shakespeare.

▦ The experience

'An ingenious comedy – fresh as a daisy, light as a feather, clean as a whistle – in which there is positively not a stitch of love interest.' *Daily Express*, 29 June 1951

'Every taste is catered for with the result that some people will be hating some of it some of the time. The film, in short, is over-insured for laughs and for every guffaw there will be a corresponding withdrawal as from a heavy finger poked in the ribs.' Phillip Hope-Wallace, *Sunday Times*, 1 July 1951

'I think Alec and I made a good team because when he is playing comedy I think he is at his best when he has another comic personality to play against, to set off his own performance. On his own – and I stress I mean in comedy, not necessarily serious roles – he needs to disguise to help him.' Stanley Holloway, 1967

▦ Can you spot . . .

* A likely cigarette girl. Neither did Michael Balcon, much to his regret. Chiquita is played by a 22-year-old Audrey Hepburn.
* A friend of David Niven. Michael Trubshawe met Niven in a Maltese cricket pavilion in 1930 and they became life-long friends. After becoming a success in Hollywood the suave star got his pal with the seven-and-a-half inch moustache several walk-ons like this, as the Ambassador at the end (see also *The Pink Panther* (1964)).
* A superior grasp of geography. It is with justification that Dutch says during the car chase that the police are getting mixed up. They have believed his report of the suspect car heading *west* along Portobello Road, an avenue that runs almost exclusively north-south. But would the cops be able to keep up with them in any case? In a flash the Mob has cruised from West London to beyond St Paul's in the City. This particular chase was inspired by Tibby Clarke's experiences as a War Reserve policeman when a patrol car was stolen. Much else pokes fun at his earlier serious police film, *The Blue Lamp* (1949).

Lawrence of Arabia

1962 Two years of World War I's Middle East campaign in the company of one of Britain's most enigmatic heroes.

▦ The talent

Peter O'Toole 29, as T. E. Lawrence; *Becket* (1964) followed. He was Henry II again in *The Lion in Winter* (1968) and a hit in the eighties with *My Favourite Year* (1982). Holds the record for most Oscar nominations without a win

Omar Sharif 29, as Sherif Ali; went on to star in Lean's next epic, *Doctor Zhivago* (1965), then lost steam but has continued on international scene as both film star and top bridge player

Arthur Kennedy 47, as Jackson Bentley; familiar lead in films at a peak in the late forties

Anthony Quayle 48, as Colonel Harry Brighton; author, director, theatrical manager and distinguished support in many films since *Hamlet* (1948) including *Ice Cold in Alex* (1958) and *Anne of a Thousand Days* (1969)

Claude Rains 73, as Mr Dryden; one of the last of a thirty-year range of solid supporting roles in many memorable films including his debut in *The Invisible Man* (1933), and *Casablanca* (1942)

Alec Guinness 48, as Prince Feisal; Lean's star in *The Bridge on the River Kwai* (1957) – also in *Doctor Zhivago* (1965) and reunited for *A Passage to India* (1984)

Anthony Quinn 47, as Auda Abu Tayi; originally a character villain who had built himself a star career. *Zorba the Greek* (1964) was to come

Jack Hawkins 52, as General Allenby; stock major British actor, well-used to military characters. This was one of his last films with his own voice, lost following an operation for cancer of the larynx in 1966

Sam Spiegel 58, Producer; German refugee whose credit read S. P. Eagle until the mid-fifties. Also made *The African Queen* (1951) and *On the Waterfront* (1954) amongst many memorable films

David Lean 54, Director; second work of the latter 'epic' phase of this most respected of directors

▦ The business

David Lean and Sam Spiegel's previous collaboration, *The Bridge on the River Kwai*, had made the producer a millionaire. That and the shower of Oscars it attracted prompted the pair to attempt a repetition of the formula with another tale of an interesting fellow in an exotic location. After some initial work they bottled out of doing a *Gandhi*, plumping instead for two years in the life of peculiar British hero, T. E. Lawrence.

Spiegel set about buying up every Lawrence-related book that he could find so as to thwart anyone who might have the same idea during Lean's lengthy preparatory work. The big rights prize was Lawrence's own memoir, *The Seven Pillars of Wisdom*, originally printed privately but a wider hit when published after his death in 1935. That went for £20,000 to Lawrence's executor, his brother Professor A. W.

Lawrence who, having approved an early draft of the script, wrote to the papers denouncing the final Robert Bolt* version and refused to let them use the 'Seven Pillars' title.

Canny and realistic, Spiegel seems to have had the measure of his perfectionist director and took the original estimates of a $2,500,000 budget and four months shooting schedule in the desert with a grain of sand. Columbia were already quite well disposed, given that *Kwai* had earned ten times its cost. Just as well; in the end the studio parted with about $13,000,000 over two years of shooting *Lawrence* in Jordan, Morocco, Spain and back in Britain.

It was the desert shooting that really inflated the costs: £50,000 a week to keep the unit going and they were out there for the best part of a year. Finally the only way that Spiegel could induce Lean to wrap it up was getting the picture booked as the Royal Command Film Performance at the end of 1962. It was one of the few deadlines the director wouldn't argue with.

It all might have cost much more had it not been for Spiegel securing the services of former Foreign Office Minister Anthony Nutting who had quit the British government over Suez and was a friend of King Hussein of Jordan. Not only did he train Peter O'Toole in the manners of a Great War Arabist but he also smoothed the way for Spiegel, a Jew, to operate amongst the Arabs. One of Nutting's greatest coups was getting Hussein to drop the price of using his army as extras from £1,000,000 to £150,000.

The stars were even less expensive. The then-obscure Shakespearean actor Peter O'Toole had been spotted by Lean playing a small part in *The Day They Robbed the Bank of England* (1960). He was signed for a three-picture deal at £50,000 a film. Omar Sharif got £40,000 for his first appearance outside Egypt.

The critics were very impressed by both new faces and with the picture itself. So were the public, especially as they had already been softened up by the Spiegel publicity machine. The film scooped seven Oscars** – as many as *Kwai* – and earned $16,700,000 in North America (so about that again abroad). Lean's next film, *Doctor Zhivago* for MGM earned less than half the Oscars but more than twice the money.***

The success of *Lawrence of Arabia* has continued over the years though only recently has it been possible to see it in the form David Lean intended. The version that he put together for the Royal premiere lasted three and three-quarter hours. He was made to trim out twenty minutes for its distribution prints and a further fifteen minutes was cut from the second half for a 1971 release.

Then at the age of eighty the director was presented with a rare opportunity to reconstruct his film from scratch. A number of archivists gathered all the rushes and Martin Scorsese assembled a rough-cut. Then Lean honed it to a final form for a highly profitable re-release in 1989.

---

*He made his name with *A Man for All Seasons* (filmed in 1966) and also wrote Lean's *Doctor Zhivago* and *Ryan's Daughter* (1970), the latter starring Mrs Bolt, Sarah Miles. Writer and director have continued to work together.
**Including Best Picture, Director, Photography and Music.
***The statistics: *Kwai* cost $2,900,000, earned seven Oscars, and $15,000,000 in North America; *Lawrence* cost $13,000,000, earned seven Oscars, and $16,700,000 in North America; *Zhivago* cost $15,000,000, earned three Oscars, and $42,000,000 in North America.

▦ Behind the screen

Not so much a picture as a way of life. It started in early 1960 at Jebel Tubayq near Jordan's Saudi frontier, where they shot Omar Sharif's spectacular introductory approach from the horizon.* He could have been delivering the drinks; the nearest water was 150 miles away. They had to cool the thermometers to stop them going pop in the 130° heat and the film stock went in the fridge next to the catered lunch. With much more hassle besides, and all the moody, gobbing camels, it's no wonder that people were quitting left, right and centre.

On the other hand David Lean revelled in it. He seems to have been, as Feisal describes Lawrence, 'another of those desert-loving English'. The director would rise before dawn, so the stories go, to contemplate the desert sunrise, and when it was time to leave for the comparative comforts of Seville in Spain he was close to tears.

The rest of the company, as did Feisal's Arabs, preferred water and green trees – particularly the props men. One of their many duties was as make-up artistes to the desert, brushing huge areas to a seeming virginity between takes and even painting it where the natural colours lacked sufficient subtlety. They made sure that the unit lorries always approached from behind the camera position.

David Lean would push his crew and his star through ordeals to obtain results which matched his vision. He might take two weeks to get a scene right or subject O'Toole to considerable discomfort, like the nineteen takes needed to capture Lawrence facing the sandstorms of Sinai with his eyes wide open.

Peter O'Toole had already suffered just to get the part. He endured surgery to straighten his nose and correct a squint, which left him a far more perfect physical specimen than the man he was to portray, who was shorter, uglier and gayer.

The young star was subjected to the full pressure of being the linch-pin in a multi-million pound production. He undertook intensive preparation. There was three months acclimatizing himself to desert life and, with guidance from Anthony Nutting, O'Toole set about studying all the books whose rights Spiegel had bought and anything else besides that he could find on Lawrence and the Middle East.

You can see the results of a more painful side of his training. Peter O'Toole's seemingly natural command of the camels is the result of 5,000 desert miles of aching practice in good camelmanship – occasionally eased by rubber padding. A joking reference to all this preparation is the scene where El Aurens gives his robes a twirling try-out, only to be interrupted by Auda – a scene that was O'Toole's idea and itself followed further extensive practice in cutting a Bedouin dash.

He must even have impressed the camels in the end because in two incidents they may have saved his life. The first was while filming the scene where Auda's men gather with Lawrence's Bedouins who have trotted across the Nefud to attack Aqaba. The 400 extras hired for the scene were city Arabs who had an extreme antipathy to the Bedou, and there was a major ruck. O'Toole was knocked to the ground and for ten minutes lost in the melee. Another dangerous moment came during the actual attack on Aqaba. A special effects machine which sprays pellets into the sand to mimic machine-gun fire malfunctioned and O'Toole was hit in the eye. He fell blinded from his camel as the horsemen were charging towards him.

---

*Not him, rather a stand-in, until the dismount.

Peter O'Toole and guardian: creature comforts

On both occasions O'Toole's mounts turned up trumps, instantly following a procedure instilled through millenia of breeding. They stood their ground over their fallen rider, diverting the deadly hooves. The camels immediately reverted to malicious type, however, when the pressure was off. One got the hump and dealt O'Toole a bite that deprived him of the use of two of his fingers for some time. This was only one of a catalogue of injuries which included sundry sprains, wrenched ligaments, a torn groin, a cracked skull and third-degree sunburn.

O'Toole insisted on doing most of his own stunts, a practice which gave Sam Spiegel the horrors for if he had been too badly injured the project would have had to be shelved. It certainly took its toll. Look at the difference between his appearance in the first scenes they shot – Tafas leading him toward Feisal's camp and, two stone later, some of the last such as the bloodbath sequence.

Peter O'Toole's emulation of Lawrence's drive to outnative the natives was the action of an actor attempting to prove to his colleagues and his director that he was not just a pretty face. The crew were sympathetic but Lean seemed unimpressed. O'Toole was given few of the creature comforts of a star, just a deckchair to sit on between takes. Alec Guinness would have none of this and was provided with a luxury caravan. Peter O'Toole was then given a hut for his deckchair but it blew away.

He was said to be near breaking point but stuck with it. His new wife Sian Phillips would turn down work to join him on location and cheer him up. On his return to Britain at the end of a six-month stint he went on a bender and got a year's driving ban.

At least it was more comfortable when the unit moved to Spain where they shot the interiors, the attack on the railway and also recreated the port of Aqaba. O'Toole and Sharif became good pals and indulged in some dedicated partying. O'Toole had been chosen by Lean despite worries about his drinking. He was quite someone to socialize with, the sort of chap who would consume three bottles of wine in order to sleep but be fine for work in the morning.* Often Peter and Omar were accompanied by comely model April Ashley. She slept chastely with Peter O'Toole but went all the way with Sharif, only then telling him about her sex-change operation.

Grand edifices built for trade exhibitions in Seville were used for all the interiors. Can you spot the priceless Spanish tapestries decorating the British headquarters walls? They were too valuable to move for the film-makers. The Arab council chamber scenes were shot in a casino.

The attack on Aqaba and on the railway were filmed a few hundred miles away near the coastal town of Almeria. The real locations for this and other incidents were either unavailable or too modern. It was a mammoth work of reconstruction which included two and a half miles of specially-laid track. Wind machines were put to good use disguising the compact filming area and much more besides. The ruined buildings at the end of the Sinai were part of an old Spanish farm which was Levantized by denuding it of all Iberian vegetation and blowing about as much sand as possible.**

If the settings were not all they seemed, what of the narrative? The real T. E. Lawrence wrote that he had already been turned into a matinee idol by the newspapers. The facts, especially the circumstances of his ill-fated spying excursion in Deraa, have been doggedly disputed. So have Lawrence's character and achievements, and the puzzle of his post-film life when, after a short continued period of high profile, he sought anonymity by re-enlisting as an aircraftsman under an assumed name.

---

*He stopped drinking in 1976.
**There was much wind machinery in the desert scenes, too. An effective example is the sandstorm blowing in the distance as Lawrence ends his night-long contemplation of the Arabs' military plight by exclaiming, 'Aqaba!' Earlier in this sequence is an example of how Lean also exploited the elements. The day-for-night tilt up as Lawrence trudges thoughtfully out across the naturally wind-rippled sand was perhaps a shot that couldn't be repeated. Can you spot the side-by-side footprints where O'Toole has been standing still waiting for his cue from Lean to start walking?

Several of the principal characters in *Lawrence of Arabia* are fictitious. Of the main ones Col Harry Brighton and Mr Dryden are mixtures of at least six different people and although Ali is mentioned in *The Seven Pillars of Wisdom* he did not play the central part represented in the film.

T.E.'s brother, A. W. Lawrence, acknowledged that though many liberties were taken with factual details and characterization in order to make *Lawrence* a good flick, O'Toole did at least capture and display a determination, courage and endurance that were quite as heroic as the real man.

▦ The experience

'Who is that pudding, that poor, coy twit with the twinkling blue eyes? My God, it's me!' Peter O'Toole on seeing the film for the first time on a hotel TV in Jordan in 1980

'*Lawrence of Arabia* must be accounted a landmark in the history of cinema: for the first time a film which has cost several million pounds and has taken years of effort by armies of men and women has proved to be worthy of consideration as a work of art.' David Robinson, *Financial Times*, 11 December 1962

'Here is a wonderful film that makes all other epics look like peanuts.' Ernest Betts, *The People*, 16 December 1962

'They used a psychological recipe. Take an ounce of narcissism, a pound of exhibitionism, a pint of sadism, a gallon of blood-lust and a sprinkle of other aberrations and stir well.' A. W. Lawrence

▦ Can you spot . . .

* Make up perspiration. Any real sweat evaporates in seconds with the dry desert heat. Whenever you see it in the film outside on location it's make-up.

* A two-year wait for a close-up. Lean decided that he needed more shots of Lawrence for the sequence where he meets Ali for the first time. So although this was one of the first scenes to be shot, the close-ups were some of the last. Look at how the ravages of the production appear from shot to shot on Peter O'Toole.

* The multi-national stand-ins. The Arab women are all imported Egyptian Christians. No orthodox Muslim Arab woman would permit herself to be photographed.

* Some related accents. Omar Sharif was flattered and bemused when Alec Guinness, recently arrived on location, had breakfast with him and spent the rest of the morning chatting. It was only later that he realized that Guinness had been listening to his accent and doing some final fine-tuning.

* The natural sound. Lean made do with little dubbing, re-recording the dialogue as wild track on location just after the take if it was marred by noise.

* The critics' favourite cut. Everyone was impressed when it went from Lawrence blowing out the match back at headquarters to Lean's sunrise celebration of the desert. Although brilliantly realized by the director Robert Bolt says that the transition was in his original script.

* Some gross discourtesy. Col Brighton seems to sit with his heels to Feisal, an insult which the Arab Prince would have been unlikely to suffer.

* A likely lad in the second unit. Nicholas Roeg, director of *The Man Who Fell To Earth* (1976) and *Don't Look Now* (1973).

The Magnificent Seven

1960 Six gunfighters and an adolescent hanger-on defend Mexican villagers from a bandit extortionist.

🎞 The talent

Yul Brynner 45, as Chris; exotic star of mysterious origin whose career finally returned to revivals of his most memorable role, in *The King and I* (1956)

Steve McQueen 30, as Vin; favourite sixties tough-guy superstar

Eli Wallach 45, as Calvera; method actor who debuted in *Baby Doll* (1956). More Western villains followed this

Robert Vaughn 28, as Lee; became U.N.C.L.E.'s Napoleon Solo four years later. Also in *Bullitt* (1968) with McQueen

James Coburn 32, as Britt; trendy sixties/seventies star

Charles Bronson 38, as O'Reilly; trendy seventies/eighties star

Horst Buchholz 27, as Chico; German mini-sensation on a good run, including *Tiger Bay* (1959), but unmemorable since

Brad Dexter 43, as Harry Luck; who? The one you can't name on a bet. Familiar stock heavy, later a producer

John Sturges 49, Producer/Director; many famous entertaining action films including *Bad Day at Black Rock* (1954) and *Ice Station Zebra* (1968)

🎞 The business

The Magnificent Seven opened in New York in 1956 to a small but appreciative audience of art-film lovers. For this was the American market title of *The Seven Samurai*, by Akira Kurosawa, which had already achieved the status of Japanese post-war classic since its original release in 1954.

Its new following in America included John Sturges, a director who had theorized that it was possible to adapt any story into a Western – even *My Fair Lady*.* *The Seven Samurai* was even more appropriate material and, as it happened, Kurosawa was a Sturges fan. He readily gave his permission for a reworking.

There followed a deal between Hollywood's up-and-coming indie producers, The Mirisch Brothers, and a company that Sturges had formed with fellow directors Billy Wilder and Robert Wise. Together they came up with the $2,500,000 *The Magnificent Seven* cost to make. Distributors United Artists left them to it apart from stipulating the inclusion of a big star like Yul Brynner.

One of the most memorable aspects of *The Magnificent Seven* is the remainder of the casting, by John Sturges. Although little known at the time at least four of the

*The plot would turn on a bet that any klutz picked off a Western street could be turned into a master gunfighter.

Steve McQueen, James Coburn, Horst Buchholz, Yul Brynner, Brad Dexter, Robert Vaughn and Charles Bronson:

remaining seven were to become substantial stars during the following decade either on film or television.

From his leading role in TV's *Wanted Dead or Alive*, Steve McQueen was the most familiar of the non-Brynners at the time. He was also the best paid, at about $100,000 a year. Initially the series' production company, Four Star (owned by Dick Powell), refused to release their leading man for the film, but McQueen crashed a rented a car and cried off his TV commitments with whiplash. However he was still well enough

Steve McQueen was scheming . . .

to do the film for his friend John Sturges* and pocket a $65,000 fee. McQueen went on to star in Sturges' next film, *The Great Escape* (1963) with Bronson and Coburn** – and became the biggest star of the lot before his early death in 1980.

*They had become acquainted shooting *Never So Few* (1959) which had also featured Charles Bronson.
**Coburn was Sturges' tip for the top: 'There's going to be a big star in the kid with the long legs.' He and McQueen were reunited in their next film, *Hell is for Heroes* (1962).

United Artists pioneered a distribution technique for *The Magnificent Seven*, later to become standard practice, termed multi-print saturation – jargon for opening it at scads of cinemas at once. It must have done the trick. *The Magnificent Seven* grossed $11,000,000 – prompting three sequels to date* but the critics were unimpressed, comparing it unfavourably with its famous Oriental precursor. However, Kurosawa liked it enough to give Sturges a ceremonial sword as a token of appreciation.

▦ Behind the screen

You are looking at a severe case of rivalry between an established star and an ambitious newcomer.

It seems that Steve McQueen started nervous plotting against Yul Brynner as soon as he got on the plane to Mexico City. Perhaps he was jealous. It is said that he coveted Brynner's star paraphernalia of cars, minders and yes-men, vowing that he would acquire the same one day. In fact it seems they were all trying to out-act their co-stars, each man under the impression when agreeing to take part that he was the principal star of the production.

At that stage and up to the start of filming much of the story was still forming in Sturges's mind. The director's reputation was sufficient to enlist their participation without an exact idea of their role. In fact it seems that Robert Vaughn's character, Lee, was never written at all; they just busked it as filming went along.

The seven-way rivalry was particularly intense in one of the first scenes to be filmed, the shots of the Seven riding across a stream. Yul Brynner, the actual star of the film, is in the lead oblivious of the not-yet-quite-so-Magnificent Six working themselves up into individual frenzies of business behind him.

The keenest upstager was Steve McQueen. He had grown up on a mid-Western farm with guns and horses whereas Brynner was from Valdivostock and more at home in a nightclub than on the trail.

Notice on the ride to Boot Hill the way Steve rattles the shotgun shells next to his ear and eases the safety catch. It seems Yul insisted that Steve use a scatter gun here so as to avoid comparisons in this first test of their shooting prowess. McQueen boasted that when he actually got to use his six-gun during the first big battle with the bandits he had let three rounds off before Brynner could shoot one. It was supposedly McQueen who taught Brynner the technique of flicking your piece backward into the holster but, according to James Coburn, it was such a hackneyed example of cowpoke schtick as to be already in the common domain.

Another, possibly apocryphal, story concerns a scene where Vin is pacing up and down while talking to Chris. Brynner had built a small perch of earth to increase his height but McQueen kicked a little away each time he passed. Not surprisingly, and to McQueen's annoyance, Brynner assigned a henchman to scrutinize him for background overacting. And even Sturges had to tell Steve to tone it down.

Inevitably tempers flared. Tales of a feud got into the papers. Yul declared that he was a star and didn't quarrel with supporting players – Steve was to contact the press and deny any friction. McQueen refused and threatened to thump him.

Elsewhere things were considerably more chummy, apart from Charles Bronson who apparently got on with no one. McQueen and Sturges became even more firm

The Return of the Seven (1966) with Brynner, *Guns of the Magnificent Seven* (1969) and *The Magnificent Seven Ride* (1972).

drinking buddies, sharing amongst other things the love of machines you can see in the actor's deft usage. McQueen was of course a keen car and bike racer but his affinity for mechanics even extended to taking pleasure in the spectacle of a washing machine go through its cycle.

Eli Wallach acquired a special circle of friends. Seeking authentic accomplices for the urbane actor cast as the bandit king Calvera, Sturges recruited real bandits from the hills outside Mexico City where he was filming. These tough nuts adopted Wallach as a protégé, teaching him to shoot, ride and snarl, and providing him and his wife with a protective shadow throughout their stay on location.

While the real banditos seemed an amiable lot the local villagers proved anything but when it came to shooting the over-acted river crossing. The stream was too shallow to provide the degree of hoof splashing that Sturges was seeking so everyone pitched in constructing an ad hoc dam. Unknown to the Hollywood interlopers this had the effect of drying up a nearby riverbank laundry. The folks who promptly turned up with machetes as arguments showed themselves to have fully outgrown the meekness of their forbears as depicted on film.

▦ The experience

'A rip-roaring, rootin' tootin' Western with lots of bite and old-fashioned abandon.' *Variety*

'Of course the film has not the looks or the exhilaration of the original and the mid-European Yul Brynner and German Horst Buchholz are as unlike Westerners as they are to the heroic Toshiro Mifune. But John Sturges' Western has a sweep of its own and touches of sub-Fordian grandeur and humour.' David Robinson, *Financial Times*, 14 April 1961

'With fifteen minutes cut out of the middle this would be one of the tensest Westerns for a long time.' Leonard Mosely, *Daily Express*, 14 April 1961

'Alright, it isn't a masterpiece as *The Seven Samurai* is a masterpiece. But it stirs, it moves.' Dilys Powell, *Sunday Times*, 16 April 1961

▦ Can you spot . . .

* Yul's bald head. Only once when he removes his hat to wipe the perspiration away as he finishes helping the townspeople to build defences.
* All the jokes. William Roberts, who was responsible for the dialogue, normally wrote comedy.
* What Sturges lifted from the original *Seven Samurai*. Aside from the overall plot the only individual touch he admitted stealing was James Coburn's character Britt examining the flowers as he is waiting for Calvera's men to retrieve their horses.
* The original colour. Only from time to time. The DeLuxe process prints faded after a couple of years.
* A favourite John Sturges shot. Notice how often he frames action in the middle distance with an individual close to the camera. He also favoured using first takes.
* The sets. Although shot roughly in the region where the action might have happened there were no towns or villages that retained the look of the 1880's and the buildings you see were all specially constructed. That is why the town, in particular, looks hardly substantial enough to support the bystanders to Chris and Vin's ride up to Boot Hill let alone the cemetery itself.

The Maltese Falcon

1941 A private detective becomes involved in the dangerous search for a priceless antique as he tries to establish who killed his partner.

▦ The talent

Humphrey Bogart 42, as Sam Spade; after a decade as supporting, heavy adulation, big money and, soon, personal happiness
Mary Astor 35, as Brigid O'Shaughnessy; forty years a film star. Later a novelist
Sydney Greenstreet 61, as Kasper Gutman; after four decades on the stage a lucrative decade as a screen villain followed this debut
Peter Lorre 37, as Joel Cairo; cult character star whose Mr Moto series had just bitten the dust with the approach of war with the Japanese
Elisha Cook Jnr 34, as Wilmer Cook; lived

alone in the mountains and would be called to work by courier. More than fifty years of character parts since 1930
Lee Patrick 29, as Effie Perine; like Cook also appeared in a sequel, *The Black Bird* (1975), with George Segal
Henry Blanke 39, Producer; production credits on many classics including *The Adventures of Robin Hood* (1938) and *The Treasure of the Sierra Madre* (1947)
John Huston 34, Director; still making great films forty years later. Later sidelined in memorable character parts

▦ The business

John Huston had built an impressive reputation as a screenwriter and worked into his contract that if Warner Brothers wanted to keep him on they would have to give him the chance to direct.

His choice for a debut was surprising. *The Maltese Falcon* was originally a magazine serial which the author, Dashiell Hammett, sold to the studio for $8,500 soon after it was published in the late twenties. Over the next few years Warners used it as the basis for two pedestrian films.*

Trotting it out again was unusual, but saved the studio having to buy the rights to a fresh property in their effort to placate an ambitious writer. The project also worked out cheaper than it might have because George Raft refused the lead role. He said that he had been promised only 'important' films and that he wouldn't have to appear in remakes. Neither did he want to chance a film with an inexperienced director.**

Raft earned in excess of $4,000 a week at the time. Bogart, who had recently made an impact in *High Sierra* (screenplay by Huston), was second on the list of casting possibles ahead of Edward G. Robinson. Bogie had been struggling to up his salary

---

*They were *The Maltese Falcon* (1931) and *Satan Met a Lady* (1936).
**Raft must hold a record for turning down smashing pictures that went to Humphrey Bogart: *Dead End* (1937), *High Sierra* (1941) and *Casablanca* (1942) are others.

from the $400 a week it had started on five years before when he was pigeon-holed by Warners as an average screen hood. Soon after the success of *The Maltese Falcon* his pay went up to $3,500 a week.

The B-picture budget wasn't going to break the bank either. At $300,000, it was about $100,000 below average, although studio records show that spending finally edged past $380,000 – perhaps because of some added shooting.

The film was an immediate hit at the previews (apart from mild confusion over the plot) and so Warner Brothers decided to promote it more heavily than originally planned. Despite this and the fact that it became one of the most admired films of all time, it wasn't a record money-spinner.

However *The Maltese Falcon* did set the style for the American film noir genre of the forties and fifties. It established Bogart as a star once and for all, got Huston's distinguished directorial career off to a cracking start and introduced a new star villain of the forties in the corpulent shape of Sydney Greenstreet.

▦ Behind the screen

All in all this must have been a very agreeable picture to work on. The principal actors and the director were either already firm friends or becoming so during the production. Much of what you see is either the run-up to or the aftermath of a leisurely get-together at the Lakeside Country Club.

Bogart counted Peter Lorre and John Huston, fellow veterans of *High Sierra*, as best friends. They met his two principal criteria: they weren't boring and they could drink a bit. 'I never trust any bastard who doesn't drink,' said Bogart, by all accounts himself a rather unpleasant drunk. 'After eleven o'clock he thinks he's Bogart,' said an acquaintance.

Typically a group including Huston, Bogart, Lorre, Mary Astor and Ward Bond, who played the cop Polhaus, would head off to the Club for an unhurried one-and-a-half hour lunch. Then in the evening it was back for a well-oiled buffet 'till late.

In this pleasant atmosphere the film was shot in sequence over a period of thirty-four days up to the middle of July 1941. But afterwards Jack Warner insisted on a number of additions.

The first thing he wanted was the scene from the murderer's point of view when Miles Archer, Sam Spade's partner, is shot. Then in August the ending was changed, in a seeming effort to soften Spade's image. Huston had filmed it straight from the book with you-know-who being turned over to the police in Spade's apartment and then a brief scene to wrap it all up in Sam's office.

But the amended result is one instance when studio interference actually contributed to film art. The changed scenes add the effective end sequence with Spade using the stairs while the murderer is already behind bars – the bars of the elevator – sombrely descending to a killer's fate. It also added the haunting description of the bird as 'the stuff that dreams are made of'.*

Finally in September, after preview cards indicated problems following the plot, Bogart was called back from his next picture, *All Through the Night*, along with Mary Astor and Jerome Cowan (who played the unfortunate Archer), to reshoot the opening interview with Miss Wonderly, as Brigid then calls herself. As first filmed she

---

*'We are such stuff as dreams are made on, and our little life is rounded with a sleep,' is from one of Prospero's great speeches in *The Tempest* (IV.i.156) if that's any help.

Elisha Cook Jnr, Sydney Greenstreet and Humphrey Bogart: call me a gonsil, will you?

appeared confused and her speeches were disjointed. The version we see now – rewritten so that even a preview audience could understand it – was completed in a short day giving ample time, no doubt, for another gathering at the Lakeside.

Perhaps the original confusion was added to by Mary Astor trying out for the first time a bit of technique she used to give clues when her character, Brigid, was lying (ie. practically all of the time). She would make herself breathless and giddy by taking a lot of deep lungfuls before each take. She may have overdone it for the first scene.

One reason for Huston sticking so closely to the original story was bound up in why he wanted to film *The Maltese Falcon* in the first place. He said that the other two screen versions had failed because they hadn't been true to Hammett's plot. But he ended up following it more closely that he might have planned. On his instructions a secretary converted the novel directly into film terms – recording the dialogue and putting it logically into scenes and shots – so that Huston could work from that base to adapt it. But it seems that Jack Warner saw and approved this raw version before Huston had even touched it.

To be fair to Huston he did do a bit of tinkering to earn his screenplay credit for the film. Spade consults his lawyer over the phone rather than face to face, thus saving a scene and an actor. And Gutman's daughter is eliminated from the proceedings which, from the look of Gutman, is just as well.

But in those days of Hollywood it wasn't enough for the head of studio to approve a script. It also had to go to the industry's morality watchdogs, the Production Code Administration. Huston had seen some of it coming and had already eliminated Brigid being made to strip to prove she hasn't stolen a $1,000 bill.

Still there was far too much sex for the public's chaperones. First on the list were Spade's relationships with Archer's wife, Iva, and with Brigid. Cuts to the script saved us from such depravity as Iva to Sam: 'You'll come tonight.' Sam to Iva: 'Not tonight.' The P.C.A also had their eye on what they termed 'the characterization of Cairo as a pansy'.

Despite their ministrations all these elements remain quite clear in the finished product and there's even one explicit reference to homosexuality which the watchdogs missed. Spade taunts Wilmer, calling him a gunsel. It sounds like a term for a diminutive hood but otherwise spelled 'gonsil' it was really American hobo slang for a homosexual side-kick as defined in a study of that year called 'The Language of Homosexuality'. Perhaps this useful work wasn't yet on the shelves of the Production Code Administration.

The vetting out of the way Huston prepared his first picture by making sketches of every scene and set-up so that he wouldn't be at a loss when he went onto the set. Like Orson Welles, who was at the same time working on *Citizen Kane* at RKO, Huston explored novel techniques – like the then rare practice of doing low shots which included the ceilings on the sets. In the event he altered most of the set-ups in rehearsal when he saw how the actors naturally played the lines.

Despite all the time spent socializing they were brisk enough about the filming, finishing in just over a month, two days ahead of schedule. There was apparently a sense that they were all on to something good and a subsequent desire to repeat the experience. Huston, Bogart, Astor and Greenstreet got back together the following year for *Across the Pacific* and many of the principals appeared later with Huston. He and Bogart made six more films together.

The family atmosphere was augmented when John's father, the actor Walter Huston, agreed to take the bit part of the ship's officer who stumbles mortally wounded into Spade's office with the bird. He evidently thought it was going to be a quick job but his son made him go through retake after retake. Huston senior got exasperated. 'Didn't expect to have to put in a day's *work*,' he complained. For a gag John got Mary Astor to telephone his father the next day posing as a secretary to tell him that the shots had been spoiled in processing. Huston senior's answer was short and to the point.

Bogart's family relationships at the time of filming were less cosy. He was married to his third wife, the minor actress Mayo Methot. His pet name for her was Sluggy (also for his yacht and his Scottie dog). The couple were known as the Battling Bogarts. She would throw things at him in public and knifed him once during a domestic argument (see also *Casablanca* (1942)). Bogie put up with it all until he fell for Lauren Bacall on the set of *To Have and To Have Not* three years later.

The details of Mary Astor's private life were common knowledge. She was emerging from the shadow of the biggest Hollywood sex scandal of the thirties. It centred on a battle with the second of her four husbands, Dr Franklyn Thorpe, for the custody of their daughter Marilyn. Dr Thorpe found Mary's diary which recounted blatant details of her affair with the witty scriptwriter George S. Kaufman. The

Doctor went through with his threat to make them public if she didn't give in. 'Ah desert night – with George's body plunging into mine, naked under the stars,' was one of the public's favourite passages. In the event Mary won the case after counter-evidence of Thorpe's own carrying-on. Her film career didn't really take a beating either, partly because of a sympathetic performance she gave at the time in the hit, *Dodsworth* (1936). She never got her diary back though. The authorities burned it as pornography.

By this time, although she didn't know it, she had truly shaken off any trace of scandal. Her performance just completed in *The Great Lie* (1941) would win her the Oscar the following year.

It was also to be a good year for Sydney Greenstreet. But although he was the most experienced actor in the company he seems to have been the most nervous. He was particularly wound up just before the first scene he appears in, the long dialogue with Spade. Mary Astor reassured him at the time but he needn't have worried. At sixty-one, in his first film after a lifetime on the stage, Greenstreet became one of the favourite screen villains of the forties. So different from the story, *The Maltese Falcon* brought good fortune to all concerned.

▦ The experience

'I had a lot going for me in that one. First, there was Huston. He made the Dashiell Hammett novel into something you don't come across too often. It was practically a masterpiece. I don't have many things I'm proud of but that's one.' Humphrey Bogart

'Two things in particular are notable and pleasing; *The Maltese Falcon* brings a new, young director, John Huston, to the surface and it gives Humphrey Bogart his best chance since *The Petrified Forest*.' Dylis Powell, *The Times*, 21 June 1941

▦ Can you spot . . .

* Where Bogart's performance changes gear. The studio heads monitored the rushes and gauged his performance to be too casual. Huston argued that it was all part of a device to make the film accelerate to where it would be 'turning like a pinwheel'. Nevertheless he got Bogart to tauten his performance from around the fourth day of shooting.
* The great dolly take. It's one of the scenes in Sam's apartment which was originally planned as a series of cuts. Instead Huston did it in one continuous shot. There were many secret cues and high tension on the set but the first take worked perfectly.

M*A*S*H

1970 Two combat surgeons' tour of duty three miles from the front line during the Korean war.

▦ The talent

Donald Sutherland 34, as Hawkeye; experienced Canadian film actor, previously in minor roles, followed this with *Klute* (1971) and has continued busy
Elliott Gould 31, as Trapper John; emerging as a top seventies star after a discouraging period as Mr Barbra Streisand
Tom Skerritt 36, as Duke; the one that didn't make it big although he keeps busy – *Alien* (1979) and *Top Gun* (1986) for example
Sally Kellerman 31, as Major Hot Lips; after past struggles for work was much praised and Oscar-nominated for this but top-flight parts have since largely eluded her
Robert Duvall 38, as Major Frank Burns; *The Godfather* (1972), *Apocalypse Now* (1979) and Oscar-winning *Tender Mercies* (1982) were to follow
Ino Preminger Producer; brother-of-Otto's first film
Robert Altman 44, Director; formed own production company to plough his individual furrow. Much critical success since but no more big money-makers

▦ The business

They had a script but no director.

At least fourteen had turned down the project or were otherwise occupied. Next on the list was Robert Altman, hired for $75,000 despite a reputation as a maverick whose unconventional techniques had got him thrown off many a TV show.

*M*A*S*H is* based on the actual impressions of medical service during the Korean war, from an ex-military doctor writing under the pseudonym of Richard Hooker. Ring Lardner Jr, who won an Oscar for his *M*A*S*H* script,* had rather different memories of the period. He was one of the Hollywood Ten, blackballed from the industry in the early fifties. Lardner's chief crime seems to have been smart alecry. His response to the House Unamericam Activities Committee's question as to whether he had been a communist was, 'I could answer that but I'd hate myself in the morning.' He had no Hollywood work for fifteen years.

Altman brought *M*A*S*H* in at $3,000,000 which was $500,000 under budget. This might have delighted the Twentieth Century Fox bosses had their thoughts not been dominated by the studio's big deal of the time, *Patton* (1970). Altman was left to post-produce his picture without interference, free to use the overlapping sound and continuity techniques that had caused problems in the past.

These loomed again when Fox got the results of some previews. The foreign press critics couldn't take the blood and walked out en masse. The man from *Variety* panned it. Happily *M*A*S*H* was saved from being withdrawn or extensively recut by a further, highly enthusiastic preview in San Francisco one Saturday night.

*Heavily revamped, as we shall see, by Altman and the cast.

Fox decided to release it as is and must have been glad they did. Riding a wave of popular anti-war films *M*A*S*H* made $36,720,000 in North America. It also received fulsome critical praise for the fresh multi-sound technique and busy visual composition. Elliott Gould and Donald Sutherland became the stars of the moment; the rest of the cast found their careers boosted. Lone dissenting voices came from the U.S. Army and Airforce authorities who banned the picture from service theatres. The Navy, who escaped its satirical targeting, were happy to let it play.

Yet more money came from selling the idea to television as the basis for one of the most successful of all situation comedies. It ran eleven years, attracting the biggest American audience in history for its final airing in 1983. This was only relatively beneficial to Robert Altman who took a flat fee up front. However his teenage son Mike, who wrote the lyrics to the *M*A*S*H* theme song, continued to receive royalties for its TV use.

▦ Behind the screen

This is entirely Robert Altman's film, but he's a very good listener and everyone who wanted to, got in on the decision-making. Before a scene was committed to film there would be a period of rehearsal and improvisation until a playable consensus had emerged. Actors were encouraged to alter, replace or simply drop their lines. New main characters were introduced.

Sally Kellerman: nine line wonder

An example is Major Hot Lips. The original part was nine lines and Sally Kellerman had come instead to read for the part of Lieutenant Dish. Altman apparently caught sight of her and started chanting, 'Hot lips, hot lips . . .' He assured her about making the part up as they went along. 'We'll try things,' he said. 'They'll work.'

Everything they tried was in a little encampment on the Fox back lot where they were filming. The team were encouraged to live together under canvas on site. They got 'riffed' each night and all vetted the rushes. Close relationships developed.

This communal feeling was not initially shared by the two stars, Gould and Sutherland, who tried to have Altman removed. Their views certainly changed with the success of the film. Gould became one of an Altman repertory of favourite actors and technicians who joined him for future projects. Sally Kellerman, Bud Cort, Michael Murphy, Rene Auberjonois and John Shuck all turned up in the director's next film, *Brewster McCloud* (1970). Only Radar, Gary Burghoff, made the transfer to the TV version.

Afterwards there was some dispute between the director and scriptwriter as to who contributed what. Altman held that any script was little more than a lure for financial backing which could also serve as a rough shooting schedule. He airily claimed to have come up with all the jokes.

Nevertheless much from the Hooker novel and Lardner script remains in the film, including Dago Red's riposte, much quoted in the reviews, to Hot Lips's rhetorical demand how Hawkeye could have achieved his position of responsibility in the armed forces. 'He was drafted,' the Padre innocently explains. On the other hand much of the first and last few scenes, the Henry/Radar exchanges, the treatment of the Colonel in Tokyo and the charnal chit-chat in the operating theatres, was a product of camping out, improvisation and, possibly, getting riffed.

When filming had finished the director began making sense of his improvised scenes, punctuating them with those sharp post-produced zooms and layering in the sound. It was here, finally, with all the material to play with, that Altman himself came up with one last character that hadn't existed either in the book, the script or even during filming: the camp tannoy.

▦ The experience

'Crazily enough, *M*A*S*H* is a comedy, except it doesn't make you laugh until it hurts; it makes you hurt while you laugh.' *Saturday Review*, 31 January 1970

'Without a moment's rest it slices up the service and service people with a keen eye for weak spots and foibles.' John Greenwald, *The Army Times*, 18 March 1970 – in a review accompanying an article on why the Army was banning the film

'It could truthfully be said that the film has no centre. It has, however, a splendid periphery.' *New Statesman*, 22 May 1970

'I spent years getting fired for things I was acclaimed for in *M*A*S*H*.' Robert Altman, 1970

▦ Can you spot . . .

* What M*A*S*H stands for. Mobile Army Surgical Hospital of course . . . but it's never explained in the film.
* Gunfire. The only time you hear a shot it's time-keeping for the football game. *M*A*S*H* is one of the few war films with no fighting, just the evidence.

One Flew Over the Cuckoo's Nest

1975 An unruly new patient disrupts a mental ward.

▦ The talent

Jack Nicholson 37, as R.P. McMurphy; newly-arrived in the top Hollywood echelon. Has remained one of the modern film superstars

Louise Fletcher 40, as Nurse Ratched; has never repeated this one-off success

Michael Douglas 33, Producer; production debut after co-starring in TV's *Streets of San Francisco*. Major eighties acting star

Milos Forman 42, Director; Czech refugee establishing himself after a difficult start in America. Few films since include hit Oscar-winner *Amadeus* (1983)

▦ The business

Kirk Douglas as R.P. McMurphy? Well, he played the role on Broadway for six months after buying the rights from author Ken Kesey when the book first came out in the early sixties.

And Douglas might have starred in the film as well but he was too old for the part by the time his son Michael, who had taken over the project, succeeded in finding finance for what seemed on paper like unprepossessing subject matter.

Indeed he had to go outside the movie industry – to a record company, Fantasy, who were keen to diversify and had $1,500,000 to spare. When Jack Nicholson agreed to play the lead they raised the ante to $4,000,000 – which included a $1,000,000 fee for the star who had recently become one of Hollywood's most sought-after talents.

Ken Kesey was another formidable, if slightly bizarre, creative force. He wrote *One Flew Over the Cuckoo's Nest* in his early twenties after working in an Oregon mental hospital. His descriptive style was said to owe much to experimentation with LSD and peyote. The book was hailed as an influential work of proto-psychedelia and the novel's trippy feel remained in Kesey's attempt at a screenplay, along with the device of using Chief Broom as narrator.

No sale. Douglas had chosen little-known Czech director, Milos Forman, partly for his realistic filming style. Both wanted the impression of madness to come from the behaviour of the characters rather than special effects and voice-over that would have been needed to convey Kesey's florid prose. Besides, it would have ruined one of modern cinema's most memorable surprises.

Already bitter at having parted with the rights in the first place for just $5,000 Kesey launched a seven-figure lawsuit claiming that he had been promised 5% of the gross, and then retired brooding to his Oregon farm.

Jack Nicholson: Mr 75%

He had more to mull over after the film was released. *One Flew Over the Cuckoo's Nest* was top U.S. money-maker of 1976 with rentals of $120,000,000 worldwide. But even more unusual was its Oscar success. It is so far the only film to repeat the feat accomplished by *It Happened One Night* (1934) in sweeping all five major categories: Best Film, Director, Actor, Actress and Screenplay.

▦ Behind the screen

Are they actors or are they really nutters? So asked the audiences of the mid-seventies, without the advantage of recognizing Danny de Vito, who was to spend another ten years emerging from TV's *Taxi* to film stardom.*

*And his *Taxi* co-star Christopher Lloyd, later to star in *Back to the Future* (1985) and *Who Framed Roger Rabbit* (1989). Brad Dourif, as Billy, was highly praised by the critics and often pops up on TV as a guest player in agitated roles.

The feeling that you are eavesdropping on a hospital ward comes from Milos Forman's shooting-from-the-hip technique, sensitive preparation and a substantial injection of authenticity. Forman had to approach more than forty mental hospitals before Dr Dean Brooks, director of Oregon State Hospital, let them use one of the wings, the sane folk of the area only being capable of filling a fifth of the institution's beds. Dr Brooks' end of the deal included a stipulation that the action be set in the original 1963 (to distance the treatment and characters from current psychiatric practice), and a part in the film. This accounts for his natural portrayal of Dr Spivey; particularly the clinical repartee in interviews with McMurphy, which like much else in the film was improvised on the spot.

So as to maximize his atmospheric absorption Forman stayed at the hospital while he polished off the script with writer Laurence Hauben. The supporting actors, who had been selected from 900 hopefuls by observing their interaction in staged group therapy sessions, were also made to immerse themselves in the Oregon State ambience for a week before filming started in the autumn of 1974.

Forman's technique was to establish a structure for the main scenes – especially the therapy sessions – and then let the actors go. There were at least two cameras running at once with Forman bustling about in the background calling shots in a whisper. Focus and framing were almost incidental to the pursuit of unexpected gestures and facial expressions. The actors never knew when they were on camera which prompted them to try like mad (sorry) every second. This directorial technique is now familiar but then it all looked very fresh to the audience – and very naff to the distinguished cinematographer, Haskell Wexler, who left mid-way through filming. Can you tell the difference? No, which sums up why he quit.*

Louise Fletcher was cast after a number of well-known actresses had turned down the unsympathetic role. Forman claimed to be influenced in his choice by the resolute line of her chin. Fletcher was just returning to work after a decade off raising a family. During filming she was on the brink of separation from her husband but new romance was on its way. She was soon being escorted by a man half her age: James Mason's son, Morgan.

Nicholson, too, was in a state of domestic turmoil. His long-term girlfriend Anjelica Huston left him twice during this period for Ryan O'Neal – prompted, apparently, by Nicholson's proposal of marriage. Nevertheless the pair were reconciled and continued to be an item for years afterwards.

Using a celebrity actor like Nicholson in the lead was deemed essential to give the audience someone to identify with in the alien hospital atmosphere, but the star was no prima donna. He got on well with Fletcher and the rest of the cast, resolving the few disagreements with Forman over how to do a scene by agreeing to play it both ways and have the best version used.

At first the supporting players set about acting crazy but Forman soon put them right. He directed them to the more realistic and touching path of conveying the inmates' pathetic attempts at a semblance of normality despite the upheavals going on in their minds.

Living in an institution for eleven weeks left its mark on the entire production. Michael Douglas joked that the only way you could tell the difference between the

*He nevertheless was nominated for an Oscar.

actors and the inmates was if you had a programme. Even the relentlessly ebullient Jack Nicholson admitted to an initial feeling of depression, particularly at the hopelessness of trying to communicate with some of the patients.

Very few genuine Oregon nuts actually appear. Look carefully at the extras in the basketball game and the characters in the background as Broom and Cheswick are dragged off for shock therapy; and that's about it. Those inmates who were involved on- and off-camera seem in general to have benefited by the experience – but not all.

One took the opportunity of pitching himself backwards out of a window whose protective screen had been left unsecured by a forgetful grip after some cable-laying. The patient fell three floors but fortunately only fractured a shoulder. That didn't prevent the largely hostile local newspapers from having a go, egged on by disgruntled local resident, Mr Ken Kesey. 'One Flew Out of the Cuckoo's Nest' was one keen sub's contribution to the art of headline writing.

The bulk of the grotesques in the background were recruited through those same local papers with an ad which read: Do you have a face that scares timberwolves?

Apart from Dr Brooks the only non-actor who took a major part was Will Sampson, the full-blooded Creek Indian who played Chief Broom. He was a former rodeo rider spotted by a casting agent at an Indian Trade fair in Washington State. In Kesey's novel the whole story is told from the character's psychotic perspective and Sampson took his role very seriously, becoming too intense for the director's liking during the shooting. The laid-back performance you see was finally elicited, says Forman, by an adequate provision of beer.

▦ The experience

'*One Flew Over the Cuckoo's Nest* is a powerful, smashingly effective movie – not a great movie but one that will probably stir audience's emotions and join the ranks of such pop-mythology films as *The Wild One*, *Rebel Without a Cause* and *Easy Rider.*' Pauline Kael, *New Yorker*, 1 December 1975

'One half of me applauds the intelligent, funny, clever, Oscar-nominated film . . . the other half is ashamed at enjoying it.' Margaret Hinxman, *Daily Mail*, 26 February 1976

'You would be mad not to see it.' Ian Christie, *Daily Express*, 27 February 1976

'I am at least 75% of every character I play.' Jack Nicholson, 1974

▦ Can you spot . . .

* Whether McMurphy is really mad or not. Neither could Forman – that's what attracted him to the story.
* The difference between Nicholson's portrayal of electroshock therapy and the real thing. Neither could a doctor who berated Forman on the subject of cruelty to actors.
* The traffic in the background. They had problems with a major road just outside where they were filming which Forman felt obliged to show in one awkward high-angle shot. As it turned out, only a matter of ten lines you hear are re-dubbed.
* The rhythm of the acting. Forman chose the background music early for incorporation in his plan of shooting. He would play it as a take was about to begin so that the actors would retain the proper pace once the cameras rolled.
* What unpleasant byproduct of rats comes to mind when pronouncing the Louise Fletcher character's surname in an American accent.

The Pink Panther

1964 A gentleman cat burglar seeking the eponymous jewel is in league with the wife of the bumbling French detective who is pursuing him.

▦ The talent

David Niven 53, as Sir Charles; charmer with a colourful military past

Peter Sellers 37, as Inspector Clouseau; became a top star – mostly as Clouseau in the seventies – until his death in 1980

Robert Wagner 33, as George; fifties screen teen-throb, later a TV star

Capucine 30, as Simone Clouseau; French former fashion model whose comedy prowess in this impressed previously sceptical critics. She soon left Hollywood for European cinema

Claudia Cardinale 22, as the Princess; latter-day Loren in the most memorable of many films

Martin Jurow 49, Producer; also produced two other Edwards hits of the time, *Breakfast at Tiffany's* (1961) and *The Great Race* (1965), before becoming a lawyer

Blake Edwards 40, Director; multi-talent who since the late sixties has concentrated on reshaping the image of wife Julie Andrews, and on the further adventures of Clouseau

▦ The business

How much different might it have been had Peter Ustinov not pulled out of playing Clouseau at the last minute, ostensibly a reaction to the departure of Ava Gardner who was the original choice for his Mme.

Peter Sellers was ripe for prominence on the world screen, following cult popularity on BBC Radio during the fifties in *The Goon Show*, a decade of British comedy films and some international exposure the previous year in Stanley Kubrick's *Lolita*. Though not yet a star he was offered what he considered to be an astronomical fee, £90,000 for five weeks work. And in Rome!

Sellers stepped off the plane to meet Edwards for the first time and found a comedy soul-mate. They shared a taste for the Harold Lloyd, Buster Keaton and Laurel and Hardy type of comedy where the central character attempts to carry on as all around collapses. There rapidly evolved between them a slapstick Clouseau whose antics budged from the limelight the original central figure, Sir Charles. However the script – by Edwards and Maurice Richlin – remained essentially the same, playful send-up of *To Catch a Thief* (1955). So if you listen to Clouseau's scripted role rather than revel in Sellers' sight gags you'll gather more of the original flavour of the part, with Clouseau one of several characters, a dignified cuckold.

Later in 1963 Blake Edwards was asked to take over filming *A Shot in the Dark*, based on a French stage play. He agreed providing he could rewrite it with Sellers again playing Clouseau. It was filmed before *The Pink Panther* came out in early 1964 and made even more than its $5,875,000. But the honeymoon was over; Sellers and Edwards quarrelled and they didn't get back together until *The Return of the Pink Panther* (1975).*

Peter Sellers was not the only major discovery of the film. Also much appreciated both by the critics and the general public was the title sequence featuring the Pink Panther itself, a creation of Friz Freleng, longtime Warner Brothers animator and his partner David DePatie in their newly-formed independent. The character has maintained a very healthy career of its own with TV and cinema cartoons plus much profitable merchandizing. There is also a cartoon Clouseau.

▦ Behind the screen

This was almost therapy for Peter Sellers, one of the happiest and easiest films he ever made. There was, of course, the money and the wide exposure with a top international cast, but more than that Sellers clearly welcomed an escape from his troubled home life, which in a way mirrored the sad absurdity of Clouseau's predicament.

His wife, Anne, had fallen in love with the architect whom they had hired to re-do their house in Hampstead. Peter said that he started to suspect something when they began to overrule all his suggestions about the decoration. Peter and Anne divorced soon after filming *The Pink Panther* ended in early 1963. Later that year she had married her architect.

Sellers threw himself into exploring the new territory of visual humour. His starting point for the character was a box of matches. Included in the manufacturer's trademark was a portrait of Captain Matthew Webb who in 1875 became the first man to swim the English Channel. His proud stance and heroic moustache evoked for Sellers a trans-Manche image of ostentatious virility he had noted being affected by French males. A master mimic, Sellers also conceived the tortuous accent. Blake Edwards was the sight-gag merchant, choreographing most of Clouseau's physical clumsiness.

It was a volatile partnership. Shared humour was one thing but Blake Edwards and his new star also matched each other in arrogance, and they differed profoundly in their approach to work – Sellers the perfectionist and Edwards more inclined to improvise. What you see is a compromise which accommodated Sellers' penchant for retakes and still left room for the unexpected.

The catchphrase, 'It's hell in there,' was painfully apt when coined as Capucine and Robert Wagner are in the bath. Wagner claims they were assured the suds were baby shampoo when in fact the tub was filled with a powerful chemical frothing agent. Capucine was burned, which perhaps accounts for the out-of-character high neckline to her night attire. Wagner, who was totally immersed, found himself blinded. The doctor prescribed four weeks in a darkened room which in the producer's view made him dispensable. But Sellers, Edwards and David Niven all rallied round insisting that they shoot round Wagner's recuperation.

---

*Alan Arkin took the lead in an unsuccessful revival, *Inspector Clouseau* (1968), directed by Bud Yorkin. The other Clouseau films with Sellers directed by Edwards were *The Pink Panther Strikes Again* (1976) and *The Revenge of the Pink Panther* (1978). After Sellers died there were two more resurrections of the series stitched together with off-cuts: *Trail of the Pink Panther* (1982) and *Curse of the Pink Panther* (1983).

Capucine, Peter Sellers and Robert Wagner: hell in there

These were uncertain times for Robert Wagner. Aside from personal worries* his film career was slowing down, actually reaching a dead halt after *The Pink Panther* with two years of unemployment until he revived cat burglary in TV's *It Takes a Thief*. Wagner has continued to prosper on the box with only occasional forays onto the big screen.

Despite thirteen years in the business, since being spotted by a talent scout at college, Wagner seems to have been offered a lot of fatherly advice on *The Pink Panther* set. Can you spot him hooding his eyes? Peter Sellers could and counselled him to quit this nervous habit. David Niven gave him some pointers on style and acted as guide to the Roman nightlife. They formed a lasting friendship.

David Niven . . . remember him? This great screen smoothie emerges with the kind of bruised poise displayed when Sir Charles excuses himself from the Princess's dinner party. His career needed a lift but this was not to be it, as Sellers stumbled away with what was meant to be Niven's film. Even the presence on set of Niven's old army friend, Michael Trubshawe, playing the novelist, was little compensation. Their days of roguish comradeship were long gone; they hadn't been close for years.

Niven was a prize raconteur but rarely included *The Pink Panther* in his reminiscences. Some years later while preparing to make a presentation at the Oscars

---

*He was between Natalie Woods. They were recently divorced and Wagner was soon to marry another actress, Marion Marshall. He remarried Natalie in 1972.

he overheard Henry Mancini rehearsing his *Pink Panther* theme tune for the Niven entrance and gently suggested they play *Around the World in Eighty Days* instead.*

However, the film proved good news for Sellers, professionally and even romantically. He soon met and within weeks married a twenty-one year old Swedish actress then called Britt Eklund. Their first date was at an early London screening of *The Pink Panther.*

▦ The experience

'*The Pink Panther* is comedy with a difference: comedy with grace. Absurd grace, but still grace.' Dilys Powell, *Sunday Times*, 12 January 1964

'Here is genius wearing its funniest face.' Alexander Walker, *Evening Standard*, 9 January 1964

'It all looks very rich and glossy but I fancy that when Peter Sellers glances back in old age over the film peaks of his prime he will prefer to forget this one.' Cecil Wilson, *Daily Mail*, 8 January 1964

'A bit of a giggle.' Peter Sellers

▦ Can you spot . . .

* The Princess's disappearing cigarette. As David Niven attempts his seduction of Claudia Cardinale on the tigerskin rug her cigarette changes magically from one hand to the other and then disappears entirely as they kiss. Very fortunate, otherwise, following continuity with the previous shot, they both would have felt a fire in their bosom. Perhaps everyone had drunk too much champagne.

* A touch of Fred Astaire. The choreographer for Fran Jeffries' rendition of 'Meglio Stasera' was Fred's old crony Hermes Pan. Sellers had another famous tutor. He learned his bossa nova for the film from regal British star, Dame Anna Neagle.

* A slimline Peter Sellers. He had been popping diet pills for the past year achieving a younger, leaner look which was to remain. Compare how podgy he looks in earlier films.

* Flare amid the flair. As Clouseau is being cross-examined by the defence lawyer, played by *Dad's Army* favourite John Le Mesurier, an unusual mistake in the way reflected light is accommodated in the lens has caused a rainbow effect when the camera is pointing towards Clouseau.

* A European single market in sleuthing. Clouseau, a French Inspector, seems to have carte blanche to investigate freely in Italy, commanding a large force of the country's police at Angela Dunning's party in Rome.

*Ironically Niven's last screen appearances were in the final two *Panther* films frankensteined after Sellers' death.

Anthony Perkins: stuffing birds

Psycho

1960 A woman steals money from her employer and flees to a new life with her lover. On the way she stops at an isolated motel to rest for the night . . .

▦ The talent

Anthony Perkins 28, as Norman Bates; forever identified with this part, and never quite as successful since
Janet Leigh 33, as Marion Crane; soon to divorce Tony Curtis. Their daughter Jamie Lee Curtis is a star of the eighties
John Gavin 32, as Sam Loomis; minor beefcake who became U.S. Ambassador to Mexico

Vera Miles 31, as Lila Crane; Hitchcock might have made her star if she hadn't got pregnant after *The Wrong Man* (1957)
Martin Balsam 41, as Milton Arbogast; one of the screen's most familiar supporting players since *On the Waterfront* (1954) debut
Alfred Hitchcock 61, Producer/Director; brilliant cinematic trickster but with little left up his sleeve after this

▦ The business

After decades at the top Alfred Hitchcock was taking a big chance with his reputation and with his pocket book. Although his eminence and consistent bankability meant that‘others were prepared to give him up to $3,000,000 a picture and no questions asked, the $800,000 *Psycho* cost to make came from his own savings. No director does this lightly, but Hitch saw it as a calculated risk based on the huge financial success of recent low-budget horror imports, from Britain's Hammer Films and others.

At one point in the post-production he lost faith in the project and was going to demote *Psycho* to an episode of his top-rated television series. But the gamble paid off handsomely. *Psycho* proved to be his most financially successful film, taking to date an estimated $20,000,000 worldwide. Hitchcock himself received more than $2,500,000 during the first four months of business and it probably netted him twice that in all.

If he was paying for it, Hitchcock was determined to keep costs low. Shooting in monochrome was a big saving to start off with, which he rationalized by claiming that the realistic style would have less impact in colour. Of course, it also would have necessitated using something other than chocolate sauce for blood.

The sets were all fragments from around the lot, now owned by Universal but then the Revue TV studio,* and most of the crew were Hitchcock TV show regulars. And there were none of the customary big-name-big-money stars like Cary Grant or James Stewart. Vera Miles was on a personal contract to Hitchcock's own company and Anthony Perkins owed a movie to Paramount who were acting as distributors. He got

---

*The Bates family home has a surprisingly less sinister history than you might think. Recognize the main tower from *Harvey* (1950)?

$40,000, the same amount as Janet Leigh's character stole from her employers.* Her fellow office worker can't have cost Hitchcock dear, either. It's his own daughter, Patricia (previously featured in his *Strangers on a Train* (1951)).

Hitchcock was a master publicist and played to the full on rumours about the movie. He wouldn't give critics or cinema owners any previews, decreed that no one should be allowed into the theatre after the film started and further teased the public with a six-minute trailer – his own droll tour of the Bates establishment.

Perhaps because of all this, and the liberal use of chocolate sauce, the critics were almost universally hostile. Hitch, who said he regarded the whole film as his little joke, laughed all the way to the bank.

Afterwards he was curious as to why the film had been quite so successful and commissioned a study by Stamford University. But when they quoted a fee of $75,000 he cancelled it. 'I wasn't *that* curious,' he explained.

The success of *Psycho* did none of the players any harm except perhaps Anthony Perkins who seems to have learned to live with typecasting, and has repeated the *Psycho* experience in remakes *II* and *III*, the last of which he also directed. For Janet Leigh the film has proved an inconvenience. Even now she is plagued with crank calls and letters whenever *Psycho* is televised in the U.S., which is up to twenty-five times a year.

▦ Behind the screen

Psycho is full of recurring symbolic themes and in-jokes but isn't really as violent as we tend to remember it. Hitchcock wanted to transfer the terror from the screen into the audience's mind as the film went on – and if you think about it there are only two real bits of all-out frenzy.

The pseudish symbols come thick and fast, though, starting with the shot that opens the action: the culmination of a three-and-a-half-mile helicopter run that needed days of rehearsal (the crew practised by buzzing a hotel in Hollywood before the location work started in Phoenix). It's all about voyeurism, you see. We begin by peeping into the room where Janet Leigh and screen lover John Gavin are enjoying some afternoon delight – a very hot scene for its time.

There's more for voyeurs in this scene than is obvious at first sight. John Gavin was nervous acting without a shirt and not really worked up enough to make things look convincing. So Hitchcock had a quiet word with the professional Miss Leigh who let her fingers do the walking beyond the call of duty and produced a more convincing reaction from slow-start John. The director claimed later that Gavin played the scene with an erection.

Hitchcock has often been portrayed as something of a cold fish himself with actors but he evidently took quite a shine to Janet Leigh. She was more experienced and accomplished than many of his leading ladies, able to fit well into his style of leaving the players to work pretty much as they wanted so long as they kept within the confines of the shots he conceived. Anthony Perkins was very enthusiastic about the film and was also favoured. But Hitchcock didn't rate Gavin and was bored with Miles, and tended to cold-shoulder them both.

---

*The first four $1,000 bills in the bundle were real. Janet Leigh, who earned $25,000 for *Psycho*, insisted on a receipt each time she handed them back after a take.

The film and Perkins' part in it are screen legend which makes it difficult to experience *Psycho* nowadays in quite the same way as was intended. The trouble is that we all know the structure of the story now (pulp novel by Robert Bloch, screenplay by Joseph Stefano). You *should* think it's a tale of theft and escape, with the seemingly mild and pathetic Norman Bates appearing at first to be just one of a series of cameo vignettes – the salacious house-buyer, the threatening policeman, the suspicious car dealer and so on. It was the unexpected shape of the piece that really got Hitchcock hooked. Who would expect the star to get bumped off in the middle of the action, and all that follows? No wonder he pleaded with the public at the time not to reveal the ending. 'It's the only one we've got,' he said.

Just before the shower scene the symbolism reaches a fever pitch, all birds and voyeurism. Birds? Well, the favourite hobby of mother-dominated 'Master' Bates is avian taxidermy, an allusion to 'stuffing birds' which would be obvious to anyone, like Hitchcock, with a British background. And his intended victim: Miss Crane from Phoenix. It's no wonder Hitchcock's next movie turned out to be *The Birds* (1963).

The voyeurism theme is continued with Norman's little peep-hole into cabin number one where Marion is preparing for the most ill-advised ablution in film history. Even the picture that covers the hole is significant – it's a copy of Rembrandt's *Susanna and the Elders*, which portrays the story from the Apocrypha of a girl brought to grief by being spied on.

This shot is significant in another way. Almost all of *Psycho* is shot through a standard 50 mm lens - the one which, on 35 mm film, most closely mimics our normal field of vision. To get through the peep-hole the cameraman attached a special lens called an Acorn which can see through a $\frac{1}{4}$-inch hole and is normally used for eye operations.

The shower scene that follows is one of the most analysed sequences in all cinema. It took almost eighty separate set-ups over the course of a week and lasts only about forty-five seconds. And the murderer is ... Hitchcock himself. He held the knife because he knew exactly where it should be. For full-length shots the knife-wielder is 24-year-old stunt girl Margo Epper. You-know-who wasn't anywhere around and neither was Janet Leigh for much of the time. The face and hands are hers but the nude torso is 23-year-old Marli Renfro. Originally Hitchcock planned to make the scene even more gory. He had the special effects men make up a fake torso that spurted blood, but had to admit that the effect was over the top. Hitch claimed that the knife never actually touched flesh but video stop-frame buffs might disagree and despite the attentions of the censors might also spot a flash of Ms Renfro's nipple. In fact, the American censors took a close look but left the shower scene virtually unaltered.* In the UK, however, it was cut from seventeen stabs (count 'em) to a more British three.

It was planned without any musical background, just the sound of screams and gurgling water, but Bernard Herrman, who wrote the all-string 'black-and-white' score to match a black-and-white film, persuaded Hitchcock to include the famous insistent-stabbing theme music.

---

*More touchy, it seems, was the later close-up of a flushing toilet which was regarded as in very poor taste. It was one of the first times that bodily functions were even hinted at in films and another conscious Hitchcock shock tactic.

Hitchcock owed much of the visual style of this famous screen murder to Saul Bass, one of Hollywood's most innovative graphic artists and designer of the titles for *Psycho*, and for *Vertigo* (1958), *North by Northwest* (1959) and many other films. Bass story-boarded the shower scene and has claimed that he actually directed it as well. He is alone in this. Many more witnesses recall Hitchcock peering down at Renfro the Torso from the platform built around the specially constructed shower set and calling all the shots.

Bass also story-boarded the death of Arbogast the detective, and this time Hitchcock *wasn't* the director, at least not for the first version. He caught a flu bug that had been going round the set and assistant director Hilton Green took over for a day using Bass's concept.

They proudly showed the results to the old master but he gave it the thumbs down. The Bass story-boards had repeated the tricks of rapid cuts and odd angles that worked so well in the shower. However Hitchcock said it just made you expect the worst for Arbogast, and that simple shooting would maintain the element of surprise.

Simple or not it is one of the most expensive sequences in the film. The camera is on a specially constructed platform ninety feet above the action, necessary so that you don't wonder too much why you don't see Mother Bates up close.* Arbogast's tumble down stairs is a back projection. The camera was tracked down the stairs and then Martin Balsam was filmed throwing his arms about. The tracking shot goes soft midway, although you're so taken up with Arbogast's aghast expression it scarcely notices. Hitch didn't bother to reshoot that element of the original Bass/Green effort, which they themselves let pass because they planned to cut in and out of it.

All of the driving sequences are back projections as well. Hitch even changes the background in mid-shot to denote passage of time without sagging the viewer's disbelief.

Now, if you haven't actually seen the film it would be best for you to skip these last few paragraphs and get right on with the critics' comments . . .

Are we alone? For those of us who already know the perils of venturing into the fruit cellar let us dwell for a moment on the mummified Mrs Bates. This rubber-coated human skull which, if anything, had more shock impact than the shower scene and Arbogast's misadventure put together, got through the censors because, like the rest of the film, it was meticulously and accurately researched.

Hitchcock had people look into all aspects of the plot. They travelled the route from Phoenix to make sure the geography of Miss Crane's flight was authentic. They researched the workings of used car lots and detective agencies, and even photographed the home and wardrobe of a woman in Phoenix who resembled Marion so that the costume designer got the proper feel.

Still, you can't help feeling that what Hitchcock really relished was the more grizzly research, like the sound a knife makes in contact with flesh (tested with melons) and what a corpse would look like in Mrs Bates' conditions of storage. A mortician's academy confirmed that if your Mummy was a mummy she'd look just like that dummy.

---

*Hitchcock further added to the confusion by making a big deal of looking for someone to play Mrs Bates. He had great fun rejecting several distinguished elder actresses who coveted this prestigious cameo.

▦ The experience

'Sicko.' *Picturegoer*

'I have just seen one of the most vile and disgusting films ever made.' Rene MacColl, *Daily Express*, 2 July 1960

'It is not just a sick joke, it is also a very sad joke. Because it is outrageous, it exhilarates, but it is a very depressing film as well.' Raymond Turgnat, *The Strange Case of Alfred Hitchcock*, 1974

'I remember the terrible panning we got when *Psycho* opened. Perhaps the films are too subtle for the critics. They seem to take about a year to sink in.' Alfred Hitchcock

▦ Can you spot . . .

* Hitchcock's traditional cameo appearance. Of course you can. He's standing outside the estate agent's office wearing a ten-gallon hat. Another cameo you may recognize is one of the arresting officers, Ted Knight, more familiar many years later as the prissy newsreader on TV's *Mary Tyler Moore Show*.

* A gruesome relation. Bloch's *Psycho* novel was loosely based on the real story of a nutter called Ed Gein who thrived in Wisconsin during the fifties and did things with women's bodies that really *would* make you sick. So was *The Texas Chainsaw Massacre* (1974).

* Three lost days. The opening caption makes it pedantically clear that the story starts on Friday, December 11th. The final date on the calendar in the Bates motel office is the 17th but according to the time we are told has elapsed it must actually be the 20th. Very mysterious.

* Another little joke. The scene at the end when Bates is in a cell is meant to echo the famous painting, Whistler's *Mother*.

* How the lens stays dry in the shot where it is pointing directly at the showerhead. It's another shot that couldn't be done with a standard 50 mm lens. Instead they employed a long lens shooting tight. The water sprays past the lens though it looks like it's actually going onto it. All that got wet was the film crew.

* A pathological error. Marion's famous post-stabbing close-up eye is contracted by the strong studio lighting. A real victim's pupil would have been dilated. Lots of opticians pointed it out and prescribed a drop of belladonna, which Hitchcock employed in later films where the circumstances warranted.

* Vera Miles' wig. She had just finished *Five Branded Women* (1960) which she played with a shaved head (her own).

* A final trick. The mother's face is superimposed on Norman's in the last shot before the end title. Or perhaps it isn't. This was an effect that Hitchcock wasn't sure about and it is only in half of the prints that were actually released.

Raiders of the Lost Ark

1981 Archaeologist races with the Nazis to discover the whereabouts of a priceless and powerful relic.

▨ The talent

Harrison Ford 38, as Indy; in Lucas' *American Graffiti* (1973) and *Star Wars* (1977). Broadened his range with *Witness* (1985). One of the biggest eighties superstars

Karen Allen 29, as Marion; in *Manhattan* (1979) and other films since but not in any of the *Indiana* sequels

Denholm Elliott 58, as Brody; one of Britain's most familiar and well-regarded character actors. Many previous films; *Trading Places* (1983), *A Private Function* (1984) and *A Room With A View* (1985) amongst many successes since

Paul Freeman 38, as Belloq; familiar face from British TV's *Death of a Princess* and other series

Ronald Lacey 45, as Toht; another of British TV's staple actors, often in comedy villain parts. Spotted by the film-makers a decade before in TV role as safe-cracker

John Rhys-Davies 33, as Sallah; impressive telly credits include *Shogun* and *The Naked Civil Servant*. Like Elliott, back for *Indiana Jones and the Last Crusade* (1989)

Frank Marshall 32, Producer; former Bogdanovich team player starting a fruitful association with Steven Spielberg, with whom he and *E.T.* (1982) producer Kathleen Kennedy formed Amblin' Productions. Involved in most Spielberg projects since

Steven Spielberg 34, Director; *E.T.* (1982) was to come. He has since branched out into production, and more adult drama

▨ The business

The story goes that after the release of *Star Wars* (1977) George Lucas retired to a beach in Hawaii. His friend Steven Spielberg joined him with confirmation of the film's success and together they began kicking around a notion combining the Saturday morning serials of their youth, the occult and a touch of James Bond. It had apparently been a toss-up which film genre George Lucas would conceptually pillage first, Flash Gordon-space or this.

The *Raiders* plot emerged through Lucas plonking himself down in front of a tape recorder for five days with some scriptwriters and talking his idea through into a structure. Chicago ad writer Lawrence Kasdan then spent the next six months filling in the words.*

Faced with the combination of George (*Star Wars, American Graffiti*) Lucas and Steven (*Jaws, Close Encounters*) Spielberg you would have thought that studios would be falling over each other to get a piece of the action. Not so. They were scared

---

*Philip Kaufman, who retained a co-writing credit, was originally to be the director but dropped out. Spielberg took over and Kaufman went on to write and direct *The Right Stuff* (1983). For *Raiders* his major contribution was the mcguffin of the Ark of the Covenant.

off by the high percentages that they expected two such talents to demand which would cut the heart out of the profits.

Eventually Michael Eisner of Paramount took the plunge but he negotiated tough penalty payment clauses for running over the $20,000,000 budget or the proposed schedule of just eighty-seven days. Lucasberger, as the team was nicknamed, readily agreed having already worked out a secret agenda which brought them in under-budget and in seventy-three days.

They had some trouble finding the leading man who was right under their noses all the time. At first their ideal was some undiscovered hunk – a concept dubbed Johnny, the construction worker from Malibu. Johnny remained undiscovered and it wasn't possible to disentangle another possibility, Tom Sellick, from his new TV show, *Magnum P.I.*

The final, now seemingly-obvious, choice was not keen to repeat what looked like a character clone of *Star Wars'* Han Solo. Part of the price he exacted was a much fuller participation in creating the film. Steven Spielberg had added key scenes to the Lucas story and Kasdan script. Harrison Ford extensively rewrote his part in the ten hours he spent flying over to Britain for filming in June 1980. His contribution continued during the shoot.

The financial result was a foregone conclusion. *Raiders of the Lost Ark* was an immediate smash when released a year later. It grossed over $8,000,000 in three days and went on to make $115,500,000 in North America alone.* Its sequel, *Indiana Jones and the Temple of Doom* (1984), was just as successful and the third adventure, *Indiana Jones and the Last Crusade* looks on course to complete the hat trick.

▦ Behind the screen

The first sequence, Raiders of the Lost Fertility Goddess as it was known to the unit, was shot in Hawaii and, as with the rest of the picture, in a rush. Steven Spielberg was faced with spending a friend's money and he knew that his customary perfectionism was costly. As a result you are looking at Spielberg's most quick-fire filming since his salad days in TV. His rate of work accelerated to fifteen set-ups a day on set and thirty-five in the open air.

Harrison Ford is of the school of action stars who does his own stunts wherever possible. His reason in this case was two-fold. The unquestionable participation of the star rather than a stand-in provided a degree of realism elsewhere scarce in the film. Furthermore, with the constant hurly-burly of the *Raiders* narrative he hardly would have got a look-in otherwise.

In the Bond-derived preamble he had to run away from the giant boulder ten times – two takes for each of five camera angles. Although you would be right in thinking it's not a real boulder, eight hundred pounds of special-effects plaster still could have made an unhealthy dent in the production.

There were some near misses. The sea plane crashed on take-off. And when they were doing the fight scene under the revolving grounded aircraft Ford slipped and almost had his leg crushed by one of the wheels.

The star himself made things marginally more dangerous for the real stunt men. For film fights they are all trained to throw everything behind a punch but miss the

---

*There were also two Oscars for technical achievement: Editing and wrath-of-God Visual Effects.

Harrison Ford: he *wanted* to do the stunts

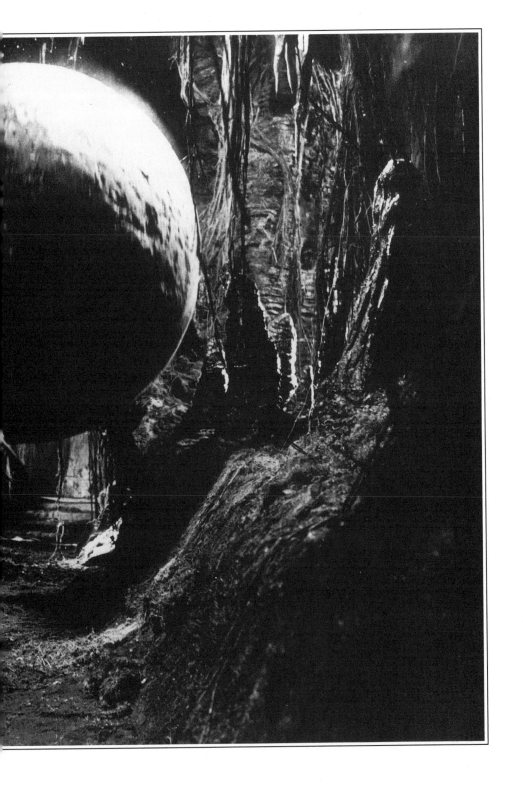

target by inches, leaving the false perspective of a camera angle to complete the illusion. Actors don't have that degree of accuracy and the stunt men get a higher average of bruises.

One incident that boosted the figures involved stunt man Martin Groce on his own. He was standing in, or rather clinging on, for Indie atop the thirty-foot-high Jackal statue in the Well of Souls. The hydraulic ram under one leg of the statue was fired too early, making it tumble. You can see that Groce has not quite got to his position yet and loses his footing. Fortunately he escaped serious injury.

This scene, filmed at Elstree, employed 6,000 harmless garden snakes imported from Holland with two bad-ass cobras spiced in for the thrill factor. Karen Allen hated them all but managed to brazen it out. However, unlike their screen counterparts, Harrison Ford has no problem with snakes and the snakes themselves are rather partial to a nice fire. The cobras were kept on a short lead by handlers. Serum was imported from India and they had an ambulance standing by. But someone failed to keep an eye on the innocuous snake masses and two thousand of them went missing. Whether they were nicked as souvenirs or set up independently in the London suburbs remains a mystery.

It all added up to the trickiest part of a production that required the degree of careful planning that Spielberg specializes in. He employed four artists to complete the story-boards, spending six months mapping out at least 80% of the action. He actually stuck to about 60% of that – most closely to the plan for the final sequence, which had to fit the separate work being done by Lucas' special effects factory, Industrial Light and Magic.

As it was all mapped out Spielberg was able to save further time and effort by not shooting the whole film himself. He directed all the sequences with Harrison Ford but crowd scenes, for example, have been shot by the second unit director, Michael Moore or, on his infrequent visits to the set, by George Lucas.*

A celebrated scene that didn't pan out according to Spielberg's story-boards was the fight with the Arab swordsman. Indie has reason to look dischuffed. He had the squits, as did many of the company.** The original elaborate fight scene would have meant four more days of dysentery but Ford had other ideas, making for one of the film's favourite gag surprises. He reasoned that in any case Jones would have been anxious to get on with finding Marion.

So all in all *Raiders of the Lost Ark* does not bear the Spielberg stamp as firmly as some of his other works. There is more violence and the camera is not permitted to linger, both the influence of George Lucas who supervised the editing. This was an isolated period of relative uncertainty for Steven Spielberg. His previous film, *1941* (1979), with John Belushi ran entirely counter to form in failing to raise a huge profit. He had also broken up with his girlfriend, Amy Irving.***

Nevertheless he seems to have thoroughly enjoyed the production and did all he could to foster a good atmosphere, treating his stars with a courtly respect and gently kissing Karen Allen after each shot.

---

*Some of the shots weren't done by anyone directly involved. Those of the plane going over the Himalayas were reportedly bought from the owners of *Lost Horizon* (1972) and some of the period street scenes from *The Hindenberg* (1975).

**Not Spielberg, who stuck to a personal store of tinned food imported from home.

***They got back together, had a son, married and then split again in the late eighties.

This may have been over-compensation. There does not seem to have been much love lost between the two. The leading girls have changed in each film. For *Indiana Jones and the Temple of Doom* Allen was replaced by Kate Capshaw, who a few years later replaced Amy Irving as the woman in Spielberg's life.

▦ The experience

'*Raiders of the Lost Ark* has it all – or, anyway, more than enough to transport movie goers back to the dazzling, thrill-sated matinee idylls of old.' Richard Schickel, *Time*, 15 June 1981

'It will have you laughing, almost crying, and perched on the edge of your seat gripped by excitement.' *The Sun*, 17 April 1981

'Despite its daring surface, *Raiders* is timid movie making: the film seems terrified of not giving audiences enough thrills to keep them happy.' Pauline Kael, *New Yorker*, 15 June 1981

'I've never enjoyed making a film as much as this one. I felt like I was playing the role. I was the Indiana Jones behind the camera.' Steven Spielberg

▦ Can you spot . . .

* Karen Allen's freckles. They were a challenge to the make-up boys.
* What a cobra is doing in the Middle East so far from its native Asiatic habitat.
* Where Indiana's name comes from. He shares it with George Lucas' pet malamute, also one of the character constituents of Chewbacca of *Star Wars*.
* Some unexpected nourishment. Paul Freeman as the villainous Belloq appears to swallow a fly. It's as he says 'You will give mercenaries a bad name,' when Indiana attempts to play hard ball by threatening the Ark with a bazooka. Freeman keeps on going, but what happened to the fly?
* Steve Edge's ankles. He was one of the animal handlers and for some of the snake shots shaved his legs and donned a white dress as Marion's pins. Despite this sacrifice it looks as if they mostly used shots of Karen Allen in the front line.
* Marion pulling a fast one. In the drinking contest she still has one glass to go after her opponent keels over.
* Where Indie got the scar. It is a genuine Harrison Ford injury caused in a 1960's road accident. He was trying to fasten his safety belt at the time.
* The producer. Frank Marshall plays the pilot of the revolving plane.
* A man with two roles. Pat Roach appears both as the Giant Sherpa and a mechanic.
* Where you've seen the sub before. It was used in the German U-Boat film *Das Boot* (1981). They filmed at a genuine ex-German base at La Rochelle in France, complete with original signs.
* Where the Ark of the Covenant really is now. Ask the Babylonians. It disappeared when they sacked the Temple of Jerusalem in BC 586.

Rambo: First Blood Part II

1985 Military superman John Rambo is looking for Americans still being held captive by the Vietnamese.

▦ The talent

Sylvester Stallone 38, as John Rambo; writer and actor who continues to make a limited image go far and pay spectacularly well

Richard Crenna 57, as Colonel Trautman; TV star, former child radio actor

Julie Nickson 27, as Co Bao; Singapore model and American TV actress

Charles Napier as Marshall Murdock; *Blues Brothers* (1980) and TV actor tending to Westerns in the eighties

Steven Berkoff 48, as Lt Podovsky; British alternative playwright. Actor villain of the moment, also in *Beverly Hills Cop* (1984)

Buzz Feitshans 45, Producer; associate of writer/director John Milius, on *1941* (1979) and *Conan the Barbarian* (1982). Produced *First Blood* (1982) when original producer fell ill

George Cosmatos 43, Director; stayed with Stallone for *Cobra* (1985)

▦ The business

John Rambo was the unlikely creation of a professor of American Literature, David Morrell, who practised a lucrative sideline contributing to the literature of gore and action. When *First Blood* was published in 1972 there was considerable Hollywood interest but the subject matter of a traumatized Vietnam War vet was still somewhat raw for current American sensibilities.

The withdrawal from Vietnam in 1975 was followed by some big cathartic movies such as *The Deer Hunter* (1978) and *Apocalypse Now* (1979). Then the Reagan years of gungho pride witnessed the emergence of a more sympathetic, even jolly, image fostered by TV's *The A Team* and *Magnum P.I.*

First Blood was now a viable film proposition and independent producers Mario Kasser and Andrew Vajna were in first, with a deal that included Sylvester Stallone. He in turn was looking for a career supplement to the *Rocky* series that had taken him in the space of a few years from penniless writer to Hollywood's highest-paid star. *First Blood* delivered $57,000,000 worth of alternative success and Stallone immediately started to speculate on repeating a good thing.

It all gelled when he received a letter from a lady in Virginia whose husband had been missing in action for sixteen years. In interviews at the time he seemed sincerely to espouse the film's basic premise that the government was attempting to suppress public knowledge of the existence of 2,500 or so M.I.A.s from the U.S. forces in Vietnam, miserably incarcerated in Laos.

Sylvester Stallone: fancy a walnut?

The $28,000,000 film with screenplay by Stallone and James Cameron* captured perfectly an eighties American recovery of military pride. In May 1985 the film opened simultaneously in over 2,000 cinemas across the country and it took more money in the first few days than all but two films in history.** *Rambo* had the honour of finally nudging *E.T.* (1982) off the *Variety* top spot.

Then, as if that wasn't enough, came the best plug in movie history. On 1 July 1985 Ronald Reagan, the most popular president since Kennedy, preparing to comment on a successful resolution to the TWA hijack in Beirut, let slip this widely-quoted review: 'Boy, I'm glad I saw *Rambo* last night. Now I'll know what to do next time.' Sales powered off, once again, totalling almost $80,000,000 in North American revenue alone.

The merchandise was extra. You could buy replicas of Rambo's cunning little combat knife and high explosive bow for $150. For the less homicidally inclined there were vitamin pills, dolls and supercharged water pistols which could deliver a soaking at ten feet. *Rambo* pin-ups outsold those of the current pop queen, Madonna, partly because the posters were snapped up by the United States Armed Forces to boost recruitment of potential Rambos or M.I.A.s. There were even Rambo-gram services where a suitably-attired testimonial to steroids would deliver spectacularly intimidating greetings or alternatively ask the boss for a raise.

Of the film's profits Stallone's cut was $5,000,000 up front plus a healthy percentage. Even Professor Morrell hit the jackpot all over again. His novelization of the film based on his original novel was a best seller. The biggest worry for the backers was a bustling bootleg video trade.

All this was in the face of almost blanket critical hostility, accusations of anti-oriental racism and allegations about Stallone's own war record. Where was Sylvester while his contemporaries were going missing in Southeast Asia? For at least part of it he was an instructor at a Swiss girls' school; it seems that Stallone had twice tried to join up but his hearing wasn't up to scratch.

No intellectual arguments could blur John Rambo's embodiment of an eighties American mood.*** It was the strongest audience participation cinema for some time, prompting rousing cheers when the killing starts. There was also a perverse involvement in the Rambo myth outside the theatre. Unpleasant gangs adopted both the *Rambo* attire and propensity for carnage, and in Britain one tragic maniac went on a mass killing spree in Hungerford soon after kitted out like his hero.

▥ Behind the screen

If Rambo looks a bit dozey it's not just the trademark slack eyelid and lip that are the result of Stallone's difficult birth. The star was dead tired as he made the film occasionally falling asleep like a horse, standing up.

And no wonder if you look at his schedule. As filming started in September 1984 he was already committed to preparing *Rocky IV*, which had a similar atmosphere of

---

*He had written and directed the Rambo-clone *Terminator* (1984) for Stallone-clone Arnold Schwarzenegger.
**The others were both sequels as well: *Indiana Jones and the Temple of Doom* (1984) and *Return of the Jedi* (1983).
***This mood was echoed throughout the world during the tense mid-eighties, particularly in Beirut where it was the biggest draw in years.

unabashed pre-perestroika confrontation. Stallone's day began at half-past four with writing, work-out and breakfast until filming at seven-thirty. The twelve-hour day, six-day week filming was the toughest he had ever faced – with unprecedented levels of running, climbing and maiming. In the evening Sly would prepare for the next day with lights out at eleven-thirty. All this in the heat of Acapulco, where the temperature was at least 95° with humidity to match.

Nevertheless he was fit enough. The stunning physique you see – likened by one wag to a condom stuffed with walnuts – had been through five months of fanatical body-building; six hours a day of rowing, jogging and weights which puffed out his chest from 44 inches to 50. He supplemented this regime with archery lessons and exercises with the Los Angeles S.W.A.T. team.

One motive for all this dedication may have been a needed diversion from problems at home. His ten-year marriage to Sasha, already strained by temptations which came with the success of Rocky, was finally coming apart. His next wife, Brigit Neilsen, arrived on the scene the following year.

The film-makers set up shop in a compound hacked out of the jungle near Acapulco at a cost of $200,000. The prisoner of war camp that Rambo is assaulting is also the unit's living accommodation and production headquarters.

In the absence of local sound stages Cosmatos improvised interiors wherever he could. A nearby conference centre served as headquarters for the double-dealing CIA men and the scene where Rambo is lovingly kitting himself out with knife and bow was shot in one of the crew's rooms at the Acapulco Plaza Hotel.

More difficult to set up was the waterfall location which was only accessible by a small advance party on donkeys. They took along some dynamite and soon the spot was accessible by helicopter too.

Does Rambo look somewhat more shaken than elsewhere on his campaign of destruction? It was here that the only real death in the film occurred, when special effects man Cliff Wenger Jr (remembered in the credits) fell 200 feet during a break in filming.

Then the area got side-swiped by a hurricane that washed away the sets and almost took the star as well. The house where Stallone was staying was threatened by a landslide and, as the roads were washed away, he set out on foot across nine miles of wilderness towards the main camp. The tension while he was out of contact was far more acute than anything the film produced.

Even given these and other mishaps this was a relatively trouble-free shoot for Stallone, who normally at least cracks a rib doing his hard-hitting stunts. His short-lived love interest, Julie Nickson, was most fearful for her own safety during her death scene. Stallone may only have been letting off blanks but those shell casings coming out of the Heckler and Koch were hot enough to make the water hiss. Ms Nickson is keeping her eyes tight shut praying she's not going to end up scarred for life.

The final set-piece destruction of the camp was unrepeatable and carefully planned with four cameras going at once and an arsenal of destructive power at the ready. So if ever you want to blow up a Vietnamese prisoner of war camp here's the recipe: take 300 gallons of petrol, 200 lbs of black powder, a mile of primer cord woven into the thatch and 400 burning tyres for that extra smokey effect. Set off with three miles of command wire and stand well back.

▦ The experience

The professional critical consensus held *First Blood* to be the superior film. The public disagreed.

'It's a vengeful fantasy tailored to the age of Reagan.' J. Hoberman, *Village Voice*, 28 May 1985

'*Rambo* is an effort to deal with a complex, painful and deep wound with simple and sentimental responses.' Arthur Egendorf, 'Healing from the War', quoted in *Time* 24 June 1985

'Obviously the sight of this marvellous physical specimen cavorting through the jungle in a series of brutally effective, strikingly photographed action scenes is a big part of the movie's appeal, regardless of ideology.' Richard Zoglin, *Time*, 24 June 1985

'*Rambo* triggered long-suppressed emotions which had been out of vogue. Suddenly apple pie is an important thing on the menu.' Sylvester Stallone

▦ Can you spot . . .

* Some pretty inefficient management. If you were cost-conscious Vietnamese would you allocate sixty men to guard a dozen Westerners used as farm hands?

* A surprising lack of survival instinct. Thirty years of guerrilla activity should have honed the Congs' ballistic skills to the pitch of being able to hit the side of a barn door. Equally you would have thought they'd know enough to duck, or similarly avoid incoming.

* A durable helicopter. How come it doesn't incinerate itself when Rambo launches rockets from the cockpit? And how did he manage to leap from the river into the helicopter?

* Just how violent it really is. Although the savagery is slow to get started there's still on average a killing every 2.1 minutes, 44 in all. *The Sun* studiously broke it down to include 5 deaths by knife, 2 strangulations, 14 by bow and arrow, 15 by fire-arm, 3 by explosion and 2 by helicopter assault.

* Shades of Cal Trask. Stallone likened his performance in *Rambo* to James Dean's in *East of Eden* (1955).

Rebel Without a Cause

1955 Twenty-four violent hours in the lives of a group of delinquent teenagers.

▦ The talent

James Dean 24, as Jimmy Stark; 'The new Marlon Brando' – an epithet he despised – in his second of three films

Natalie Wood 16, as Judy; her first grown-up role. Mrs Robert Wagner two, and again seventeen years later. Starred in many films including *West Side Story* (1961)

Sal Mineo 16, as Plato; ex-Broadway child star who was also with Dean for *Giant* (1955)

Jim Backus 42, as Jimmy's father; the voice of Mr Magoo, in his first non-funny role. A year's run of the TV comedy *I Married Joan* was just ending but TV's *Gilligan's Island*, and much else, was to come

Ann Doran 42, as Jimmy's mother; familiar character actress who had been in pictures for twenty years and was still busy twenty years later

Corey Allen 20, as Buzz; his first year in films, later a director

David Weisbart 40, Producer; chosen especially by Nicholas Ray for this, he had edited *A Streetcar Named Desire* (1951). Later produced *Valley of the Dolls* (1967)

Nicholas Ray 42, Director; started with Orson Wells and John Houseman in the Mercury Theatre. Largely inactive after 1963

▦ The business

Warner Brothers bought the rights to a psychology tome called *Rebel Without a Cause* written in 1944 by Dr Robert Lindner. It collected juvenile delinquent case histories extracted through hypnosis.

The studio tried to find a film there for Marlon Brando but the script apparently wasn't much cop and nothing came of it. Then Stanley Kramer starred Brando in *The Wild One* (1953) for Columbia and suddenly, with MGM's *The Blackboard Jungle* (1955), the new Hollywood buzz-phrase was 'crazy, mixed-up kids'.

Meanwhile Nicholas Ray had his own idea for a teen rebellion piece which he called *Blind Run*, a term used to describe the homo/sui-cidal game of automotive chicken. After several drafts a TV scriptwriter, Stewart Stern, finished off a screenplay which acceptably combined the available elements.

The director decided to go for a production which would be an authentic exploration of the subject. Ray took the scriptwriter on an eight-month tour of research interviewing police, judges and youth leaders. They walked on the wild side with a youth gang, spent days in court and took advice from one of the psychologists who had worked at the Nuremberg trials.

Ray's cast, too, would be picked for what they could contribute to the image and substance of the story. He chose well. James Dean had made a big impression in *East of Eden* (1955) and was in any case under contract to Warner Brothers for nine pictures in six years. His salary was rising from the $18,000 he received for his first film to a rate of $100,000 which was promised but which Dean never actually got to collect.

Neither the director nor her parents were keen for Natalie Wood to take the role of Judy, but then she did just the right thing. Ray saw her drive off with an adolescent male companion who sported a fresh facial knife scar. This apparently was judged by the director as a successful clearance of the authenticity hurdle and she got the part. A short time later she was in a car crash while travelling with Dennis Hopper. A doctor attending them called her a juvenile delinquent. Natalie begged for her parents not to be told but presented the anecdote to Ray as a further casting qualification.

The rest of the company, however minor their part, had to produce similar maladjustment bona fides. Personal screening by the director and producer for each of the hundreds of applicants involved questioning about how they got on with their parents, and other indicators of youth rebellion. One young actor brought his criminal record along as concrete evidence.

The film cost $600,000, shooting for two months to the end of May 1955. Then Dean went straight on to make *Giant* which wrapped in September. By this time well and truly shagged out, he set off in his Porsche Spyder for the races at Salinas. Dean had always been a speed freak, fascinated by fast cars and capable of hair-raising motorcycle stunts. He crashed head-on while overtaking and died shortly afterwards.

Rebel Without a Cause had not yet been released but already the Dean image was building and with the news of his death his cult took off. The film struck a profound chord with teenagers of the time, and did well at the box office, earning $4,600,000 in North America alone.

Two years after his death the studio was still receiving 6,000 letters a month for him. There were rumours that Dean was still alive though disfigured. Recently speculation about sinister motives in his death has resurfaced including wild theories like Rock Hudson having the brakes of Dean's car tampered with as part of some lover's quarrel.

Most of the principal youngsters in the film died young. Nick Adams, who played Moose succumbed to a drug overdose in 1968, Sal Mineo was murdered in an alley in 1976, and Natalie Wood drowned in 1981. And the man who started it all, Dr Robert Lindner, died the year following the film's release at the age of forty-one.

One great survivor was Dennis Hopper, who played Goon in the film and was greatly affected by Dean's death. He made it big with *Easy Rider* (1969) and by the eighties was creating some striking character portrayals.

The most durable, in his way, was Jimmy Dean. A generation grew up to adopt him as their alienation model and still today his picture adorns many a high school locker.

▦ Behind the screen

The monkey that Jimmy is playing with at the beginning of the film is a relic of footage that was lost when, early on in the production, Warners decided to do the film in colour. Ray had already shot an upbeat little scene which was to go before the existing opening with an old man being mugged by a group of youths who burn the parcels he is carrying. The monkey was the only one of his purchases left strewn on the street.

These first minutes of *Rebel Without a Cause* are typical in the degree to which they were extemporized. They had been filming for twenty-three hours. It was dawn. James Dean just asked the director to roll the cameras and he improvised the drunken reverie that you can just about see behind the titles. Beverly Long, who played Helen, claimed that afterwards everyone wept. Tears of fatigue, perhaps.

In his brief time after *Rebel Without a Cause* Dean boasted that he co-directed with Ray, a claim supported by Jim Backus, but others say that his real contribution was in developing the central character. It produced some memorable moments, like cooling his brow with the milk bottle. This was a piece of business that was first improvised in the director's kitchen, then re-filmed on the set.

Nicholas Ray was something of a beatnik, given to wandering round in jeans and bare feet in an age when jacket and tie, or at least cravat, were regulation director wear. He invited contributions from any source. This involvement in the creative process and a commitment to the material prompted an exceptionally family-like atmosphere. Sal Mineo described it as spiritual.* Look at Natalie Wood's excitement at being able to reverse the cigarette that Dean has accidently put in his mouth filter-out.

Sprinkled liberally through the dialogue are exchanges that betray the overlapping uncertainty of a theatre workshop. Scriptwriter Stewart Stern felt the impulse to attack the screen when he heard the liberties taken with his script and the banal lines improvised by the young stars.**

The company looked up to Dean, who could be easy and helpful with his acting colleagues, though very uptight when out of his milieu. He got the assistant director to avoid shouting 'Roll 'em', restricted the distraction of visitors to the set and was always there, intently viewing every scene.

What of the real Jimmy Dean behind the anguished Jimmy Stark? Biographers of such a short life have found much to say about a mercurial personality which, as witnessed from his performance in *Rebel*, could flash between extremes of charm and withdrawal. Dean's sex life has been especially well raked through. He was apparently bi-sexual, but a reputation for perversion which grew after his death ('the human ashtray') has since been discounted. Sal Mineo said they never had an affair, but that he would have liked to.

Dean's lack of interest could have been due to preoccupation with a broken heart. His great love, actress Pier Angeli, had left him out of the blue three months previously to marry Vic Damone. Dean was particularly upset when she told him she was pregnant. It was a couple of days before his crash.***

James Dean was obsessive in his method. He prepared for the scene where he batters the desk by working himself into a drunken frenzy in his trailer. He then emerged and did it in one take. Don't try it at home, kids. You are apparently watching him break two bones in his hand for art. The musical punctuation that follows was added after it was noticed that preview audiences tended to choose this point to have the giggles.

---

*Allegedly at odds with this prevailing cooperative spirit was Nick Adams, who played Moose. Watch him trying to upstage at any opening.
**Stern later wrote *The Last Movie* (1971), Dennis Hopper's universally-panned follow-up to *Easy Rider* plus several other films which have been very well-received.
***The marriage lasted only a few years. Pier followed the tragic trend: overdose, aged 39.

James Dean and Corey Allen: a stab at method acting

Dean wanted the knife fight to be as realistic as possible. Fortunately Frank Mazzola, the lad portraying Crunch, had some experience to offer as the real-life leader of a gang at Hollywood High called the Athenians. He was able to block out some good moves and got Nicholas Ray in to witness a fight between two girls for some extra background.

Neither Dean nor Corey Allen, playing his opponent Buzz, had ever participated in a rumble but both were very keen. Despite some body armour they were using real knives and Jim Backus says it was a wonder no one was badly hurt. During one of many takes Jimmy got nicked and it drew blood. Much to his annoyance the shot was spoiled because of Ray yelling for first aid.

It may be presumed that Frank 'Crunch' Mazzola was not consulted on the staging of the chickie run sequence. In his view it did not come close to the realism of the fight. There were two fundamental errors: no one would use such smart cars in this particular sporting event and in any case they shouldn't have been heading toward a cliff. They should have been heading straight for each other.

▦ The experience

'This is a performance with much of Marlon Brando's dramatic power, nearly all his technique – and an innate, sensitive charm which Brando has never shown.' Harold Conway, *Daily Sketch*, 20 January 1956

'Half-ferocious, half-sentimental, wholly melodramatic, the film is remarkable for the acting and direction of all its young savages.' Dylis Powell, *The Sunday Times*, 22 January 1956

'I'm a serious-minded and intense little devil, terribly gauche, and so tense I don't see how people can stay in the same room with me.' James Dean

▦ Can you spot . . .

* The importance of colour. Once it had been foisted on him Ray used the spectrum as a code. Plato's red and black signifies confusion; Jim changes from browns to rebellious red; Judy's wardrobe turns from red to pink. Nicholas Ray: 'When you first see Jim in his red jacket against his black merc it's not just a pose. It's a warning. It's a sign.'
* Maxwell Smart's boss, Edward Platt, who played the chief in TV's *Get Smart*. He plays 'Ray' who, as the only figure of real authority, has the director's name.
* Where you've seen Plato's house before. In Billy Wilder's *Sunset Boulevard* (1950). It used to be on Calabasas Road but has since been pulled down.
* Two Platos. The character was apparently modelled on Jack Simmons, who was a friend of Dean's. But Simmons was too self-conscious as himself and so he took the role of Cookie instead.
* How blue the jeans are. They all had to be dyed specially to show up properly in Warner colour.

Road to Morocco

1942 Jeff sells Turkey to a Moroccan princess and plans to reclaim him, but at first his pal doesn't want to be rescued.

▥ The talent

Bing Crosby 38, as Jeff Peters; giant of American popular song soon to win an Oscar in *Going My Way* (1944)
Bob Hope 39, as Turkey Jackson; radio comedian who became the elder statesman of the American entertainment industry
Dorothy Lamour 27, as Princess Shalmar Hanoun; her star did not survive the forties
Dona Drake 22, as Mihirmah; Mexican singer, reputedly a handful, in pictures for the next decade or so

Anthony Quinn 27, as Mullay Kasim; small-time heavy despite being C.B. DeMille's son-in-law. A decade away from two Oscars and twenty-three years before *Zorba the Greek*
Paul Jones 41, Producer; Paramount comedy specialist
David Butler 47, Director; former actor, a director for forty years without making much else that is memorable

▥ The business

Hollywood legends attract Hollywood myths, and stories about the genesis of this classic series abound. *Road to Singapore* (1940), the first of the batch,* was apparently intended to carry Burns and Allen or Fred MacMurray and Jackie Oakie. Then, following a particularly jocular golf outing with Bob Hope and Bing Crosby, Paramount director Victor Schertzinger** is said to have suggested recording their bantering rapport on film.

He had been treated to a tested routine. Hope and Crosby had appeared together as an occasional pairing on stage since the early thirties. It continued on their respective top-rated radio shows – and since both were signed to Paramount, the *Road* movies in some form seem almost a foregone conclusion.

The third member of the team, Dorothy Lamour was an ex-New Orleans beauty-queen turned singer and Paramount contract player, firmly type-costumed in a sarong because of her dusky, jungle maiden looks.

The recipe immediately hit the spot with a wartime public taste for relaxed escapism at the movies. *Singapore* proved the biggest Paramount film of the year and until the advent of the James Bond canon in the sixties the *Road*s were the most successful film series. *Road to Morocco* made about $4,500,000 and the *Road*s as a whole about $50,000,000, forming the basis of two of the largest personal fortunes in Hollywood, those of Messrs Hope and Crosby.

*Followed by *Road to Zanzibar* (1941), *Road to Morocco* (1942), *Road to Utopia* (1945), *Road to Rio* (1947), *Road to Bali* (1952) and *Road to Hong Kong* (1962).
**He made the first two *Road*s but died before *Morocco*.

Bing Crosby, Dorothy Lamour and Bob Hope: fun, fun, fun?

They were already doing well. The money from radio was good and both Bob and Bing were movie stars in their own right. Crosby had been an onscreen crooner for a decade whose current rate reached $175,000 a picture. Hope was a comparative newcomer, first popping up in *The Big Broadcast of 1938* (1937!) with a song that has remained his musical calling card, 'Thanks For the Memory'. By the time of *Road to Morocco*, considered to be the best of the batch, he was on a run of cracking comedy films* and pocketing $100,000 each time. Paramount considered Dorothy Lamour one of their big attractions valued at $5,000 a week.

But in the long run it was Dottie who missed out on the loot. Hope and Crosby felt they were losing too much to the tax man and so about the time of *Road to Morocco* they were starting to invest their cash carefully and at the same time tussling with Paramount for a new deal ('Still under contract for five more years . . .'). By the time of

---

*Such as *The Cat and the Canary* (1939) which really established him. *The Ghost Breakers* (1940), and *My Favourite Blonde* (1942).

Road to Rio (1947) they were splitting the financing of the films and their immense profits three ways with the studio.

The deal did not include Lamour, who found herself dropped by Paramount in an economy drive about the same time the boys struck their lucrative bargain (although, of course, she was in all the *Road* movies). She managed to trade for laughs on her old sarong image into the seventies but by this time Bob and Bing were each worth hundreds of millions.

▦ Behind the screen

Camel spit is smelly, as Bob Hope found out, but a camel spitting is funny and so they kept it in. It was one of several out-takes in this, the most relaxed and typical of the *Road* crop.

Among the few folk not quite so amused were the scriptwriters, Frank Butler (a British former actor and old Oxonian) and Don Hartman (another former actor, later a producer and director). They shared a grim jest of their own, shouting 'bingo' if they heard one of their original lines used. Hope, who later was to have a retinue of gag-men, on an annual payroll in six figures, already had a team of jokers working to outfunny a similar gag-gle in Crosby's employ. Part of the amusement in watching the films with this in mind is that for at least part of the time neither star is sure of what the other is going to come out with next. Dorothy Lamour discovered as early as *Singapore* that there was little point in learning a script which at best served as a rough guide to the proceedings. The sound policy was to look fetching and see about getting a word in edgeways.

Scriptwriters' revenge was possibly one reason for the emergence of the carefully set-up sight gags which started with *Morocco*, like Bob's Arabian booties uncurling, the hall of nodding heads and the camels with their animated wisecracks. The boys also started going out of character more often, with the digs at each other and their contractual arrangements with Paramount. They even extended an already thin running joke from the previous two *Roads*, getting caught out by their own patty-cake routine.

Was it as much fun offscreen? Of course all concerned are bound to say yes and indeed by almost all accounts it was. Only comparatively recently have different stories started to come out.

It was the worst of times for a world at war but on the surface these three stars were at an exciting peak. Lamour was a pin-up queen to rival Betty Grable, able to sell a million War Bonds with a single wiggle. She, like Hope, was embarking on a series of gigs at American bases, something Hope was to continue for forty years, through U.S. involvement in Korea, Vietnam and Lebanon. All three had healthy non-*Road* movie careers. Bing, in particular, had just completed *Holiday Inn* with Fred Astaire, the movie that introduced the world's most popular pop song, 'White Christmas'.

As for their personal lives, at the time of making *Road to Morocco* Dorothy Lamour was concluding an affair but she was soon to meet her second husband with whom she would remain until his death in the 1970's. Bob Hope was a decade into one of Hollywood's longest and most loyal marriages, coping with the happy demands of a brood of adopted children.

Bing Crosby has always been the image of relaxed success but there has been a crop of knocking copy since his death. The ideal husband and father of four sons presented to the public of 1942 was chipped away at most ruthlessly by Donald Shepherd and Robert Slatzer in *Bing Crosby: The Hollow Man*. The world's favourite crooner is painted as cold, moody and withdrawn, a strict disciplinarian who had few friends and an alcoholic wife. His attitude to Hope is said to have been ambivalent, his offscreen quips at his *Road* partner often barbed and hostile.

Still, it seems inconceivable that one of cinema's classic double acts could be utterly without some basis in mutual affection. They certainly did a few business deals together and shared some interests, golf in particular, but their lives were very different. Bob Hope kept the lifestyle and late hours he had cultivated as a nightclub turn but Crosby was in bed by ten and on the links by six before drifting to his nine o'clock call at the studio.

The Bingoclasts turn this around to hypothesize that Hope was possibly the isolated Crosby's best friend, perhaps because he wasn't pushy about it and happy to leave Bing alone.

About Hope himself there seems a consensus assessment of geniality more in keeping with his latter TV persona than the rascally coward image in movies of *Road* vintage. A curious light on Crosby and his feelings for his old friend emerged after his death in 1977. He had made it a provision of his will that Bob Hope attend the funeral.

▦ The experience

'Whenever Hope and Crosby get cracking funniness revives. There are pretty surrealist touches. Miss Lamour keeps drifting in. Oh, I know that many people can't live from one day to the next without dreams of Miss Lamour, but I can. She has for me the unsullied charm of putty.' William Whitebait, *New Statesman*, 14 January 1943

'It was fun from the very first day.' Dorothy Lamour

'Hope was a premier gagster who could sing. Crosby was a supreme singer who was clever with a quip.' Bob Thomas, *The Associated Press*, 1977

'They had an immense respect for each other's talent and an affection that was quite wonderful.' Delores Hope of her husband and Bing

▦ Can you spot . . .

* A soon-to-be-Lamour-clone, Yvonne de Carlo, aged 20, is one of the hand-maidens. Nowadays the clearest memory of her is as the monster Mom in TV's *Munsters*.

* Who's happy in costume. According to veteran wardrobe mistress Edith Head, Hope loved all the costumes and had what she termed the 'perfect average male figure'. Although he's looking considerably more dumpy in *Morocco* than in previous *Roads*. Perhaps it was the rich palace food. Crosby, who was colour-blind and often ribbed by Hope about his dress sense, felt out of his element togged up.

* The ring on Hope's left pinkie. It was a present from Delores on their wedding day.

Singin' in the Rain

1952 A dance musical. Silent movie star finds love and a renewed career with the advent of talkies.

The talent

Gene Kelly 39, as Don Lockwood; cinema's most inventive hoofer in last popular dance role

Donald O'Connor 27, as Cosmo Brown; dance man born too late for heyday of musicals. By this time was Francis the Talking Mule's co-star. Later quit films for a serious composing career

Debbie Reynolds 19, as Kathy Selden; string of minor comedy leads followed but greatest fame came when husband Eddie Fisher ran off with Elizabeth Taylor in 1959

Jean Hagen 28, as Lina Lamont; much praised in the reviews but subsequent TV and film career never took off

Cyd Charisse 31, as the Broadway Rhythm girl; her star waned with the musicals, but she's still working

Arthur Freed 57, Producer; illustrious film musical career blighted, with the rest of them, by sparcer sixties market for the genre. But *Gigi* (1958) was still to come

Gene Kelly Director; later made *An Invitation to the Dance* (1956) and *Hello Dolly* (1969)

Stanley Donen 28, Director; parted with Kelly a few years later for average directing career

The business

Singin' in the Rain's budget was generous at $2,500,000, which included an extra $600,000 spent on the Broadway Melody section plopped into the latter part of the film. But this was a case of the producer giving himself a treat.

Arthur Freed was one of the most successful exponents of the Hollywood musical and wanted to make use of a particular catalogue of songs newly acquired by MGM. They were the hits he himself had written in his equally successful songwriting partnership with Nacio Herb Brown in the twenties and thirties.

The writers, Adolph Green and Betty Comden, were serenaded with a bunch of twenty-year-old songs and told to write a picture around them. It was one of the last written-for-the-screen musicals. In the following years Hollywood turned to re-processing stage successes.

There was a marked disparity between the payment given to the principal actors. Debbie Reynolds was being made into a star by MGM boss Louis B. Mayer and this was her first leading role. She was on $300 a week and had to take three buses to get to the studio each morning. Donald O'Connor was well established and on loan from Universal for a transfer fee of $50,000 which he indicates he was able to keep. By far the biggest star was Gene Kelly, on $2,500 a week. This soon doubled . . . prompting him to become one of the first Hollywood stars to seek tax exile in Europe.

His career thereafter sloped down, as did those of most of the principals involved in this film, partly because of the decline of the popularity of musicals. What you see on the screen is some of the best work that any of them ever did and one of the last chances to use their talents in this way.

The film was overshadowed on release both financially and critically by *An American in Paris* (1951). It was even withdrawn from distribution in favour of that other Gene Kelly hit when it won the best picture Oscar. Still *Singing' in the Rain* managed to scrape into the top ten earners of that year and finally made about $7,500,000. Since then it has come to be regarded as one of the best musicals of all time and regularly features in the lists of all-time favourites.

▦ Behind the screen

Although this comes across as one of the lightest and most carefree of pieces it's really a case of an enthusiastic amateur struggling to keep up with two masters of dance. Debbie Reynolds worked her guts out under the stern and disparaging eye of Gene Kelly. Kelly and Donald O'Connor had been dancing professionally since childhood. Debbie was in movies on the strength of being a teenage Miss Burbank.

Gene Kelly did nothing to hide his displeasure when he was called into Louis B. Mayer's office and told in front of Debbie that she was to star opposite him. Kelly put her through an impromptu audition which she failed miserably and then, after fruitless argument with Mayer, he packed the kid off to be whipped into shape by his dance workout team.

Debbie proved to be a real trooper. Her creditable display of footwork is the result of weeks of gruelling training sessions lasting up to ten hours a day. But although a crash course in hoofing might prepare any starlet for the 'All I Do' sequence where she jumps out of the cake and shakes it all about with some other dancing girls, the real test came with 'Good Morning': side by side with Kelly and O'Connor.

Shooting went on all day with constant barracking from Kelly and co-director/sidekick Stanley Donen: 'Dance harder. More energy!' That flop down on the sofa at the end of the number finally came at eleven o'clock in the evening. What *was* she whispering to Donald O'Connor just before they all began laughing? At any rate the laughing soon stopped; moments later Debbie fainted. She had burst blood vessels in her feet dancing all day in those dreadful high-heel block shoes. Ordered off work for three days by the doctor she only stayed away for one.

Donald O'Connor needed a full three days in bed after his solo spot, the incredibly energetic 'Make 'Em Laugh'. This most memorable of numbers was something of an afterthought. The hero's piano-playing buddy was a role originally conceived for the acidic Oscar Levant, but the presence of Donald O'Connor merited a speciality dance number so Freed knocked the song off the night before rehearsals began. It's a palpable lift of Irving Berlin's 'Be a Clown' which Freed had used in *The Pirate* four years earlier. It seems that no one had the temerity to draw Freed's attention to this at the time and perhaps he thought he'd written it himself in the first place.

At rehearsal O'Connor started jumping around and going through all his old Vaudeville-based routines while Gene Kelly sat taking notes, much as he is placed in the film when Cosmo does his stuff. The routine with the hand on the dummy's knee is based on a true incident when a man tried to grope Donald in a New York subway. Kelly's only contribution was the gag where O'Connor can't straighten his face.

The overall effect was breathtaking – more so for the young dance man because at the time he was on four packs of cigarettes a day. He did the filming and had his three days in bed, only to be told that the negative was spoiled. So he had to do it all over again, and have another three days off.

One reason they all worked so hard is that they were scared stiff of Gene Kelly. Mostly, it seems, he was as charming on set as he is on screen but he had a vicious temper. He would mainly take it out on O'Connor because he feared that if he directed his anger at Debbie she would burst into tears and ruin her make-up. In fact his teenage co-star seems to have been little affected by his attitude and when it came to the one scene where she *has* to cry – running down the cinema aisle at the end – they had to use onions. Debbie explained that she couldn't make herself cry because nothing really sad had ever happened to her.

Donald O'Connor became so wary that when Kelly got the bar-chair sequence in 'Good Morning' all wrong he was too scared to point it out. That made Kelly even more mad when he found out.

Sometimes, though, the anger was only for effect. The two of them had just finished shooting 'Moses Supposes', the only song other than 'Make 'Em Laugh' which was written specifically for the film, this time by the scriptwriters. Gene insisted on straightaway doing another scene, the violin act in 'Fit as a Fiddle' from the flashbacks near the start of the picture. O'Connor was tired and dropped his bow near the end of the number whereupon Kelly smashed his own fiddle to the ground and stalked off the set. When O'Connor plucked up the courage to knock on his door a few minutes later Kelly was smiling broadly. He'd only used O'Connor's mistake as a pretext because he was pretty tired himself.

Debbie Reynolds continued to rub Gene Kelly up the wrong way. He would only sanction one number alone with her, where he leads her to a sound stage and croons 'You Were Meant For Me'. It looks smooth as silk but the young lovers had just been having a tiff. In the film Gene wraps himself athletically round the ladder but somewhere on it Debbie had secreted the gum she'd been chewing just before the take. It got stuck in Kelly's hair.

On the whole all the efforts of the MGM professionals and a lot of hard work on her own behalf leave Debbie looking pretty good on screen. But Gene Kelly continued to be patronizing. 'She didn't know what the hell was going on half the time, which was just the right quality we wanted,' he said afterwards.

In fact Debbie ended up getting the same sort of treatment that her screen nemesis, Lina Lamont, was given. She wasn't able to reach all the high notes so they were dubbed on for her and when her character is dubbing 'Would You' for Lina that's actually Jean Hagen singing it herself; in reality she had a fine speaking and singing voice. Even the tapping in Debbie's dancing was dubbed – by Gene Kelly.

The last section to be filmed was the musical-within-a-musical, *Broadway Melody*, and Gene Kelly was stuck without a partner. Donald O'Connor was committed to work on a TV show and Debbie just wasn't expert enough. So Kelly wrote the piece around Cyd Charisse, a contract dancer at MGM. Although looking as lithe as ever she was a new mother striving to keep her hips slim and regain her fitness.

The most complicated scene of the film, according to Gene Kelly, was Cyd's dance with the long scarf. It was supposed to be one of the fifty-foot variety, looks rather shorter, but whatever its length needed three aircraft motors to blow it around choreographed with the ballet – conventional wind machines just didn't have enough puff. The engines supplied so much gale force that special effects men had to conduct experiments in how not to blow the performers off their feet. A fringe benefit was the discovery of some useful scarf/wind management techniques which they employed to jazz up the item. How else could you learn how to make yards of material ruffle artistically or stand up straight in the air on demand? The result looks pleasingly ethereal, but can you imagine how it was for the dancers? Forget the swelling orchestral soundtrack. It was like dancing in an aircraft test hanger. The performers and fan operators are carefully counting beats to get their cues just right in the deafening roar.

The titles claim that the film was suggested by 'Singin' in the Rain' but although Freed insisted that the picture be called after his most famous hit the story was actually written around all the other numbers and this one slotted into the action at a late stage in planning. It is one of the favourite sequences in all cinema. MGM's 'East Side Street' set was prepared with a canopy of tarpaulin to make it seem like night even though they were filming in daylight. This covering was lined with sprinkler pipes to provide the rain (water with milk for greater visibility) and depressions were scraped in the road to let that famous puddle form. Rehearsals were done without the rain, as Gene Kelly struggled to coordinate the movements of his umbrella, the trickiest task of the number for him.

The shooting, with all that water and the heat of the California day, was like thirty-six hours in a steambath. So look carefully at Gene Kelly and that immortal blissful smile. You are watching a man who is soaked to the skin in a thick woollen suit, suffering through a heavy cold – and in a typical foul temper.

▦ The experience

'Perhaps the most enjoyable of all movie musicals – just about the best Hollywood musical of all time.' Pauline Kael

'Arthur Freed has produced another surefire grosser for Metro in *Singin' in the Rain*. Musical has pace, humour and good spirits a-plenty, in a happy, good natured spoof on the film industry itself.' *Variety*, 12 March 1952

At the time, although there was much praise for the film and, in particular, for Jean Hagen's performance the critical consensus was that the Broadway Melody sequence was too long – and in any case they were all still raving about *An American in Paris.*

▦ Can you spot . . .

*The caricatures of real personalities. The star-spotting radio announcer at the beginning is supposed to be the powerful gossip columnist Louella Parsons. The real Louella loved the film. The director, Roscoe Dexter, is based on Busby Berkeley and the studio boss, R. F. Simpson, is none other than Arthur Freed. A particular dig is the otherwise inexplicable dialogue after Broadway Melody where Simpson tells Don and Cosmo that he can't quite visualize the number, he'll have to see it on film. This is just the sort of thing Freed would have said, and tripping over the cables on the set which he does at another point is also typical.

* Real film history. Almost all the shots in the films-within-the-film are based on actual silent sequences, and the costumes and equipment they use are accurate copies. The difficulties experienced in the early sound days are also authentically

Gene Kelly: welcome to the sauna

parodied. One particular example is Don Lockwood improvising the dialogue in a love scene by repeating 'I love you' over and over. John Gilbert did just that in a scene which hastened the demise of his talkie career. The fight scene footage in the Laughing Cavalier is lifted from *The Three Musketeers* which Kelly had made five years previously.

* A technical fault for the picky – it's at the end of the experimental sound movie preview given by the producer, R. F. Simpson. When he rises his shoulder is clipped by a screen which is supposed to be behind him, a clear and surprising case of sloppy optical printing.

* Cyd Charisse can't stand up straight. Or not when she's anywhere near Gene Kelly. Her dance sequences were worked out carefully so you don't notice she's taller than the star.

* Cyd Charisse's pubes. Well you probably can't any more although you're supposed to if you look carefully enough, particularly in the scarf sequence. I can't see anything. There were great problems during filming because despite some discreet shaving her costume still seemed to have the ghost of five o'clock shadow. Happily, at last costume designer Walter Plunkett was able to make his immortal announcement: 'Don't worry fellas. We've got Cyd Charisse's crotch licked!'

Snow White and the Seven Dwarfs

1937 A fairytale princess threatened by her witch-queen stepmother finds refuge with seven dwarves living in the forest.

▥ The talent

Walt Disney 35, and his 750 staff
David Hand 38, Supervising Director; also supervised *Bambi* (1942)

▥ The business

By the early 1930's Walt Disney knew that he had to move on from just producing eight-minute Silly Symphonies. The cost of animation was high and rising, and cartoon programme fillers couldn't attract the rentals commanded by principal features. So in 1934 he began to divert most of his resources into the production of this, the first cartoon feature, with a budget originally estimated at $500,000. Costs rose rapidly as Disney invested in new equipment and techniques. He ended up borrowing to the hilt amid scepticism from all the Hollywood knockers. They called it Disney's Folly.

His business partner brother Roy forced him to show the rough semi-complete cut to Joseph Rosenberg, the banker responsible for okaying continued massive loans. The presentation was of some completed sections stitched together with rough pencil drawings and Walt's commentary on what was going on. Rosenberg seemed unmoved during the showing but his comment on leaving was 'That thing is going to make a hatful of money' – and Disney got the $1,500,000 the picture finally cost.

It was such a success that Disney had all his loans paid off in six months. At the premiere in Los Angeles the audience stood and cheered and *Snow White* broke attendance records all over the world. It was the most successful movie of all time until overtaken by *Gone With the Wind* (1939). Two of the songs, 'Heigh Ho! It's Off to Work We Go' and 'Whistle While You Work', became worldwide hits.

With the Disney practice of re-releasing all his pictures every seven years or so *Snow White and the Seven Dwarfs* has earned more than $40,000,000 in North American rentals (so about twice that worldwide). The Disney staff who had worked nights and weekends to complete the project all got bonuses. They were in any case well paid for animators, generally a poorly rewarded section of the film industry.

Snow White re-established Disney as the pre-eminent animation tycoon. And he got a special Academy Award - one big Oscar accompanied by seven little ones.

▦ Behind the screen

Disney himself was always central to the planning and execution of his films. This one contains two million drawings and although each character, background and special effect is the responsibility of a different person they all took their cue from Walt.

When he had chosen the story from Grimm's *Fairy Tales* he spent two hours relating it to key animators. This was the basic version that was used, subsequent details emerging from Disney at numerous editorial meetings. A stenographer was always present to take down his inspiration which imbued every nuance of the production.

After that, committing the free flow of Walt Disney's imagination to film required astonishing organization. Every element has its own animator, so every scene was worked out meticulously with all concerned knowing exactly how much time was required for each movement and how it was to fit in. One side-effect is that large sections of the film are set to a musical beat.

The move from eight minutes duration to over an hour involved new techniques. Some were simple, like enlarging the drawing format so that enough detail could be fitted in to sustain interest.

The most influential development, though, was the multi-plane camera. This tower of glass animation surfaces was created by Disney's long-term partner Ub Uwerks (sometimes credited with creating Mickey Mouse as well). It enabled the camera at the top of the structure to apparently zoom through the various layers of the animated landscape giving a greater sense of reality and depth. Based on a technique which had already been used to good effect for *King Kong* (1933), it still wasn't fully developed for *Snow White* but created a memorably impressive effect in certain scenes, most notably when our heroine is lost in the forest.

Disney also filmed real people as the basis for animating the action of some of the characters. Snow White's template was the wife of one of the animators, Marjorie Champion, who later modelled for characters in *Pinocchio* (1939) and *Fantasia* (1940) as well. She even achieved a career in her own right as a dancer.

The voices were also important, especially Snow White. Disney had a speaker in his office so he could hear the auditions taking place on the sound stage without being influenced by the look of the talent. He turned down Deanna Durbin (she sounded too mature) but he knew instantly when Miss Right came along: eighteen-year-old Adriana Caselotti, a trainee opera singer.

Character development was as detailed as everything else. Disney said that Snow White should be a fourteen-year-old Janet Gaynor and the Prince an eighteen-year-old Douglas Fairbanks.

The Dwarfs went through several mutations before developing their final form. Film historian Rudy Behlmer lists alternative names proposed for them as Hoppy, Weepy, Hungry, Dirty, Thrifty, Nifty, Shifty, Woeful, Doleful, Soulful, Snoopy, Gabby, Blabby, Neurtsy, Gloomy, Daffy, Gaspy, Hotsy, Jaunty, Biggy, Biggy-Wiggy, Biggo-Ego and Awful who was heralded by the planners as the most lovable and interesting of Snow White's benefactors: 'He steals and drinks and is very dirty.'

Let's count ourselves lucky we were left with the familiar Doc, Grumpy, Happy, Sleepy, Bashful, Sneezy and Dopey.

Of these finalists Dopey got the most attention. He emerged at last as an ambitious combination of Harry Langdon, Stan Laurel, Buster Keaton and Harpo Marx. The name was a worry, though. Disney's advisers thought Dopey sounded too modern and smacked of drug abuse. But Walt found a reference in Shakespeare, so that was that.

The atmosphere at the studio was one of intense excitement. They were breaking new ground and everyone worked very hard to make it a success. Disney himself, though, was not in the best of health. He had suffered a nervous breakdown a couple of years earlier and was being treated for a suspected thyroid deficiency during the making of *Snow White*.

The final product set him up for life, but despite almost universal admiration there were criticisms that parts of the film were too frightening. In Britain it got the sort of certificate where children could only see it with an adult.

But it might have been scarier still. Scenes which were planned but later dropped included the Prince in chains about to be drowned, Snow White's mother dying in child-birth, a dungeon scene with dancing skeletons and the Huntsman being led away by torturers.

And if you think the end of the wicked Queen is a bit grim when she falls off a precipice, consider the original story intended for children. The appropriately named Grimm's fairy tale has Snow White getting her own back at her wedding by condemning the Queen to dance in red hot shoes until she dies.

▥ The experience

'The studio was alive with creativity, a marriage of many minds and talents. We made life happen in cartoon form,' Wolfgang Reitherman, Disney animator, 1967

'We're all a little bit tired of it. I've seen so much of *Snow White* that I am only conscious of where it could be improved. I wish I could yank it back and do it all over again.' Walt Disney at the end of production

▥ Can you spot . . .

* Related Dwarfs. The voices of Sleepy and Grumpy are done by the same man – Pinto Colvig. He was later the voice of Goofy, and a freelance Munchkin.
* An error they couldn't afford to correct. While watching the just-completed film the Disney brothers noticed a fault in the way the Prince moves as he is about to kiss Snow White in the glass coffin. Walt was all for re-shooting but Roy persuaded him that he had borrowed all the money he could and that the cost would be prohibitive. 'Forget it,' he said, 'Let the Prince shimmy.' And they did.

Some Like It Hot

1959 Two musicians masquerade as women to escape gangsters after witnessing a St Valentine's Day massacre.

▦ The talent

Marilyn Monroe 33, as Sugar Kane; genius or bewitching klutz? Cinema's sex symbol in last great comedy role

Tony Curtis 34, as Joe; trying hard at the time. Has since relaxed into fun mediocrity

Jack Lemmon 34, as Jerry; became one of the most versatile and admired screen actors

George Raft 64, as Spats Colombo; the start of his financial Indian summer

Joe E. Brown 67, as Osgood Fielding III; long retired from low-budget comedies of the thirties

Billy Wilder 53, Producer/Director; creative powerhouse on the crest of his best work

▦ The business

The Mirisch Company had recently been formed by Walter Mirisch and his two brothers as an alternative to the big studios, who were generally having a hard time. They wanted to encourage independent talents, and gave Billy Wilder the $3,000,000 *Some Like It Hot* cost to make.

It was a good investment. Although some critics of the late fifties found the central transvestite gag and the callous violence too strong to stomach, audiences all over the world flocked to see the film. It was number three in the box office that year and the most successful comedy up to that time, earning $8,000,000 in North American rentals, so about twice that worldwide.

Despite several nominations there weren't too many Oscars left that year after *Ben Hur* had bagged a record eleven and *Some Like It Hot*'s only Academy Award was for Costume Design.

Tony Curtis was on loan from Universal where he was in the middle of a seven-year contract and on about $25,000 a week (thirty weeks a year). Marilyn, however, had formed her own production company and was on a 10% profit-sharing deal. It was the continuing income from *Some Like It Hot* that paid off the debts after her death. She only completed two more films.

The movie gave both Jack Lemmon and Billy Wilder a springboard to some of the best years of their careers. They have made six more successful pictures together.

And the Mirisch brothers went on to become one of the most successful small production companies. In addition to other Billy Wilder films they financed *The Magnificent Seven* (1960), *West Side Story* (1961) and *The Great Escape* (1963) in the following few years, and many more since.

⊞ Behind the screen

It was a risk for Tony Curtis and Jack Lemmon taking parts which would mean that they would appear for much of the time as women. But all three stars of *Some Like It Hot* were at turning points in their careers and took risks that seemed worthwhile. It worked out for Curtis, Lemmon and for Billy Wilder – but not for Marilyn Monroe.

Wilder hired a female impersonator to show Jack and Tony all those little feminine touches – the secrets of how to walk and that a limp wrist means your muscles won't bulge. The final test for manner and make-up was visiting the ladies' toilet unchallenged.

Curtis said he based his character, Josephine, on Grace Kelly. 'I decided that I was going to be rather aloof and stylish. I wasn't going to be no easy lay who hit the sack for just anyone.'

Despite the fact that Jack Lemmon was to become one of Wilder's favourite performers neither he nor Tony Curtis was the first choice for the film. With his scripting partner I.A.L. Diamond, Wilder had adapted *Farfaren der Liebe*, a German comedy of the early thirties, for a partnership of Bob Hope and Danny Kaye. When that didn't work out Wilder adapted the Daphne part specifically for Jack Lemmon, whom he had admired in *Operation Madball* the previous year.

Fine. But then the hapless Lemmon – dithering on the edges of stardom and in need of a break – was fired in favour of Frank Sinatra, considered to be a better name to have over the title. The other two principals were to be Curtis and Mitzi Gaynor. Lemmon got offered the picture again when Marilyn Monroe agreed to do it. Poor Mitzi Gaynor had just made *South Pacific* (1958) (which history has judged a turkey) and a film career that this role might have prolonged quickly fizzled out.

Marilyn Monroe was looking for a comeback film after a two-year absence from the screen. She said that Billy Wilder was the cleverest director in Hollywood and more than that 'there's no question of who's the star if I'm in his movie'. She was also looking forward to singing and to working with the fanciable Tony Curtis.

Another factor was money. She and her husband, the playwright Arthur Miller, had been inactive for some time and – according to a biography by her maid, Lena Pepitone – Miller convinced Marilyn that they needed the cash. She signed without even reading the script.

When she did read it she was horrified. It was back to being a dumb blonde, and one that couldn't even see through two men in drag. 'I've been dumb, but never that dumb,' she moaned.

She also objected to the film being shot in monochrome but Wilder insisted that the effect of colour on the make-up really would have rendered the drag illusion untenable. He told her that as long as Sugar believed it onscreen, so would the audience.

It didn't bode well for an easy shoot, especially as Marilyn then embarked on an extended food binge so that she would be too fat for the part. And there began a theme that runs through most recollections of the filming from August to November 1958: what hell Marilyn was to work with.

Tony Curtis summed up the general feeling after her death: 'Always people have said to me "Wasn't it a terrible tragedy about Marilyn Monroe?" Well, I can't lie. I didn't like her. She was a really mean person. During *Some Like It Hot* she gave us a

Tony Curtis and Marilyn Monroe: kissing Hitler

terrible time. I think Marilyn was as mad as a hatter. She had a woman's body but the mind of a four-year-old. If she hadn't had that sexy look and 38-inch bust she'd have been locked up for sure.'

Billy Wilder said she had breasts like granite and a brain like Swiss cheese. 'I have never met anyone as utterly mean as Marilyn Monroe. Nor as utterly fabulous on the screen.'

She *was* fabulous in *Some Like It Hot*, as you can see – but what an effort to get there! She was repeatedly late on set and required innumerable takes. The shot where she comes into 'the girls'' hotel room in Florida and asks 'Where's the bourbon?' is her fifty-ninth attempt.

She was spot on, though, when she predicted who would be the star of the movie. Wilder scrapped takes that showed other players to their best advantage in favour of anything that shone with full Monroe wattage. It didn't increase her fan club on the set and especially needled Tony Curtis.

For all his comments on Monroe's sanity he was no psychological oil painting himself. He had been attending analysis up to four times a week for some time and since the mid-fifties had spent thousands on psychiatric fees. Part of the problem was his career. He had been desperate to break away from roles as a pretty-boy swash-buckler with a Bronx accent. Now at last he seemed to be on his way. The role of a shabby press agent in *Sweet Smell of Success* (1958) had shown some dramatic range and *Some Like It Hot* put a lot of comedy parts his way. At the same time there were problems at home. His marriage to Janet Leigh was moving towards their divorce a few years later although their second daughter, Jamie Lee, was born around the end of filming.

In fact it seems that babies were the key to the problems in making *Some Like It Hot*.

According to Lena Pepitone a short time before filming started Marilyn's outlook changed to one of uncharacteristic contentment. She learned to play the ukelele and started practising her songs in earnest (she liked 'I Want to be Loved by You' best but would sing 'I'm Through With Love' when she was a bit down).

The reason for the change of attitude – and why Marilyn looks so especially radiant? She was pregnant. It was the child she and Miller had longed for.

Marilyn had suffered a miscarriage not long before and, according to Pepitone, was determined that nothing should jeopardize the baby's health. This included lack of sleep, so when she found it difficult drifting off (which was often) she would lie in until fully rested. If that meant arriving hours late on the set then so be it.

She partly blamed the multiple-takes syndrome on Billy Wilder, whom she began to call Little Hitler soon after filming started. Wilder's mood must have been made all the darker by the pain of bursitis and a back ailment which meant that he had to sleep in a chair. He insisted that the script be strictly adhered to. Marilyn liked to change things here and there to suit her delivery better. There was a clash of wills and a demoralizing repetition of takes.

One person she did seem to get along with was the affable Jack Lemmon. They would confide with one another their nervousness in front of the camera. But she was hurt by the complaints and jokes about her from Curtis and Wilder which began even before the production had finished, especially as she had been looking forward to working with Curtis in particular. Her favourite scene was where she seduces him, out of drag for once and holding forth as a Cary Grant with sexual problems.

The Grant impression, which became a feature of later performances, was a skill Curtis had learned during the war as a signalman on the U.S.S. Dragonette. They only had one film on board during his two years, Cary Grant in *Gunga Din* (1939). The ship's company got so familiar with it that for variety they would dispense with the sound and take turns dubbing the dialogue. Curtis developed a keen 'Cary Grant'. He actually starred with Grant in his next film, *Operation Petticoat* (1959), and the two became good friends.

The most famous jibe from Curtis referred to that seduction scene. He said it was like kissing Hitler. Marilyn retorted, 'He only said that because I wore prettier dresses than he did.'

It seems that neither Curtis nor Wilder knew she was pregnant. In the event her precautions came to nothing; Marilyn miscarried again soon after filming. This began the break-up of her marriage to Arthur Miller. She's said to have blamed him for urging her to go ahead with the film because they needed the money. They divorced two years later, just after completing her last picture, *The Misfits* (1961), which Miller had scripted. Eighteen months after that Marilyn was dead.

It seems only one person was really pleased with her impossible delays during *Some Like It Hot*, the veteran film gangster George Raft. The new Castro regime in Cuba had just closed down his Havana Casino without compensation and he was feeling the pinch. His original contract was for a week's work but her carrying on resulted in him being retained for the full four months. Manna from Marilyn!

▤ The experience

'Wild and whacky fun.' *News of the World*, 17 May 1959

'Marilyn's latest is a riot.' *Sunday Dispatch*, 17 May 1959

But twenty-five years before Boy George other critics weren't so sure . . .

'The painted girl-boys struck me as so ugly, the mixture of machine-gun blood bath and female impersonation so intolerable, and the jokes about physical geography so wearisome, that I slipped out of the theatre by a side exit, leaving the end to stronger nerves than mine.' C.A. Lejeune, *Observer*, 17 May 1959

'I have discussed this with my doctor and psychiatrist and they tell me I'm too old and too rich to go through this again.' Billy Wilder, soon after filming

▤ Can you spot . . .

* George Raft's in-joke. He sees a young hood flipping a coin and says 'Where did you pick up that cheap trick?' Of course it's a piece of business he made famous in *Scarface* (1932), his big break in Hollywood. The hood he's speaking to is Edward G. Robinson Jnr, the son of his old screen rival.

The Sound of Music

1965 A would-be-nun-turned-nanny changes the lives of a strict Austrian captain and his seven children through love and music – but the Anschluss is looming.

▦ The talent

Julie Andrews 28, as Maria; screen favourite of the mid-sixties, soon out of fashion
Christopher Plummer 36, as Captain von Trapp; Canadian Shakespearean whose career flits between stage classics and screen money-spinners
Richard Haydn 59, as Max Detweiler; stage comedy in Britain, character film fixture, sometime director
Eleanor Parker 43, as the Baroness; glamourous star of the forties and fifties
Peggy Wood 72, as the Reverend Mother; star of sentimental fifties TV favourite *Mama*, this the last of her few films
Charmaine Carr as Liesl, **Heather Menzies** as Louisa, **Nicholas Hammond** as Freidrick, **Duanne Chase** as Kurt, **Angela Cartwright** as Brigitta, **Debbie Turner** as Marta, **Kym Karath** as Gretl; some TV work – Angela was Penny in TV's *Lost in Space*
Robert Wise 49, Producer/Director; edited *Citizen Kane* (1941), made many fine films including *West Side Story* (1961). Ended up directing *Star Trek – The Movie* (1979)

▦ The business

The $8,000,000 budget was about five times over the odds for a film in the mid-sixties but Twentieth Century Fox ended up spending a staggering $12,000,000 on top of that – on promotion, and enough prints to furnish one in ten of the world's cinemas.

But at least they were throwing good money after good for a change. The $44,000,000 spent and largely lost on *Cleopatra* (1962) had seriously rocked the company and so imagine the relief at last to hear the Sound of Cash Registers. Receipts were mounting up to the tune of $1,000,000 a week at one point, reaching a worldwide total of $160,000,000.

In twenty-two months *The Sound of Music* had broken the twenty-five-year-old *Gone With the Wind* box office record. Forty million people saw it in the first two years – although this might be a bit inflated by the few fanatics who sat through it several hundred times. There was even one man in Oregon who sent Fox a copy of the script he had transcribed from memory.

Loads of money all round: the $1,200,000 paid for the screenrights to Rodgers and Hammerstein's last outing together seems modest compared to the 10% of the gross they shared with their fellow Broadway backers. And Robert Wise was wise enough to take a percentage which must have been good for $10,000,000.

So Julie's one-off fee of $225,000 plus $75,000 in overtime (because the hills were alive with the sound of rainstorms) made her pretty good value at the time even though she hadn't yet had a picture released. This was after missing out on recreating her stage role as Eliza Doolittle in *My Fair Lady* (1964) because Jack Warner didn't want to risk an unknown screen quantity. She would have asked $75,000 and thrown in the vocals as well. Audrey Hepburn charged $1,000,000 without singing. Still, it left Julie free to do *Mary Poppins* (1964) for Walt Disney, taking home $125,000. Disney was left with a measly $90,000,000. He could smell success in the rushes and was so excited he took the unheard-of step of showing them to outsiders, including Robert Wise, who snapped her up before anyone else.

Julie actually made more from the music. At the time she was bigger than the Beatles – the soundtrack album overtook her previous recording of *My Fair Lady* as biggest-ever seller. And even the movies started paying during her few years at the top: $700,000 and up a film.

In fact it seems that only the critics (and Christopher Plummer) had any reservations about *The Sound of Music* and *everyone* (apart from Christopher Plummer) was whacky about Julie. So would she pick up a second Oscar after just winning Best Actress for *Mary Poppins*? *The Sound of Music* took four Academy Awards – two for Wise as producer and director.* Presenting Best Actress was her *My Fair Lady* co-star, Rex Harrison, who should have known better. He paused sadistically as he read the winner: Julie . . . Christie.

▦ Behind the screen

Isn't the scenery lovely? But Salzburg in the spring of 1964 was better suited to Alpine ducks than film crews and it took them days to get the opening helicopter shots. Notice how threatening the clouds look in the opening song? It was bitterly cold as well.

The mountains became mudslides with the crew having to resort to ox carts instead of jeeps to lug the gear, only to be kept sheltering for days waiting for a patch of blue sky.

And what did they do during all the delays? They listened to a comprehensive music-hall revival from Julie Andrews. One of the pervading memories of the whole event was how incessantly civil and cheery she was.

She took them all on outings and there's the story of her riding up the hills on an ox cart, resplendent in mink, keeping the rain off the cameras with an umbrella. One old hand snarled that he'd never worked with someone who said thank you so much, and Christopher Plummer said it was like being hit over the head with a greeting card every day.

Her dear old step-dad, Ted Andrews, was a music-hall turn who discovered that the little girl had a four-octave range when she piped up in an air-raid shelter sing-along. He said she played herself in both *Mary Poppins* and *The Sound of Music*. But he was her dear old step-dad. Another hardened crew member's assessment was 'a nun with a switchblade'.

So will the real Julie Andrews please stand up. The real Julie Andrews was a deeply worried woman. She had recently started what would turn out to be five solid years

*The other two were for Irwin Kostal's score and William Reynolds' editing – see Can You Spot. . .

Duanne Chase, Nicholas Hammond, Heather Menzies, Angela Cartwright, Kym Karath, Julie Andrews and

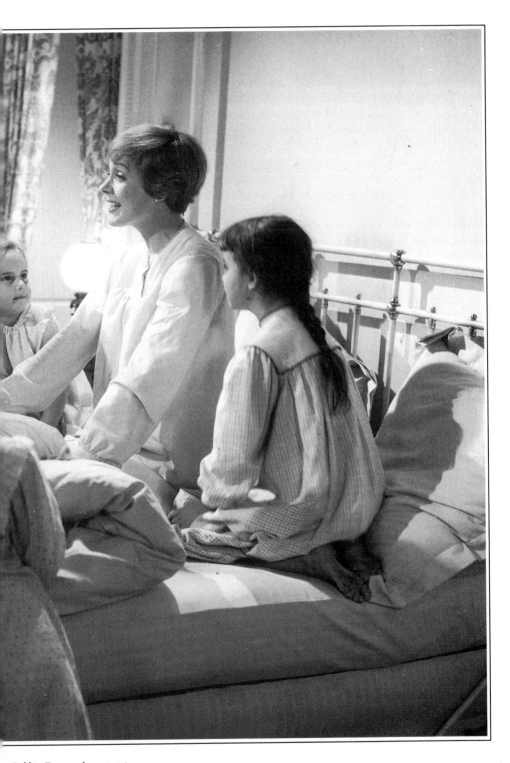

Debbie Turner: the entertainer

of psychiatric treatment, up to five times a week. Her dear old step-dad diagnosed too much sudden success but Julie herself diagnosed her dear old step-dad, taking the troubles back to the break-up of her parents' marriage.

And then there was her own marriage to Tony Walton, a boyfriend since her early teens. He had been the designer on *Mary Poppins* but seems to have felt increasingly threatened by her success and was now working in New York while she was with their young daughter filming in Austria. Every day there would be long telephone conversations, letters and tape recorded messages sent by air. They separated soon afterwards. She had already met her future husband and the mentor for her second successful career in films of the eighties, *Pink Panther* director Blake Edwards.*

Her *Sound of Music* colleagues knew little of Julie's traumas under all those layers of jolly. And who could help but respect a seasoned professional with such a splendid talent? Robert Wise was quite smitten, and grateful for the way she held the production together during the trying (and, in all that rain, drying) times. An example is the first scene they actually shot, Maria in bed with the children singing 'My Favourite Things'. Some of the little ones were ill at ease so Julie launched into her repertoire of pratfalls and stage business to instant effect. You can especially see how well it's working with Marta and Gretl under each arm. Kym Karath, who's playing Gretl, is so taken with it all that she keeps missing her cue to duck at the thunder.

Julie wanted to use a lot of physical comedy on camera as well and this is one of the few elements over which she clashed with Robert Wise. He vetoed the bit where she gets her guitar caught in the door of the bus on her way to her first visit at the von Trapps but finally let it go. And you'll notice that he confined most of her business to the 'I have Confidence' sequence and the early bits running in late at the abbey.

It is sometimes hard to believe that a lot of what you see on screen is an attempt by both Wise and Andrews to tone down the inevitably saccharine nature of the story. As Julie said, 'What can you do with nuns, seven children and Austria?'

So that is why the colours are deliberately muted and the setting as realistic as possible. And it also lies behind the casting of the distinguished but largely unknown Christopher Plummer – to give his character bite and dimension.

Plummer didn't see it that way. He looks back on the role with distaste – 'it's very sad to be remembered for something as lightweight as that' – though he admitted that it made it easier for him to fill theatres afterwards. He found Julie 'terribly nice but terribly nervous'. She thought he was 'a dear', a man whose introspection was confused by some as unfriendliness. Our Julie, as polite as ever.

▦ The experience

This from Judith Crist in the New York *Herald Tribune* was about par for the critics: 'One star and much scenery do not a two hour and fifty-five minute plus intermission entertainment make. Calorie counters, diabetics and grown-ups from 8 to 80 had best beware.'

---

*Blake restarted her career after good roles and popularity dried up in the late sixties, with some raunchier productions a decade later, like *10* (1979), which broke with her old image. Maybe he got a clue from the way she had introduced herself to him. She learned of him remarking that she was so sweet she must have violets between her legs. Julie sent him a bunch of violets.

Christopher Plummer was more succinct: 'The Sound of Mucus'.

But the critics loved Julie: 'This girl is not just a great star; she is a whole whirling, dazzling constellation.' James Powers, *Hollywood Reporter*

And even Kenneth Tynan who had called the original musical 'Rodgers and Hammerstein's great leap backwards' said, 'But it is Julie Andrews of the soaring voice and thrice-scrubbed innocence who makes me, even in guarded moments, catch my breath.'

'I wasn't trying to say a damned thing in *The Sound of Music*. People just feel good when they see it.' Robert Wise

▦ Can you spot . . .

* Some poor geography. The family would have been well and truly von trapped if they had driven up into the hills overlooking Salzburg and walked across the mountain border, as the Captain tells the Mother Superior. The border there is with southern Germany. The real von Trapps made it out through Italy, not Switzerland, and settled in New England after numerous singing tours.

* A familiar voice. Marni Nixon, who was Audrey Hepburn's singing voice in *My Fair Lady*, appears in her only onscreen role as the forgettable sister Sophie.

* A familiar opening sequence. Wise used a similar device for his previous mega-hit, *West Side Story*.

* A pioneering technique. Master ex-editor Wise shot many of the songs with a disdain for the conventions of continuity, jumping seamlessly between locations – now a standard pop video device.

* A crate of oranges marked produce of Israel (in Austria?! A decade before the Jewish homeland?!) Neither can I. Wise seems to have shot round it but you can see it in some publicity stills.

* Who's really singing. Margery McKay helped Reverend Mother Peggy Wood climb every octave but Christopher Plummer refused a vocal stand-in. Doesn't he look uncomfortable when he has to sing? They let him have his way and played the takes back to him. It changed his tune. In the end Bill Lee, who sang in commercials, sold us the eidelweiss.

* Two new songs. Richard Rodgers wrote the linking song 'I Have Confidence' and 'Something Good' for the film but didn't have the benefit of the late Oscar Hammerstein's clever lyrics. Notice the difference? Julie said she liked them both, but wasn't keen on Hammerstein's tongue-twisting 'Lonely Goat Herd'. In the event she got it perfect on the second take.

Stagecoach

1939 Nine people travel by stage in Indian country.

■ The talent

Claire Trevor 29, as Dallas; much admired actress in typical role. Never really made it out of the 'B's, though an Oscar for *Key Largo* (1948)

John Wayne 31, as the Ringo Kid; a legend in the making

Andy Devine 33, as Buck; born where the story takes place. Favourite Western character

John Carradine 32, as Hatfield; eccentric artist playing dark character roles into the 1980's. Three sons became actors including *Kung Fu* star David

Thomas Mitchell 46, as Doc Boone; journalist, playwright and a versatile actor.

Scarlett O'Hara's dad the same year, but an Oscar for *Stagecoach*

Louise Platt 24, as Lucy Mallory; lasted only five years in pictures

George Bancroft 56, as Curly Wilcox; more often a villain. Soon turned to ranching

Donald Meek 58, as Peacock; spot his Scots accent? His roles usually suited his surname

Berton Churchill 62, as Gatewood; former labour organizer in typical officious, heavy role. He died the following year

John Ford 43, Producer/Director; master film-maker at the peak of a half-century of achievement

■ The business

John Ford hadn't made a Western in more than ten years but he saw the potential in a short story he read in *Collier's* magazine called 'Stage to Lordsburg' and bought the rights for $2,500.

He was freelancing at the time and the attitude of the studios was that 'people don't make Westerns anymore', although what they probably meant was people like *John Ford* didn't make Westerns. They had continued to form a staple crop of the lower class, B-movie sector.

It took the shrewd judgement of independent producer Walter Wanger* to see something in Ford's pet project and figure out how to keep the cost down to around the $220,000 budget. That accounts in part for *Stagecoach* being in monochrome, featuring crack character players rather than big stars.

It is ironic that the least accomplished of the company was to become one of the most enduringly popular stars of all. John Wayne was a standard B Western actor, recently fallen on harder times after an attempt to switch from stock herding to stockbroking. He could make as much as $16,000 a picture but hungry for work at the start of a new contract with Republic, he may have only got $6,000 for *Stagecoach*.

At least he chose his friends superbly. About a decade before, Ford had got to know a set dresser called Michael – or Duke – Morrison (never Marion to anyone who valued their dentition) and helped him to get onscreen. After the years spent by

*Shrewd in his professional if not always his private life. He married Constance Bennett but served time in the fifties for shooting her agent.

Duke Wayne trotting along in the slow lane only Ford could see his full promise. When the director raised the subject with Wayne of who should play *Stagecoach* hero Ringo the actor had no hesitation. 'Lloyd Nolan,' he replied.

Stagecoach was one of the most popular films of a very strong film year. Consider the impact of Monument Valley's debut as the classic Western setting, especially as back-projection was then order of the day for most movie action sequences. But equally impressive to the public and critics of the time was the depth to which *Stagecoach* explored human and social themes from within the Western genre. All the normal horse opera explored was rootin', tootin' and shootin'.

There were Oscars for Thomas Mitchell and for the score of reworked 1880's folk-tunes but the coach passengers continued on life's journey largely unaffected by this splendid vehicle. It was the Duke who got noticed and, to begin with, Republic who coined it with greatly inflated John Wayne hire charges. Soon, though, he could write his own contracts. Wayne was toughing it out and topping the popularity stakes into the 1970's.

▦ Behind the screen

The John Wayne you see is being dragged up by the stirrups from mediocrity and finding it a rough ride. Typical of the helpful direction being offered by his old drinking buddy in those first days of shooting in November 1938 was, 'You walk like a drunken hippo. Your face looks as though it will crack if you smile.' Ford demanded so many retakes that Wayne got a sore face in the scene where he has to dry himself with a towel.

But it was all in a good cause, and even added to the authenticity of his fellow stagecoach passengers' supportive attitude to Ringo. All his co-stars sympathized with Wayne under the onslaught from the fearsome Ford.

Several knew what he was going through from first-hand experience. John Carradine claimed that Ford would pick at least one member of the company during any film to bully, and reckoned that the main butt on Stagecoach was Thomas Mitchell.

Ford was quite capable of letting fly at several members of the cast at once. Plucking up his courage one day ex-props man Wayne observed to Ford that the studio back-projection shots of Andy Devine driving the stagecoach might look more realistic if there was a spring attached to the reins. Ford gathered everyone from the production and announced that Wayne thought they were all doing a good job but that Andy Devine's performance stank.

Ford soon softened his approach with Wayne but Claire Trevor said that the Duke learned 'eight volumes about acting' during the production. Sometimes, though, the effort to eke out the right effect from his protégé became too much even for Ford. When all else failed during a scene with Claire Trevor, Ford's instruction to Wayne was 'Just raise your eyebrows and wrinkle your forehead.' Recalling the incident later in life Wayne remarked that it had been a mainstay of his technique ever since that time.

After more than twenty years in the director's chair Ford had a formidable reputation amongst the crew. His cool mastery meant that what you see of the film is by and large all that he shot. He is described as cutting with the camera, taking hardly any of the safety shots that might allow for uncertainty in putting it together. He didn't view the rushes or hang around the editing room.

However he could bend with the wind, or the snow. The photogenic qualities of a rare blizzard on the Arizona location were woven into the script by the addition of a couple of comments from Andy Devine. And it even brought Ford his authentic-looking extras – chilly Navajos on the move because of the bad weather, who were paid the same daily rate as the white extras on Ford's insistence, against the wishes of the film's moneymen. He was made an honorary chief as thanks for the thousands of dollars he brought to the hard-pressed Indian community of the area, an episode at odds with Ford's image as a right-wing film-maker who stereotyped Hispanics as funny-devious and Native Americans as the bad guys.

In fact everyone on a John Ford picture generally did well for creature comforts. In a throwback to his silent days he would have live mood music, often from an accordian, to soothe the members of the production between takes. And though he only actually spent a few days on location he insisted on the best food and an easy pace, finishing in the early evening.

Perhaps he wanted to enjoy the scenery. This was the first time that John Ford used the backdrop that was to become his trademark, the remote Monument Valley on the border between Arizona and Utah (though despite its dominance, notice that it is only in a few shots). The Indian chase was shot closer to home, at Victorville in the Mojave desert not too far from Los Angeles. As with many of the other action

Arizona snow

sequences it was masterminded by one of cinema's most colourful characters, Yakima Canutt, an ex-rodeo star who was Hollywood's master stunt man and second unit director for decades. He got a farmer to soften the area with his plough before he and the Indians set about falling off horses for the cameras. The climax was the stunt where Canutt – standing in for John Wayne and for the Brave pursuing him – jumps onto the team of horses.*

Look at the sequence carefully and you'll see what he went through, particularly as the Indian raider. The pinto he was riding shies at the last minute and it is a long and difficult jump to the stage team. That accomplished, comes the painful bit. In the next sequence as his character is shot and falls down you can see him cut by the horses' hooves.

The stunt where he is dragged underneath the stage and out the back was an old trick Canutt had perfected through numerous Westerns. It was actually safer the faster the horses were going (about 40 mph in this case) because they were less likely to swerve. If ever you're hanging from the bottom of a stagecoach with a team of whipped-up nags thundering around your ears, try to remember Yakima's little tip to keep your legs limp. That way you won't roll underneath their hooves. The bit at the end where he rises up briefly and then flops down was his own little touch. Incredibly no one got hurt on the *Stagecoach* shoot and Yakima Canutt himself died in 1986 at the age of ninety – in bed.

▦ The experience

'A movie of the grand old school, a genuine rib-thumper and a beautiful sight to see.' Frank S. Nugent, *New York Times*, 1939

'It is rather unfair to call it a Western at all; it plays in Arizona but it has none of the dare-devil impossibilities, the perfunctory whipping up of emotions or the honest-to-goodness black-and-white psychology of the standard, shop-soiled article.' Peter Galway, *New Statesman*, 17 June 1939

'Westerns? I never look at them but I love to make them.' John Ford

▦ Can you spot . . .

* Why the Indians didn't just shoot the horses to end the chase, a favourite question of movie-buff smart-alecs. Ford's answer was that it was the horses that the Indians were after in the first place.
* Lots more in the Indian chase. The tyre tracks from the cars the cameras were mounted on. You may also notice that some of the shots 'cross the line' – are shot from opposite sides so that the action seems to jump in reverse. Ford said he had to shoot it that way because he was losing the light. And if your ears spot some pretty repetitive horses it is because they only bought in a ten-foot loop of hoof sound effects.
* A familiar head. Chief John Big Tree, who plays the Indian scout, was the model used for the American 'Indian Head' nickel first issued in 1912.
* Where the story comes from. A fave bit of literary trivia is that it's based on de Maupassant's first published novella, *Boule de Suif* (Ball of Lard), about a coach on the outskirts of Paris during the Franco-Prussian War. The Prussians were the Indians.

---

*If you want to see what he looks like up close just ask yourself if the cavalry scout looks familiar.

Star Wars

1977 A beautiful rebel princess in distress, a young man with a mystic mission.

▦ The talent

Alec Guinness 62, as Obiwan Kenobe; illustrious career of characters which have enhanced many great films since the forties, particularly with Ealing and David Lean

Mark Hamill 23, as Luke Skywalker; mainly TV soaps and commercials before. Only emerging slowly from Skywalker image in the late eighties

Carrie Fisher 19, as Princess Leia; produced by crossing Debbie Reynolds with Eddie Fisher. Film debut as jailbait in *Shampoo* (1975). Few appearances since aside from the *Star Wars* trilogy

Harrison Ford 34, as Han Solo; former carpenter also in Lucas' *American Graffiti* (1973), later Lucas' Indiana Jones and thus the lead in half of the all-time box office top ten earners

David Prowse 41, as Darth Vader; familiar in Britain as road safety icon the Green Cross Code Man, and from many TV roles

Kenny Baker 42, in R2D2; nightclub performer in partnership with chief Jawa, Jack Purvis

Anthony Daniels 30, as CP30; actor on stage with London's Young Vic. Later voice of Elf King in *Lord of the Rings* (1978)

Peter Mayhew 42, as Chewbacca; London hospital porter endowed with Britain's biggest feet

Gary Kurtz 36, Producer; co-produced, with fellow Roger Corman protégé Francis Ford Coppola, George Lucas' *American Graffiti*. Also made *The Empire Strikes Back* (1980), *The Dark Crystal* (1982) and *Slipstream* (1987), which starred Mark Hamill

George Lucas 31, Director; Coppola's former assistant whose few films have mostly returned historic profits

▦ The business

Universal could have had this one cheap but they rejected the sixteen-page résumé that George Lucas submitted. This may seem strange in view of the fact that his previous film for the studio, *American Graffiti*, had made a 50:1 profit but the economics of sci-fi were quite different. The most acclaimed recent example of the genre, MGM's *2001: A Space Odyssey* (1968), had taken five years to turn a profit on its $11,000,000 budget.

Nevertheless, Twentieth Century Fox's Alan Ladd Jnr (son of the actor) displayed a faith in Lucas and the project that never wavered, despite boardroom pressure, a budget which itself wavered well over its $8,500,000 target and a product which continued to look quite unimpressive until its very final stages. Imagine seeing, as he did, a forty-minute rough cut of live action sequences without the benefit of the special effects or John Williams' Oscar-winning score.

Williams wrote the music in two months after seeing a more complete assemblage of the film. The then-revolutionary special effects took longer and cost more. They came courtesy of an inventive collection of hippie types at Industrial Light and Magic, a firm Lucas had set up with $1,000,000 of his *American Graffiti* loot. The 365 SFX shots sent spending way over the $2,500,000 allocated in the budget. Each of the 24 frames a second averaged out at $150. The spaceship models formed a hefty portion of this; the Star Destroyer alone cost $100,000.

No one had ever seen anything like *Star Wars*. The film hit the marketplace in the spring of 1977 and everything else was out for the count. The $9,500,000 outlay was recouped on the first day. It has so far taken $193,500,000 in North America alone, the most for any film until *E.T.* (1982). Fox stock doubled in value and Alan Ladd Jnr was made the company's president.

George Lucas also profited immensely from the success. He had taken modest up-front fees of $50,000 for the script and $100,000 to direct, whereas his market value following *American Graffiti* would have been more like $500,000. Instead he went for a 40% slab of the profits plus what seemed like lesser concessions which included the music and merchandizing rights. Fortunes were being made at the box office but with *Star Wars* the potential for product licensing was exploited as never before. Manufacturers clamoured for the chance to link their goods with the film's success. There were toys, comic books, souvenirs, clothes and myriad other items tied in with the *Star Wars* theme. Total sales are estimated at more than $2,500,000,000.

The film's performers received varied slices of the action. David Prowse, the champion body-builder who played Darth Vader, was paid a total of about $12,000 and James Earl Jones, who over-dubbed Prowse's gentle West Country burr, $10,000. Both have done better in sequels, as have Hamill, Fisher and Ford who this time each got a $\frac{1}{4}$% of the profits as a latter gesture by Lucas.

The picture's biggest established star, Sir Alec Guinness, had already been promised $2\frac{1}{4}$% for deigning to do the film in the first place. It gave him financial independence for the first time in a distinguished and busy career.

The saga continues. *Star Wars* is properly called *A New Hope* and is the fourth part of a nine-part *Star Wars* cycle. Lucas went on to mastermind the next two sections, *The Empire Strikes Back* (1980) and *The Return of the Jedi* (1983). Each made around $300,000,000 worldwide and are numbers three and four behind *E.T.* (1982) and *Star Wars* in the top box office charts.

▦ Behind the screen

You miss much of the film's impact if you're watching *Star Wars* on video. The experience of the Star Destroyer seeming to lumber directly over the cinema audience in the first scene was the clincher that made everyone go potty with enthusiasm from the premiere onwards.

This and all the other spacecraft shots were made possible by using a system called Dykstraflex, developed by chief Industrial-Light-and-Magician John Dykstra. The principle seems quite straightforward; the only thing that is really moving is the camera. All the spaceships you see are inanimate, propped on blue neon poles. They are filmed from a rig that can be programmed to repeat precisely any particular movement. All the elements are then filmed individually and carefully matted together. Never before had it been possible to be so much part of the action.*

---

*Can you spot where you've seen the dog fights before. They used action from *The Bridges at Toko-Ri* (1954) and *The Battle of Britain* (1967) as templates for the Dykstraflex treatment.

To complete the illusion successfully the 75 models had to be fashioned in exquisite detail. The Star Destroyer apparently had a quarter of a million individual portholes. The Millenium Falcon was designed by a firm of British marine engineers and was complete down to miniature pin-ups in the cockpit.

The models themselves stretched the expertise of the special effects people through vast discrepancies in scale. In that first scene, for instance, the massive Star Destroyer is only half the size of its apparently tiny quarry. When the ship carrying the princess is being sucked into the Empire flagship you are watching a six-foot model being drawn towards a six-inch aperture. The biggest of the models was the bombing run trench of the Death Star, three feet deep and fifty feet long.

It all took a long time to develop and when Lucas got back to California from filming the live action he found that little actual footage had been shot. There was a dreadful row and although the Industrial Light and Magic staff got bonuses with the success of the film none got points like the actors.

Lucas' mood after live filming was understandably black. The strain had been enough to give him stomach pains and insomnia. They started off in Tunisia in March 1976 with just eleven days to get all the desert shots, actually ten if you count the first day as wasted in trying unsuccessfully to get R2D2 to move.

Poor Kenny Baker, all 3'8" of him, was stuffed inside the egg-like robot with a set of controls which didn't work because of interference from local radio transmissions. Any time you see R2 moving during the desert shots he is being dragged along on skis by a nylon rope. When the costume *did* work the motors and relays were so noisy that the only way to let Baker know when a take was finished was to bang the exterior with a hammer.

The Tatoonie homestead scenes were shot in a village called Jerba built as an arrangement of caves around a central hole. This gave the locals protection from the area's endemic sandstorms which ravaged the production, pitting the camera lenses and tearing apart the land cruiser. This massive structure, two stories high and ninety feet long, took a day to re-assemble.

It wasn't simply technical problems in Tunisia. Although George Lucas had spent his time since *American Graffiti* on the project he found writing difficult so the script and story weren't yet finalized as filming began. It was Lucas' wife, Marcia (who also had a hand in the film editing), who suggested killing off Obiwan Kenobe comparatively early. Alec Guinness found out when he arrived for shooting in the desert and apparently threatened to walk off the picture. There was hasty renegotiation of plot line giving Guinness's character even more of its mystical dominance over the entire proceedings.

Back at Elstree in Britain things were no better. It was just as uncomfortable as Tunisia, one of the hottest summers on record. To make matters worse they had to use fiercely powerful lighting so that the matting process would work.* Several people fainted and Peter Mayhew suffered heatstroke in the furry confines of his Chewbacca costume. It seems that everyone in costume endured discomfort. When Luke comments that you can't see anything in the Storm Trooper's helmet he isn't kidding. They were forever running into one another. One of the troopers even suffered concussion.

*Some of the cockpit shots with space behind were regarded by the makers as the least convincing example of the matte-maker's art. Look particularly at all the blue fringes around Chewbacca's fur.

Hamill, Ford and Fisher had a grotty time of it when they were stuck for ages in the watery rubbish disposal, though at least they had wet suits on underneath their costumes. Carrie Fisher had her breasts taped to a chaste stationary condition as befits a fairytale princess.

Anthony Daniels, the skeletal Shakespearean actor who played C3PO, had to spend days completely naked apart from a coating of vaseline and plaster as his costume was designed along the contours of his ectomorphic frame. Peter Cushing, as Grand Moff Tarkin, took it more in his stride. Finding his boots uncomfortable he played every scene where his feet were out of shot in carpet slippers.

The atmosphere at Elstree was poor. Lucas and his producer appeared to the uncooperative British crew immature, shambling and withdrawn. One problem was that no one apart from Lucas seemed to have an idea of how great the final product would look. Without his vision of the special effects and with no coherent idea of the plot it all looked a mess to them.

Even more senior technical staff had little idea of what Lucas was trying to do. He clashed with his veteran cinematographer Gilbert Taylor who refused to use soft focus. And production designer John Barry was less than pleased at Lucas going around deliberately scuffing his sets. Lucas had, of course, grasped that to make the future realistic you had to make it look lived in.

One impediment to understanding was the jumbled way that the picture was shot; out of sequence and sans SFX it was incomprehensible. Things went from bad to worse as the production was guillotined by head office before they had completed some of the key early scenes in the narrative.

As the axe was falling Lucas had three separate units working at Elstree mopping up the missing sequences. So the sense of danger is real when Princess Leia is loading her message in R2 and for Darth Vader's key introductory appearance. Most of the initial battle was filmed during this last week with producer Kurtz handling the scenes with the invading storm troopers.

The cast were just as puzzled by proceedings as the back-room boys. Mark Hamill compared the experience of acting in *Star Wars* to being a raisin in a fruit salad and not knowing who the other fruits were.

There was no rehearsal, not even a run-through. Carrie Fisher remembers a typical direction along the lines of 'Act more like a princess'. Lucas' favourite note seems to have been 'Faster, more intense'. One of the few definite rules was that everyone should take it seriously. There was to be no mugging to the camera, no self-conscious double-takes.

The script was no help. Alec Guinness called it ropey. Harrison Ford, on the other hand, displayed the forthright bluntness that won him the role of Han Solo in the first place. 'You can type this shit, George,' he said to Lucas, 'but you can't say it.'

Guinness does not seem to have been best pleased with his most lucrative performance, admitting to not knowing who he was playing. His worst moment was when Ben Kenobe, sensing that Alderan has been destroyed, puts his hand to his forehead. This hammy gesture made him wince.

No one can doubt the overall success of the result. However, since the experience of *Star Wars* Lucas, while maintaining his guiding hand on further episodes of the galactic saga and on the *Indiana Jones* series, has largely left the dialogue and direction to others.

Carrie Fisher and Mark Hamill: fear of heights

▦ The experience

'A remarkable confection: a sublimal history of the movies, wrapped in a riveting tale of suspense and adventure, ornamented with some of the most ingenious special effects ever contrived for film.' *Time*, 1977

'*Star Wars* loots a form; it is the biggest exploitation movie of them all.' Michael Moorcock, *New Statesman*, 16 December 1977

'Lucas is completely wrapped up in the cinema, he is only happy talking film.' Alec Guinness

'It's a film that is totally uninterested in anything that doesn't connect with the mass audience. There's no breather in the picture, no lyricism; the only attempt at beauty is the double sunset.' Pauline Kael, *New Yorker*, 26 September 1977

▦ Can you spot . . .

* The different musical themes for each of the main characters. There's one each for the Princess, for Luke, for Ben, for Darth Vader and for the Death Star itself.
* Where some of the names come from. R2 D2 is film editor's jargon for Reel 2 dialogue 2. And Luke Skywalker? Here's a clue: Luke S.
* The most dangerous shot. It's when Luke and the Princess swing across the chasm. It was actually thirty feet high and there were no doubles. They only dared try it once. See how scared Carrie Fisher looks?
* Some references to other films. In the cantina when the alien thug says 'You just watch yourself. We're wanted men. I have the death sentence on twelve systems,' is roughly what a samurai says in Akira Kurosawa's *Yojimbo* (1961). The burning farm is a reference to John Ford's *The Searchers* (1965).
* How the light sabres work. They had revolving four-sided blades with reflective material which scintillated in the beam of a light mounted on the camera. The blade's seeming emergence from the handle is due to the way it reflects as the motor starts up and the stuff of camera angles. The best place to spot the workings is in Obiwan's duel with Darth.
* The life and death of Biggs. This was an extra character, Luke's best friend from home, who survives in the film mainly in references. Luke mentions him a couple of times on Tatoonie and is briefly reunited with him in his formation attacking the Death Star. The third member of the wing, Red 2 also known as Wedge, gets hit and limps off. Poor Biggs gets blown away, before we've been properly introduced.
* Where you've seen Wedge before. It's Dennis Lawson, star of *Local Hero* (1983). And Don Henderson, TV's *Bulman*, is pillar of the Empire, General Taggi.
* A spaced-out space princess. Carrie Fisher was developing a taste for drugs at the time of *Star Wars*, allegedly taking cocaine and LSD at the weekends. She subsequently had treatment and re-arranged her experiences in a novel entitled *Postcards from the Edge*.
* A werewolf. The cantina scene is considered a highlight of sci-fi film history but they ran out of masks and sneaked in a naff joke-shop example. While imagination ran riot with the appearance of the creatures patronizing this interstellar dive, practicalities of terrestrial respiration were forgotten and they had to slit the masks at the throat for breathing holes. The scene itself was made possible through an extra $20,000 prised from the Fox board by Alan Ladd Jnr who told them '*Star Wars* is possibly the greatest picture ever made. That is my absolute statement.'

The
Third Man

1949 A hack novelist searches Vienna for clues to the death of an old friend.

▦ The talent

Joseph Cotten 44, as Holly Martins; most memorable with Welles, as in his *Citizen Kane* debut. Worked steadily for more than thirty more years but he'd had his share of classics

Orson Welles 34, as Harry Lime; boy genius going magnificently to seed

Alida Valli 28, as Anna Schmidt; brave Italian anti-fascist tipped at the time for big international stardom that never materialized – especially after involvement in a sex, drugs and murder scandal in 1954

Trevor Howard 34, as Major Calloway; five years into a sturdy four-decade career

Bernard Lee 41, as Sergeant Paine; character actor who became most familiar as James Bond's boss, M

Wilfred Hyde-White 64, as Crabbin; many similar parts in straight comedy, Pickering in *My Fair Lady* (1964)

Carol Reed 43, Producer/Director; film artist at his peak – an Oscar in the end for *Oliver* (1968)

▦ The business

The setting of Vienna was Alexander Korda's idea. As the film's backer, he was looking for a repeat of his previous successful pairing for *The Fallen Idol* (1948) of one of Britain's finest directors, Carol Reed, with one of its premier novelists, Graham Greene.* The deal Korda struck with *Gone With the Wind* producer David Selznick was a reverse of those generally arrived at today: the Americans would provide the stars (Welles, Cotten and Valli) and the Brits would supply the money.

Korda sent Greene to Vienna for two weeks so that, in the proper atmosphere, the writer might flesh out an idea he had once jotted down on the back of an envelope. Three days before he was due to leave Greene was no further advanced from his original notion of a resurrected central character. Then he got talking to a British intelligence officer whose conversation covered a range of topics including the apolitical sprawl of the divided city's sewers and the deadly trade in black-market penicillin.

Carol Reed sold the unusually brief starring part to Orson Welles over dinner. When the director explained the appearance of Lime half-way into the film Welles replied that he'd much rather come in two-thirds of the way through. He was offered a 20% stake or $100,000 up front and took the ready money to finance his own production, *Othello* (1951), and satisfy the immediate requirements of the American Internal Revenue Service. But given the immense success of the film it was an expedient he regretted.

*The Man Between (1953) and *Our Man in Havana* (1959) brought them less successfully together again.

Welles loved *The Third Man* in any case. It was the only one of his movies he would take the trouble to catch on TV every two or three years. The critics loved it too. They hailed *The Third Man* as the best British film of the year and worldwide it was a great audience-puller, helped to some degree by a teen cult of the time which centred on bobby-soxers vying with each other for the highest number of viewings.

Amongst the burghers of Vienna there was general tolerance, even enthusiasm, for Reed's vision of their home town as a fragmented den of thieves but the feeling was that they would have preferred a soundtrack featuring lush strings. Trevor Howard claimed to have discovered Anton Karas busking with his zither outside a Vienna restaurant and recommended him to Carol Reed. The musician was transported to Britain, chained to a movieola and subjected to 500 or so runs of the film. The resulting soundtrack was a haunting synthesis of traditional folk tunes and some original themes which became one of the biggest-selling records, four million in Britain alone. Karas later bought the restaurant.

Now anyone can share in the success of *The Third Man*. In an extraordinary oversight copyright holders EMI Films failed to renew their claim to the picture when it came up for renewal in 1978, meaning that like many other, though older, classics *The Third Man* is now irretrievably in the public domain.

▦ Behind the screen

One of the things that immediately set *The Third Man* apart for contemporary audiences was the authentically oppressive atmosphere of post-war Vienna, a result partly of Reed's unusual decision to film on location. This would inevitably mean privations for the company. Joseph Cotten had been warned about the shortages in Europe at the time by Alexander Korda who advised him over the trans-Atlantic telephone to pack a couple of lemons for his gin and tonics.

But Cotten's first real taste of the tyranny of occupation bureaucracy came when he was thrown off the train thirty miles away from the city because he didn't have the right documentation. He called Reed for help, spelling out his name for the hotel receptionist as ending 'N for never again'.

Orson Welles had a rather smoother arrival. He was in the throes of filming and romance in Italy but managed to reach a deal with Carol Reed whereby if given two days warning he would be on location. Welles kept to the deal stepping off the train early in the morning and immediately taking part in his first scheduled scene, where he walks across the Prater to the Big Wheel and says a few words to Cotten. It was in the can by 9 a.m. Welles, who had just shot his version of *Macbeth* (1948) in a breathless twenty-one days, was impressed. 'Jeez, this is the way to make a picture,' he said.

Reed might have disagreed. Faced with cramming shooting into five difficult weeks on location and seven in the studio he had divided the team into a night and a day unit. But the director was needed all the time and so the masterpiece you see has been shot between snatches of sleep taken mid-morning and at dusk.

Still Carol Reed found the inspiration to improvise brilliant touches that weren't in Greene's script, like the first time you actually see Welles in the darkened doorway. Seeking a more intriguing entrance for Harry Lime than just being spotted by Holly he used the fact that the cat placed in Valli's apartment as set decoration refused to play with the flowers proferred by Cotten. Reed planted a reference in the dialogue to the cat only liking Harry and let puss do the introductions.* The motivation for the mog's display of affection for Welles was a strategically-placed smear of sardines.

If Orson Welles looks like he's had his sardines it is because he had just succeeded in bedding some Italian actress after a long and arduous pursuit, this in the midst of divorcing Rita Hayworth. In retrospect he regretted that his appetites had been sated to the extent that he didn't bother to try it on with his beautiful co-star Alida Valli, especially as their hotel rooms were next door to each other.

Then again perhaps it was the flu. Welles demanded that Reed use a stand-in when it came to filming in the sewers because he was recovering from a virus and didn't want to aggravate it by getting wet. Wellesian enthusiasm, however, rapidly took over. He was soon offering plenty of suggestions, and cavorted around for retake after sopping retake.

Welles has often been credited with writing and directing some of his own scenes, particularly the 'cuckoo clocks' speech extolling the virtues of no income tax, but this doesn't seem to have been the case. He might have wished it otherwise. For the rest of his life the band would strike up the Harry Lime theme whenever he made an entrance. He was never so publicly identified with any of his own works.

It seems to have been a happy, even slightly boozy shoot. Joseph Cotten had taken seriously Korda's advice about lemons. He managed to get in contact with the genuine Harry Lime fraternity and his room became the unit's social headquarters, an oasis of scarce good food and drink. However this was evidently insufficient for Trevor Howard who went out on the razzle one night still in his colonel's costume. Everyone thought the World War Two paratroop hero was real Top Brass and didn't dare intervene as he got louder and louder. Finally, when the MPs did take the plunge he got done for impersonating an officer and might have been in deep sewer water but for some fast talking to the authorities.

It was the Russian authorities who caused the film-makers the most problems, particularly over the shots of the four-power patrols in the introduction, which finally had to be posed by actors, and the scenes in the Vienna train station, which was in the Soviet sector.

Carol Reed had been forewarned by a local film producer that the commissars would surely confiscate the equipment. Fortunately, said the Austrian, they chose his studio to store it in and he would steal the film back.

All this went according to form except that the Soviets took their cue early and swooped when shooting was only partly completed. So what you see is a mixture of Russian sector and studio mock-up.* Most of the set was just about passable but the flimsy prop Austrian train was so pathetic that Reed just used it in silhouette and to outline lights shining through smoke. The effect of this expedient was one of the film's most critically acclaimed shots.

Another was the final shot of the film. Graham Greene's script didn't have an ending and the problem of the film's resolution for once divided writer and director. Greene viewed *The Third Man* as one of his 'entertainments' and too light for a sad ending. Reed thought that so soon after Lime's final demise anything else would have been inappropriately cynical. Greene later conceded that his friend got it spot-on.

---

*Pusses, really. There were several different cats on the street in Vienna and on the set in Britain, as you can tell from the rapid changes of fur patterning.

In that last shot Cotten has no idea what is happening. Remember that only the director knew that he was going to use Anton Karas' insistent music to pace out the time. Cotten is at first expecting Valli to stop and speak to him, he lights a cigarette to fill, waiting for Reed's call of 'cut' which never seems to come.

▦ The experience

'*The Third Man* is not a work of art. It is the work of two great artists on holiday (Reed and Greene) who between them have produced a surpassingly good thriller.' Paul Dehn, *Sunday Chronicle*, 4 September 1949

'It is the little things that make this film a joy to watch and hear: a child's face, a careless word, an idle gesture – and running through it all Mr Reed's (or perhaps Mr Greene's) delightful sense of humour.' *The Standard*, 1 September 1949

'Carol Reed and I have something in common – we are both awfully patient with me.' Orson Welles

▦ Can you spot . . .

* How Anton Karas managed to play the Harry Lime theme on the zither. Neither could other zither players – it isn't possible. Karas jumped the gun on modern recording stars and did it with over-dubs.

* The director's voice. That's him narrating the introduction.

* The director's hand. He stood in for Harry's mitt clasping desperately through the sewer grating. And if you're familiar with the sewers of Vienna you'll know that what's happening just on the other side is a mock-up on set. The real Vienna sluices don't have natty little stairways going up to the manholes.

* A transient style. All those lopsided shots were Reed's experimental expression of something crooked going on. Fellow director William Wyler gave him a spirit level later for a joke and Reed never revived the style in his future work.

* An intermittent soldier. As the setting shifts from location to studio in the sequence when Anna is being arrested, actor Geoffrey Keen, playing the most talk-ative of the squaddies, keeps on being replaced from shot to shot by someone else. Later he was to replace Bernard Lee as the James Bond film authority figure.

* A touch of the props men. It wasn't that rainy in Vienna and they spent much time and money hosing down the cobbled streets for the wet look. You can see a hosing truck as Holly speeds by on the sinister taxi journey that ends up at the British Cultural Centre. And props men on ladders also supplied the fluttering leaves for the final shot.

* Harry didn't know his cuckoo clocks. They originate in the German Black Forest, not Switzerland.

Tootsie

1982 Temperamental actor can only get work by impersonating a female.

▦ The talent

Dustin Hoffman 44, as Michael Dorsey; a panning for *Ishtar* (1986) and an Oscar for *Rain Man* (1989) were to come
Jessica Lange 33, as Julie; survived the odium of *King Kong* (1976) to win an Oscar here and nominations for her two subsequent films
Sydney Pollack 48, as George Fields; he says he wouldn't act and direct again, it interfered with his concentration
Teri Garr 30, as Sandy; Richard Dreyfuss' screen wife in *Close Encounters of the Third Kind* (1977). Ex-TV comedienne and busy co-star of the eighties.
Bill Murray 32, as Jeff; Canadian graduate of TV's *Saturday Night Live*. *Ghostbusters* (1984) was waiting
Sydney Pollack Producer; a new move into production. He continued with his next picture, *Out of Africa* (1985), for which he won an Oscar
Dick Richards 46, Producer; another director moving into production
Sydney Pollack Director; made *They Shoot Horses Don't They?* (1969) and a lot of Robert Redford films

▦ The business

They had to send three boxes full of scripts to the Writers Guild for them to adjudicate the writing credits for *Tootsie*. The original concept, at least, was Dustin Hoffman's. It was in the aftermath of his first Oscar win, which came not for one of his brilliant character leads, but rather his very conventional role in *Kramer vs. Kramer* (1979). Hoffman wanted a real challenge, and he started discussing with playwright Murray Schisgal what it would be like to be himself, but a woman. The actor called this female persona Shirley. He felt he'd always had a Shirley in him.

This was at a time when transsexuality was being more openly explored in the cinema. Two big contemporary films with related themes were *Victor/Victoria* (1982) starring Julie Andrews and Barbra Streisand's *Yentl* (1983) which was in production at the same time as *Tootsie*. In the end Schisgal shared the credit with Larry Gelbart, one of the key men behind TV's *M*A*S*H*, but the script you hear is largely the result of an Elaine May rewrite. She didn't claim a credit but accepted instead a reported $450,000 for three weeks work. The total writer's tab came to about $1,500,000.

The directors came and went almost as readily as the writers: Hal Ashby, then Dick Richards (who nevertheless retained a co-producer credit) and finally Sydney Pollack. This may have been Hoffman's baby but it was Pollack's picture and one of his conditions was that he got final say. Another condition was a fee of $2,000,000.

Hoffman's fee was $4,500,000 which, with those of Pollack and the writers, plus filming and preparation delays, pushed the final cost of *Tootsie* up to $21,000,000, about twice the average for the early eighties. Although justifying the production expenses Sydney Pollack, as co-producer, still sometimes shuddered to the bottom of his wallet. It came home to him particularly when he looked down the street during a break in filming the final scene to see a substantial fleet of pantechnicons all being maintained by the production for make-up, wardrobe, lighting and the like.

Columbia were apparently unruffled at the cost and by the reported conflict between star and director, all of which had earned the production's nick-name, Troubled Tootsie. They were undoubtedly paying top rates for volatile talent but both Hoffman and Pollack had secure enough track records to let the accountants sleep easily.

Hoffman had a brilliant history of successful and well-regarded films which he had topped with his new Oscar. Pollack was skilled and experienced at working with big stars. More to the point, six of his eight previous films had made good money and he'd brought in his last picture, *Absence of Malice* (1981), $500,000 under budget.

Studio confidence proved quite justified. *Tootsie* was an instant hit with the public and the critics. It was eclipsed in the earnings stakes by its contemporary, history's number one, *E.T.* (1982), but still made an astounding $95,000,000 in North America, becoming Columbia's most successful film and remaining the highest-selling pure comedy.

▦ Behind the screen

Dustin Hoffman said he based elements of Dorothy's character on his mother, who was very ill through his long preparation for *Tootsie* and died a few months before they started shooting. He took the film's name from a childhood game when she would throw him in the air saying 'How's my tootsie wootsie?'

He was very attached to Dorothy, becoming so involved that he broke down when asked during a screen test if she would ever have children. 'I think it's a little late in the day for that,' he replied and began to sob.

Nevertheless he maintained that he wouldn't do the picture he had conceived and nurtured unless he passed his own screen test. It couldn't be a drag act. He had to look convincing.

Clothes were the least of their problems. Dorothy's TV role as hospital administrator enabled him to conceal a sixteen-inch neck and outsize adam's apple in scarves and high necklines. His breasts were made by a firm specializing in prosthetics for mastectomy patients.

The voice was more difficult. They went to the extent of fiddling about with an oscilloscope at Columbia University so that Hoffman could tune his vocal chords to an authentic womanly wave pattern. The problem was that he could do a fine falsetto, but only in a French accent. The notion of making Dorothy a southerner came in the shower. Like the French, sentences inflect upwards down south. He auditioned the new voice to his *Kramer* co-star, Meryl Streep, performing extracts from *A Streetcar Named Desire* as Dorothy as Blanche.

The make-up artists went the way of writers and directors on this picture. Credibility and the speed of application were equally essential. However no weapon in modern make-up's arsenal could withstand the swift and inexorable rallying of the Hoffman beard. It restricted the Dorothy sequences to three- or four-hour days following a couple of hours getting prepared.

This was a more extreme version of Michael's onscreen routine. It involved shaving Dustin's legs, arms and even the backs of his fingers (in a sauna, extra close) and taping back his facial skin to tighten his features. Hoffman has manly teeth, big and

Sydney Pollock and Dustin Hoffman: made up at last

irregular, hence the daintier false choppers. His eye make-up was the same as that for Bo Derek. The glasses also helped.

What didn't help was the summer heat of 1981 which caused his face tapes to snap. And beneath all the greasepaint Dustin Hoffman was suffering a recurrence of what he described as the worst case of adolescent acne in Los Angeles.

They improvised a number of trials to test the disguise. Hoffman was introduced to his daughter's teacher at school without being recognized. He also offered to fellate Jose Ferrer when they found themselves sharing a lift. Ferrer could scarcely wait to get out at his floor. 'Who was that scumbag broad?' he asked someone with him.

Hoffman found that his experiences as Dorothy offered some thought-provoking insights. Although perfectly understandable, especially in Mr Ferrer's case, he came face to face with a special form of rejection rarely experienced by straight men, as a fellow's eye strays beyond you to find a more attractive girl.

In fact, as they started filming, the tests didn't look all that good. Hoffman projected the image of a female prison warder. Both he and Pollack were worried. Although things improved, they began shooting the soap opera scenes before the cosmetics were perfected. You can see the difference once we get to the sequences in Julie's apartment.* All the way through, though, you may be able to spot slight differences in Hoffman's look from shot to shot.

Director and star maintained a healthy dialogue during filming about how Dorothy should be played. It would be so easy to tip the character into the realm of the grotesque or absurd. Hoffman's interest was towards outrageously comic exploration of the craft of acting. Pollack, who was unused to comedy, tried to mellow this as far as possible by developing the relationships. Both men play down reports of their vigorous disagreements claiming there was hardly ever a raised voice and that they never argued in front of the crew. Pollack said that it would have been impossible to make the film had there been the degree of rancour described in the press.

*The locations, incidentally, were the same: New York's National Video Centre.

The character of Michael was more straightforward than Dorothy. It was a lot like Dustin, or at least the Dustin who might have been without a lucky break in *The Graduate* (1968). Hoffman, with his reputation for single-minded pursuit of excellence, might well have expounded like Dorsey on the motivation of a tomato. This was the crew's favourite scene. Doesn't the actor's actor look a little as if he's playing to an appreciative live audience?

Hoffman kept his transformation into Dorothy strictly business. His feminine facet, Shirley, had not prevented him from remarrying just six days after a divorce which followed *Kramer vs. Kramer*. The Hoffmans had a daughter shortly after *Tootsie* came out. His co-star, Jessica Lange, like her character, was soon to change partners – from ballet dancer Mikhail Baryshnikov to actor and writer Sam Shepherd. Lange had been cast by Sydney Pollack. Bill Murray, who is said to have improvised most of his part, was Hoffman's choice.

Hoffman also finally got his choice to play Michael's agent. Sydney Pollack had started as an actor but was unwilling to step back in front of the camera. However Hoffman kept on at him, even sending him a bunch of roses with a card saying, 'Be my agent, Love Dorothy'.

The crew apparently applauded this piece of casting, enjoyed Pollack's scenes immensely, and not just for the acting jokes. Normal problems were forgotten as they watched their director getting attacks of the nerves just like anyone else. Apparently his hands were shaking before he went on camera.

▦ The experience

'Mr Pollack and the writers of the screenplay have taken a wildly improbable situation and found just about all of its comic possibilities, not by exaggerating the obvious but by treating it with inspired common sense.' Vincent Canby, *New York Times*, 17 December 1982

'I had no desire to do anything grotesque. But I love doing this, I feel really emotional about this character.' Dustin Hoffman, 1982

'He gives a master actor's performance: he's playing three characters and they're shaped so that Dorothy fits inside Michael, and Emily fits inside Dorothy. Even Hoffman's self-consciousness as an actor works in this performance; so does his sometimes grating, rankling quality (which is probably his idea of sincerity).' Pauline Kael, *New Yorker*, 27 December 1982

▦ Can you spot . . .

* Teri Garr isn't looking as good as she could. Early on in the production it was noticed that director of photography Owen Roizman (*The French Connection* (1971), *Exorcist* (1975)) was making her appear too pretty. So Roizman, who enjoys his cinematographer's power of bestowing or withdrawing good looks, tampered with her lighting.
* How Michael manages to assemble his audition wardrobe so quickly.
* An injured hand. Hoffman caught it in a door. A particularly painful patch was the final scene of the film when he had it in a sling between takes.
* The scriptwriter. Murray Schisgal is one of the party guests.
* Dorothy's posture. Hoffman's shoulders naturally slope and he found it particularly strenuous carrying a shoulder bag.

Top Hat

1935 Boy meets girl. They dance. Boy loses girl. Still they dance. Boy gets girl. More dancing.

▦ The talent

Fred Astaire 36, as Jerry Travers; cinema's greatest hoofer just started on his screen career. Many more memorable films, with and without Ginger, to come

Ginger Rogers 24, as Dale Tremont; two or three films a year for another twenty years but always most associated with Fred

Edward Everett Horton 49, as Horace Hardwick; favourite ubiquitous comedy character. Still working in films and as cartoon voice-over until 1970

Helen Broderick 45, as Madge Hardwick; Broadway comedienne in second film role. Broderick Crawford's mum

Erik Rhodes 29, as Alberto Beddini; Oklahoma-born character actor who debuted in *Top Hat* predecessor *The Gay Divorcee* (1934). Soon returned to the stage

Eric Blore 48, as Bates; British butler-type in typical role

Pandro S. Berman 29, Producer; RKO's equivalent of MGM's prodigy production chief Irving Thalberg. Many notable movies through to the sixties

Mark Sandrich 35, Director; mainstay of Astaire/Rogers and other musicals including 'White Christmas' smash, *Holiday Inn* (1942). Died in 1945

▦ The business

RKO decided to pull out all the stops for this, their fourth pairing of Astaire and Rogers, a combination whose nine films* for the studio were its financial backbone during the thirties. Studio boss and producer Pandro S. Berman lavished $620,000 on *Top Hat* commissioning the music from the world's most popular songwriter, Irving Berlin.

And what songs! Imagine the impact as Astaire, who was Berlin's favourite song stylist, first delivered numbers which have since become standards, particularly 'Dancing Cheek to Cheek' and 'Top Hat' itself. At the time, however, more attention seems to have been paid to the trendy 'Piccolino'. It now sounds like a museum piece but in 1935 it was thought of as the successor to 'The Continental', from Fred and Ginger's previous-hit-but-one, *The Gay Divorcee*.

Top Hat was also the first of the musicals to be specifically written for the pair rather than adapted from a successful stage show. But while Pandro Berman was willing to risk original tunes from the masterly Mr Berlin he decided to play safe with the storyline. The author of the original theatrical version of *The Gay Divorcee*, Dwight Taylor, was brought in to write *Top Hat*. How's this for a set of uncanny similarities: both films have Fred as a well-known American dancer falling for Ginger at first sight but thwarted by a case of mistaken identity. In both Edward Everett

Flying Down to Rio (1933), *The Gay Divorcee* (1934), *Roberta* (1935), *Top Hat* (1935), *Follow the Fleet* (1936), *Swing Time* (1936), *Shall We Dance?* (1937), *Carefree* (1938) and *The Story of Vernon and Irene Castle* (1939). They also co-starred in *The Barkleys of Broadway* (1948) for MGM.

Horton plays his English friend, Eric Blore a servant and Erik Rhodes an Italian (Tonetti in *The Gay Divorcee*, Beddini in *Top Hat*).

It was a huge success all over again. Astaire and Berlin (who was already a million-aire) were each on 10% of the profits, worth $285,000 in the end. *Top Hat* proved second only to *Mutiny on the Bounty* as top grosser of the year. It made $135,000 in its first week alone.

Ginger Rogers was considered by the studio the less valuable of the duo* but she was not to be done out of equal billing, equal publicity and a share of the loot. She retired in a huff to her mountain pad until RKO caved in on all points except a percentage. She had to make do with a comparatively measly bonus of $10,000 and a pay rise to $3,000 a week.

▦ Behind the screen

They were sick of appearing together by now, especially Ginger who despite a wide variety of screen roles at the time rightly feared that she was becoming regarded principally as fifty per cent of a type-cast product. As for Fred, this was only his fifth screen appearance, all but one with Ginger.

Ginger Rogers didn't particularly want to be a musical star, but it was still a continued irritation that her dancing was universally compared unfavourably to his. She was an all-round entertainer who happened to come into the business after winning the Texas Charleston championships. Fred had been a professional dancer since the age of seven. His well-off parents had commissioned the finest tutors Omaha, Nebraska could offer. Fred and sister Adele (who retired to marry a British Lord) could earn a hefty $200 a week on Broadway before they were much older.

The Astaire/Rogers chemistry, so obvious from the start in *Flying Down to Rio*, was strictly reserved for the screen. They had, in fact, dated a few times but that was five years before *Top Hat* when both were appearing in different shows on Broadway. They went dancing a few times socially** but there doesn't seem to have been anything serious in it and by 1935 they were living entirely separate lives offscreen.

Fred became an expectant father as shooting on *Top Hat* began in spring of that year. He had been married to Phyllis Potter for two years and theirs remained one of Hollywood's happiest marriages until her death in 1954.

Ginger had married *All Quiet on the Western Front* (1930) star, Lew Ayres, at about the same time Fred and Phyllis tied the knot but they had already separated. Lew was the second of five husbands. Her mentor and constant companion was her mom, Lela, a former scriptwriter. Mother and daughter ensconced themselves chez Rogers, which boasted a well equipped soda fountain. The non-drinking, non-smok-ing star would gain a stone between pictures.

She'd soon lose it again working out for any picture with Fred Astaire. It was the job of Fred's friend and choreographer, Hermes Pan, to drill Ginger through the routines he and Fred had spent five weeks blocking out. They would dance eight hours a day to prepare her for the remorseless professionalism of Astaire. Fred himself would rehearse for up to two solid weeks per routine to get the fluid ease you see on screen. He was so finicky that he wouldn't even trust anyone else to hammer

---

*Despite the RKO adage which even-handedly explained the pair's immense popularity: she gave him sex (appeal), he gave her class.
**Oddly enough, Fred is said not to have been any great shakes as a ballroom dancer.

the taps into his shoes, nor would he take the normal screen short cut of having the tapping sound re-recorded by a drummer beating on coconut shells. He would dub it all by foot, time and again if necessary. Ginger's taps were done the same way – if needed, at the same time – by Hermes Pan.

Astaire could get quite tetchy in his quest for perfection and it's said that after each, in his view, substandard take in the *Top Hat* routine he snapped a cane, finally getting through seven of the nine spares that Hermes Pan had thoughtfully called on the props men to provide. Astaire was especially jittery as he prepared for the shooting-with-the-cane sequence because Jimmy Cagney was looking round the set. Cagney was best known on screen as a gangster but he began in vaudeville as a dancer, a talent he was to show off to brilliant effect in *Yankee Doodle Dandy* (1942). He was impressed by what he saw of the *Top Hat* number, especially take two. He told Astaire not to bother to shoot any more as he would never better it, and despite more attempts take two is the one they used.

'Dancing Cheek to Cheek' is one of the most admired dance numbers Hollywood has ever produced. But the silky pas de deux you see is the morning after one of cinema's most celebrated night befores.

The problem was that dress. Exactly what happened depends on whose account you believe. Fred Astaire in his autobiography, *Steps in Time*, casts a fairly benevolent light on the incident amid fascinating insights on the mechanics of movie musicals.

Ginger took the unusual step of rehearsing in a dress rather than regulation slacks (a swirling gown becomes, in Fred's words, '*our*' dress and has to be included in the choreography), but nothing could prepare them for the feathers.

Accounts vary of her entrance after a half-hour getting into this ice-blue creation. Fred says he thought the dress was rather fuller than he expected but okay. Another version has the suppression of laughter by all concerned made more difficult by a call of 'Tweet, tweet' from the lighting gantry.

But it was when the dancing started that the feathers really began to fly, to such an extent that the shots were being obscured by a fluffy blizzard. They got everywhere including, it seems, into very accessible Astaire orifice. By all accounts there was a set-wide set-to with Lela, Ginger's formidable agent-mother weighing in as well (which Fred recounts as 'Lela trying to help').

You can still see the odd feather drifting off the dress if you look closely at the number but that was after all those extras had been retained for an additional, expensive day and the costume department had been marshalled into an all-night stitching session, securing each feather in place.

The fabulous result is a neat encapsulation of Fred and Ginger's professional relationship – a perfect, relaxed display after all those ructions. But the incident must have made a lasting impression. Thereafter Fred is said to have changed his pet name for Miss Rogers from 'Ginge' to 'Feathers' and at the end of the production presented her with a feather-shaped pin. He and Hermes Pan also composed a pastiche on 'Cheek to Cheek' which began, 'Feathers, I hate feathers . . .'

▓ The experience

'It's gay . . . it's glamorous . . . it's glorious . . . see the screen's top dancing stars in their biggest musical success.' RKO blurb for cinema hoardings

Fred Astaire and Ginger Rogers: feathers, I hate feathers . . .

'*Top Hat* has a plot which exists solely for the pupose of bringing these two artists together, separating them and bringing them together again – not to put too fine a point on it, a thin plot.' *Daily Telegraph*, 14 October 1935

'When *Top Hat* is letting Mr Astaire perform his incomparable magic or teaming him with the increasingly dexterous Miss Rogers it is providing the most urbane fun that you will find anywhere on the screen.' Andre Sennwald, *New York Times*, September 1935

▦ Can you spot . . .

* Lucille Ball as the flower clerk. She had also made an appearance in the preceding Astaire/Rogers flick, *Roberta* (1935) and had a $50-a-week contract. Twenty-three years later she bought the studio.

* Something lacking near the end. There was supposed to be another song, 'Get Thee Behind Me, Satan', just before the 'Piccolino' song at the end, also to be sung by Ginger Rogers but they cut it. Never fear, if you want to hear it watch their subsequent outing together, *Follow the Fleet*.

* Two cool characters. Both Jerry Travers and his producer Horace Hardwick are out on the town the night before their show opens in the West End and aren't even bothered about Jerry appearing for the first big Saturday night performance. They're off instead to Venice.

* The Lido colour scheme. Of course not, unless you're watching a colourized version. But for your information and as guidance to the colourizers, RKO turned over two connected soundstages to make the Lido, with candy-coloured buildings and a red bakelite dancing surface. Even in monochrome you can tell that to make it more visible they dyed the canal water black.

* A film technique for musicals which has become standard. Astaire insisted on full-length shots with no cutaways so that the audience knew for sure that the stars were performing all the Terpsichorean feats without the aid of trickery.

* Just how kinky Alberto's family are. No, because the Hays office allegedly made them change the Beddini motto to 'For women the kiss, for men the sword,' from the original, 'For men the sword, for women the whip!'

2001: A Space Odyssey

1968 Two major steps in the evolution of man, with a little help from God's monolith.

▤ The talent

Keir Dullea 29, as Dave Bowman; normally played neurotics before this. He returned in 1985 for a sequel, *2010*

Gary Lockwood 29, as Frank Poole; started as an extra, stunt man and stand-in. This has been his only memorable film

William Sylvester 44, as Dr Heywood Floyd; familiar character in British and American productions

Stanley Kubrick 37, Producer/Director; former photographer. A cinematic artist who had already made *Lolita* (1962) and *Dr Strangelove* (1963). Few films since included *A Clockwork Orange* (1971) (which he subsequently withdrew), *The Shining* (1979) and *Full Metal Jacket* (1987)

▤ The business

Stanley Kubrick invested £85,000 in MGM shares after completing *2001*, so confident was he of its success.

The studio bosses were not so sure. First there were protracted and involved preparations which went so far as rewriting Arthur C. Clarke's short story, 'The Sentinel', first into a novel* and then into a screenplay. The costs to MGM drifted upwards from the original $6,000,000 to a final $10,500,000, this at a time when the once dominant studio found its fortunes stagnating.

More than half of the inflated budget went on the stiffly formal, though still convincing, special effects. Remember that this was before the public were so accustomed to the sophisticated televising of space events but when interest in extra-terrestrial exploration was at its peak.

The impact of the film's space scenes was re-inforced with the new footage which soon became available. Notice, as people did at the time, the similarity between the *2001* lunar pod landing in a puff of compressed air and the shots of the Apollo rocket taking off from the moon. They did get the view of earth from the moon wrong, though, as a white disc rather than the cloudy green we have become used to gazing at.

Reviews were mixed when the film first came out in early 1968 but movie-goers instantly acclaimed it a classic. One sizeable element in the initial following were hippies who returned repeatedly for the trip sequence towards the end.

The film grossed about $40,000,000 worldwide, though not very quickly. Nevertheless in the end Kubrick probably got a good return on his MGM shares.

---

*Which was released in 1968 and proved a best seller.

▦ Behind the screen

The star of *2001* is Stanley Kubrick.* He was involved in every stage of the production from the writing through to the music and costumes, marking a turning point in movies becoming recognizable to the public for the director as much as the leading actors.

But he didn't do it alone. The MGM publicity machine made the best of the film's long gestation by blurbing all the technical expertise being consulted by the director. A corps of designers were advised by scientists and technical manufacturers on the likely look of the twenty-first century jet set.

Some of their predictions have acquired a quaint, Dan Dare look but the degree of advancement which they foresaw and which now, closer to the millennium, seems *unlikely* is what really dates the production. Kubrick assumed the contemporary view that scientific knowledge would double every five years and could be matched by finances of sixties magnitude. Man was to become a slightly cold, space-orientated creature with no buttons on his clothes.

Most of the live action was shot at Borehamwood, north of London, apart from the first scenes to be filmed, which couldn't be fitted into any of the sound stages and had to be transferred to Shepperton. These were the excavations on the moon, shot in a pit made of ninety tons of sand, specially dyed to fit in with the moon colour.

Despite all the futuristic trickery the scenes which seemed to cause the most problems were those at the beginning of the film, The Dawn of Man. All of the participants are human, apart from two baby chimps, and the challenge was to get them to look like apes.

This was a problem also being tackled at Fox by the makers of *Planet of the Apes* (1968) roughly at the same time. In *2001*, rather than the monkey heads on human bodies of *Planet*, Kubrick wanted man's ancestors to have simian bodies as well. So his recruits were small-limbed dancers and mimes. Diminutive British comedian Ronnie Corbett was apparently a postulant Dawn of Man ape but was rejected as too stocky.

The *Planet of the Apes* apes were certainly more expressive, as befits their greater evolutionary advancement. But the *2001* special effects men showed a creditable level of ingenuity in the system of toggles and levers in each mask which were operated by the occupant's tongue. These curled back lips and operated the false monkey tongue. All you can see of the actors is their eyes. The masks were also quick-fit compared to those of the star *Planet* apes, on in half-an-hour rather than five.

Considered more clever at the time to the technical crowd was the way the director got his scenery. Spending had gone through the roof and even Kubrick was loath to see it enter orbit by filming in the remote African locations that would have been the ideal primaeval backdrop. Instead he used a new super-reflective material for a 3,600-square-foot backdrop onto which were projected 8″×10″ slides of the region.

It all begs the question of why you can't see the backdrop beamed as well onto the apes or any shadows in the background. The answer was to have the projector, specially built to accommodate that size of slide, aligned with the camera and at very low intensity. You can still see the slide because the newly-developed screen was so

---

*A close second is the villainous computer, HAL, the people's choice as by far the most interesting onscreen participant.

reflective and you can't see shadows because the figures in the foreground perfectly mask their own shade. You can, however, see the golden glow of the front projection on the fur of the apes.

The space special effects, which crossed new boundaries of believability, were achieved with a mixture of technical innovation and meticulously realized conventional trickery. Many of the shots are grafted together from numerous separately-filmed pieces of action or model-work using the careful technique of mattes which has been a staple of special effects spectaculars since *King Kong* (1933).

The docking with the space station is typical of a sequence which lends itself to the use of geometrically arranged boxes with carefully timed images filmed in perspective. Notice how few objects actually overlap anywhere in *2001*, lessening the chance of any tell-tale raggedness.

The planets are generally paintings on rotating perspex. An exception, the moon, is an actual photograph. And if some of the space craft seem familiar you may have put bits of them together yourself. Kubrick sent a team to a German toy fair to scout out the cream of that year's plastic models. The rockets you see in the film are generally two to three feet long, detailed with metal foils and tubing, but based on box cars, battleships, aircraft and good old Gemini capsules. A size exception was the Discovery space craft – ninety-six feet long in one version and fifteen feet for another which was used in distant shots. Their stately choreography to classics, which included a well-worn snippet of Richard Strauss' *Thus Spoke Zarathustra*, was immensely impressive at the time, and the soundtrack has become a cliché for space adventure.

Much of the trickery inside the space craft concerned creating the illusion of weightlessness. Some is simple, like Dr Floyd's floating pen. It is dangling from a piece of nylon until the stewardess plucks it from the air by which time it has been fixed to a clear revolving disk. Can you spot a giveaway? The food in Dr Floyd's weightless inflight meal slips back down the straws. It would stay put in zero G.

The hostess's other trick of walking around in a complete weightless circle was achieved by fixing the camera to the centre of a revolving drum-like set rather than actually relying on velcro shoepads.

Much the same principle was used for the impressive living area of the Discovery probe taking Poole and Bowman to Jupiter. This was a centrifuge built specially by the arms engineers Vickers for $750,000. It was thirty-eight feet high and revolved at three miles per hour, not enough to simulate the force of gravity at Borehamwood but quite hairy enough for those inside.

It was a self-contained unit, self lit from the control panels. Shots could be taken in two ways. Either the camera and operator would be fixed to the floor and subjected to a sickening 360° circuit while Poole jogged at ground level. Alternatively the camera would be on a little dolly frantically tugged by grips clambering up the revolving drum. Everyone offscreen wore hard hats because of the hazard of tumbling debris. Kubrick prudently stayed out of it, directing via a video link.

The HAL that Dullea and Lockwood are actually playing to has an English accent. Apparently Kubrick, who had been a British resident since the early sixties, thought it would raise the level of their performance. At one point a voice like that of Jackie Mason, the New York-Jewish comedian, was considered for the final version but it was Martin Balsam who provided the first voice track. However his delivery was

Gary Lockwood: safety helmet and sick bag

judged too emotional and so instead Kubrick used the actor who was originally to have provided a narration for the story, Douglas Rain. HAL is talking blind. Rain never saw the completed script or any of the footage as he knocked off his part in a nine-and-a-half hour stint.

He missed out on a good time. By all accounts the set was a happy one. At the end of shooting the live sequences the crew of British technicians, not always known for being well disposed towards American clientele, gave Kubrick a model of a lunar landscape as a memento. Mindful that he was on his way back to face the budgetary music at MGM his first assistant, Derek Cracknell, announced at the presentation 'It's our personal Oscar to you, guv – no matter what the other lot think.'

The experience

'The year is 2001. The six-day weekend is over and people are returning to work. Mr Smith rises refreshed after his satisfying three hours sleep, breakfasts on synthetic tea or coffee and checks with his boss on the closed-circuit television.' MGM background blurb

'I would say that *2001* reflects about 90% on the imagination of Stanley Kubrick, about 5% on the genius of the special effects people, and perhaps 5% on my contribution.' Arthur C. Clarke

'It attempts to communicate more to the subconscious and to the feelings than it does to the intellect. I think clearly there's a basic problem with people who are not paying attention with their eyes.' Stanley Kubrick

'As a technical achievement – a graduation exercise in ingenuity and the making of film magic – it surpasses anything I've ever seen. In that sense it is a milestone, a landmark (or a spacemark) in the art of film.' *Los Angeles Times*, 5 April 1968

'Kubrick is a clever man. The grim joke is that life in 2001 is only faintly more gruesome in its details of sophisticated affluence than it is now.' Penelope Gilliatt, *New Yorker*

▦ Can you spot . . .

* Why 2001 rather than any other year? It was supposedly Kubrick's act of homage to Fritz Lang's *Metropolis* (1926) which was set in 2000.
* The only intentional joke. Lots of people found the film very funny in bits but Kubrick said that the only real gag was the instructions for the gravity-free toilet.
* Two familiar faces from British TV. Star comic actor Leonard Rossiter – Rigsby and Reggie Perrin – as the Soviet scientist Smyslov and Margaret Tyzack, of *The Forsyte Saga*, as Elena.
* A hidden meaning to the name HAL. Substitute the next letters along in the alphabet and you'll see what many noticed but was said by Arthur C. Clarke to be coincidence. HAL is supposed to stand for *H*euristically-programmed *Al*gorithmic computer.
* Some genuine professionals amongst the actors. The mission controller was difficult to cast so, despite the protestations of the actors' union Equity, Kubrick used a U.S. Air Force traffic controller, based in Britain, Chief Warrant Officer Franklin Miller. The BBC 12 news is brought to you by a well-preserved Kenneth Kendall, a BBC 1 and 2 newscaster of the sixties and seventies. And Dr Floyd's video-phone daughter is the director's own Vivian.
* How they did the psychedelic bit, officially called the Star Gate sequence. They used a machine called a slit scan, really a camera rig with a focal length of fifteen feet to half an inch, apparently normally employed for making the afterimage whooshes on advertising lettering.
* What it's all about? The monoliths were supposed to be both abstract images of God and signalling devices. In an early version of the script they had images projected on them. The monolith on the moon responded to the first rays of light hitting it, after being unearthed during the fourteen-day lunar night, by signalling to Jupiter. Man had shown himself sufficiently advanced to be drawn there for the next stage in his evolution.

Who Framed Roger Rabbit

1988 Cartoon character Roger hires a private eye to clear him of a murder charge.

The talent

Bob Hoskins 46, as Eddie Valiant; British star of the eighties, from TV's *Pennies From Heaven* through smallish-budget successes like *The Long Good Friday* (1980) and *Mona Lisa* (1986)

Charles Fleischer 35, as Roger Rabbit; nightclub comedian with bit in *Nightmare on Elm Street* (1984)

Christopher Lloyd as Judge Doom; cornering the nutty character market from *One Flew Over the Cuckoo's Nest* (1975), the *Back to the Future* series and TV's *Taxi*

Joanna Cassidy 44, as Dolores; also in *Blade Runner* (1982) and *The Fourth*

Protocol (1987) – and *Bullitt* (1968) if you're quick enough to spot her

Steven Spielberg 41, Executive Producer; the hands-off motive force behind several SFX-intensive films, including Zemeckis' *Back to the Future* (1985), in addition to his Midas directorial skills

Kathleen Kennedy 36, Executive Producer; *E.T.* (1982) producer and joint founder of Spielberg's production company, Amblin'. Involved in all his major projects

Robert Zemeckis 34, Director; made *Back to the Future* and *Romancing the Stone* (1984)

The business

Spielberg, a master of live-action fantasy, had already ventured into the world of old-style, high quality animation with *An American Tail* (1986). His next cartoon adventure would go a step further, combining actors and drawings in a way never successfully achieved before.

It also meant Spielberg working with the Disney organization, a dream combination of which Walt would have thoroughly approved. He would have also applauded the choice of animator to fill the fifty-five cartoon minutes of the film – required to have Disney's own élan toned up with the wit of Warner Brothers and the adrenalin of Tex Avery.*

Richard Williams had already impressed the great cartoon industrialist himself in the late forties. At the age of fifteen he mooched his way into a free run of the Disney studio after bussing down from his native Toronto and showing off his sketches of Mickey and Donald. By the mid-eighties Williams was long settled in Britain, plying a lucrative trade animating movie title sequences (e.g. *The Charge of the Light Brigade* (1968)), commercials (e.g. Long Life Beer) and short animated features (e.g. *A Christ-*

*Warner characters included the more sassy and adult-oriented Bugs Bunny, Daffy Duck, Roadrunner, Porky Pig and Tweety – all voiced by Mel Blanc. Avery was one of the most influential animators at Warners and elsewhere, founder of the eyes-popping-out-off-the-head-on-springs school of cartooning.

mas Carol (1972) for which he received an Oscar). But the profits had been bled over twenty-three years by the animator's obsession with a project called *The Cobbler and the Thief*. So far he had lavished £2,000,000 and produced just fifteen minutes of completed footage.

Spielberg heard rave reviews of *The Cobbler* when Williams arranged a special Los Angeles screening for his cartooning hero, the relatively obscure Disney animator Milt Kahl.* *Roger Rabbit* co-producer Frank Marshall also recognized the right stuff when he caught Williams' Long Life Beer ad which ran in Britain and featured a cat rapidly expending its nine lives (Most people would prefer a Long Life – geddit?!).

After being persuaded by Warners master animator, Chuck Jones, that it would be worth devoting two and a half years of his life to the project Williams assembled a crew of thirty-four animators,** mostly based in London. All were made to sign a three-page secrecy agreement. They then set about their work, which was to end up costing about $400,000 a minute. The original budget was $27,000,000 and despite rumours of it almost doubling the producers say it came in at about $35,000,000, plus almost as much again on prints and publicity.

The cheaper end of the production was the live action, directed by Spielberg protégé Robert Zemeckis. It was shot at Elstree in Britain with a crew assembled by Spielberg to make *Indiana Jones and the Last Crusade* (1989) but abandoned when he decided to go off and do *Empire of the Sun* (1988) instead.

Critical opinion of *Who Framed Roger Rabbit* divided across the Atlantic. In the States they were very enthusiastic, but by the time it opened in Britain the reviewers' expectations had been jaded by the ballyhooing publicity. The public were in no doubt. The film grossed $150,000,000 in its first five months and was topping the video charts the following year. Of this Bob Hoskins – once described by a friend of Pauline Kael as a testicle on legs – is said to be in for as much as £5,000,000 and Richard Williams is likely to have enough cash to finish *The Cobbler and the Thief*.

▓ Behind the screen

Shooting the live action was likened by Steven Spielberg to filming *The Invisible Man*. For Bob Hoskins it was the toughest challenge of his acting career.

There he was, running around sets which were propped ten feet off the ground, where furniture moved seemingly of its own accord and whiskey glasses drained themselves. Down below dozens of puppeteers and special effects men fiddled with the wires and pullies that made his surroundings come alive with the influence of the Toons. The contraption that makes Roger come alive up Hoskins' jumper was wired through one of the actors legs.***

Zemeckis and Spielberg had reasoned that past Disney attempts to interact live action with cartoon, such as *Song of the South* (1946) and *Mary Poppins* (1963), had been limited by the animators. The actors were shot with the flat lighting and static point-of-view of most cartoons, spoiling the illusion.****

*He did Alice in *Alice in Wonderland* (1951) and bits of *Jungle Book* (1967).
**Plus their numerous assistants and support staff that keep the credits rolling through a marathon of 739 names.
***There is also the odd mismatch. In the first sequence that mixes Toons and actors doesn't director Raoul's coat tail reach out to meet Roger before he actually tugs at it?
****One reason that the opening cartoon sequence looks quite unlike anything that would really have been produced in the 1940's is the elastic perspective.

Bob Hoskins and Jessica: using his imagination

For *Who Framed Roger Rabbit* the camera was to move as freely as it liked and the animators, despite many moans, would have to follow. For their part however, the live action end would have to acknowledge the participation of the Toons with realistic physical reaction. When Roger sits down there is a puff of dust and the chair takes his weight. The principle was termed rather grandly by Steven Spielberg 'multi-dimensional interactive character generation'.

That left Bob Hoskins having to make it seem as if the drawings were not added later. For this he took coaching from his then three-year-old daughter Rosa who had a circle of invisible friends. It was this ability to interact with thin air that got him the job over the heads of such as Eddie Murphy and Bill Murray. Another pre-requisite was the faultless exchange of his native London tones for an American accent.

At one point he feared it was getting to him. Apparently, like the mad ventriloquist in *Magic* (1978), Hoskins began engaging in agitated conversations with empty space during his time off. His wife told him to cool it or she would get him professional help.

An added threat to his sanity was Charles Fleischer who claims he wore a rabbit costume for all his scenes with Hoskins. He is supposedly just off camera, in fur and whiskers, delivering his lines and going through all Roger's movements. It was something like watching a man and a rabbit do the tango from opposite sides of the dance floor. Hoskins meanwhile was himself handling most of the stunts, and the tricks in his hyena-slaying routine, drawing on his training as a professional circus performer. The upshot was that he had to wear a shirt on the beach during a holiday which followed production to cover up the bruises.

If Roger was all in the mind, at least Hoskins had something more substantial to play to with Jessica. During filming, her space was amply filled by one Betsy Brantley. Later all evidence of Betsy was painted over with Jessica, who herself has been somewhat more painted over than at first. As well he might, Zemeckis looked carefully at her slit skirt (which, apparently, is a sewn-up version of the original animator's conception). This would pass but he insisted that her cleavage be more discreetly robed. Perspicacious daddies at the Disney theme parks will perhaps note with disappointment that Jessica is displayed within those sanitary portals even more demurely than on screen.

The character is loosely modelled on Rita Hayworth and Lauren Bacall. Her speaking voice is provided uncredited by Kathleen Turner. the rendition of the old Peggy Lee number 'Why Don't You Do Right' was by Spielberg's then wife Amy Irving.

Of all the scenes it was Eddie Valiant's tour of Maroon Studios that was most challenging, with 140 different elements to be jigsawed together. All the extras were taken through how the final scene would look with directions like: 'There's a giraffe on your right and a hippo on your left and the hippo is taller so look up.'

Shooting at Elstree went on for six months from December 1986, relying on storyboards to coordinate the special effects. Then came the task of adding the Toons. The final form of Roger himself wasn't decided until a late stage. Steven Spielberg wanted him to look like Thumper, Zemeckis favoured something of Jimmy Stewart but in the end, as scribbled by Richard Williams on a restaurant napkin, he's a derivation of many characters.*

---

*Apparently his closest relation is a mouse in Tex Avery's 1947 *King Size Canary.*

Each frame of live action was photocopied and worked on individually. Richard Williams did the mini-cartoon at the beginning by himself but later on, in a complicated scene, up to ten animators would be crowded round drawing by hand. At twenty-four frames a second to match the live action, not the twelve of cartoon convention, there were about 80,000 individual images.

Even then it wouldn't have looked right without the added touch of George Lucas' special effects workshop, Industrial Light and Magic. It was they who actually grafted together the cartoon and live images, adding shading and shadows to complete the brilliant effect. It was all very painstaking and time-consuming, and they only just beat the deadline. Years in the making, *Who Framed Roger Rabbit* was in its complete form only twelve hours before the American premiere.

▦ The experience

'*Roger Rabbit* careers like a Toontown trolley and boasts a technical dexterity that Walt Disney could only have daydreamed of.' Richard Corliss, *Time*, 27 June 1988

'Because the film drags when Toons aren't on screen and over-accelerates when they are, there are moments when *Roger Rabbit* is less great than grating.' J. Hoberman, *Village Voice*, 5 July 1988

'It is a measure of the distance this movie establishes that many audiences applaud after the showiest sequences rather than laugh during them.' John Powers, *Rolling Stone*, 11 August 1988

'If you sit there thinking "How'd they do that?" then I've failed.' Robert Zemeckis

'A lot of actors say things like "Well, I was on stage with Olivier or Gielgud, but I'll say I was on film with some of the real big guys – Bugs Bunny and Mickey Mouse. That's something to brag about!" ' Bob Hoskins

▦ Can you spot . . .

* Popeye and Felix amongst all the Disney, Warners and other cartoon regulars of the forties. No, because their owners didn't fancy the deal offered: $5,000 a character and their non-use in trailers or publicity.
* An anachronistic appearance. The Roadrunner wasn't created by Chuck Jones until 1948, a year later than the movie is set. Ah, say the film-makers, he was really just hanging around Toontown but hadn't found work yet.
* The strain. Richard Williams took much more time on and was happy with the first third but thought after that the pressure and volume of work showed. You can see the odd jump in the images, despite the attention of the umpteen checkers and final checkers listed in the credits. Jessica, for instance, displays a nasty judder as she passes behind a table during her song, quite out of keeping with her customary grace.
* Betty Boop's boobs. They were included in a flashframe for a joke but excised by the hand of Disney.
* Some good old cartoon voices. Mel Blanc is doing his bit as the authentic Daffy Duck, Bugs Bunny, Tweety Pie and Porky Pig – one, or rather four, of his last assignments before his death. Betty Boop's original voice, Mae Questel, is there and June Foray, the voice of Rocky the Flying Squirrel, plays several roles including the Toon Hag that Eddie mistakes for Jessica. Fleischer pops up as other characters: Benny the Cab, Greasy and Psycho. And you can even hear the man who made them all move. Richard Williams is the voice of Droopy.

The Wizard of Oz

1939 A girl and her dog get blown by a tornado from Kansas to the magical land of Oz. Only the Wizard can get them home.

▥ The talent

Judy Garland 16, as Dorothy; no star ever gave more to cinema, nor suffered more in the process

Bert Lahr 44, as the Cowardly Lion; his most memorable foray into films from his natural stage habitat

Ray Bolger 35, as the Scarecrow; dancer more at home on Broadway than on film

Jack Haley 40, as the Tin Woodsman; comedian, another stager, whose son Jack Haley Jnr made *That's Entertainment* (1974)

Frank Morgan 49, as the Wizard; ubiquitous MGM character actor averaging five films a year in the thirties and forties

Margaret Hamilton 37, as the Wicked Witch; former kindergarten teacher whose hatchet face was her fortune. She was still hard at work in the seventies

Billie Burke 54, as Gilda; widow of Florenz Ziegfeld. Long, varied career from Broadway star to film character roles

Charlie Grapewin 70, as Uncle Henry; typical role from the peak years of his character career

Clara Blandick 59, as Auntie Em; her most memorable role. She committed suicide twenty years later

Mervyn Le Roy 39, Producer; versatile director. Made both *Little Caesar* (1930) and *Golddiggers of 1933*. Still active in the 1960's

Victor Fleming 56, Director; former racing driver who though regarded as a very average director turned out some splendid films

▥ The business

One theory is that *The Wizard of Oz* was actually designed to lose money, one of the 'prestige' pictures that MGM would put out every so often to bolster its claim to being the biggest, most opulent production house in Hollywood.

They certainly didn't skimp. The budget was $2,777,000 – a million dollars more than for a normal big MGM production and the shooting schedule was just as extravagant: twelve weeks of rehearsal followed by almost six months filming, compared to eight weeks on average for any other picture.

The Wizard of Oz finally did make a profit though MGM had to wait twenty years. Audiences were large and enthusiastic at first, and for a re-release ten years later, but they were mostly children benefiting from reduced admission prices. Box office takings in North America were about $4,000,000. The big money came from television. This was one of the first films to be sold to the rival medium and with repeated, wildly popular showings it has brought in more than $10,000,000 from the television companies.

All the principal actors became linked with their characters as screen immortals, not that it did much for anyone's career apart from Judy Garland. Bert Lahr said that afterwards he was type-cast 'and there aren't all that many parts for lions'. In any case the largest and most appreciative audience watched it on television and by then Dorothy's friends and foes were either dead or beyond caring.

Salaries on this production are particularly well documented so here's a rundown of what you could be earning in pictures in 1939:

Judy was paid the least apart from Terry, the Cairn Terrier who played Toto. The dog's trainer, Carl Spitz, got $125 a week. Next came Judy, on contract to MGM at $500 a week (which she had to share with her domineering mother). Her salary was raised to $2,000 a week with the success of the picture.

Charlie Grapewin and Clara Blandick (who only worked a week or so) each got $750 a week, Billie Burke $766 (and, as Ziegfeld's widow, a smarter-than-average trailer), Margaret Hamilton $1,000 ($18,000 for the whole picture), Bert Lahr and Frank Morgan $2,500, and Ray Bolger $3,000 a week.

Jack Haley got $3,000 too but he was moonlighting on a radio series and had to give $1,000 a week back to the studio to be released. Does he look a bit tired? He needed to catnap between takes but couldn't sit down in his Tin Woodsman's costume. Instead he had to lean against a special board, normally used by costume drama ladies encumbered by hooped skirts.

The Munchkins, 124 midgets gathered from all over America and Europe, got a miniature $50 a week each. The ones that doubled as the Wicked Witch's Flying Monkeys could multiply that with an additional $25 per piano-wired flight, a hazardous way to become a rich midget as the wires sometimes broke.

The director, Victor Fleming, got $2,500 a week. But the best paid by far was the producer, Mervyn Le Roy. He was normally a director but had been brought in by the studio boss Louis B. Mayer as a new golden-boy executive producer after the death of Irving Thalberg. Le Roy was on $6,000 a week and when it leaked out there was a steady flow of furious producers through Mayer's office demanding rewritten contracts.

▓ Behind the screen

The first and last scenes in the film – monochrome Kansas – were actually the last to be filmed. Did they run out of colour stock? Did something go wrong with the developer? No, it was always planned that way to contrast Dorothy's drab no-place-like-home with the brilliance of Oz. It's just as well because by that time the scarce Technicolor cameras were needed elsewhere: on the set of *Gone With the Wind*, which David Selznick had just begun shooting in a co-production with MGM.

Selznick got the cameras and he got the director, too. The Kansas scenes were shot by King Vidor. He was the fifth director to work on *The Wizard of Oz*, the sixth if you count the producer, Mervyn Le Roy, who went back to directing soon after *Oz*, had definite ideas of what he wanted. Richard Thorpe and Lewis Milestone were dispensed with in quick succession and, aside from Fleming and Vidor, the only director to leave a mark on the film was George Cukor.

The studio originally put Judy Garland in a blonde wig and sought to alter the shape of her face with heavy make-up. Cukor said that she should be completely natural, a little bit of Kansas in the unreal fantasy of Oz. This was agreed but Cukor

was soon replaced by Fleming – who also replaced him in *Gone With the Wind*.*
King Vidor had been offered the Civil War epic but didn't want to take it on with so
little preparation. So he stepped in for the Kansas scenes while Fleming commuted
between the two pictures supervising *The Wizard of Oz* editing.

This gave King Vidor the only opportunity of his long career to stage a musical
number, though he never acknowledged his part in the film until after Fleming's
death ten years later. What a secret to keep about one of the best-loved musical
numbers ever: 'Over the Rainbow'. It went on to win the Oscar for best song, despite
being cut out at first by the studio after unfavourable reaction from a preview.
Doesn't it still look as if it has been re-inserted?

The main theme of 'Over the Rainbow' came in easy inspiration to the composer
Harold Arlen but the middle section was a stumbling block. His lyricist, Yip Harburg,
suggested using the sound Arlen made whistling to call his dog. Try it: Some day I'll
wish upon a star . . .

The Wizard of Oz is credited with being the forerunner of later musicals where the
songs were fully integrated with the story, and characters burst out singing for no
logical reason. So Harburg's lyrics were central to the script and added touches like
the Lullaby League and the Lollipop Guild.

'Over the Rainbow' stayed with Judy Garland for the rest of what became a tragic
career. But as you see her in *The Wizard of Oz* she was by most accounts a bright
teenager who loved to laugh and was looking forward to her high school graduation.
Ray Bolger would help her with her homework.

Sometimes Judy laughed too much. The scene where she meets the bullying
Cowardly Lion and reduces him to tears with a slap is the tenth retake. Bert Lahr, the
film's premier ham, gave the scene so much vaudeville business that she burst out
laughing each time. Finally Fleming lost patience. He slapped her face and sent her off
the set. Judy came back a little later and the take you see was a more solemn
occasion.

It wasn't all laughs for Bert Lahr though. He was a troubled man, guilty and
anxious about his wife who had been mentally ill for some time. The following year
he married his long-term mistress. Margaret Hamilton too was having personal
problems. She had recently divorced and was struggling to bring up her young son.

Judy Garland's main problems were still to come. However, even then it seems she
was on a diet imposed by the studio because they thought she was running to fat. It
was not long before she was using pills to help keep slim, then to get to sleep, finally
all the time . . .

Fat or no fat Garland's healthy bust was not the thing for little Dorothy. Her
landscape was rendered more like the Kansas prairie by a tight corset. Even so she
probably suffered less discomfort than her three travelling companions.

The main problem was heat from the intense lighting that early Technicolor
cameras needed. Because of this, filming could only go on for a limited period before
the sound stage doors were flung open to give everyone some air. What we see of the
film was grabbed in short takes, scenes often carrying on for several days and
everything needing careful continuity matching using the previous days rushes.

---

*Chopping and changing of directors was not uncommon and did nothing to harm the careers of these top
professionals.

Jack Haley, Ray Bolger, Judy Garland and Bert Lahr: that sobering slap

Even Judy in her light gingham dress was apt to wilt so imagine Bert Lahr underneath fifty pounds or more of real lion skin, his tail being worked by an assistant on an overhead walkway. To make matters worse his Lion face meant that he couldn't even eat lunch. He had to suck what nourishment he could through a straw. The three vaudeville cronies who played Dorothy's companions were all so heavily made up and so grotesque that they were ordered not to eat in the normal canteen. They ate (or sucked) together in a trailer, the only advantage being an unspoken arrangement that this way the studio paid for lunch.

Bert Lahr seems to have always been the choice for the lion – the part makes full use of his comic stage persona – but as with so many films most of the others got there by chance. It might have been Shirley Temple as Dorothy, Ray Bolger as the Tin Woodsman and Buddy Ebsen as the Scarecrow. Bolger was an ace comic dancer and particularly wanted to use his talents as the Scarecrow. Ebsen agreed to exchange parts. It was his biggest mistake. He rehearsed twelve weeks, he recorded all the songs, he tried out the make-up . . . and found himself in an iron lung. His 'tin' face was an aluminium spray which blocked up his tubes giving him breathing problems right into later life. Ebsen's film career headed straight downhill after this misadventure and it was some twenty years before he finally made his fortune as Jed Clampett, patriarch of TV's *Beverly Hillbillies*. With Jack Haley the once-bitten make-up department used an aluminium paste, which still gave him an eye infection. The rest of his costume consists mainly of painted bookbinding material.

The part of the Wizard was written for W.C. Fields and also offered to Ed Wynn but they both turned it down. So it fell to MGM contract character actor Frank Morgan, who brought at least one Fieldsian touch to the set. He arrived each day with a briefcase housing a discreet martini kit.

Shirley Temple was to have been borrowed from Fox in exchange for the services of Clark Gable and Jean Harlow. That fell through when Harlow died before the deal could be completed, so Judy got her big break.

Shortly before her death Garland claimed that Bolger, Lahr and Haley tried to upstage her, pushing her to the back in scenes but the surviving Bolger and Haley denied it. They were constantly ribbing each other, though, during the filming as only old vaudeville cronies could, and with the discomfort of their working conditions they needed their good humour.

More difficult to keep under control were the 124 Munchkins, many of whom spoke little English (no pun intended) and most of whom had no experience of acting. Their songs and voices were dubbed, by the then new process of speeding up a soundtrack recorded at low speed (the same process was used in reverse for the Wicked Witch's Winkie guards). There are numerous tales of Munchkin orgies and knife-fights, and of normal size studio workers having to fend off the explicit advances of female midgets, but surviving Munchkins have claimed that this is a libel.

Perhaps the rowdy behaviour of a few tearaways reinforced a repellant image in the minds of non-midgets. Judy Garland certainly claimed she was propositioned by a selection of optimistic Munchkins and it is widely documented that the head of the Witch's Winged Monkeys got drunk and was discovered stuck in the toilet.

There were further dangers for them to face . . . several of the Winged Monkeys ended up in hospital when the piano wire carrying them on their lucrative flights broke. And Margaret Hamilton was off work for six weeks after her exit from Munchkinland went wrong.

The plan was that she would stand on a platform which would lower her quickly as smoke went off, then fire would appear the instant after she had disappeared. But the fire came too soon. It burned her hat and broom . . . and her face and hands. It was the best take, though, and that's the one you see. Later when a similar technique was used to make her melt, substituting the more controllable effects of dry ice, all went well.

This is just one of a myriad of special effects on what was a completely set-bound production, spreading over all MGM's twenty-nine sound stages. The sixty-five sets would have covered twenty-five acres if they'd all been up at the same time and hardly any of them could be used again.

Special effects mean special problems. Some solutions were simple. The colour for the yellow brick road was the subject of detailed experimentation but nothing seemed to give quite the right effect. In those early days of colour, extensive tests were needed on every element on camera to see that it photographed in the proper shade and didn't clash with anything else. They finally used cheap yellow fence paint for the road and it looked fine.

The Wicked Witch's skywriting – 'Surrender Dorothy or die' – took special effects man Jack McMaster two months to prepare. The witch is a model three-eights of an inch long, her broom a hypodermic needle through which McMaster squirted a solution of milk and dye onto a 'sky' which was an oil and water mixture. The sky was opaque so you can't see McMaster in the background struggling to write upside down and backwards.

Some of it was plainly tedious work like the week that twenty props men spent planting 40,000 wire poppies. Other simple effects were fiddly like the Horse of a Different Colour who pulls the four travellers to the gates of the Emerald City. It was actually a succession of white horses which would have just been painted if the animal welfare groups hadn't found out and objected. In the end they had to use flavoured dessert jelly which the horses loved and kept licking off.

Much of the sense of space and distance was achieved with mattes, paintings of scenery on pieces of glass which were than married with the partially exposed frames of live action.

But how do you make a tornado? It was Buddy Gillespie's problem and he first wasted $8,000 on a thin rubber cone that didn't spin properly. There is a romantic story that he finally used a lady's silk stocking and a wind machine but Gillespie's version to author Aljean Harmetz is far more businesslike: a thirty-five-foot muslin wind sock seeded with dust. It was pulled up from a gantry and whirled through a miniature landscape beneath noxious sulphur clouds. Auntie Em's house is only three feet high and when it is sucked up that's reverse action of it being dropped by hand.

Somewhere over the rainbow lurks an MGM special effects man.

▦ The experience

'The songs are charming, the Technicolor no more dreadful than illustrations to most childrens' books, and the sepia prologue on the Kansas plain ... and the tornado twisting across the horizon ... very fine indeed.' Graham Greene, *The Spectator*, 9 February 1940

'Suggestive of neon-lit cocktail bars mixed with Arthur Rackham illustrations, and Things to Come, it gives full play to Technicolor, trick photography and bad taste.' *New Statesman*, 3 February 1940

'As art, the movie is flawed by its sentimentality, by its cheerful insistence that "east, west, home is best", and by the decision to void Dorothy's experience by making it into a dream. As art, it is salvaged by its musical score, by actors who manage to make a Scarecrow, a Tin Woodsman, a Cowardly Lion, a Wicked Witch, and a fraudulent Wizard credible, and by Judy Garland's absolute sincerity.' Aljean Harmetz, *The Making of the Wizard of Oz*, 1977

▦ Can you spot ...

* A problem that just disappears. We never find out in the end whether Miss Gulch finally gets Toto in her clutches.
* A production number that just disappears. When the Wicked Witch is watching Dorothy and company in the haunted forest she tells her monkey flunkies that she will send a little insect that will take the fight out of them. This is all that remains of 'The Jitterbug', a scene where all the principals sing and the Lion gets bitten by a Jitterbug. It took five weeks to film, cost $80,000 and by all accounts turned out very well but the picture needed cutting down from its original two-hour length and this was sacrificed along with several other numbers.

Index

Picture Acknowledgements

The photographs used in this book, kindly supplied by the Kobal Collection, are stills issued to publicize films made or distributed by the following companies: Alfran; Amblin Entertainment; Anglo-Amalgamated; Argyle; Cineguild; Columbia; Danjaq SA; Delphi; Ealing; Embassy; Eon; Horizon; Hoya; Lucasfilm; Malpaso; MCA; MGM; Mirage; Mirisch; Omni-Zoetrope; Pando/Raybert; Paramount; Pathe; Proscenium; Rank; RKO; Selznick; Seven Arts; Shamley; Tatira/Hiller; Touchstone; Turner Entertainment; Twentieth Century Fox; Two Cities; United Artists; Universal; Walter Wanger; Warner Bros.
We apologize in advance for any unintentional omission or neglect and will be pleased to insert the appropriate acknowledgement to companies or individuals in any subsequent edition of the publication.